797,885 Books
are available to read at

www.ForgottenBooks.com

Forgotten Books' App
Available for mobile, tablet & eReader

ISBN 978-1-5278-0695-5
PIBN 10903345

This book is a reproduction of an important historical work. Forgotten Books uses state-of-the-art technology to digitally reconstruct the work, preserving the original format whilst repairing imperfections present in the aged copy. In rare cases, an imperfection in the original, such as a blemish or missing page, may be replicated in our edition. We do, however, repair the vast majority of imperfections successfully; any imperfections that remain are intentionally left to preserve the state of such historical works.

Forgotten Books is a registered trademark of FB &c Ltd.
Copyright © 2017 FB &c Ltd.
FB &c Ltd, Dalton House, 60 Windsor Avenue, London, SW19 2RR.
Company number 08720141. Registered in England and Wales.

For support please visit www.forgottenbooks.com

1 MONTH OF FREE READING

at

www.ForgottenBooks.com

By purchasing this book you are eligible for one month membership to ForgottenBooks.com, giving you unlimited access to our entire collection of over 700,000 titles via our web site and mobile apps.

To claim your free month visit:

www.forgottenbooks.com/free903345

* Offer is valid for 45 days from date of purchase. Terms and conditions apply.

English
Français
Deutsche
Italiano
Español
Português

www.forgottenbooks.com

Mythology Photography **Fiction**
Fishing Christianity **Art** Cooking
Essays Buddhism Freemasonry
Medicine **Biology** Music **Ancient Egypt** Evolution Carpentry Physics
Dance Geology **Mathematics** Fitness
Shakespeare **Folklore** Yoga Marketing
Confidence Immortality Biographies
Poetry **Psychology** Witchcraft
Electronics Chemistry History **Law**
Accounting **Philosophy** Anthropology
Alchemy Drama Quantum Mechanics
Atheism Sexual Health **Ancient History**
Entrepreneurship Languages Sport
Paleontology Needlework Islam
Metaphysics Investment Archaeology
Parenting Statistics Criminology
Motivational

Nº

PURCHASED FROM
BILLINGS FUND

TEMPORARY COLLECTORS.

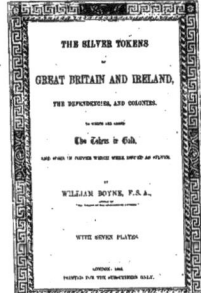

THE
NINETEENTH CENTURY
TOKEN COINAGE

OF

GREAT BRITAIN IRELAND THE CHANNEL ISLANDS AND THE ISLE OF MAN

TO WHICH ARE ADDED

TOKENS OF OVER ONE PENNY VALUE OF ANY PERIOD

OF THE

CITY OF BOSTON

BY

W. J DAVIS

Inspector of Factories to Queen Victoria Member of the London and British
Numismatic Societies . Author of " The Token Coinage of Warwickshire "

LONDON
PRINTED BY J. DAVY AND SONS AT THE DRYDEN PRESS LONG ACRE TO BE
HAD OF SPINK AND SON PICCADILLY W. CORNISH BROTHERS BIRMINGHAM AND
SIMMONS AND WATERS LEAMINGTON SPA

1904

Guarantee.

This Edition is limited to Two Hundred and Fifty=eight copies, of which this is No. 65

Author.

Billinge
Dec. 6. 1904

All Rights Reserved.

INDEX TO INTRODUCTION.

Token Authors, p. vii.
    First mention of a token. Tokens to pay wages. Early lead tokens. Pledges of tokens by Queen Elizabeth. Want of small change. Cotton's estimate of persons in London issuing tokens. Lord Harrington's patent. Proclamation by the Dublin Lord-Deputy and Council. Farthings of Charles II. Stringent laws passed against tokens. Extract from an essay on tokens, 1644. State of the coinage during the Civil War. The Commonwealth pattern farthings. Farthings of Oliver Cromwell. Richard Cromwell. The great seventeenth century token period of Charles II., state of the coinage.

The Origin and History of Tokens. p. viii.

Sir William Parkhurst urges necessity of small money. Indifference of the Government. Corporate and private tokens. Proclamation by Queen Elizabeth making tokens unlawful after All Saints' Day. Solitary seventeenth century token of Scotland. Petitions against tokens. Token devices. Evelyn's prediction. Token legends. Proclamation that no form of coin to be legal except made at His Majesty's mint. The copper coinage of Charles II. Superiority in design and quality of copper.

    Coinage neglected by George III., its debased state. Regal coinage almost extinct. Power of governments. The 1797 copper coinage, and its influence. Council on the coinage, held at the Cock Pit. Money of necessity. Commerce and tokens. Eighteenth century tokens almost supersede the national copper currency. Quantity of copper consumed in tokens. The forgery of regal copper specie. Government orders. Matthew Boulton to strike the 1797 copper coinage. Pingo's penny of 1788. Perfection of the 1797 coinage. Restrikes. Traders make thirty per cent. profit on the issue of tokens. The trade of counterfeiting, Colquhoun's treatise on. Price of copper, its effect on coinage. Government contract with Boulton. Copper coinage of 1799. Advertisements to defraud. Heavy coins worth more when melted down. Fluctuations in the price of copper. Pince's prices from 1800 to 1820. The Anglesea penny tokens. The expansion of trade. Copper coinage of 1806, 1807, and of 1821. List of Soho productions in coins, tokens, and medals.

Cause and Effect. p. xv.

    Why they appeared. Bank tokens, shilling and sixpence, of 1787. Yeo's shilling of 1763, Dorrien and Magén's shilling of 1798. Spanish dollars. Spanish dollars captured and carried from Plymouth to London. Forgery of counter-marks. Bank dollars of 1804. Complaints for the want of small silver coin. Mayor of Newcastle-on-Tyne convenes meeting, 1807, to petition Parliament for a new silver coinage. The stoppage of the Bank of England. Directors of the Bank ridiculed. Commencement of nineteenth century silver tokens. Sir Edward Thomason on his production of tokens. Agitation in favour of tokens. The Earl of Lauderdale's questions. Firm supporters of tokens in Parliament and the country. The height of token popularity. Fereday's tokens. Token note found by H. B. Bowles. Protest against ten per cent. appreciation of dollars by the Bank of England. A criticism by "A Briton." Overseers', private bankers and tradesmen extensively circulate tokens. Bank of England issue tokens for three shillings and one shilling and sixpence. Weight of the tokens. Price of silver in 1811. Number of Bank of England tokens issued. Expansion of factory system. The demand for tokens in 1812. Value of a guinea in 1812.

Nineteenth Century Silver Tokens. p. xxi.

    Wellesley Pale fails to obtain permission to issue a new gold and silver coinage. J. B. Monck issues a gold forty shilling token. Hon. S. Percival, Prime Minister, interposes.

Token Decay. p. xxviii.

    Public discover the coinage is absorbed in making tokens. Morgan's Agency. Halliday's and Thomason's Factories. Weight of coins and tokens compared.

INDEX TO INTRODUCTION.

Nineteenth Century Copper Tokens. p. xxx.
Government indifference causes their appearance. No regal copper coinage struck between 1807 and 1821. Absence of Act of Parliament against the issue of copper tokens. Petitions to Parliament fail to redress. Scarcity of small change. Petition from Birmingham. Debates in Parliament on the coinage. Copper tokens suppressed by Act of Parliament 1817. Immunity preceding the Act. Character on design compared with eighteenth century work. Weight of tokens compared. Bogus companies varied devices. The departure of tokens. The Dudley petition. Sir Edward Littleton's Bill passed. Birmingham and Sheffield Overseers granted extension of time. The silver coinage of 1817. The people support the act of suppression. Montagu on the dignity of reigning sovereigns. Want of contemporary collectors. Sharp on token collectors. Sir George Chetwynd's sale of tokens. The increase of token collectors.

Irish Tokens. p. xxxv.
The earliest Irish tokens, denomination of. Royal Proclamations of 1660, 1661 and 1673. Aquilla Smith on money of necessity. Tokens pass current until 1679. Patent granted to Sir Thomas Armstrong. Protest by the Governor of Ireland. St. Patrick's Halfpence, when circulated. The Tynwald Act. Butcher's Halfpence. The copper coinage of Charles II and James II. Gun money. Copper coinage of William and Mary. Queen Anne ignores the currency. Wood's Halfpence, weights compared. The Duchess of Kendal. The want of small money. Dean Swift on "raps." The Drapier controversy. George II copper issues. *Voce populi* Halfpence and Farthings. McMinn's token. Mossop's Pattern Penny. Bank of Ireland and Six Shillings token, weight compared with the English Dollar. Slap tokens. Bank tokens, Thirty, Ten and Fivepence Irish. The copper coinage of 1805. Private tokens. Wyon's pattern for One Penny. Ireland without copper coin for nearly forty years. The coinage of George IV.

Counter-marked Tokens. p. xl.
Why issued. Silver a standard value. Copper countermarked tokens. The custom of countermarking.

Tokens a Lawful Tender. p. xlii.
Parliamentary sanction. Bankers receive permission to issue tokens. The act of 1812. Crowns and Dollars melted to make tokens. Meeting held in support of tokens. The extension of the Tokens Act. The Act of Suppression finally passed and put into force. Bank of England tokens. Wyon's Pattern Ninepence. Depreciation in the value of silver. The public lose confidence in tokens. Wellesley Pole appointed Master of the Mint. The price of silver from 1813 to 1816. The cry for more silver coin. Tokens undated to avoid the final Act until the end of 1815. The coinage of 1817 supplies public demands. The weight of coins and tokens compared.

Tokens Admitted. p. xlv.
Great Britain until the end of George III.'s reign. Ireland 1822. The Isle of Man 1831. Farthings and other pieces without date or value expressed omitted. Several names on one token. Truck money excluded.

Acknowledgments, p. xlvi.

INTRODUCTION.

THE Seventeenth Century Tokens, issued by Corporations, tradesmen and others, were dealt with by William Boyne in his great and laborious book published in 1858.

Token Authors. The year 1889 saw the publication of G. C. Williamson's extended work, embodying the efforts of former writers, with original observations on numerous token issuers; the result being a compilation which meets with general approval. Although it has not exhausted the subject, nor dealt with every existing token or variety, it will not be superseded for years to come. The Eighteenth Century Tokens, more than a century ago, received from James Conder of Ipswich, and Charles Pye of Birmingham, a treatment which established a solid interest in them, and speaks volumes for the energy of collectors, who lived in an age which knew nothing of the facilities afforded either by railways, telegraphs, telephones, or a cheap and rapid postal service.

During the following twenty or thirty years that interest appears to have languished; collectors apparently were few and unenterprising, no further work upon tokens appearing until 1834, when Sir George Chetwynd commissioned Thomas Sharp, the Warwickshire antiquary, to catalogue his collection of Eighteenth and Nineteenth Century pieces. The catalogue was issued when Sir George was in the prime of life. The worthy numismatic baronet, by his personal acquaintance with James Conder, Charles Pye, Thomas and Peter Wyon, E. W. Percy (whose collection of tokens Chetwynd purchased) George, and George Hollington Barker, Francis Blick, Matthew Young, John Harding, William Till and other eminent collectors and dealers, had a vast knowledge of tokens, and this knowledge was embodied in Sharp's work for the advantage of students.

It remained, however, for James Atkins, in an exhaustive work on the Eighteenth Century Tokens, to bring together or focus the token issues of that period, and to show the great variety of dies and edge readings. A long period must elapse ere any want for a re-issue of the book in an extended form can make itself felt. The arrangement was the best that could be chosen thirteen years ago; for even so recently tokens were but little appreciated, and co-operation difficult to obtain.

In 1866, William Boyne published *The Silver Tokens of Great Britain and Ireland*, which, although containing much information, is rather a suggestive catalogue than a completed epitome. Indeed, the author was of the same opinion, for he says "Nearly the whole of the tokens described are specimens in my own collection; there may be others which I have not seen."

In this brief review of the principal works relating to the old trading currencies, reference to local efforts should not be omitted. Indeed, the stimulus for standard works emanates from local zest. Akerman and Burn's London, Boyne's Yorkshire, Cotton's Worcestershire, Davis' Warwickshire, Golding's Suffolk, Simpson's Lincolnshire, Waters' South London, show the deep interest of the local antiquary in token coinages.

The best authority on the laws respecting tokens, as on coins, is Ruding.

The Origin and History of Tokens.

The first mention of a token by this or any other author is interesting. He says "I have met with an account of money struck, by this monarch, upon a material very different from those usually selected for coinage." He then quotes the writer of the *History of Allchester*, 1622, as follows: "King Edward (1272-1307), his leathern money bearing his name, stamp and picture, which he used in the building of Carnarvon, Beaumarish and Conway Castles, to spare better bullion, were, since I can remember, preserved and kept in one of the towers of Carnarvon Castle." Ruding continues: "If the statement of this anonymous author be correct, the above must have been rather tokens, or a kind of promissory note, than money."*

The anonymous writer was probably correct, as, by the subse-

---

* *Vide* Ruding, vol. II, p. 130.

quent history of tokens, it will be seen that they were mainly used by tradesmen, and especially for paying the wages of workers.

Ruding also informs us "that private tokens were used to supply the want of silver coins" at the commencement of the reign of Henry VIII (1509), or at the end of his father's; and he refers to Snelling, as mentioning that Erasmus spoke of "*Plumbeos Angliæ*," or tokens made of lead. As Erasmus visited England in 1497, and wrote *Adagia*, alluded to by Snelling, before he (on the invitation of Henry VIII) revisited this country in 1510, it would seem that the leaden tokens were in circulation at the latter end of the monarchy of Henry VII.*

There is historical evidence, that such contrivances were in vogue (1558-1603) in the time of Queen Elizabeth. Ruding tells us: "The use of private tokens for money, which were stamped by inferior tradesmen, was at this time grown to such an excess as to be the subject of frequent complaints." And Snelling† says: "they were made of Lead, Tin, Latten, and even of Leather. Of these base materials were found Farthings and Halfpence, to the great derogation of the princely honour and dignity, and the great loss of the poor, since they were only to be repaid to the shop from whence they were first received." Queen Elizabeth, for the ease of her subjects, caused "Pledges and Tokens" to be made of "pure and fine copper" to pass current as halfpence and farthings. The copper coinage of Elizabeth was, however, only issued in Ireland. This would seem to have been the first recognition by the State of anything resembling a copper currency since the Anglo Saxon *styca*.

Several patterns for English copper coins made their appearance during Elizabeth's reign, but were not put into circulation.

The people's want of a convenient and ready medium of exchange received no practical attention. The discontent was so great when James I (1603-1625) came to the throne, that cordwainers, butchers, vintners, chandlers, and others, issued farthing tokens of lead. Sir Robert Cotton estimated that there were 3,000 persons in London alone, who "cast yearly Five pounds apiece in leaden tokens." Such was the dissatisfaction then prevailing, that the King granted, in 1613, a monopoly to John Lord Harrington, of Exton, by

---

* *Vide* Ruding, vol. II, p. 411.
† *Vide* Snelling, "View of Copper Coinage," p. 2.

Letters Patent, to make a "competent quantity of Farthing Tokens of Copper" to circulate in place of the base leaden ones, which were prohibited by Royal Proclamation. The regal tokens were mean in appearance, weighing only 6 to $8\frac{1}{2}$ grains each, and were unpopular.

This attempt to be rid of an old abuse gave rise to a new one. In order to force these tokens into circulation, Lord Harrington had been enjoined to give twenty-one shillings nominal value in tokens, for twenty shillings in sterling money. This, Ruding says, "did breed an inconvenience, because many, for the gain of twelve pence in twenty shillings, would take the tokens in great sums, and so with the same, and some money, pay handicraftsmen for their labour at the week's end." The abuse, however, gradually discontinued, but not without the aid of a new proclamation, ordering that "the tokens should be freely exchanged backwards and forwards, for their equal (nominal) value only, in silver money, and providing facilities for the same." A similar proclamation was issued by the Lord Deputy and Council, at Dublin, in 1622, in which it was stated that His Majesty's English subjects had derived benefit from this special provision, and the circulation of the tokens.

Charles I (1625-1648) continued the use of these farthing tokens, but, unfortunately, with a return to the practice of exchanging them in the ratio of twenty-one shillings for twenty shillings in sterling money, and often labourers were compelled to take their whole weekly wages in tokens. The murmurings of the people, on the renewal of the abuse, led to a decree that no one should pay above two pence in farthings to any person at one time. The forgery of the tokens had helped to "breed an inconvenience," and the most stringent laws were passed against the offenders. Notwithstanding, things went from bad to worse.

Snelling* gives the substance of a tract, published in 1644, which reveals a semi-State approval to the private venture tokens of the period. The author says :

<small>Our projectors soon found the advantage that accrued to a private tradesman by his farthings being sometimes lost, and, under pretence of the good of the subject and of the poor, obtained a patent to make thousands of pounds' worth ; and, amongst other ways to get rid of them, some merchants would sell unvendible commodities for tokens, and then would press them upon their workmen whom they dealt with, and by that means, even chandlers, bakers and victuallers had their hands full. Their profit was exorbitant, as</small>

---

* Vide Snelling, "View of Copper Coinage," p. 9.

out of 10 oz. of copper, which cost them one penny,* they made 20 pence in tokens. This could not hold long, but others, more eminent persons, must have a share, and so the first makers were dismissed, and their patents disannulled, and all the tokens left on the subjects' hands, who were to sell them to the braziers at 10 pence or 12 pence a pound, for they had a patent to distribute them, but the poor subjects had no patent to force the makers to take them again.

The next token makers, we all know who they were, the public farthing token offices in London do witness it, and this was done with a more large profit to the makers; they had their officers to attend the sale of them daily, and had a pretty way to vent them, by giving one shilling over in twenty to those who came to buy them, which occasioned many to fetch them, and force 5, 10, yea 20 shillings at a time away; so that in a short time there was an infinite quantity dispersed abroad, to the excessive profit of the makers, but the excessive loss of the takers. The City of London and the adjacent counties of Kent, Essex, Suffolk and Norfolk were so loaded with them, that there was scarce any silver or gold coin left, but all was farthing tokens.

During the troublesome times of the great Civil War, the coinage fell back to its worst state, and a "petition of the poor" was presented in the House of Commons, in 1644, complaining that "there was no exchange for their farthings, to their great damage, even to their utter undoing." There appears to be no record that any serious attention was given to the grievances complained of; but at this particular time, Charles I. must be excused, if he gave a little more attention to the head on his shoulders than the copper tokens of the period.

The Commonwealth (1648-1653) was prolific with patterns for a copper coinage; the legends resembling more the token sentiment than regal inscriptions; such as:—

THE · FARTHING · TOKENS · FOR THE RELEFE OF THE PORE ·

ENGLANDS · FARDIN. · FOR NECESSARY CHANGE ·

¼ OUNCE · OF · FINE · PEWTR FOR NECESSARY · CHANGE ·

THE · FARTHING · TOKEN · OF · THE · COMMONWEALTH · OF · ENGLAND ·

These were more a pretence than an actual coinage, as the great rarity of these farthings prove they were not generally circulated. Nor did Protector Cromwell (1653-1658) recognise his obligation to the people in the matter of small change; although on some pattern farthings his effigy appears with legends, OLIVAR · PRO · ENG · SC · IRL · THVS · VNITED · INVINCIBLE · and on another reverse CHARITIE · AND · CHANGE · 1651 ·

During the brief rule of Richard Cromwell (1658-1660) there was no possibility of dealing with the question of a new coinage, all interest and attention being absorbed by the larger and more urgent question of the Restoration of the Monarchy. Consequently, in that period, as in preceding years of Oliver's Protectorate, private tokens

---

* A silver penny is here referred to.

increased in number, ushering in one of the greatest token-periods known in the coinage history of England and Wales, and Ireland.

At the Restoration, which brought Charles II to the throne (1660-1684), one of the things the nation badly wanted, and which the people hoped to secure, was a sufficient supply of copper coin. This desire and hope seemed to be full of promise, as patterns for a farthing were made freely in the first year of the re-established Monarchy. Among the legends were SVCH · GOD · LOVES ·   THVS · . VNITED · INVINCIBLE ·   TRUTH AND PEACE   And on others   THE KING'S · GRACE · IS · THE POORES · RELIEFE ·   This pattern-making went on for some years; it was seen that they were mere playthings, and there was no intention to come to THE · POORES · RE LIEFE ·

The poor badly wanted relief, and the substitution of Regal halfpence and farthings for the tokens then in use was pressed on the Government. Sir William Parkhurst, in 1660, urged the necessity for small money, to obviate the inconvenience of Tradesmen's tokens, and complained that the practice of coining tokens was so common that the implements to produce them were openly sold.

The indifference of the King and his Parliament to supply a medium of exchange in the lower denominations of our coinage was not only the cause of, but warranted, so to speak, corporate bodies, chamberlains, companies, merchantmen, artificers and retailers, in establishing a general token coinage to facilitate easy purchase and ready settlement.

From 1660 to 1672 corporate and private tokens were freely coined and circulated without let or hindrance. As there was no State prohibition, except which had become obsolete, until 1672— the year of the real establishment of the English copper coinage— these tokens must be regarded as the authorised copper currency of the period, though they were not so technically. Indeed, in 1662, a legality by inference was established for the use of private tokens.

A proclamation stated "all persons who should, *after* the first day of September 1672, make, vend or utter any kind of pence, halfpence, farthings, or other pieces of brass or copper base metal, were to be chastised with exemplary severity." In like manner, Queen Elizabeth, nearly a century before, in a negative sense, made existing private tokens lawful; for, in 1574, Her Majesty by proclamation "forbid the making or using any such (private tokens) *after* the Feast of All Saints next (November 1st) ensuing *without special warrant or commission from Her Majesty.*" A special license was granted by the Queen to the Mayor and Aldermen of the city of Bristol to make farthing tokens.

Mr. Williamson, in a note to the only Seventeenth Century token issued in Scotland (Combes, Dunbar), says :—"This is very surprising... as there seems to have been no special law in Scotland against their issue, any more than in England and Ireland."

From England there were numerous protests and petitions, one stating that "brass and copper tokens, pence, halfpence, and farthings, which the owners now refuse to receive back, saying they are exempted therefrom by His Majesty's pardon of such offenders" and praying "some means of redress to prevent their utter ruin."

The devices on the tokens were many; including tavern and shop signs, articles of dress sold by the issuers, implements of trade, processes of manufacture, animals, articles for domestic use, heraldic signs, the mail coach, views of public edifices, and punning legends. Under these heads, Boyne, in his work, gives interesting descriptions. The tokens were mostly halfpence and farthings; no pence were known until after 1660.

A contemporary observer thus expressed himself on how the tokens would be regarded in after years.

> The tokens which every tavern and tippling-house (in the days of the late anarchy among us) presumed to stamp and utter for immediate exchange, as they were passable through the neighbourhood, which, tho' seldom reaching further than the next street or two, may happily, in after times, come to exercise and busie the learned critic what they should signifie.*

There were some curious legends, among which the following are selected as examples :—

Richard Bakewell, of Derby, in 1666, issued a valentine token, with two doves billing; legend, GOOD · MORROW · VALINTINE ·

At Braintree, one Allen put forth a token with the legend, TURNE A PENNY, encircling a representation of a soldier.

Sam Endon, of Macclesfield, put on his token, WELCOM · YOV · BE · TO · TRADE WTH ME ·

An issuer, named *Swindell*, also of Macclesfield, had for his legend, SQVARE · DEALINGE · IS · BEST · His token was struck on a square piece of metal.

* Evelyn's "Numismata."

Thomas Cotton, of Middlewich, frankly states, ALTHOVH · BUT · BRASS · YET · LET · ME · PASS ·

Thomas Thorpe, of Hepworth, in 1667, adopted the legend, HIS · HALFE · PENNY · THAT · GOES · TOOE AND FROE ·

Edward Lewis, of Maideley Market, announces around a collier's pick, MADELY · WOOD · YIELDS · COAL · THATS · GOOD ·

Two remarkable Christian names, America and Amisist, occur in the family of Baggerley, at Thingden.

In 1652 a token was made payable AT WOMORSLE · CHAPEL · TURTON ·

At Exeter, in 1651, Mary Moore put on her token a Communion cup, with the legend, DRINK YEE ALL OF THIS

Richard Lucas, of Wycombe, declares (1670), around a lion rampant, RATHER DEAD THAN DISLOYAL

The only token, throughout Great Britain and Ireland, where the issuer's name began with Z, was Francis Zacacy, who was a brewer in Limehouse, Middlesex.

On July 25th, 1672, there appeared in the *London Gazette* an advertisement "that it was his Majesty's pleasure that no person or persons should for the future make, coin, or exchange, or use any Farthings or Tokens, except such as should be coined in his Majesty's Mint, his Majesty having given directions for the speedy making of a considerable quantity of farthings, to be made current for exchange of his Monies by his Proclamation."

This proclamation was hailed with approval, but some had doubts, and were, from past experience and disappointment, not to be considered disloyal if they had but little confidence in the King's promise.

It transpired, however, that his Majesty was serious, and had it not been for the fulfilment of the undertaking by the issue of a copper currency, worthy the demand and the times, it may be questioned if the tokens of the period would have been suppressed. As it was they lingered, but the undoubted superiority, both in design and weight, of the Farthing of 1672 was what was wanted to restore confidence to the State in its capacity as provider of copper money.

In 1674, Parliament at last recognised that the practice of private persons passing into circulation their own currency had become a source of unfair profit to the few, an inconvenience and pecuniary loss to the many, and must cease. On the 15th of December of that year it was, by proclamation, announced that those who should "make or utter Farthings, Halfpence, or pieces of Brass, or other base metals, with private stamps," would be prosecuted.

The denominations of the new coinage were halfpenny and farthing. They were of pure Swedish copper; the weight of the halfpenny was 175, the farthing $87\frac{1}{2}$ grains. The coins became at once popular, and the farthings were turned out at the Royal Mint in great numbers. The superiority of the coins in design, execution, and weight, did more than any Act of Parliament or proclamation to stamp out tradesmen's tokens. The supply of copper currency being sufficient, tokens disappeared.

In the third decade of King George III., who had grossly neglected the coinage, a token production and circulation was again brought into existence. The debased state of the coinage justified it, and the result was that, at least for a few years, the regal copper coinage became almost extinct. The English Government has, in many matters, the power to do equitably and efficiently for the public that which cannot be done so well by private enterprise. It may be slow to recognise a danger or to perform a duty, but by virtue of its power it may set aside any attempt to usurp its authority. The issue of the approved copper coinage of 1797 did completely that which was wanted to stamp out the eighteenth century tokens; and this as effectively as the copper coinage of Charles II. did in its day.

Cause and Effect.

Had the Council in 1787 given speedy effect to its resolve, quoted below, it would have put a check on the token specie.

In consequence of a Council held at the Cock Pit (Whitehall) to take into consideration the present state of the copper coin of the Kingdom, Lord Effingham, who is Master Warden of the Mint, attended, and repeated the various representations that had been officially made to him, in order to prevent the present abuse of that species of coinage. It was then determined immediately to commence a new coinage; and in order to put a total stop to counterfeit halfpence and farthings, which are now so great a burden to the public, it was resolved, that in the new arrangement one pound of copper should be made into 24 halfpence instead of 48, which has been the practice hitherto, and the farthings in the same proportion of size and weight.*

It has been seen that tokens were brought into vogue from the neglect of the Governments of the times to provide a proper coinage. Like siege coins, they were a money of necessity; this condition alone sufficiently justifying an issue of trader's tokens mainly for the purposes of small change.

* *The European Magazine*, December 1787.

A ready circulation of money is one of the essentials of commercial life. Tokens forced the Commonwealth, under the Protectorate of Cromwell, to think of an issue of farthings. Tokens caused the issue of a regal coinage of small value under Charles II, continued as need arose by his successors down to the second decade of George III, during which long period tokens disappeared as needless.

The lapse in the copper coinage, from 1775 to 1797, was responsible for the revival of tokens in the latter end of the XVIIIth century. The issue of these tokens became so vast that Sharp said they "almost superseded the national currency," which statement is borne out by the fact that 600 tons of copper were used from 1787 to 1797 in the coinage of tokens in Birmingham, to which must be added those struck in London, absorbing many additional tons of metal. At the Royal Mint, prior to 1797, halfpence and farthings only were made. By forgery this copper currency was debased and degraded. One-fourth only of the halfpence, and scarcely one-tenth of the farthings, were struck at the Mint. As a consequence the people ignored them. On the other hand, the eighteenth century tradesmen's tokens were popular, containing as they did almost their nominal value in weight of metal. Soon, however, the fabricator's art was brought into requisition by manufacturers and traders. The public, especially the wage-earning class, were victimised by a token coinage almost as base as the coins supposed to be of Government issue. The question of the copper coinage was often before Parliament during this period, and although the Government had repeatedly promised to put it in order, it was not until 1797 that Matthew Boulton received instructions to strike the twopenny and penny pieces once so famous.

After this tardy treatment it is remarkable that the Government confined itself to these two denominations, rejecting the halfpenny and farthing (patterns for which still exist)—remarkable inasmuch as previous issues had been for halfpence and farthings alone. The pattern penny, prepared by Pingo in 1788,[*] not having been approved cannot be recognised.

The copper coinage of 1797, struck at the Soho Mint, possessed beauty of design, good quality and weight of metal, and was so excellently wrought as to defy the forger's art.

[*] *Vide* Montagu, p. 104.

No contemporary counterfeit of Boulton's copper money of 1797 is known; but, years after, dies from the Soho Mint came into lawless hands, and brought his proof coins into disrepute: the deception did not consist in imitating them, but in striking from the original dies, which were repolished, or, as it is technically termed, "lapped."

Young, Till, and Taylor, the two former, dealers in coins and tokens, muled Boulton's dies somewhat extensively.

Another influence in the disappearance of the token currency after 1797 was undoubtedly the avarice of some traders, who sought to make as much as 30 per cent. profit from the issue of their tokens.

The counterfeiting of coin was a trade, illegal of course, but a profitable business, connived at in proportion to public submission. P. Colquhoun, an eminent magistrate, in "A Treatise on the Police of the Metropolis," 1797, informs us that there was a rolling mill in London, well known, where all the dealers and coiners of base money resort for the purpose of having their plates prepared, from which, when finished, blanks were cut out of the size of the money to be counterfeited. He also said: "The artizans who stamp or coin these blanks into base money are seldom interested themselves. They work as mechanics for the large dealers, who employ a capital in the trade." Colquhoun estimated that the annual turnover of counterfeit coin was £200,000, and states that "the great dealers execute orders for the town and country with the same regularity as manufacturers in fair branches of trade. Scarce a waggon or coach departs from the Metropolis which does not carry boxes and parcels of base coin to the camps, seaports, and manufacturing towns."

The maintenance of a copper currency, either by the Crown or by private persons, was, to a great extent, controlled by the price of metal. In 1793 copper was £105 per ton, a price the Government considered too high to justify a new coinage. In 1797 the Government undertook to supply Matthew Boulton with copper ingots at £108 per ton. The contract stipulated that Boulton should charge that sum, plus 4d., for every lb. avoirdupois of coins struck. Eight twopenny pieces and sixteen pennies were to weigh 1 lb. respectively, exactness being insisted on, so that the coins might be useful as weights. The cost of the coinage was £140 per ton, leaving the Government £9 6s. 8d. as a profit, out of which had to be defrayed the cost of carriage and the distribution of the coins. This would leave but a small margin (if any) for Brassage. The nation was, however, secured against loss by the continued appreciation of copper. The Boulton "cart-wheel" penny was so heavy that an artizan who was paid his wages of 20s. in those coins would have to carry 15 lbs. in weight from the pay-table. Early in 1799 the Government announced that a further contract had been made with Matthew Boulton for halfpence and farthings, at a rate of 36 halfpence and 72 farthings to the lb.

This decrease in weight occasioned confusion and unrest, which was taken advantage of to defraud the public, and not without success, as attempts were made to *bear* the currency, which the following advertisement will show :

> J. Owen acquaints his Friends, and those who have on hand Bad Halfpence, that he has received a quantity of Woollen Cloths, Kerseymeres and some Drapery Goods, which will be sold on Thursday, Friday and Saturday, by private Sale, half payment in Bad Halfpence, no Promissory will be taken, those who have quantities will find it worth their notice.*
>
> Also : *Aris' Birmingham Gazette*, in March, 1799, contained an advertisement stating that "Base copper coin, that will not pass in this country, will be taken for eight days, and positively no longer : as the ship sails in a few days after, and they cannot be taken afterwards."

The company who issued this advertisement offered goods in exchange for what they called " base copper coin " knowing at the time that no order had been made either in Parliament or in Council. At the end of 1799 the new coinage made its appearance; and, while it did not give the same satisfaction as the 1797 issue, it was on the whole well received, and gave much relief to the commercial classes.

In the meantime copper was still increasing in value; indeed, so scarce had it become, that the heavy Boulton coinage found its way into the melting-pot, to the profit of the metal workers at the various centres of that industry. Ruding quaintly says : " Whenever copper happened to rise in price the lean coins soon devoured the fat ones."

In consequence of this melting process, small change gradually again become scarce. As will be seen from the table below the price of copper, too, was constantly changing, and this in itself made the question of the coinage difficult to deal with.

By 1805 " the greater part of the penny and twopenny pieces

---

* Bath Journal, Jan. 20, 1799.

disappeared, being worth, when melted down, nearly one-third more than their value as coins. The Anglesea penny tokens, of 1787 and 1788, then in general circulation, and which were of

PINCE'S PRICE CURRENT.
COPPER, BRITISH, IN CAKES.—PER CWT.

First Qr. s. s.	Second Qr. s. s.	Third Qr. s. s.	Fourth Qr. s. s.	YEAR.
— —	— —	— —	133 —	1800
— —	— —	— —	117 —	1801
— —	— —	— —	111 —	1802
— —	130 140	140 —	— —	1803
140 —	156 —	— —	165 —	1804
— —	165 —	200 —	— —	1805
— —	200 —	182 —	— —	1806
— —	162 —	147 —	— —	1807
— —	147 —	200 —	— —	1808
Uncertain till April	160 —	160 —	— —	1809
— —	160 —	Uncertain	— —	1810
— —	150 156	140 146	— —	1811
— —	140 146	130 135	— —	1812
— —	130 135	— —	— —	1813
None till December	— —	140 —	120 a 130	1814
— —	130 140	120 130	— —	1815
— —	120 130	Uncertain to Nov. 85	—	1816
— —	105 —	133 —	— —	1817
133 —	123 —	No price after April	—	1818
— —	No price	— —	— —	1819
— —	„ „	— —	— —	1820

the same quality and even of a greater weight than the Boulton coinage, suffered the same fate.

Through the continued expansion of trade, which brought the Nation an increased turnover, a greater need than ever was felt for a ready exchange, and the demand, instead of being a pleasure to the Government, was esteemed a trouble.

The Government was, however, compelled to provide a further supply of small money, and, in 1806 and 1807 pennies were issued representing 150 tons of metal; halfpennies, 427½ tons; farthings, 22½ tons; altogether 600 tons. There were 24 pennies, 48 halfpennies, and 96 farthings to the lb. avoirdupois.

This order was the last which Boulton executed for copper coinage; and, strange as it may appear, no further issue of copper money made its appearance until 1821, when a farthing (by the famous artist Pistrucci) became current in the reign of George IV.

The following account, contained in a circular letter printed by Boulton and Watt, is extremely interesting

Medals & Coins
Struck at
Soho Mint, Staffordshire.

Medals.

Emperor of Russia.
King's Preservation.
Assassination of King of Sweden.
Restoration of King of Naples.
Final interview of the King of France.
Execution of King of France.
Execution of Queen of France.
Prince and Princess of Wales on their marriage.
Marquis Cornwallis, on the peace with Tippoo.
Earl Howe, on his Victory of the first June.
Hudson's Bay Company.
Slave Trade abolished.
Chareville Forest.

General Suworow on his success in Italy.
Empress Catharine of Russia.
In commemoration of British Victories.
Union with Ireland.
On the Peace 1802.
Serment du Roi.
Lafayette.
J. J. Rousseau.
Respublica Gallica.
The Death of George III.
Battle of Trafalgar.
Frogmore Medal.
Prince Regent of Portugal.
Manchester and Salford Volunteers.
A Specimen Prize Medal.
Emperor Alexander of Russia.

Coins.

British Government.

1797 {Twopenny Piece. / Penny.
1799 {Halfpenny. / Farthing.
1806 {Penny. / Halfpenny. / Farthing.
1797. Specimen of proposed Penny.
1797. Specimen of proposed Guinea.

1805 {Irish Penny. / Irish Halfpenny.
1806 Irish Farthing.
1798 {Manx Penny. / Manx Halfpenny.
1804 {Bank of England Dollar. / Bank of Ireland Dollar.} *Silver*
1811. Proposed Bank of England Token.
A Soho Mint trial Piece.

Foreign Governments.

1790. 5 Sols Pacte Federatiff.
1792. 5 Sols Hercule.

1822. Buenos Ayres Decimo.
1792. 2 Sols Liberte.

Provincial Tokens.

1791. Anglesey Halfpenny.
1795. Bishop's Stortford do.
1791. Cornish . . . do.
1789. Cronebane . . do.
Dundee . . . do.
1800. Enniscorthy . . do.
1791. Glasgow . . . do.
Hornchurch . . do.

1794. Inverness Halfpenny.
1794. Lancaster . do.
1793. Leeds . . . do.
London . . do.
Penryn . . do.
1791. Southampton do.
1793. Wilkinson's . do.

Colonial.

Bencoolen.

1804 {
4 Köping.
3 Köping.
2 Köping.
1 Köping.
}

Bombay.

1804 {
1 Adell.
½ do.
¼ do.
⅛ do.
}

African Company.

1786 {
1 Akie, or 1 Crown Piece.
½ Akie, or ½ do.
2 Takoe, or ¼ do.
1 Takoe, or ⅛ do.
}

Sierra Leone.

1796 {
100 Cent, or 1 Dollar Piece.
50 . do.
20 . do.
10 . do.
1 . do.
1 Penny Piece.
}

Madras.

1794 { 4 Faluce.
2 do.

1803 {
20 Cash.
10 do.
5 do.
1 do.
}

Ceylon.

1802 {
48 to 1 Rupee.
96 to do.
192 to do.
}

Miscellaneous.

1791. Bermuda Penny.
1804. Bahama Halfpenny.
1821. St. Helena Halfpenny.
1830. Guernsey 1 Double.
  ,,   Do. 4 Doubles.
1831. Sincapore 1 Köping.
  ,,   Do. 2 Köping.
1809. Portuguese Dollar.
  ,,   Proposed Indian Coin 1 Pice.
  ,,   Do . . ½ do.
Copper Company of Upper Canada Halfpenny.

Prize Medals
of various
Colleges, Societies, &c.,
of which
Specimens are furnished only to their order.

Nineteenth Century Silver Tokens. A renewal of the failure to supply coin, a token coinage—the last this country has seen—was taken in hand by traders, for gold, silver and copper. The first Bank token coinage which appeared in this century was in 1804. No silver coins had been issued by the Royal Mint since the shilling and sixpence of 1787; indeed, this was the only silver coinage of George III during the forty years he reigned in the eighteenth century. The shilling of 1763, by Yeo, and the Dorrien and Magens' shilling of 1798, although they appear in English numismatic works, must be regarded as tokens rather than coins, as the former was struck for the Earl of Northumberland, limited to 2,000 pieces, and the latter minted in error, and forbidden circulation by an order in Council. Previous to the issue of the Bank dollar of 1804, Boulton and Watt, at their Soho Mint, had countermarked 3,744,583 Spanish dollars.

The capture of the Spanish specie by the British was naturally popular in this country. On one occasion a haul was made of no less than one and a quarter million dollars, as will be seen from the following account:

"Wednesday, Dec. 4, 1799.
"This day six waggons, loaded with the treasure taken in the two Spanish frigates, reached the Bank from Plymouth. At 9 o'clock, the waggons arrived at Kensington, where they were met by a Captain's guard of the Grenadier battalion of the Guards, and the procession moved along Piccadilly, St. James's-Street, Pall Mall, the Strand, Fleet-street, and Cheapside as follows:

"Military Band of Music
A Detachment of the guards;
A commissioner of the customs, and a lieutenant
of the navy, on horseback;
Six waggons with the treasure, drawn each
by eight horses;
"Each waggon had flags on it, the English surmounting the Spanish. Sailors rode on the outside of the waggons.
"A detachment of the 16th regiment of light
dragoons closed the procession.
"The horses were decorated with ribbons. When the cavalcade reached the Mansion-House, the Lord Mayor, the Lady Mayoress, and the gentlemen of his household came out in front of the house, and drank from out of a gold cup, 'Success to the British Navy,' the band playing *Rule Britannia*, while the honest tars, who were regaled at the same time, gave his lordship three cheers. (Twelve or fourteen waggons more are since come up. The whole of the specie taken on board the two ships amounts to the vast quantity of *forty tons*.)"*

The forgery of the countermarks, and of the dollars, had become such a scandal, that as many genuine pieces as could be collected were sent to the Soho Mint, to be restruck by the new machinery invented and used there. The design had the bust of the king and his titles on the obverse, and, on the reverse, in an oval, Britannia with her attributes; legend, BANK OF ENGLAND FIVE SHILLINGS DOLLAR 1804. They were in striking contrast to the silver crowns issued by previous monarchs, and welcomed on account of the paucity of silver coin. The new dollars were excellently well struck, and although they did not defy the forger's art, they supplied the public with a good medium of exchange.

There were, however, great complaints, owing to the absence of coins of lesser values. Silver was scarce, and the Government did not see the importance of the question; merely promising that

* Gentleman's Magazine, January, 1800.

the matter should receive due attention, and that it was preparing to provide a new supply of silver coin.

From 1804 to 1811, no new coinage made its appearance. The inconvenience was keenly felt, and the old methods of the Bank of England, whose great idea was that a paper issue was enough to serve the public, had become antiquated. Maberly Phillips, Esq., F.S.A., recently informed the Institute of Bankers, that such was the condition of things that "merchants, traders, overseers of the poor, and the City Corporations, were floating their promises to pay, and publicans issued small notes which they could not redeem in specie, and so indorsed the drinks of the holder on the back until the debt was *liquidated*.* In Ireland, we read of a country gentleman who had to abandon a dinner party he was to give, as no one would trust him with goods, or could give him change for a note." Archd. Reed, the Mayor of Newcastle-on-Tyne, in response to a numerously signed requisition, convened a meeting of the principal inhabitants of that city on the 13th July, 1807, to petition Parliament for a new silver coinage.

The Government had no definite proposals as to silver and copper coin. It was, moreover, unable to rehabilitate confidence in the Bank of England, since its stoppage of payment in 1797.

The Directors of the Bank had also brought ridicule on themselves by adjusting the standard value of countermarked foreign coin. Commercial men cried in vain for a sufficient medium of exchange, and the poor were alike inconvenienced. This intolerable strain was working its way again to tokens, the production of which literally verifies the adage that necessity is the mother of invention. In 1810, such was the contempt in which the Government was held on the question of the coinage, and the public indignation so great, that history repeated itself, and traders again, with public approval, resolved to supply a token coinage, in order to facilitate the trading propensities of the Nation.

The Nineteenth Century Tokens proper commenced in 1804, by Clark, West & Co., of Dublin, and in 1809 with Bishop de Jersey & Co., of Guernsey, who commissioned Boulton and Watt to strike

---

* The italics are my own. Bruce's Licensing Act made the recovery of debts for drink consumed on the premises illegal, until which there was a custom to have drink, in slang phraseology, "on the strap." To clear the "strap" at the public house "hard by," workmen have been known to pay more than half their wages.—W. J. D.

over dollars, their bank tokens for five shillings. In the following year, orders were extensively forwarded to Birmingham for great quantities of tokens in silver and copper. Sir Edward Thomason, in his Memoirs, states:

> The copper and silver change, in the year 1810, became so extremely scarce and inconvenient throughout the country, that the demand for the manufacture of tokens, to enable the masters of manufactories and others to pay their workmen their weekly wages, was so great, that I had endless applications for both, as I was, at this period, making the silver crowns, half crowns, shillings and sixpences* for the Douglas Bank in the Isle of Man. And I manufactured, during this year, silver and copper tokens for Wales, Brecon, Gainsborough, and Newcastle-on-Tyne, and for many different establishments in the neighbourhood.

In 1811, there was an agitation, in and out of Parliament, for and against local tokens. The Earl of Lauderdale, who at the time was defending the issues of private tokens, wrote to Edward Thomason (afterwards Sir Edward) as follows:—

DUNBAR HOUSE, DUNBAR.
SIR, *August* 31, 1810.†

In a letter I received last night from Mr. B. Thomson, manager of the Burichie Main Colliery, Newcastle, in reply to a printed letter I had sent him, as an issuer of tokens, he says—"I would recommend your applying on the subject of your letter to E. Thomason, Esq., of Birmingham, who, I apprehend, can give you more general information in relation to it than, perhaps, any other individual."

I have to urge this as my apology for enclosing one of my circular letters to you, and to assure you that I will be grateful for any information you can give. A list of the names and addresses of those you know to be engaged in circulating local tokens will be particularly acceptable. I am, Sir,
Your most obedient humble Servant,
LAUDERDALE.

In his letter, his Lordship states:—

In the last Session of Parliament, I opposed the Bill, entitled *An act to prevent the issuing and circulating of pieces of gold and silver, or other metal, usually called tokens, except such as are issued by the Banks of England and Ireland respectively.*

Much as I could wish for the credit and welfare of the country, that a general revision should take place of the principles upon which our circulation is now conducted, I was then, and am now, perfectly convinced that the measure of annihilating all local tokens in the month of March next, unless it should be attended with some further arrangements, must prove highly injurious.

I am indeed of opinion, that there is just reason to believe that, if this Act is not repealed immediately on the meeting of Parliament, the commerce of the country will sustain a most severe shock. For, in my view of the subject, it will deprive the master-manufacturer of the power of paying the wages of his workmen, and leave the poorer consumer without the means of dealing with the retail trader, whilst it would prove a source of infinite inconvenience to the community at large.

There were fifteen queries submitted at the end of the letter for Thomason to answer:—

1. What is the denomination of the tokens you have issued?
2. What is the average weight of each species?
3. By how many dwts. in every twelve ounces is the metal of which they are composed inferior to standard silver?
4. What is the average intrinsic value of each species?
5. Are there any local tokens circulated in your immediate vicinity, besides those you have issued, and by whom?

---

* If a sixpence was intended it was never issued.
† Sir Edward dates the letter in error; it should have been 1811.

6. What do you compute to be the total value of the local tokens circulating within the district in which you reside?
7. What proportion do the local tokens bear to the halfcrowns, shillings and sixpences, that are in circulation near you?
8. What do you conceive to be the average intrinsic value of these halfcrowns, shillings and sixpences?
9. Are there many tokens of the Bank of England circulated in your vicinity?
10. Has it been common to refuse change for a banknote, unless a large proportion of copper is taken?
11. Have you known a premium given to get silver for a twenty shillings bank note?
12. Has there been any attempt to issue paper notes or tickets under the value of twelve shillings?
13. Have you not known master manufacturers pay their workmen's wages with paper tickets, under the circumstance of a shop being established in the neighbourhood, where the workmen are furnished with goods in exchange for those tickets?
14. Where this has occurred, has it not been customary for the retail trader to settle his accounts monthly or quarterly with the manufacturer by whom the tickets were issued?
15. Is there a disposition to petition the two Houses of Parliament, at their next meeting, for the repeal of the Act, which has recently passed, prohibiting the circulation of local tokens?*

It is to be regretted that Thomason does not give the reply to this important letter, as in all probability particulars of a valuable character would have been handed to us.

Tradesmen's tokens were once despised and ignored because they never were strictly a legal tender. Tokens had firm supporters, both in Parliament and the country; who, in consequence of the failure of successive Governments to provide a constant flow of coin, believed that commerce could not be developed without such aids. Indeed, it will be presently seen that by Acts of Parliament they were, if not a legal tender, lawful for specific periods. A distinction certainly, but one which the people failed to see.

Throughout the year 1811 the rage for tokens was at its height, and such was the hold they had on the public that meetings were held in different parts of the country to promote them. In Sheffield, at a public meeting held on October 24th, 1811, it was resolved that "the denomination of 2s. 6d. and 1s. be stamped and sent into circulation to an amount not exceeding £10,000 and not less than £5,000." Nor was there any sign of abatement in their popularity during the year. Thomason says: "In 1811 I manufactured above two million of copper tokens for Samuel Fereday, the then greatest Ironmaster in the world. He (Fereday) stated, upon examination before the House of Commons, that he had nearly 5,000 persons in his employ. . . . The tokens which I manufactured for him to a very large amount were all of copper.

* Sir Edward Thomason's Memoirs, p. 44.

. . . He used to send a carriage to my establishment every other Friday, during the continuance of the pressing of these, to enable him to satisfy his numerous workpeople."

Silver and copper tokens were now firmly established; indeed, thanks to H. B. Bowles, Esq., it has been discovered that a token bank was started at Bristol. This bank issued a token note for one pound, which is the only known instance of a bank circulating a token paper currency as such. During the year the price of silver had so much increased that the Bank of England failed to issue a new supply of its tokens. A correspondent, writing in the *Statesman* on March 10th, 1811, appeals to stockholders to resist the attempt of the Bank to levy a tax of 10 per cent., and deprecated any excuse for abusing the public confidence.

Christopher and Jennett, of Stockton, who had their own tokens, printed a scathing criticism in 1811 on Bank Tokens, written under the *nom de plume* of "A Briton." The writer voiced the opinions of the extremists who advocated the abolition of the Bank of England's protection by the State. He trusted that "a House of Commons, before whom all Europe trembled, would see (so *he* wrote), that the *marriage à la mode* between the Bank and Treasury . . . will be speedily dissolved by Act of Parliament." * Although this reasoning was untenable it throws a flood of light on the bad state of the coinage of the time; the *inertia* of the Government, and the incapacity of the Bank, or its unwillingness to meet the emergency which had too long existed for an adequate coinage. The fluctuation in the price of silver from 1804 to 1811 had, of course, much to do with the chaos, and made matters extremely awkward for the managers in Threadneedle Street; but an enlightened policy, coupled with an acceptance of responsibility to find the country necessary money, would have saved the situation, and private tokens might have been prevented.

During the controversy, the Overseers of the Poor, private banks, and tradesmen, jointly and separately, were sending out their own tokens, and, as they were freely accepted, trading was expedited, which further tended to strengthen the opposition to Parliament in its desire to suppress the issues.

* Discussing Mr. Manning, M.P., in defending the Bank directors' actions, this critic says: "I wonder he has not proceeded to coin crowns of tin; to assure the ducal diadem of Cornwall; to divert the prince (Wales) of that which bound
His baby-brow with sovereignty."

INTRODUCTION.

In 1811 the Bank of England issued tokens for three shillings, and one shilling and sixpence. They were of less relative weight than the countermarked dollar and the dollar of 1804, being in proportion 76, as against 83·3 grains per shilling. There was no complaint as to their weight, and relief was given by their circulation. Much of the difference was accounted for, as the standard value of the dollar was 5s. 6d. Their lightness was a benefit to the community, as, although a large quantity was put into the melting pot to make private tokens, they were, for this purpose, ignored when dollars could be obtained.

The dies were engraved by Lewis Pingo. Of the three shillings and one and sixpence the obverses bore the King's bust in armour, with his short titles, as on the dollar of 1804. The reverse indicated the denominations within a wreath of oak.

The price of silver in August, 1811, was 6s. 4d. per oz.; in October it had risen to 6s. 11½d., and before the year was out had advanced to 7s. per oz.

The countermarked dollars were issued in 1797 at 4s. 9d. each, and, as they weighed only 63 grains under the ounce, it will be seen how, without a firm, clear, and definite policy on the part of the Government, the coinage would be demoralised. The report of the Bank of England—February 9th, 1810—informs us that "Dollars issued by the Bank of England," to the 8th of February of that year, were:—

Dollars stamped and issued 1797 .	2,325,099
Dollars of 1804 .	1,419,484
And 1809 and 1811 inclusive .	1,073,051

There were also issued between the 9th of July, 1811, and the 10th of December, 1812, Bank tokens for three shillings 9,548,690= £1,432,303 10s., and for one shilling and sixpence 4,708,937= £353,170 5s. 6d.—total £1,785,473 15s. 6d.,* a supply quite inadequate to the nation's needs.

The expansion of the factory system had created or developed an increased demand for small change with which to pay wages, and in these circumstances all attempts to put an end to the private token were ridiculed, and resulted in failure.

The *Gentleman's Magazine*, in 1811, announced that "a rise of ten per cent. of the stamped dollars in circulation took place this day (March 19th). The increase in the price of silver has become so great, that the dollars or tokens issued by the Bank sell for more for bullion than they are current at as coin. The directors of the Bank gave notice that they would receive them at 5s. 6d. In the House of Lords Lord Grenville, commenting on

* *London Star*, Dec. 1812.

the action of the Bank directors, censured it as violating the constitution, by an assumption of the rights of sovereignty. Earls Bathurst and Roise defended on behalf of the Government."

At the commencement of 1812 there was no falling off in the public demand, for such it was, for a continuance of token issue.* Sir Edward Thomason says : " In this year an English guinea was "worth twenty-seven shillings, according to the Mint price of gold; "and so scarce was the coin, and the panic so great, that every "maiden lady hoarded up all the gold she received. The Master of "the Mint at this period (The Honourable Wellesley Pole) could "not obtain permission from the Government to proceed with a "new gold and silver coinage; and the country could not afford "the loss which naturally attends the calling in and re-issuing of a "new coinage of gold and silver. Berkley Monck, Esq., M.P. for " Reading, in Berks., the principal banker at that place, determined "upon issuing both gold and silver tokens; and desired that I "would proceed with manufacturing as soon as the dies could be "completed conformable to his drawings. For the obverse he "adopted the likeness of Alfred the Great, with following motto on "the legend :—' PIGNORA CERTA PETIS DO PIGNORA CERTA, 1812.' "And on the reverse :—' 40 Shillings. Berks Token. Standard "gold, 6 dwts, 18 grains. Reading.' On the legend :—' Payable in "bank notes, at 6s. the dwt., by I. B. Monck, Esq.' The weight "being struck upon the gold pieces, fully proved the Mint price of " gold at this period.

" The Hon. Mr. Percival, the Prime Minister, requested that "I would suspend proceeding with the *gold* tokens until he should "see Mr. Monck. No more were manufactured, and only £1,600 "worth were struck, and the pieces were eagerly bought up at as " much as the sum of £5 each, to be retained as mementos of the "only gold token ever struck, and to confirm the price of gold at "this eventful period in his country." †

Token Decay.
There was a coming awakening to the danger of permitting private parties to coin their own money. It was gradually discovered that tokens issued by the Bank of England were melted down for the purpose of making tokens of less intrinsic value.

* The Earl of Lauderdale, speaking on the Local Token Bill, on July 21, 1812, said he " opposed the Bill, as it would be sure to injure the retail trade of the country, which could not be carried on without these tokens. It would also be the means of introducing again those local notes, which were good for nothing, whereas the tokens were worth three-fourths of their nominal value."

† Sir Edward Thomason's Memoirs, p. 48.

There had also been working an insidious malady, which was eventually sure to kill private enterprise. H. Morgan, of London, publicly advertised that he was a licensed maker of tokens; but it would appear that his statement was made without warrant, at least no record for any such authority having been granted him has come to light. He was probably the agent of Thomason or Halliday, of Birmingham. Halliday was a die engraver and manufacturer, whose business premises were in Newhall Street, in that town, and near to Thomason's works, in Church Street. Halliday engraved most of the token dies for Thomason as an outworker, but Morgan's orders were engraved and struck in Newhall Street, at Halliday's works. Morgan gradually reduced the weight of his tokens to suit his customers. The Birmingham Overseers' shilling weighed 73 grains, as against 83·3 in each fifth part of the 1804 dollar. A Bristol shilling sold by Morgan weighed only 60 grains, or a difference in value of thirty per cent. in favour of the dealer and trader. The Marlborough Old Bank circulated shillings, the specific gravity of which was reduced to 53 grains. The imposition continued, and was practised openly—firstly, because Parliament was indifferent; and, secondly, in consequence of the relief the public had received from a ready system of barter.

The subjoined interesting calculation is taken from a journal of the period:—

SILVER TOKENS.

The following table of the weight and value of several of the Provincial Tokens, which at present form a large part of the silver circulation, has been drawn up by Mr. North, of the Assay Office, York, from the assays made by him. The intrinsic value is said to be calculated according to the present price of silver (but the price is not mentioned), and the weights on an average of several pieces. The fourth column states the inferiority in every 12 oz. to standard silver:—

	s.	d.	Weight. Dwts. Gs.		Worse. Dwts.	Intrinsic Value. s.
The Bank Dollar of	5	6	17	8	9	5 5
Ditto	3	0	9	11	9	2 11½
The Gloucester	2	6	6	8	20	1 10¾
The Newcastle	2	6	7	3	11	2 2½
The Hull	1	6	3	14	11	1 1¼
Ships, Colonies and Commerce	1	6	3	18	21	1 1¼
The Doncaster	1	0	2	21	30	0 9¾
The Leeds	1	0	3	1	29	0 10¼
The Newcastle, by Robertson	1	0	2	22	10	0 10¾
The Newcastle, by Kelty	1	0	2	18	11	0 10
The York	1	0	2	16	10	0 10
The Lincolnshire	1	0	2	12	30	0 8½
The Whitby	1	0	2	16	10	0 10
The West Riding	1	0	2	16	18	0 9½
The Scarborough	1	0	2	16	20	0 9½
The Stockton	1	0	2	16	23	0 9¾

SILVER TOKENS—(*Continued*).

			Weight. Dwts.	Grs.	Worse. Dwts.	Intrinsic Value.	
The Newark	1	0	2	12	20	0	$9\frac{1}{2}$
The Sheffield	1	0	2	23	23	0	$10\frac{1}{4}$
The Shaftesbury	1	0	2	10	20	0	$8\frac{1}{2}$
The London's (Warren's)	1	0	2	15	11	6	$9\frac{3}{4}$
The Bristol	1	0	2	16	14	0	$9\frac{3}{4}$
The Bridlington	1	0	2	10	19	0	$8\frac{1}{2}$
The Derby	1	0	2	12	48	0	$7\frac{3}{4}$
The Lincoln	1	0	2	13	11	0	$9\frac{1}{4}$
The Gainsborough	1	0	3	1	29	0	10
The Charing Cross, London	1	0	2	7	15	0	$8\frac{3}{4}$
The Stamp Office	1	0	2	15	46	0	$8\frac{1}{2}$
The Bradford	1	0	2	20	28	0	$9\frac{1}{4}$
The Fozely (*sic*)	1	0	2	8	24	0	8
The York	0	6	1	5	10	0	$4\frac{1}{2}$
The Britannia	0	6	1	7	32	0	$4\frac{1}{4}$
The Hull	0	6	1	6	11	0	$4\frac{3}{4}$
The Derby	0	6	1	2	48	0	$3\frac{1}{4}$

It has been seen that silver tokens originated from the indifference of Governments to the needs of the populace in respect to the mediums of exchange. The same causes which brought in silver tokens operated with greater force on the issue of copper ones, and, as this metal was more or less plentiful during the nineteenth century, there was less excuse for the neglect. Early in the century many people received their wages wholly in copper specie, because traders were bound to find ready cash of some kind. The traffic in truck was indirectly forced into existence in olden times by the failure of monarchs and Governments to supply a sufficient coinage.

Nineteenth Century Copper Tokens.

It has been already mentioned, from 1807 until 1821, no copper coins were issued by the State either in Great Britain or in Ireland.

Early in the century, as previously dealt with, copper had become so high in price that the heavy coinage of 1797 had been put into the crucible, because it was worth more when melted down than its indicated face value; but this only aggravated the unsatisfactory condition of the regal coinage, and should have induced Parliament to grapple with the difficulty by providing, for the time being, a coinage of less specific gravity. The *apathy* of the State caused tradesmen to bring on another token period, which received tacit official recognition in the absence of any Act of Parliament to prohibit its issue until 1818.

The people wanted regal coin, and repeatedly petitioned Parliament to provide it.

In 1811 copper coins were so scarce that the *Gentleman's Magazine* noticed that a merchant of Truro had offered to give Bank of England paper for one thousand pounds worth of small money which, in those days, was regarded as a wonderful undertaking.

In September of the same year the High Bailiff of Birmingham, in pursuance of a requisition, forwarded to the Privy Council, on behalf of the town and neighbourhood, a memorial:—

"that trade suffereth great and serious evils from the want of small change. . . . That there are in this town and neighbourhood many thousands of persons whose weekly labour does not produce more than from three to ten shillings, and that their employers being compelled to pay several together in pound notes, they are under the necessity of going to public-houses to get change, where, of course, some of the money must be spent to induce the publicans to supply them therewith, or they must buy some articles which they do not want, or in many cases must take the articles of food on credit at an extravagant price, paying for the same when what they have had amounts to a pound. That the issue of Bank Tokens, although of great and essential service, is by no means adequate to the remedy of the evil. And your memorialists, therefore, most earnestly request that your lordships will speedily order a coinage of copper penny and halfpenny pieces, which would effectually remove the evil they labour under."

On the second reading of the Silver Tokens Bill, June 13th, 1813, Mr. Huskisson asked the Chancellor of the Exchequer: "Is it intended by the Bill to prohibit the circulation of local copper tokens, as there is an immense quantity made of spurious metal,* the circulation of which has a tendency to enhance the price of first necessaries, being issued by large manufacturers, and exchanged at par for bills at twelve months after sight?" Sharp, in a footnote written as early as 1833, after quoting this statement, doubts it, as he found no evidence on which it was based. The same member further stated that "shopkeepers consequently charged their articles higher, and that the labouring classes are obliged to submit to the imposition, from the difficulty they have of procuring employment." This general statement supports the contention, if such it may be termed, that tokens were largely used in paying wages to labourers and artizans. On the third reading of the Bill, June 29th, 1813, Mr. Grenfell, M.P., in calling attention to the depressed state of copper specie, said: "The bad halfpence, when taken by the shopkeeper, are sold by him as base metal at 8d. per lb., whereas 16 good penny pieces weigh 1lb., and it takes 73 of these halfpence to produce the sum of sixteenpence, so that the difference or loss is as 32 to 73."†

---

* I have not found many tokens which are not of the best copper. Mr. Huskisson's remarks would well have applied to the spurious regal coinage.—W. J. D.

† Hansard, v. 26, c. 961.

On July 27th, 1817, the circulation and issue of copper tokens were dealt with by Act of Parliament. Copper tokens had enjoyed a long life, as from 1811 to 1817 no official interference checked their circulation. This immunity gave to the issuers a free hand, and, as a result, many of the industrial districts secured a ready medium of exchange, remarkable from its matter of fact type. The eighteenth century tokens aimed at the picturesque; the nineteenth were severely Spartan, some with nothing but inscriptions or legends, both on the obverse and reverse, and when character was delineated it was represented by busts of eminent men, workhouses and mills. The reverses were largely devoted to the figures of Britannia and Commerce, and in Ireland the harp naturally predominated. Many tons, mostly the penny denomination, were circulated, and though they fell short of the just standard of the 1797 coinage, they successfully competed with the regal issue of 1807. There was, however, much difference in the specific gravity of the various tokens, that of the Birmingham Overseers being the heaviest of all. This disparity in weight gradually became more marked, and led to dissatisfaction. On many there was no "promissory" to redeem, as was the case with most of the silver tokens. Bogus companies, with a promissory of imaginary persons and legends, overshot the market, and an undoubted reaction enabled the Government to deal with the subject by public consent.

The design, or devices, of the tokens, silver and copper, were very varied and included:—

Gods of classical literature, saints, emperors, kings, queens, the Druid, and warriors; men of mark, figures of Britannia, Justice and Commerce; heraldic arms of country, cities, towns, the nobility, and gentry; diadems, crests and monograms; statues, cannons, military trophies, musical instruments, and the stage coach.

Animals, birds, and fishes. The Phœnix and the Griffin.

Mountains, cathedrals, churches, castles on land and on rocks at sea; light-houses, ships, sea views, public and private buildings interior and exterior; bridges, mills; furnaces and collieries.

Engines, machinery, including the loom, the plough, water wheels, windmills, the wheatsheafs; trade appliances, agricultural and horticultural implements; bales of merchandise; beehives and casks.

The time had come for these tokens to depart. Many of those who had issued them had either become bankrupt, or refused to redeem them. For the purposes of commerce, it was gradually perceived that as vouchers they were insecure. As these evils grew the public became uneasy, and a movement commenced, which found a ready response in the House of Commons, where the private issue of tokens had always been disliked; and sanctioned only on the ground of expediency.

A petition was presented in the House of Commons, from Dudley, by Mr. Grenfell, on April 25th, 1817, complaining that the copper tokens were not half their nominal value, and praying that their issue might be forbidden. At the time of the petition, tokens were so plentiful that the wage earners had a difficulty in purchasing, and were forced to accept in exchange for them less of the common necessaries of life, which in effect raised the price of commodities but did not bring a corresponding increase to their earnings.

The grievances of the people were real, and Parliament was not long in giving effect to the Dudley petition.

Sir Edward Littleton, member for Stratfordshire, introduced a Bill to prohibit the making of copper tokens, and to render the circulation of such tokens illegal after January 1st, 1818.

The Government succeeded in passing the Bill on July 27th, 1817.* It contained, however, a proviso that the penny tokens issued by the Sheffield Overseers of the Poor, in 1812, 1813, 1814, and 1815, were to remain a lawful tender until March 25th, 1823; and another to the same effect in respect to the Birmingham Overseers of the Poor, and their tokens bearing the dates 1811, 1812, 1813, and 1814,† which were lawfully permitted circulation until the 25th day of March, 1820. The ground for such exceptions as stated in the Act was that "the immediate suppression of which would be attended with great loss to the said townships, and to the holders of such tokens, being for the most part labourers and mechanicks, as well as with great inconvenience to the inhabitants."

The new silver coinage, which was now in general circulation, contained a plentiful supply of shillings and sixpences; and, consequently, not so much copper specie was required.

A study of the subject will also show that a greater power than Parliament had decreed that tokens could no longer be tolerated in England and the Principality of Wales. For nearly three years (with the exception of the twopenny piece of Rugeley, a few farthings, and the Sheffield Workhouse token of 1815) none were issued

---

* Ruding, vol. iv, 139.

† Ruding, who was evidently quoted by Sharp, gives the additional date of 1815, but this is an error, as the Birmingham Overseers did not issue tokens after 1814.—W. J. D.

were almost regarded as a regal issue, and, though there is much obscurity as to how and when this interesting coinage was first produced, probably Mr. Grueber is right in that it was not issued so early as thought by Simon and Lindsay, as he says "the style of work shows that it is of a much later period, and it seems more probable still, according to Dr. Aquilla Smith, that the issue took place between the cessation of the copper tokens and the striking of a regal currency." This opinion Mr. Grueber bases on the fact that " these coins formed part of the currency of the Isle of Man in 1678 and 1679, being especially referred to in an Act of the Tynwald of the 24th June, 1679," and that "also in 1682 they were the authorized currency of the State of New Jersey."

The Tynwald Act referred to was an Act to suppress the circulation of " Butchers' halfpence, Patrick halfpence, copper farthings, or any other of that nature after the 1st day of January, 1679." As the Isle of Man was at this time in the possession of the Earl of Derby, and it had the sovereign right of issuing its own coinage, it does not follow, because of the Tynwald Act referred to, that the Saint Patrick money was not a regal issue for Ireland. Even Ruding had no information, and Simon is content to quote Rymer, who only "supposed that the copper pieces called Saint Patrick halfpence and farthings were struck by the rebel's authority."

In 1680, Charles II. gave to Ireland what it needed to effectually stamp out private tokens.

In this and the two years following, under another patent granted to Sir Thomas Armstrong, halfpence of good workmanship and weight were circulated; and tokens ceased to be made.

The next issue was the halfpenny of James II., which was struck 1685-1688. Then followed, during the troublesome times of this monarch, the appearance of the gun and tin money, the former of which was, in Ireland, known as " brass money." After the abdication of James, William and Mary, from 1690 to 1694, supplied a currency in the form of a copper halfpenny, and in 1695 and 1696 William III. issued halfpence. Queen Anne, during the twelve years she was on the throne, ignored the currency of Ireland altogether; and it was not until George I. had reigned eight years that a patent was granted for coining copper money in Ireland, which Dr. Philip Nelson says, in his account of the life of Wood, was originally granted the Duchess of Kendal, who sold the patent rights for £10,000 to William Wood, and that the halfpence and farthings of 1722-24 were issued or minted in Phœnix Street, Brown's Gardens, Seven Dials, London.

The *Hibernian Patriot*, p. 44, quotes the report of the Committee of Privy Council.

Whitehall, July 24, 1724.

The want of small money in Ireland has now grown to such an height, that considerable manufacturers were obliged to pay their men with tallies or tokens in cards signed upon the back, to be afterwards exchanged for money; and counterfeit coins called raps, * were in common use, made of such bad metal, that what passed for a halfpenny was not worth half a farthing.

Dean Swift wrote: "It having been many years since copper halfpence and farthings were last Coined in this Kingdom, they have been for some time very scarce, and many counterfeits pass about under the name of raps."

In 1730 Mr. Prior, in "Observations on Coin in General," quoted by Aquilla Smith, noted "the constant drains of money out of the Kingdom, for the support of our gentlemen abroad, and the scarcity of money occasioned thereby."

Wood's currency was very unpopular, occasioned perhaps more by the informal way the coins were sent to Ireland than to the specie itself. The prescribed weight, 128 grains, compared favourably with the preceding copper currency, and which had become very worn. It must also be recorded that the failure of successive Governments to keep up a sufficient supply of copper had caused a want of small change, and as private traders were preparing to reissue a token coinage it is assumed that the opposition was strengthened by this interest. Indeed, during the next twelve years, no effort was made to satisfy the legitimate requirements of Ireland in its coinage; of either gold, silver, or copper; therefore, as Ruding states, "several persons in the North and other parts of that kingdom were under the necessity of making copper and silver tokens, which they passed as promissory notes amongst their workmen, customers and neighbours, those of copper for twopence, and those of silver for threepence." It was during this period that the "Drapier" (Dean Swift) controversy arose; and there was, until 1736, practically no restriction to the issue of private tokens.

---

* This seems to be the origin of the saying "Not worth a rap."

INTRODUCTION.

In 1736, it was decreed that his Majesty (George II.) was graciously pleased, at the humble request of the Lords Justices and Council, to direct a contract for fifty tons of copper to be made into halfpence and farthings for his Majesty's subjects in Ireland, and that the profit of such issue should go to the public revenue of that kingdom. From the legend was omitted " Dei Gratia," which was much noticed at the time. Halfpence and farthings were issued until 1755, and private tokens disappeared apparently without a royal proclamation. No further regal copper coinage appearing, there was created, in the words of Mr. Grueber, "another occasion for the striking of copper tokens." The *voce populi* halfpence and farthings " struck by Roche (or Roach) of South King Street, Dublin, who was a manufacturer of metal buttons for the army," were extensively circulated in 1760, and were recognised as Pretender money. In the same year F. McMinn issued a private token for twopence, and as Ireland, until 1766, had to find its own coinage there was no other way but to resort to tokens. At intervals, from 1766 to 1783, halfpence were coined of twenty-six pence to the pound avoirdupois, the number struck was inadequate, but sufficient to check private token venture. From 1783 to 1804, Ireland was, in the matter of its specie, left to its own resources.

Efforts were not wanting to induce the royal authority to maintain its copper coinage. Mossop, the Irish die engraver, in 1789 submitted a pattern for a penny, the design of which delineated national feeling. On the obverse was a striking portrait of the King with the legend GEORGIUS III REX, and under the head a harp. On the reverse the figures of Britannia and Hibernia, with their attributes, hand in hand before a lighted altar. Legend CON COR DIA. (Unanimity) 1789. The King evidently thought well of it, as he was graciously pleased to retain two of the specimens out of the six, which, it is said, were struck.*

In 1804 there were struck for the Bank of Ireland six-shilling pieces. The obverse was similar to the English dollar, but with the reverse Hibernia seated, supporting a harp, and the legend, BANK OF IRELAND TOKEN 1804 SIX SHILLINGS. The design was by the renowned die engraver C. H. Küchler. The peculiarity of the pieces was that they were struck over the Spanish dollars;

---

* *Vide* Montagu, lot 240, Sotheby, Wilkinson & Hodge, July 16th, 1897.

were of the same date and weight as the English dollar, and yet represented a shilling more in value. Previous to the issue of this token no regal silver coins had been minted for Ireland since the reign of Charles II.

So much had Ireland been neglected that worn shillings and sixpences, without any trace of the obverse or reverse designs, were in circulation, countermarked with the initials and names of various tradesmen and shopkeepers. These were called "slap tokens," from being countermarked by another trader, probably to induce acceptance. They were almost as thin as a hammered English silver penny, and, like the imitation regal halfpence and farthings of the second decade of George III., show the depressed state into which the coinage of Ireland had fallen—indeed, had almost disappeared.

In the two succeeding years the Bank of Ireland issued tokens for tenpence and fivepence, which were a great convenience. Those dated 1805 were the most abundant. Mr. Grueber, in his excellent work on the "Coins of Great Britain and Ireland," ignores the second issue, but the tenpenny and fivepenny tokens of 1806 were plentiful, and as the latter carries the obverse of 1805 there can be no doubt that the Bank of Ireland caused them to be struck in 1806. The Bank of Ireland in 1808 brought another relief to facilitate the medium of exchange, in the form of a half-crown token, or XXX PENCE IRISH. The designs of this, as well as of the tenpence and fivepence, were by Pingo. Ireland here established another peculiarity, inasmuch as the Bank of England issued no tokens from 1804 until 1811. The last silver token of Ireland was struck and circulated by the Bank of Ireland in 1813; it was for tenpence. The obverse was the same as the pattern for the English ninepence by Wyon.

In 1805 the dies for a regal penny, halfpenny and farthing, were engraved by Küchler, and struck at the Soho Mint, Birmingham, in the following year a farthing only. The farthings were circulated in large quantities, but the penny and halfpenny are usually found as proofs.

The issue of private silver tokens commenced in 1804, and consisted of three types, each for one shilling. With the exception of the "Pro Bono Publico" token, only a limited number seem to have been circulated, which is accounted for by a sufficiency of Bank silver specie.

In 1813, an attempt was made to supply a new copper coinage, and for this purpose two patterns of merit were submitted from Soho. The first has, on the obverse, the bust of the King laureate and draped, under the bust a rose, beneath T. W (Thomas Wyon), legend GEORGIUS III D:G: BRITANNIARUM REX. The reverse a large harp similar to those on the tokens of the period, legend HIBERNIA 1813. The second pattern has a broader but similar bust with the rose omitted, and W on the shoulder, legend GEORGIUS III D:G: REX* This obverse was afterwards used for the Colonies of Essequibo and Demarary, one stiver token of 1813. Neither pattern was accepted for Ireland.

For nearly forty years, except in 1805 and 1806, Ireland was without copper money. Private tokens, as a result, began in 1801 and continued until 1822-3, when the last regal coinage of Ireland was struck at the Soho mint, from dies engraved by William Wyon, who, for the King's portrait, was supplied with a model by the famous Pistrucci.†

The assimilation of the Irish coinage with that of Great Britain, and its regular supply, finally ended the desire or the necessity for private tokens. There did appear at a later date work (or truck) tickets, but these will be dealt with in a forthcoming book on badges, society, garden, and theatre passes.

Early in the nineteenth century there was issued a trading coinage of a remarkable character. This currency, for such it was, is now known as the "Countermarked Tokens." The seal, or countermark, of the issuer was intended to be taken as security for the full indicated value. The token issue was again directly caused by the failure of the Government to supply sufficient silver coin for public requirements, which was the more keenly felt, as people were naturally averse to accept foreign dollars, which bore effigies and inscriptions they did not understand. To meet this antipathy mill owners and merchants, perforce, impressed

---

* *Vide* pl. 3, Montagu sale, July 16th, 1897.
† *Vide* Grueber 133.

on foreign coins their own promissory stamp, and such was the desire for something reliable that the issuers could almost demand the acceptance of their countermarked money. These countermarked pieces are described, and, so far, form a complete list of all known to exist.

At the period in question silver had its intrinsic, or standard, value, almost as gold has now; and it is more than conjectured that the various values were stamped on the coins in proportion to the appreciation or depreciation of that standard.

The smaller denominations in copper also show that the public had more confidence in the mill owners' than in the regal coinage—*pre* the Soho productions. These pieces were generally countermarked over worn English and Scotch halfpence; also on eighteenth century tokens, many of which were in circulation at this period. Some few indicate that dollars might still exist with these countermarks, but, up to the present, research has failed to find them in silver.

The countermarked pennies of Bradford Workhouse, and of the Keighley Overseers—also those crossed G R, J M and W W—were issued by local authority. At the time money being scarce, puncheons were resorted to, to save the expense of a pair of dies, and to give an additional promissory that tokens in circulation, but struck for another county, were to be accepted on good local security.

The countermark was most favoured in Scotland, which is attributed to an old custom of re-issuing coins at a rate different from that at which they were first circulated. During the reign of James VI., the testoon and other coins of Mary were countermarked with a crowned thistle, and re-issued at an advanced value.

The ryal, or sword dollar, struck 1567-1571, was in 1578 similarly countermarked, which process was resorted to in consequence of the appreciation of silver. The testoon, so countermarked, was made current for tenpence more than its original recognized value, and the sword dollar four shillings and threepence above its face value, in the method of the Scotch calculation.* This appears to be the origin of the countermark in Great Britain, and, as it was first applied in Scotland, accounts for the preference given to this form of a token.

* *Vide* Grueber 193, 134.

There can be no doubt that the tokens of 1811 and 1812 were a lawful tender by Act of Parliament. This, it is admitted, was made imperative by the necessity of the times, but it is not a sufficient justification for excluding all tokens from the coinage of the country; to do so is to make a similar mistake to that of the historian, who passes lightly over the Cromwellian period, in a descriptive chronological record of our Monarchial system. A Parliament that decrees a certain coinage for a given period, and afterwards extends such time of official recognition to that form of coinage, confers on such a circulation its highest mandate, short only of a royal warrant.

Tokens a Lawful Tender.

By an Act of Parliament, passed in 1809, it was required that local tokens, when presented to the issuer, were to be met in Bank of England notes. This not only accounts for the promissory legends to honour the tokens in the highest security of the times, but conveyed the impression that they were allowed to circulate with official sanction.

The Statesmen informed the public on September 18th, 1811, that "All the Country Bankers have received permission to issue silver tokens for small change."

On July 20th, 1812, it was enacted* that after the 25th day of March, 1813, no tokens, except those issued by the Banks of England and Ireland, should be current. The penalty for the issue of each private token was to be not less than five pounds or more than twenty at the discretion of the Justices of the Peace, who should hear and determine the offence. Ruding says: "The copper tokens were not mentioned in this Act, and consequently their circulation was not forbidden." Thus, for eight months, private tokens were clearly a lawful tender.

During this period of official recognition no regal coinage was struck, except Bank tokens. Crowns and dollars, especially the crowns, were fast finding their way into the melting pot for the production of tokens, to the great loss of the community.

This absorption aggravated the situation, and, as time advanced, the dearth of regal coin was such that much anxiety was manifested as to how the commerce of the country was to be conducted.

* 52 George III. c. 157.

INTRODUCTION. xliii

Citizens held meetings and expressed their disapproval of the extinction of tokens. At Reading, on September 19th, 1812, a meeting of traders and the inhabitants generally thanked J. B. Monck for the issue of his tokens, and condemned the Act forbidding the circulation of gold and silver tokens.

In the beginning of 1813 there was no improvement, as, although the Government had passed the Act of prohibition, it failed to substitute coins for tokens, and was, as a result, ultimately compelled to give a new lease to the traders who provided them. Therefore Ruding says: "It became necessary to extend the circulation of private tokens to the 5th day of July next following." This extension Act was passed on March 13th, 1813, and again on July 10th of the same year* it was enacted that the "time for the circulation of private tokens be extended to the space of six weeks after the commencement of the next Session of Parliament, and in order to remove doubts which had arisen it was enacted that the issuers of local tokens should be liable in Law, upon demand made, of the value denoted upon such tokens to pay the same." On November 25th, 1813, Parliament again considered the question, but the Government had no definite proposals to make as to the immediate prospect of a new regal silver coinage except Bank tokens. It enacted that private tokens should remain in circulation as a substitute until " six weeks from the commencement of the next Session of Parliament." This Act,† which received the Royal Assent November 26th, 1813, is the last on record which in any way gives parliamentary sanction to the circulation of tradesmen's silver tokens.

The Bank of England had, during the token periods, issued the three-shillings and one-shilling-and-sixpence of the Pingo type. The directors had also given large orders to the Soho mint for tokens of similar denominations. These were engraved by William Wyon, and were circulated in the years 1812-15. The three-shilling token was also struck in 1816 but not circulated. In 1812 a pattern by the same artist for ninepence was submitted which, however, was not approved.

Bank tokens, by their superior make and intrinsic value, were,

---

* Statute George III. c. 106.
† Statute 54 George III. c. 4.

xliv   INTRODUCTION.

on their merit, doing more to suppress private tokens than the final Act of 1813, again showing that, without a sufficient official coinage, Acts of Parliament were almost abortive.

"The time had come even for Bank tokens to cease as it was announced.* The first of May is the last day on which the five shillings and sixpence Bank dollars will be exchanged by the Bank, after which time they will not be received in payment but must be sold for old silver. The Country Banks in general have intimated to their customers that they cannot take dollars later than to day."

The general public, rather suddenly, was changing its opinion on the question of private tokens, and members of the House of Commons, whose protests against the wholesale issue of commercial tokens had been made in vain, now found ready support for their final extinction.

Another agency came to the aid of the Government. The price of silver began to fall. The movement in this metal went on until the Spanish dollar, in November 1815, which had been honoured by the State Bank for five shillings and sixpence, was not worth more than about four shillings and threepence.

On September 30th, 1814, the Hon. William Wellesley Pole was appointed Master of the Royal Mint, and proved himself to be equal to all that was required to reinstate a regal silver coinage commensurate to the commercial necessities of the times, and, since the coinage which he introduced in 1816, there has been no need for tradesmen to set up a token silver specie, and therefore none have been issued. The continued depreciation of silver was an important factor, as will be seen from the following table :—

DOLLAR SILVER PER OUNCE.

		s.	d.			s.	d.
1813.	May	6	7		September	5	6
	June	6	8	1815.	January	5	7
	July	6	9		February	5	10
	August	7	0		April	6	9
	September	6	11		May	6	8
	October to December	7	0		June	6	5
1814.	January	6	11½		July	5	7
	February	6	11		October to December	5	3
	April	6	6	1816.	January	5	3
	July	5	11		April	4	11½
	August	5	7½		July	4	10

From the time of the final Act of suppression, however, to the issue of the silver coinage, which from various causes was delayed until 1817, there were loud cries for silver coin.

A writer signing himself "An Englishman,"† dealing with

* Northampton Mercury, Apl. 26, 1817.
† Monthly Magazine of 1814.

the lightness of silver coin, says : " I find that a crown piece is equal in weight to twenty-two sixpences, and to eight country tokens which pass for one shilling each."

Tokens were now an illegal tender by Act of Parliament, but were, in the absence of a new coinage, still being made, undated so as to evade the law, and were in general circulation until the latter end of 1815.

There are various opinions as to where the series of nineteenth century tokens should end, and what pieces should be admitted.

Tokens Admitted. The course taken is, that in Great Britain tokens are described where they express a value, or are dated prior to the end of the reign of George III.

In Ireland, where no specific Act appears to have been passed for their suppression, they are recognized until the regal coinage of 1822 was struck. In the Isle of Man until 1831, the date of the last token.

Tokens are included which at sight leave no room for doubt but what they were circulated and used as coin. Many pieces of farthing size have been omitted which do not express a value or a date; to include such would bring in doubtful pieces, issued probably in the eighteenth, or too late in the nineteenth century.

Many of the silver tokens have, on the reverse, the names of several tradesmen, notably those issued in the towns of Bath, Bristol, Haverfordwest and Newark. These tradesmen had, as it were, a small combine to assure the public that the issuers or the company were able to meet their liability.

Mr. Sydney Sydenham found that Culverhouse, Orchard, Phipps, Whitchurch, and Dore, were tradesmen who carried on business in different parts of a street, or in various streets, in the City of Bath. This form of partnership applies to the issue of tokens in many towns.

All tokens, other than purely truck money, expressing values exceeding one penny, are recognized as necessary to complete a distinct section of numismatics.

Acknowledgment. The present work aims at finality, both of die and variety. The great assistance which the author has received from advanced collectors, eager to help, has made the task lighter than such an undertaking would otherwise have been, and considerably added to the pleasure of its production, which kindness and zeal he will always remember gratefully, and thankfully acknowledge.

Most esteemed assistance has been rendered by Mr. James Atkins, who for some years diligently laboured to get together varieties of the nineteenth century tokens. The manuscript is in the author's possession, and has been found invaluable for reference.

Mr. Thos. Bliss kindly lent the whole of his choice countermarked collection, and other tokens, from which plates H, L and M have been entirely prepared.

Mr. H. B. Bowles, of Clifton, has minutely examined his splendid cabinet of silver tokens, and from time to time reported varieties of die, the knowledge of which has done much towards making the long series complete. In many ways Mr. Bowles' contributions have enriched the work.

Mr. Lionel L. Fletcher, of Caterham, who is an authority on the early Irish series, and whose cabinet is particularly rich in farthing tokens, has contributed the specimens illustrated on plate N.

Mr. William Norman, of Newcastle-on-Tyne, whose collection of nineteenth century copper tokens is one of the most perfect, has been ardent in the desire to afford aid; and who also most willingly forwarded any token required for description or illustration.

Messrs. Spink and Son have given willing and excellent assistance, and readily supplied the blocks for some of the woodcuts.

Mr. Sydney Sydenham, of Bath, has waded through piles of old newspapers and periodicals, and found many important facts to justify the issue of tokens.

Mr. A. W. Waters, of Leamington, by research, has been able to furnish much information on the literature of the subject, and assisted the undertaking in many ways.

The author is also indebted to the following gentlemen for their valuable assistance: Mr. A. H. Baldwin; Mr. J. H. Dormer; Mr. Herbert A. Grueber, British Museum; Mr. S. H. Hamer, Halifax; Mr. F. G. Laurence, Sutton; Messrs. Lincoln and Son; Mr. F. E. Macfadyen, Newcastle-on-Tyne; Mr. J. Macmillan; Mr. T. C. Martin, Clifton; Mr. W. Sykes, Hull; Mr. J. Verity, Dewsbury; Mr. W. C. Weight; and Mr. W. C. West.

Indeed, it is not possible for the author to express adequately his indebtedness and gratitude for the genial aid, which so many have given in the effort to classify this interesting branch of numismatology.

Moseley, 1904.

xlvii

ARRANGEMENT OF PLATES.

CONTEMPORARY COLLECTORS.
TITLE PAGES OF TOKEN WORKS.
MATTHEW BOULTON ... ... *Page*	1
LADY CHETWYND AND AUTOGRAPH LETTER OF SIR GEORGE CHETWYND ... ... ,,	29
THOMAS SHARP ... ... ,,	31
MATTHEW YOUNG... ... ... ,,	71
D. T. BATTY ... ... ,,	91
TOKEN BANK NOTE OF BRISTOL ... ... ,,	103
JAMES CONDER ... ... ,,	135
VIEW OF SOHO FACTORY... ... ... ,,	143
BIRMINGHAM OVERSEERS' TOKEN NOTES ... ... ,,	147
BUST OF CHARLES PYE ... ... ,,	157
CHARLES PYE: AUTOGRAPH LETTER ... ... ,,	159
WILLIAM BOYNE: AUTOGRAPH LETTER... ... ... ,,	167
J. K. PICARD ... ... ,,	177
SIR EDWARD THOMASON ... ... ,,	181
JOHN LINDSAY ... ... ,,	213
AQUILLA SMITH ... ... ,,	229
ISLE OF MAN BANK NOTE ... ... ,,	243

AUTOTYPE PLATES A TO N AT THE END.

REFERENCES TO WOODCUTS.

MIONNET SCALE ... ... ,,	11
BOLTON COUNTERMARKED DOLLAR ... ... ,,	17
PT. GLASGOW COUNTERMARKED DOLLAR.... ... ... ,,	21
DEVONSHIRE TWOPENCE ... ... ,,	41
BUST OF SAMUEL FEREDAY... ... ... ,,	121
BIRMINGHAM SIXPENCE ... ... ,,	147
BIRMINGHAM SIR ORIGINAL HALFPENNY ... ... ,,	156
HANCOCK'S WORKSHOP AT SOHO ... ... ,,	158
VIEW OF STAVERTON FACTORY ... ... ,,	160
DUDLEY PENNY ... ... ,,	162
BUST OF NELSON ... ... ,,	185
SOWERBY BRIDGE SEVEN SHILLINGS ... ... ,,	186
PEEL CASTLE TWO SHILLINGS AND SIXPENCE ... ... ,,	243
ATLAS HALFPENNY ... ... ,,	246

ABBREVIATIONS.

O = OBVERSE.   E = EDGE.
℞ = REVERSE.   Ex = EXERGUE.

CORRIGENDA.

Page 75, *no.* 49, *read* " PIDCOCK'S."

Page 190, *omit the first* D *in* " GLANCLY(D)WEDOG."

Page 227, *Co. Mayo. Since including these Tokens, the Author has received the following important communication from Earl Altamont:*—

"I am sorry to say that, I fear the tokens of which you wrote to me, and whose rubbings you sent to me, are not Irish Tokens at all. I have found a set among some odds and ends. They are described as having been used for paying negro slaves in Jamaica. My family at one time owned large estates and many slaves. The head "garden" or estate was known as "Kelly's." These estates came into the family about the middle of the eighteenth century, by marriage. My grandfather, the second Marquis, sold them about 1840. He went out to Jamaica as Governor-General in 1834, to carry out the Abolition of Slavery, as, tho' a large slave owner, he had scruples, and spoke strongly in the House of Lords in favour of abolition. It is likely that tokens were in use long before his time, when small money was scarce, but whether or no these represent early or late specimens, I cannot tell. The date, however, must be between 1800 and 1834."—*London, 3rd March,* 1904.

Matt^w Boulton

24th June 1787

From a Wax Medallion modelled from life in the possession of
Mr John Ranose.

THE
Nineteenth Century Token Coinage.

BANK OF ENGLAND.

SHIELD DOLLAR, 1798.

SILVER.

1. ○ Laureate and draped bust to the right, GEORGIUS III DEI GRATIA REX. Truncation mark C.H.K., the first leaf of laurel points to the *centre* of the E in DEI

℞ M. B. F. ET. H. REX. F. D. B. ET. L. D. S. R. I. A. T. ET. E. 1798. (Magnae Britanniae, Franciae, et Hibernae Rex; Fidei Defensor; Brunsvicensis et Lunenbergensis Dux; Sacri Romani Imperii Archi Thesaurarius et Elector); the royal arms surmounted by the crown which divides the date, *a proof pattern.* *R.r.r.*

2. A Copper Proof.

3. Similar, but the first leaf of laurel points to the *first* limb of E IN DEI *R.r.*

4. A Copper Proof. *R.*

5. Similar, but truncation mark ..K. and the first leaf of laurel points to the *centre* of E in DEI *R.r.r.* *Küchler.*

This variety was sold at Preston's sale (Lot 118) for £14.

BRITANNIA DOLLAR, 1804.

BUST TO RIGHT.

6. ○ Laureate and draped bust to right, GEORGIUS III DEI GRATIA REX. Truncation mark C.H.K. *well spread;* top front leaf of laurel points to the *centre* of E in DEI

℞ BANK OF ENGLAND 1804 Britannia seated, with her attributes, between a beehive and cornucopia; К incuse under the shield, *inverted;* all within an oval band inscribed FIVE SHILLINGS DOLLAR and surmounted by a mural crown.

Boyne 7.

7. Also in Copper.

Boyne 10.

8. ☉ Similar, but truncation mark C.H.K. *close,* and the first leaf of laurel points to the *end* of E in DEI

℞ Similar, the ℣ under the shield *inverted and expressed.*

9. Also in Copper.

10. ☉ Similar, but the first leaf of laurel points to the *centre* of E in DEI

℞ Similar, but with K under the shield *proper and expressed.*

11. Also in Copper, struck on flans of different sizes and thicknesses.

12. ☉ Similar, but truncation mark C.H.K. again *close;* the first leaf in laurel points to the *end* of E in DEI

℞ Similar, but the ℣ under the shield *inverted* and *incuse.*

13. Also in Copper.

14. ☉ Similar, truncation mark C.H.K. The first leaf of laurel points to the *centre* of E in DEI No period after REX

℞ Similar, but K under the shield *proper.*

15. Also in Copper.

16. ☉ Similar, but with a period after REX. ; the first leaf of laurel points to the *first limb* of E in DEI No period between C H

℞ As last. *R.r.*

17. ☉ Similar, truncation mark C.H.K.

℞ As last. *R.*

18. Also in Copper. *R.*

19. ☉ Similar, but the first leaf of laurel points to the *centre* of E in DEI

℞ Similar, but ℣. under the shield *inverted and expressed. R.*

A vagary of the time is well placed by a contemporary writer who, with commendable shrewdness, passed it to the antiquary of distant ages. He wrote:

Mr. URBAN, *London, Sept. 17.*

The following curious phenomenon, occasioned by the present state of British currency, deserves to be recorded; and may be of use to the future Historian who shall consult your pages.

	£	s.	d.
A Guinea made of Standard Gold, weight 5 dwts. 9 grs., passes by law for only	1	1	0
A Guinea 3 grains *lighter* is worth as Bullion	1	5	6
A Crown Piece made of Sterling Silver, weight 19 dwts. 8 grs., passes by law for only	0	5	0
A Bank Dollar weighing 2 pennyweights *less,* and the silver 2½d. an ounce *worse,* is current for	0	5	6

A Half Crown Piece of Sterling Silver, weight 9 dwts. 16 grs.,
    passes by law for only 0 2 6
A Bank Token weighing 5 grs. *less*, and the Silver 2½d. an ounce
    worse, is current for 0 3 0
    The lesser Bank Token for Eighteenpence weighs 1 dwt. 2 grs. *less* than a Shilling and a Sixpence, and the Silver is also 2½d. an ounce *worse*.
    Any person who buys an ounce of Standard gold, and pays for it in Coin, will receive Ten-pence in change out of Four Guineas and Two Seven Shilling Pieces.
    The One Pound Bank of England Note purports to be the representation of full 5 dwts. 3 grs. Standard Gold; but at the present nominal price it will purchase not quite 4 dwts. 4 grs.: its deficit is full 23 grains, and its consequent depreciation 3s. 8½d.
                                                             Yours &c. B. S.
Gent. Mag., *Sep.* 1811.

It does not appear that any notice was given by the Bank to assimilate the value of the Regal Crowns to the Dollars, which apparent neglect was probably due to a legal difficulty.

GARTER DOLLAR, 1804.

20. O Laureate and draped bust to the right, GEORGIUS III DEI GRATIA. Truncation mark :·C.H.K The first leaf of laurel points to the *first* limb of D in DEI *Four* berries in wreath.

℞ BRITANNIARUM REX FIDEI DEFENSOR The royal arms within a garter; motto, HONI SOIT QUI MAL Y PENSE surmounted by a crown dividing the date 1804. Under the shield DOLLAR *R.r.r.*

21. Similar, but truncation mark ·:C.H.K *R.r.*
                PLATE J, no. 5.

22. Also in Copper.
        Glendining & Co. (lot 183) April 29, 1903.

23. Similar, but truncation mark ·: K *R.r.r.*

24. Similar, but truncation mark .. K and REX added to the legend, the first leaf in laurel wreath; points to the *upright* limb of E in DEI

25. Also in Copper.
            In Mr. Bowles' Cabinet.
All the above described Tokens were from dies engraved by Küchler.

FIVE SHILLINGS AND SIXPENCE, 1811.
BUST TO LEFT.

26. O Laureate and draped bust to the left, GEORGIUS III DEI GRATIA REX Truncation mark ✿ · ✿ The first leaf of laurel points to the first limb of D in DEI There are *five* berries in wreath.

℞ Britannia seated, holding in her right hand a spear, her left resting on a shield; BANK OF ENGLAND TOKEN Ex. FIVE SHILLINGS & SIXPENCE 1811 *R.r.*
                PLATE A, no. 1.

27. Also in Copper.

28. Similar, but there are *six* berries in the wreath. *R.r.r.*
                                                        Phillp.

29. O. As no. 26.
℞ As no. 1 Shield Dollar of 1798.
O by Phillp; ℞ by Küchler.
This rare mule is in copper, and in Mr. Bowles' cabinet.

BUST TO RIGHT.

30. O. Laureate and draped bust to right, GEORGIUS III DEI GRATIA REX. Truncation mark C.H.K The first leaf of laurel points to the *centre* of E; four berries in wreath.
℞ Britannia seated, holding in her right hand a spear, her left resting on a shield; BANK OF ENGLAND TOKEN Ex. FIVE SHILLINGS AND SIXPENCE, 1811 *R.r.r.*
Boyne 16.

31. Also in Copper. *R.r.*

32. Similar, but the first leaf in laurel points to the *end* of E in DEI

33. Also in Copper. O by *Küchler*; ℞ by *Phillp*.

BUST TO LEFT.

34. O. Laureate and draped bust to the left, GEORGIUS III DEI GRATIA REX. Truncation mark ✣ · ✣ *Six* berries in the wreath.
℞ BANK TOKEN 5s. 6d. 1811 within a wreath of oak; stem of wreath turns slightly *downwards;* I.P under the tie of wreath. *R.r.*
Boyne 11.

35. Also in Copper.
Boyne 13.

36. O. Similar, but with *five* berries in the wreath.
℞ Similar, but the stem of wreath turns slightly *upwards;* I.P. under tie. *R.r.*

37. Also in Copper. *R.*

38. Also a Proof in Brass. *R.r.r.*
In Mr. Bliss' cabinet.

39. O. As last
℞ Blank, *a trial piece, copper. R.*

40. O. Blank,
℞ As no. 36, *a trial piece, copper. R. Nos.* 34-40 *by Phillp.*

41. O. As no. 34.
℞ Britannia in an oval garter 1804 as No. 10, with K proper and expressed. *R.r.* O by *Phillp*; ℞ by *Küchler*.
This mule is in copper and until recently was not known.

BUST TO RIGHT.

42. ○ Laureate and draped bust to right, GEORGIUS III DEI GRATIA REX. Truncation mark C.H.K Top front leaf of laurel points to the *centre* of E Four berries in wreath.

℞ BANK TOKEN 5s. 6d. 1811 within a wreath of oak; under the tie knot I.P. *R.r.*

43. Also in Copper. *R.*

44. Similar, but the first leaf of laurel points to the *end* of E in DEI *Küchler and Phillp.*

"The Bank has lately had £100,000 worth of dollars new stamped at Boulton &° Co.'s Manufactory at Birmingham. The charge for stamping is only one farthing each."—*Bath Chronicle, Oct.* 12, 1809.

"£800,000 in stamped Dollars will shortly be added to our Silver currency. They were sent a few days ago from the Bank to Birmingham to be restamped."—*Bath Chronicle, Dec.* 21, 1809.

These notices must have referred to the Octagonal Countermarks, as the large denominations coined at Soho subsequent to 1804, were not circulated, and were without exception proof patterns. These were the 5s. 6d. and the FIVE SHILLINGS &° SIXPENCE 1811.

THREE SHILLINGS 1811.

ARMOURED BUST.

45. ○ Laureate and draped bust to right in armour, GEORGIUS III DEI GRATIA REX The first leaf of laurel points to the *first* limb of E in DEI *Five* berries in wreath.

℞ BANK TOKEN 3 SHILL. 1811 within a wreath of oak with *twenty-four* acorns. *R.r.*

Boyne 17.

46. ○ Similar, but with the first leaf of laurel under the *space* between D and E of DEI

℞ Similar, but a wreath of oak of *twenty-five* acorns. *R.r.*

47. ○ As last.

℞ BANK TOKEN 3 SHILL. 1811 within a wreath of oak with *twenty-six* acorns. *R.r.*

48. Similar, but the first leaf of laurel points to the *end* of E in DEI

49. ○ As last.

℞ Similar, but a wreath of oak with *twenty-seven* acorns. *R.*

1812.

50. ○ Laureate and draped bust to the right in armour, GEORGIUS III DEI GRATIA REX The first leaf of laurel points to the *end* of E in DEI *Four* berries in the wreath.

℞ BANK TOKEN 3 SHILL. 1812 within a wreath of oak with *twenty-seven* acorns.

Boyne 19.

51. Also in Brass. *R.* *Nos. 45 to 51 by Pingo.*

HEAD LAUREATE, 1812.

52. O- Laureate head to right, GEORGIUS III DEI GRATIA REX The top leaf of laurel is *under* the space between I of DEI and G of GRATIA
℞ BANK TOKEN 3 SHILL. 1812 within a wreath of oak and olive.
PLATE J, no. 1.

53. A Proof in Gold is in the British Museum. *R.r.r.*

54. A Proof of the obverse only, in Gold, is in the British Museum. *R.r.r.*

55. O- Laureate head to right, GEORGIUS III DEI GRATIA REX The top leaf of laurel points to the *centre* of D in DEI
℞ As No. 53. *R.r.*
Boyne 20.

56. Also in Platinum. *R.r.r.*
Boyne 21.

1813.

57. O- Similar to last, but the top leaf of laurel is *between* the I in DEI and the G in GRATIA
℞ BANK TOKEN 3 SHILL. 1813 within a wreath of oak and olive.
Boyne 22.

1814.

58. O- Same as last.
℞ Similar to last, but BANK TOKEN 3 SHILL. 1814
Boyne 23.

1815.

59. O- Same as last.
℞ Similar to last, but BANK TOKEN 3 SHILL. 1815
Boyne 24.

1816.

60. O- Same as last.
℞ BANK TOKEN 3 SHILL. 1816 *R.r.r.* Nos. 52 to 60 by *T. Wyon.*
Boyne 25.

EIGHTEEN PENCE.

ARMOURED BUST, 1811.

61. O- Laureate bust to right in armour, GEORGIUS III DEI GRATIA REX The end of the centre ribbon turns *upwards.*
℞ BANK TOKEN 1s. 6d. 1811 within a wreath, an *acorn* over B in BANK.   *Pingo.*
PLATE J, no. 2.

BANK OF ENGLAND.

62. O· Similar, but the end of the outer ribbon turns *downwards*.
    ℞ Similar, but the acorn over the B in BANK is *omitted*.
    Unknown.
    Probably a forgery of the period.

1812.

63. O· Same as last.
    ℞ Similar to last, but BANK TOKEN 1s. 6d. 1812   *Pingo.*
    Boyne 29.

LAUREATE HEAD, 1812.

64. O· Laureate head to right, GEORGIUS III GRATIA REX
    ℞ BANK TOKEN 1S. 6d. 1812 within a wreath of oak and olive.
    Boyne 30.
Proofs are rare.

1813.

65. O· Same as last.
    ℞ Similar to last, but BANK TOKEN 1s. 6d. 1813
    Boyne 32.

66. O· Similar to last, but the terminating centre leaf in the laurel wreath is the same *length* as the outer ones, whereas in the last it *projects*.
    ℞ Similar to last, but the tops of the ones point to the *right* instead of to the *left*. *Unknown.*
    This is in brass, and in Mr. Bowles' Cabinet.

1814.

67. O· Similar to last, but projecting leaf as before.
    ℞ Similar to last, but BANK TOKEN 1S. 6d. 1814
    Boyne 33.

1815.

68. O· Same as last.
    ℞ Similar to last, but BANK TOKEN 1S. 6d. 1815
    Boyne 34.

1816.

69. O· Same as last.
    ℞ Similar to last, but BANK TOKEN 1s. 6d. 1816
    Boyne 35.

70. O· As last.
    ℞ As obverse, but incuse.

The Dollars and especially the Three Shilling and Eighteen Pence Tokens were extensively forged. In consequence the government announced that the law would strictly be enforced, as will be seen from the notice here reproduced.

"Bank Tokens. Counterfeiters are liable to seven years transportation; Utterers, first time, six months imprisonment; second time, two years imprisonment; third time, fourteen years imprisonment."—*Bath Chronicle, August* 15*th*, 1811.

NINEPENCE.

71. ☉ Laureate head to right, GEORGIUS III DEI GRATIA REX
℞ BANK TOKEN 9D 1812 within a wreath of oak and olive. *R.r.*

Boyne 36.

72. Also in Copper.

Phillips, p. 34.

73. This obverse was muled with the reverse of a Farthing of George IV, and struck in Platinum. *Nos. 62 to 72 by T. Wyon.*

Montagu, p. 120.

The Ninepence was submitted as a pattern, but was not approved, the obverse was afterwards used for the Irish 10 Pence Token.

BANK OF IRELAND.

SIX SHILLINGS.

BUST TO RIGHT.

74. ☉ Laureate and draped bust to the right, GEORGIUS III DEI GRATIA REX.; truncation mark C.H.K The first leaf of laurel is under the *end* of E in DEI.
℞ Hibernia seated to left; in her right hand a palm branch, her left resting on a harp; K on the ground; BANK OF IRELAND TOKEN Ex. 1804 SIX SHILLINGS.

Boyne 37.

75. Also in Copper.

Boyne 38.

76. Similar, but truncation mark C.H.K *close* together.

77. Similar, but the first leaf of laurel points to the *centre* of F. in DEI The truncation mark : C.H.K

78. Also in Copper.

79. Similar, but *without* the period after REX

80. Also in Copper.

81. Similar, but the first leaf of laurel points to the first limb of E in DEI

82. Also in Copper. *These were engraved by Küchler.*

BANK OF IRELAND.

BUST TO LEFT.

83. ○ Laureate and draped bust to the left, GEORGIUS III DEI GRATIA REX. Truncation mark ✿ . ✿

℞ Hibernia seated to left; in her right hand a palm branch, her left resting on a harp; K on the ground; BANK OF IRELAND TOKEN Ex. 1804 SIX SHILLINGS *R.r.r.* *Phillp and Küchler.*

This is in Copper. Lot 197, Lawrence Sale; Sotheby, Wilkinson &° Hodge, May 3rd, 1900. The piece is obviously a restrike, but of an early date.

The singular feature about the Bank of Ireland Six Shilling Tokens is that they were struck on similar blanks, and were of the same specific gravity as the 1804 Bank of England Five Shilling Dollars.

HALF CROWN.

84. ○ Laureate and draped bust in armour to the right, GEORGIVS III DEI GRATIA REX Under the bust 1808

℞ Hibernia seated to left; in her right a palm branch, BANK TOKEN In the exergue XXX PENCE IRISH Top of harp points *between* the O and K in TOKEN

Boyne 39.

85. Similar, but the top of harp points *to* the O in TOKEN *Pingo.*

PLATE A, no. 2.

TENPENCE.

1805.

86. ○ Laureate and draped bust to the right, GEORGIUS III DEI GRATIA The first laurel leaf is under the E in DEI

℞ BANK TOKEN TEN PENCE IRISH 1805

Boyne. 40.

87. Similar, but the first laurel leaf is under the D in DEI *R.*

1806.

88. ○ Laureate and draped bust to the right, GEORGIUS III DEI GRATIA The right hand laurel leaf is under the E in DEI

℞ BANK TOKEN TEN PENCE IRISH 1806 *Pingo.*

Boyne 41.

1813.

89. ○ Laureate head to right, GEORGIUS III DEI GRATIA REX The outer end of the ribbon lines *to* the E IN GEORGIUS

℞ BANK TOKEN 10 PENCE IRISH 1813 within a wreath of shamrock. *T. Wyon.*

This obverse is the one engraved for the English 9D of 1812.

Boyne 42.

90. ℺ Similar to last, but the outer end of the ribbon lines *between* the E and O in GEORGIUS

℞ Similar, but the 1 in 10 *touches* a shamrock leaf, whereas in the last it is *distant* from it.   *Unknown.*

Probably a forgery of the time.

FIVEPENCE.

1805.

91. ℺ Laureate and draped bust to the right, GEORGIVS III DEI GRATIA

℞ BANK TOKEN FIVE PENCE IRISH 1805

Boyne 43.

1806.

92. ℺ Laureate and draped bust to the right, GEORGIVS III DEI GRATIA

℞ BANK TOKEN FIVE PENCE IRISH 1806   *Pingo.*

Boyne 44.

COUNTERMARKED TOKENS.
ENGLAND.

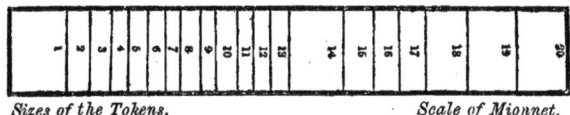

Sizes of the Tokens. *Scale of Mionnet.*

The size of the circles or ovals on which the legends appear are given in Mionnet's scale.

DOLLAR.

SMALL OVAL STAMP.

SILVER.

1. Bust of George III countermarked in a small oval on the obverse of a Spanish dollar.
    Boyne 1.

2. Similar, but with G R also countermarked at the side.
    Meili 8.

3. Similar, but with s c s also countermarked at the side.
    Meili 52.

4. A specimen countermarked on an *American* Dollar of 1795.
    Meili 5.

This stamp was the same as used by the Goldsmiths' Company, and the Dollars were an equivalent for 4/9.

5. Similar, but countermarked with 5/ *incuse* and without the small oval.

6. Similar, but value 4/9.
    In Mr. Bliss' cabinet.

7. Similar, but G R 5 ORD countermarked on a Spanish Dollar. R.r.r.
    PLATE A, no. 3.

This is said to have been countermarked for the Board of Ordnance.

8. Similar, but in a rectangle M; 2 x 2½. H C T CO no value expressed.
    In Mr. Bowles' cabinet.

9. Similar, *without* the small oval, but with bust of Washington (?) to left, R B and dagger at the side, all incuse.

Meili 50.

The Bank reported 1816: " The order for stamping these was given in March 1797 and in the year 2,325,099 at 4/9 each were issued." In 1797 an attempt was made by the Treasury to supplement the deficiency of silver coinage by the issue of the Spanish dollars, and half, quarter, and eighth dollars, countermarked on the obverse with the bust of George III, the stamp, an oval one, being that used by the Goldsmiths' Company for stamping the plate of the Country. The dollars were to be current for 4s. 9d, which gave rise to the saying " two Kings' heads not worth a crown."—*Coins of Great Britain and Ireland,* no. 865. H. A. GRUEBER.

OCTAGONAL STAMP.

10. Bust of George III in an octagon, countermarked on a Spanish dollar.

Boyne 5.

The stamp was the one used for the Maundy Penny, not the Fourpence as Boyne incorrectly states.

11. Similar octagonal countermark on a Spanish Dollar; but in addition, counterstruck over the large bust with the small oval head.

This singular piece is probably unique, and was sold in the Marshall sale at Sotheby's, lot 568, March 1852. It suggests the query " If two Kings' heads are not worth a Crown, what are three worth ? "

The octagonal countermark was by the Order of the Treasury, and was resorted to in 1804 in consequence of the extensive forgeries of the mark of the Goldsmiths' Company.

BANK OF ENGLAND DOLLAR 1804.

12. COUNTERFEIT W Z countermarked on a forged Bank of England Britannia Dollar of 1804. *R.r.r.*

This piece was forged by S. and S. J. Ingleby, who were tried and convicted at the Warwick Assizes in 1814, and transported for 12 years. The specimen here described is said to have been the identical forgery countermarked COUNTERFEIT by authority for the purposes of conviction.

On February 9th, 1810, Henry Hase, the chief Cashier of the Bank of England; produced evidence before a special committee appointed by the House of Commons on the currency, that the dollars stamped and issued between the years 1797 and 1810 numbered 4,817,634.

HALF DOLLAR.

13. Bust of George III in a small oval as on no. 1.

Boyne 3

14. A specimen countermarked with a bust of George III in a small oval on the reverse. *R.r.*

Meili 2.

15. Bust of George III on an octagonal, similar to no. 10. *R.r.*

PLATE H, no. 1.

QUARTER DOLLAR.

16. Bust of George III in a small oval, similar to no. 1. *R.*

PLATE H, no. 2.

17. Bust of George III in an octagonal, similar to no. 10. *R.*

ONE SHILLING.

18. Bust of William III ; on a shield M And on another shield R (Mary Regina ?) (*M.* 1.)
In Mr. Bowles' cabinet.

19. Bust of George III in an octagon, similar to no. 10. *R.r.r.*
Meili 56.

20. E.S. surmounted by a crown, struck over a George II Shilling.
In the Murdoch collection of tokens.

ONE EIGHTH OF A DOLLAR.

21. Bust of George III in a small oval, similar to no. 1. *R.r.*

HALFPENNY.

COPPER.

22. Bust of George III in a small oval, similar to no. 1, on a London and Middlesex Halfpenny of 1792. *R.r.r.*
Atkins 140 ; 740. PLATE H, no. 3.

This countermark is from the genuine die of the Goldsmiths' Company and perfectly struck.

PRIVATE BANKERS' AND TRADESMEN'S COUNTERMARKED TOKENS.

ENGLAND.

DERBYSHIRE.

DOLLAR.

SILVER.

23. CROMFORD DERBYSHIRE. in a circle ($M.$ 3) ; and, in the centre, 5 struck on a Spanish Dollar. $R.$

PLATE H, no. 4.

24. The same, but with a *small* c countermarked on bust. CROMFORD. DERBYSHIRE. 4/9. $R.r.$

Boyne 27.

25. The same, but *no value* expressed. $R.r.r.$

Issued by Arkwright & Co., Millowners and Bankers.

DORSETSHIRE.

SHERBORNE.

DOLLAR.

26. STERLING countermarked in a small rectangle ; the monogram *PP & W* 1754 engraved ; countermarked and *engraved* on a Spanish Dollar.

In Mr. Bowles' cabinet. Preter, Pew & Whitty, Bankers at Sherborne, it is said issued a Five-shilling Piece in the eighteenth century.

POOLE.

SHILLING.

COPPER.

27. O W. BEST in a garter, &c.

℞ A female seated ; ONE SHILLING &c., as Poole no. 8 ; countermarked on a Walsall Church Penny.

PLATE I, no. 4.

This rare piece is in Mr. Bliss' cabinet.

DURHAM.

HALF CROWN.
SILVER.

28. On a shield, a ship in full sail to right; above, S° Shield, (*M.* 2).; struck on a Charles II Half Crown. *R.r.r.*

SHILLING.
29. Also struck on a Shilling. *R.r.r.*

HALFPENNY.
COPPER.

30. Also struck on a Halfpenny of George III. *R.r.*

(The last three are in the Murdoch collection of tokens.

LANCASHIRE.

CARK-IN-CARTMEL.

31. CARK COTTON WORKS 1787 in a ribbed circle (*M.* 5); no value expressed; countermarked on a George III Halfpenny.

PLATE K, no. 1.
In Mr. Norman's cabinet.

MANCHESTER.

32. MARY . HAMPSON . & . SON in a circle; a rose divides MARY and SON (*M.* 5).; in the centre, MAN CHES TER a period over MAN and under TER No value expressed; countermarked on a George III Halfpenny. *R.r.*

MIDDLESEX.

HALF CROWN.
SILVER.

33. DAVIS WINE & BRANDY MERCHANT 46 HOUNDSDITCH LONDON in a circle; no value expressed; also countermarked *above* with the figure of Sir John Falstaff.

34. Similar, but with the first D in HOUNDSDITCH *omitted*.

This countermark is generally found on Charles II Half Crowns. John Davis, White Rose Co., Wine and Brandy Merchant, Colem Street, Houndsditch, existed in 1790.

PENNY.
COPPER.

35. Similar to no. 34, but struck on a Penny of George III.

HALFPENNY.

36. CLARKE above, a lion couchant in a square compartment ; LON DON surmounted by the Royal crown in a rectangle ; *no value expressed*; countermarked on a George III Halfpenny. *R.r.*
PLATE J, no. 3.

37. Also struck on a Halfpenny of George III.*

These countermarked pieces were issued in the silver token period by Davis, of the Falstaff Inn. There is a public house of that sign in Houndsditch at the present time.

38. O A lion couchant gardant fondling a dog, EXETER CHANGE LONDON PIDCOCK

℞ A beaver eating a root, THE BEAVER 1801 countermarked on a George III Halfpenny.
Davis catalogue, Sotheby's, March 11, 1901, lot 147.

39. IOHN TATE & SON. LONDON. in a circle (*M.* 5) ; and within an inner circle, a woolsack, countermarked on a George III Halfpenny.
In Mr. Norman's cabinet. PLATE K, no. 2.

NORTHUMBERLAND.

SILVER.

40. Ships in quay, a cart unloading, MAY NORTH SHIELDS FLOURISH On the reverse, the cipher $\mathscr{IPR}$ Under, 1795 Within a wreath of laurel NORTHSHIELDS HALFPENNY (*M.* 8) ; counterstruck on a Spanish Dollar.
Atkins, 161, 25.
In the British Museum. The device is well spread and the Token very sharply struck.

NOTTINGHAMSHIRE.

EAST RETFORD.

DOLLAR.

41. An Ampers and, and a crown thus :—$\&$ No value expressed, countermarked on a Spanish Dollar.
Boyne, 28, 37.
In the British Museum. Boyne says : "In the MS. catalogue it is said to have been issued from the Revolution Mill, East Retford." This town was famous for its mills early in the nineteenth century, and the reputation is still maintained.

SUFFOLK.

BURY.

FARTHING.

COPPER.

42. BURY W. HOUSE countermarked both on the obverse and reverse of old Copper Farthings. *R.*

"There was also, at the time of the Reformation, a college in this town, named Jesus College, and was situated in College Street ; it had a Guild attached to it, and consisted of a Warden and six Associates or priests. This building is now converted into a workhouse. The College was founded by King Edward I."—*History of Bury, by Gillingwater.*

---

* No. 37 should read as no. 35.

WARWICKSHIRE.
BIRMINGHAM.
TWO SHILLINGS AND SIXPENCE.
COPPER.
43. O A female seated extending *alms*, etc., countermarked w (Workhouse).

℞ TWO SHILLINGS AND SIXPENCE etc. countermarked w (Workhouse). R.

PLATE I, no. 1.
For full description see Birmingham.

ONE SHILLING AND SIXPENCE.
44. O A beehive and bees; INDUSTRY HAS ITS SURE REWARD An ornament at the bottom.

℞ $\overset{S\ D}{1.\ 6}$ incuse countermarked on a blank reverse. *Wyon.*
Boyne 24.

ONE SHILLING.
45. O Bust to left, ADM$^\text{L}$ L$^\text{P}$ NELSON Victory AT THE Nile, August. 1. 1798.

℞ 1 incuse countermarked on a blank reverse. R. *Wyon.*
PLATE I, no. 2.

YORKSHIRE.
BOLTON.

SILVER.
46. O The ruins of a fortress, BOLTON CASTLE. YORKSHIRE.

℞ An urn, surmounted by a flaming torch, between sprigs of laurel and scythes, arrows crossed, a skull, and an hour glass at foot; TIME DESTROYS ALL THINGS 1797. (*M.* 8); counterstruck on a Spanish Dollar with the additional countermark of the small oval of George III.

Atkins 249, 1.
A specimen of the Token was sold at the Davis sale, in March, 1901, for £29 10s.

BRADFORD.

THREE SHILLINGS.

47. BRADFORD WORKHOUSE no value expressed; countermarked on a Three Shilling Token of the armour type. *R.*

PLATE H, no. 5.

ONE SHILLING AND SIXPENCE.

48. BRADFORD WORKHOUSE no value expressed; countermarked on a 1s. 6d. Token of the armour type. *R.r.*

THIRSK.

SHILLING.

49. SCURR THIRSK on a rectangle (*M.* 1); countermarked on a Thirsk Association Shilling. *R.r.*

PLATE H, no. 6.

BRADFORD.

PENNY.

COPPER.

50. BRADFORD WORKHOUSE countermarked on various copper Nineteenth Century Tokens.

Warwickshire Token Coinage, 752.

Kelly's Directory says, "the present Workhouse was erected in 1852, cost £40,000, has a large Infirmary attached, and is available for 1000 inmates." Most likely it supplanted an older building.

KEIGHLEY.

51. KEIGHLEY and on the reverse KEIGHLEY in a straight line at the top, and KEIGHLEY in a curved line at the bottom; countermarked on various Nineteenth Century Penny Tokens.

Warwickshire Token Coinage, 751.
These were issued by the Keighley Overseers of the Poor, to pay the paupers in 1818.
Boyne Yorkshire Tokens, no. 107.

52. As last, with the *additional* countermark G R.

53. As no. 51, but with the *additional* countermark J M.

54. As no. 51, but with the *additional* countermark W W.

SCOTLAND.

AYRSHIRE.

FIVE SHILLINGS AND SIXPENCE.
SILVER.
55. CATRINE. COTTON. WORKS No. in a circle (M. 3); within an inner circle the value 5/6 countermarked on a Spanish Dollar. $R.r.r.$

FIVE SHILLINGS.
56. CATRINE WORKS. in an oval (M. 7); No. ; and in the centre the value 5/ countermarked on a Spanish Dollar. $R.r.r.$

FOUR SHILLINGS AND NINEPENCE.
57. CATRINE. COTTON. WORKS No. 3505 (M. 6) and value 4/9
PLATE H, no. 7.
In Mr. Bliss' cabinet.

58. GALSTON. SOC.y. No. above; the value 5 s countermarked on a Spanish Dollar. $R.r.r.$

59. MUIR KIRK IRON WORKS + in a circle (M. 4); within an inner circle the value 5/6. On the reverse a view of the blast furnaces at work; with the date 1809 under; all within a circle (M. 3); countermarked on a Spanish Dollar. $R.r.r.$
Meili 40.

60. O the same as last, but *without* the blast furnaces on the reverse. $R.r.r.$

BUTESHIRE.

DOLLAR.
61. ROTHSAY COTTON WORKS. in a beaded circle (M. 2); in a cable circle the value 4/6 and date 1820. countermarked on a Spanish Dollar. $R.r.$
PLATE H, no. 8.

HALF DOLLAR.
62. PAYABLE AT ROTHSAY MILLS × in a circle (M. 4); and in an inner circle the value 2/6 countermarked on a *segment* of a Spanish Dollar. $R.r.$
PLATE H, no. 9.

63. Similar, but the value expressed on a *rectangle* (M. 1); and a *star* countermarked at the right.
In the Murdoch collection of tokens.

ONE-THIRD OF DOLLAR.
64. PAYABLE AT ROTHSAY MILLS + in a circle (M. 4); and within an inner circle the value 1/8 countermarked on a *segment* of a Spanish Dollar. $R.r.r.$
PLATE A, no. 4.

COPPER.
HALFPENNY.

65. Also in Copper; countermarked on a George III Halfpenny and on Eighteenth Century Tokens, but no value is expressed.

66. PAYABLE AT ROTHSAY COTTON MILLS in a circle (*M*. 5); in the centre a woolsack; no value expressed; countermarked on a George III Halfpenny. *R.r.*

CLACKMANNANSHIRE.
SILVER.

67. PAYABLE AT ALLOA COLLIERY + in a circle (*M*. 4); in the centre 5/. incuse; countermarked on a Spanish Dollar. *R.r.r.*

68. Similar, but with the *additional* small bust of George III struck at the left of 5/.

PLATE H, no. 10.
In Mr. Bliss' cabinet.

SHILLING.

69. Similar to 67, but countermarked on a Shilling of George III; without the cross after COLLIERY and *no value* expressed.

In the Murdoch collection of tokens.

COPPER.
HALFPENNY.

70. Similar, but countermarked on George II and III Halfpennies.

ELGIN.
DOLLAR.
SILVER.

71. BALLINDALLOCH * in an outer circular legend (*M*. 3); and in an inner circular legend COTTON * WORKS * in the centre a large 5/ countermarked on a Spanish Dollar. *R.r.r.*

PLATE H, no. 11.

COPPER.
HALFPENNY.

72. BALLINDALLOCH COTTON WORK in a circle (*M*. 7); and in the centre a woolsack; no value expressed; countermarked on a George III Halfpenny.

In Mr. Bliss' cabinet.

LANARKSHIRE.
DALZIEL FARM.
DOLLAR.
SILVER.

73. PAYABLE AT DALZELL (*sic*) FARM * in a circle (*M*. 3); in the centre 5/ countermarked on the reverse of a Five-Franc Piece of the French Republic. *R.r.r.*

74. Similar to last, but *no value* expressed. R.r.r.
PLATE H, no. 12.

75. Similar to last, but DALZELL FARM. R.r.r.

GLASGOW.

DOLLAR.

76. GLASGOW BANK + in a circle (*M.* 2); within an inner circle the value 5/. countermarked on a Spanish Dollar. R.r.
PLATE H, no. 13.

Issued by the Glasgow Bank Company whose London Agents were Morland, Ransom & Co., 56, Pall Mall.

77. ROB^T CRICHTON P^T GLASGOW + in a circle (*M.* 3); within an inner circle the value 4/6 countermarked on a Spanish Dollar. R.r.r.

From a Block in possession of SPINK & SON.

78. + A. STEVEN & SONS P^T GLASGOW in a ribbed circle (*M.* 3); and within a cable circle the value 4/6 countermarked on a Spanish Dollar. R.r.r.

THISTLE BANK.

FIVE SHILLINGS.

SILVER.

79. THISTLE BANK · in a circle (*M.* 2), and, within an inner circle, the value 5/ On the reverse *a thistle* in a circle (*M.* 2); countermarked on a Spanish Dollar. R.r.r.

FOUR SHILLINGS AND NINEPENCE.

80. The same as last, but value 4/9 R.r.
PLATE H, no. 15.

81. The obverse same as last; but the *thistle* countermark on the reverse *omitted*. R.r.

FOUR SHILLINGS AND SIXPENCE.

82. Similar, but 4/6   *R.r.r.*
   In the Murdoch collection of tokens.

These tokens were issued by the Thistle Bank Company, Glasgow, whose London agents were Smith, Payne & Co., George Street, Mansion House.

The Order of the Thistle, known also as the Order of St. Andrew, was first mentioned in the inventory of the effects of James III, who probably adopted it as an appropriate illustration of the royal motto, " In defence."

LANARK.

DOLLAR.

83. PAYABLE AT LANARK MILLS- in a circle (*M.* 5); and in the centre 5/ incuse countermarked on a Spanish Dollar.   *R.r.*
   PLATE H, no. 14.

84. Similar, but value 4/9 in large *incuse* figures.   *R.r.r.*

85. PAYABLE AT LANARK MILLS ✽ in a circle (*M.* 4); and in the centre 4/6 *incuse*.   *R.r.*

86. Similar, but with the *additional* countermark ꝑ at the right.
   In the Murdoch collection of tokens.

HALF DOLLAR.

87. PAYABLE AT LANARK MILLS in a circle (*M.* 5); and in the centre 2/6 *incuse*; countermarked on a Half-ecu of France.   *R.r.*
   Boyne 30.

FARTHING.
COPPER.

88. LANARK. COTTON. MILLS. in the centre; a shield of arms under thistle sprigs; crest, the monogram *J C D* (*M.* 5); countermarked on a William III Bodle of Scotland.   *R.r.*
   PLATE K, no. 3.

" On Wednesday week about mid-day the preparation house at Lanark Mills was set on fire, in consequence of part of the teazing machinery becoming red hot by friction. The fire was soon extinguished, but not before £200 worth of cotton was destroyed."—*Star Newspaper, Oct. 29th,* 1813.

MIDLOTHIAN.

HALFPENNY.

Mr. Bowles has, in his cabinet, an old countermarked Halfpenny, WILKISON · EDINBURGH ·   In the centre a *thistle*.

PERTHSHIRE.

SILVER.   HALF DOLLAR.

89. ADELPHI COTTON WORK in a circle (*M.* 6), and, in the centre, a woolsack; the right hand knot is over the R in WORK no value expressed; countermarked on a Half-ecu of France.   *R.r.r.*
   PLATE H, no. 16.

COPPER.

90. ADELPHI COTTON WORK in a circle (*M.* 6), and, in the centre, a woolsack; on the reverse Four Shillings and Six Pence 1786 countermarked on a George III Halfpenny.

PLATE K, no. 4.

This is in copper and is in Mr. Norman's cabinet.

HALFPENNY.

91. As 89, but countermarked on George III Halfpence.

92. ADELPHI * COTTON WORK * in a similar circle, but the knot at the right lines to the O in WORK; countermarked on Copper Halfpence.

The woolsack first made its appearance in the House of Lords, during the reign of Edward III, to remind the Peers of the importance of England's staple trade.
In the reign of Queen Elizabeth an Act was passed to prevent the exportation of wool.—BREWER: *Phrase and Fable.*

DEANSTON.

DOLLAR.

SILVER.

93. DEANSTON COTTON MILL in a circle (*M.* 7), and in the centre 5/' R.r.r.

PLATE H, no. 17.

HALFPENNY.

COPPER.

94. The same in Copper, but without the value expressed; on a Charles II Bawbee of Scotland; also on Halfpennies of George III. R.

Boyne says: "I cannot learn where it was used."

These Mills were the Deanston Mills, but were known as the Adelphi Cotton Works, and were situated on the West bank of the river Teath. In 1794 the owners were James and Archibald Buchanan *&* Company.

LOCHEARN.

HALFPENNY.

95. DUN. M^CLAREN MERCH^{T.} · LOCHEARN. in a circle (*M.* 7); no value expressed.

PLATE K, no. 5.

Countermarked on a Coventry Eighteenth Century Token. All efforts to trace the countermark on a silver coin have failed.

RENFREWSHIRE.

GREENOCK.

SILVER.

96. R & G. BLAIR. GREENOCK. in an oval (*M.* 4 x 2), and, in the centre 4/6 countermarked on a Spanish Dollar. R.r.r.

PLATE H, no. 18.

97. PAYABLE BY I & W SCOTT GREENOCK countermarked on a Spanish Dollar; the value 4/9 expressed on a rectangle (*M.* 1).
In the Murdoch collection of tokens.

98. A KING GREENOCK. 5/- countermarked on a Spanish Dollar. *R.r.r.*

99. Similar, but value 4/6. *R.r.r.*

100. J. M^c K· & Son GREENOCK. in a toothed circle (*M.* 3), and, in the centre, 4/6 countermarked on a Spanish Dollar. *R.r.r.*
PLATE H, no. 19.

101. M^c FIE LINDSAY & COY * GREENOCK * in a beaded circle (*M.* 5), and, in the centre, 4/6 countermarked on a Spanish Dollar. *R.r.r.*
PLATE H, no. 20.

102. The same, but S *incuse*, under the figure 4. *R.r.r.*
Meili 37.

103. J & A. MUIR * · * GREENOCK in a beaded circle (*M.* 4), and, in the centre, 4/6 countermarked on a Spanish Dollar. *R.r.r.*

104. A MUIR * GREENOCK * within a beaded circle (*M.* 4), and, in the centre, 4/6 countermarked on a Spanish Dollar. *R.r.r.*

LEVERNBANK.

105. S · D · & Co LEVERN · MILL· in a circle (*M.* 4), and, in the centre, 5/6 countermarked on a Spanish Dollar. *R.r.r.*

106. The same, but with an additional countermark S · D in a small beaded circle; a puncheon mark over all to obliterate the value.
PLATE H, no. 21.

107. S · D · & Co LEVERN · MILL · ; same as no. 105, but for value 5. *R.r.r.*

LOCHWINNOCH.

108. A. GIBSON & Co. LOCHWINNOCH. in a circle (*M.* 6), and, within an inner circle, the value 5/- countermarked on a Spanish Dollar. *R.r.r.*
PLATE H, no. 22.

PAISLEY.

109. CORCER PAISLEY. in a circle (*M.* 2), and, in the centre, 5/- countermarked on a Spanish Dollar. *R.r.r.*

110. JOHN LANG MERCHT PAISLEY in an oval (*M.* 6); the value *obliterated* by a puncheon mark; countermarked on a Spanish Dollar. *R.r.r.*
In the Murdoch collection of tokens.

111. (PAY)ABLE BY W. LANGM... in a circle (*M.* 7), and, in the centre, 5/3 countermarked on a Spanish Dollar. *R.r.r.*

112. Similar, but the arms of Paisley in the centre, and on the reverse PAISLEY...SOCIETY in a circle (*M.* 6); counshed on a Spanish Dollar. *R.r.r.*

Meili 33.

113. J. MUIR Manuf. PAISLEY. in a plain and beaded circle (*M.* 3), and, in the centre, 5/. On the reverse the Prince of Wales' plumes and motto in a circle (*M.* 3); counshed on a Spanish Dollar. *R.r.r.*

PLATE H, no. 23.

STIRLINGSHIRE.

CULGREUCH.

DOLLAR.

114. PAYABLE AT CULGREUCH MILL ✷ in a circle (*M.* 4), and, in the centre, the value 5/- *R.r.r.*

115. Similar to last, but CULGREUCH MILL 5/- *R.r.r.*

HALFPENNY.

COPPER.

116. Similar to no. 114, but *no value* expressed, and, in the centre, THO^s WHYTE counshed on Eighteenth century Halfpenny Tokens. *R.r.*

PLATE K, no. 6.

SILVER.

117. FORSTER & CORBE HOTCHESON TOWN in a circle (*M.* 3), and, within a double circle, the value 5/- counshed on a Spanish Dollar. *R.r.r.*

118. Similar, but FORSTER & CORBE HOTCHESON MILL. *R.r.r.*

<small>The factory at Culgreuch was erected in 1796. For this information I am indebted to Mr. William Paterson, Chief of the Glasgow Fire Brigade.</small>

FINTRY.

COPPER.

119. P. (Payable) BY. ROBERT M^{c}NEE FINTRY ✷ in a circle (*M.* 6), counshed on a Glasgow Eighteenth Century Token.

In Mr. Norman's cabinet.

IRELAND.

(Co.) DOWN.

HALFPENNY.

COPPER.

120. PAYABLE AT M^{RS} SOMERVILLS. DOWN in a circle (*M.* 6); no value expressed; countermarked on a George III Halfpenny.
In Mr. Bliss' cabinet.

(Co.) DUBLIN.

SHILLING.

SILVER.

121. O GIBBONS bistruck, and MD
℞ The monogram *J R*
Boyne 10b.

122. O I. Three four-leaf shamrocks in as many compartments.
℞ Blank.

123. O I T in a rectangle.
℞ W R and the monogram *J R*

124. O M^C CORMIC W MURPHY and in a rectangle I T
℞ W R with C under.

125. O M^C O'GRADY three times countermarked.
℞ As obverse.

126. O J M^C QUOID
℞ BOLTON bistruck.

127. O O'BRIEN
℞ M D

128. O O'NEILL
℞ M

129. O J SHORT The monograms *C C* and *S B*
℞ POWELL and S under.

130. O TOOLE also in a rectangle R
℞ Blank.
Boyne 10a.

131. O WILSON bistruck.
℞ Blank.

SIXPENCE.

132. O͝ A M B
℞ H

133. O͝ POWELL and ℳ
℞ S

Aquilla Smith says "about the year 1804, many traders issued silver pieces, which passed as shillings. They were thin pieces not worth more than sixpence each, usually stamped with the name or initials of the issuers, and frequently countermarked." Mr. Fletcher has two irregularly shapèd silver pieces, from the Gillespie collection, which, without any device or countermark, circulated as coin. The dearth of silver being such as to command exchange on the merits of its intrinsic value.

(Co.) KILKENNY.

CASTLECOMER.

DOLLAR.

SILVER.

134. PAYABLE ᛫ AT ᛫ CASTLE ᛫ COMER ᛫ COLLIERY ᛫ in an oval ($M.$ 4 by 3); and in the centre within a wreath, the value $\overset{S}{5}\ \overset{D}{5}$ countermarked on a Spanish Dollar.

PLATE H, no. 24.

Aquilla Smith, in his Silver Tokens of Ireland, 1855, p. 5, says—"I am indebted to Mr. T. G. Robertson of Kilkenny, for the following account of this countermarked Dollar— 'A friend of mine, who has often seen the coin, says that, about fifty years ago, Anne Countess of Dromore, not wishing to lose by the depreciated value of Spanish Dollars, of which she had at that time a large number, caused all she had to be stamped with the legend 'Castle Comer Colliery, Five shillings and five pence.' Coals for that amount being given for them at the pits, Kilkenny traders used to take them in exchange for their commodities, knowing that they could give them afterwards to colliers in payment of coals."

(Co.) MEATH.

HILL OF DOWN.

HALFPENNY.

COPPER.

135. I᛫ MITCHELL. H. DOWN in a circle ($M.$ 5); *no value* expressed; countermarked on a George III Halfpenny.

In Mr. Bliss' Cabinet.

ISLE OF MAN.

SHILLING.

COPPER.

136. A incuse; countermarked on the reverse of a Peel Castle Shilling token. *R.r.* *Halliday.*

Nelson, pl. III, no. 9.

Dr. Nelson informs me that there are four specimens known of this Countermark and, in a note on p. 34 of his work, gives the names of three gentlemen who possess one each. They appear to be all struck in copper.

LOCALITY UNKNOWN.

CROWN.

SILVER.

137. JAS. MEESON *No value* expressed, countermarked on a William III Crown. *R.r.*

In Mr. Bowles' cabinet.

138. OATES & CO. 5 SHILL^S countermarked on a Thaler. *R.r.r.*

HALF CROWN.

139. OATES & CO. 2 SHILL^S 6 countermarked on a Half-ecu of France. *R.r.r.*

Sir George Chetwynd presents his
Compliments to Mr Cullen, and
has just an enquiry, that the Com-
of the Reform Club, have any knowl-
-ledge of his Work now in pro-
or that they intend purchasing it
the Library —
Sir George is much too humble a
Individual, to think of having a
Memoir or Portrait published —

New Palace Yard,
November 15, 1845.

W. C. Ross pinxt.   J. Cochran, sculp.

LADY CHETWYND.

OVERSEERS', PRIVATE BANKERS' AND TRADESMEN'S TOKENS.

BERKSHIRE.

READING.

FORTY SHILLINGS.

GOLD.

1. O. Bust of the King to left, with sceptre ; ALFRED below the bust, and 1812 under ; PIGNORA CERTA PETIS DO PIGNORA CERTA (Pledges sure thou askest, I give sureties faithful). DWTS. GR.

℞ 40 SHILLINGS BERKS TOKEN STAND^D GOLD 6 . 18 READING in a circle ; legend PAYABLE IN B^K NOTES AT 6^S THE DWT. BY I. B. MONCK ESQ$^{RE}_{..}$ *R.r.*

PLATE A, no. 5.

2. The same, in Silver. *R.r.r.* *Halliday.*

In Sir Edward Thomason's Memoirs it is stated that the gold tokens were eagerly purchased at £5 each as mementos of the only issue of tokens struck in gold.

The Sheffield 10/6 and the proof of the Bank of England token in gold were, however, struck subsequently : the former at Halliday's works, and the latter at the Soho mint.

HALF CROWN.

SILVER.

3. O. The arms of Reading, azure ; five busts in saltire, the central one (Queen Elizabeth) between E R legend LABIMUR IN PEJUS DONEC MELIORA REVERTANT. 1811. (We pass into the worse until the better may return).

℞ HALF CROWN TOKEN SPAN. DOLL. SILVER 6 DWTS between sprigs of palm ; legend PAYABLE IN BANK NOTES BY I. B. MONCK ESQ^{RE} READING. X.   *Halliday.*

Boyne 186.

The arms were granted to Reading in the reign of Queen Elizabeth.

EIGHTEEN PENCE.

4. O. Similar to last, except in size.

℞ Similar to last, but 18 PENCE TOKEN SPAN: DOLL. SILVER 4 DWTS The left top sprig of palm points to the *centre* of the T in TOKEN and the 8 is under the Y in BY

Boyne 187.

5. O. The same as last.

℞ Similar, but *without* a period after DOLL and the 8 is under I. and the left top sprig to the *space* between PENCE and TOKEN   *R.*

6. O. The same as last.

℞ Similar as regards the position of the 8, but *has* a period after DOLL. and the sprig *terminates* at the T in TOKEN   *Halliday.*

J. Berkeley Monck was a Member of Parliament.

BUCKINGHAMSHIRE.

HIGH WYCOMBE.

SHILLING.

SILVER.

1. ◯ The arms of the borough, a swan gorged and chained, not in a shield; HIGH WYCOMBE & BUCKINGHAMSHIRE TOKEN XII PENCE

℞ View of the Town Hall; JAMES GOMME   Ex: MDCCCXI

Halliday.

Boyne 100.

The issuer of this token was a cabinet-maker and auctioneer.

From a Print in the possession of the Author.

CAMBRIDGESHIRE.

MARCH.

SHILLING.

SILVER.

1. O The golden fleece, PAYABLE BY MESS^{RS} ⁙ S. RATCLIFFE E. ELAM & J. THURBON ⁙

℞ MARCH SILVER TOKEN ONE SHILLING in a circle TO FACILITATE TRADE ⁙ ISSUED NOV^R 1 1811 *   *Halliday.*

PLATE A, no. 6.

Stephen Ratcliffe and Edward Elam were grocers, John Thurbon a brewer. About 1,400 of these shillings were issued. Boyne says "After the tokens had been current a short time it was discovered that there were more in circulation than the proprietors had issued. They were in consequence withdrawn from circulation and the silver sold in London." If this statement is founded on fact the same dies were used for those wrongly circulated as no variety of the token exists.

E. W. Elam, grocer, March, was declared bankrupt May 20th, 1817.—*London Gazette.*

CHATTERIS.

FARTHING.

COPPER.

2. O A sugar-loaf labelled W C—C and two canisters inscribed HYSON and SOUCHONG CHATTERIS FARTHING. 1813

℞ W. CURTIS. GROCER & TEA DEALER LINNEN & WOOLEN DRAPER. WHOLESALE & RETAIL.

3. O W. CVRTIS. 1813. CHATTERIS FARTHING. with an ornament above CVRTIS.

℞ ONE FARTHING 1813. FOR PUBLIC ACCOMODATION. *R.r.r.*

W. G. Searle, Cambridge Tokens, p. 25.

4. O Blank.
   ℞ As last.

5. O As no. 3, but *reads* CURTIS
   ℞ Blank.   *Halliday.*

MARCH.

6. O JOHN SMITH 1820 MARCH ISLE OF ELY An ornament under MARCH

℞ LINEN & WOOLEN DRAPER & TEA DEALER WHOLESALE & RETAIL

Boyne was under a wrong impression with respect to the extreme rarity of this token, as they are not difficult to obtain.

The issuer was the successor to Edward Elam, and in 1825 he had a similar farthing struck. John Thurbon, as late as 1827, also issued tokens of farthing size.

CHESHIRE.

NANTWICH.

SHILLING.

SILVER.

1. ☉ Arms (quarterly first and fourth or, second and third gules, a bend sable over all); NANTWICH TOKEN VALUE ONE SHILLING

℞ AT THE OLD BANK within a garter; inscribed PAYABLE 1811 ONE POUND NOTE FOR 20 TOKENS

Boyne 149.

2. Similar to last, but PAYABLE 1811 is *incuse* upon a plain broad band. *R.r.*

In Mr. Bliss' cabinet.

3. ☉ VALUE ONE SHILL. within a wreath; BROUGHTON. SPROUT. GARNETT. & SUTTON ✱

℞ AT NANTWICH BANK within a circle; ONE POUND BANK. NOTE FOR 20 TOKENS ✱ . *R.r.r.* *Halliday.*

The persons whose names are on this token were the proprietors of the Nantwich Bank, whose London Agents were Stevenson & Salt, 80, Lombard Street. "C. O. Broughton and J. J. Garnett, Bankers, Nantwich, were declared bankrupts January 13th, 1826."—*London Gazette.*

STOCKPORT.

SHILLING.

4. ☉ Beehive and *sixteen* bees, T. CARTWRIGHT & G. & R. FERNS... STOCKPORT...

℞ Female seated on a bale to right holding scales and cornucopia; on the ground a sword; the initials Y & D under the *hilt;* a small H on the bale; a ship in the distance; ONE SHILLING SILVER TOKEN 1812

5. ☉ Similar to last, but G & R. FERNS & T. CARTWRIGHT .. STOCKPORT .. with *fifteen* bees.

℞ Similar, but without the H on the bale.

Boyne 213.

6. Similar to last, but Y & D under the *sword* at the right. *R.*

7. Similar, but *seventeen* bees; STOCKPORT ... CHESHIRE ... *R.*

These reverses also occur on tokens of Mansfield and Doncaster. George and Robert Ferns were tallow chandlers in the Market Place. George Ferns was declared bankrupt March 9, 1821.

SIXPENCE.

8. ☉ Beehive and *fifteen* bees; T. CARTWRIGHT ... STOCKPORT ...

℞ Female seated as before, but *without* sword, the initials Y & D are partly under the bale and the figure; the small H omitted; SIX-PENCE SILVER TOKEN. 1812. *Halliday.*

PLATE A, no. 7.

This reverse occurs again at Doncaster. Thomas Cartwright was a draper in the Market Place.

CORNWALL.
COUNTY.
SHILLING.
SILVER.
1. O Arms (fifteen bezants, 5 over 4, 3, 2 and 1), NORTH CORNWALL. 1811
 ℞. ONE SHILLING VALUE within a wreath.
Boyne 57.
2. Also a copper proof. *R.r.r.*
This reverse occurs also on Devonshire County, and London, Charing Cross.
3. O The same as last.
 ℞ SILVER ✻ TWELVE PENNY TOKEN SOLD BY MORGAN ✻ 12 RATHBONE PLACE ✻ LONDON ✻ displayed with various ornaments. *R.*
Boyne 58.
See Charing Cross.
4. O Arms as before, but the bezants are *not expressed*; between two sprigs of olive, CORNWALL. 1811.
 ℞ A TOKEN FOR ONE SHILLING within a wreath. *R.*
5. Also a copper proof. *R.r.*
6. Similar to last, but date is *omitted*.
Boyne 59.
All efforts, up to the present, have failed to trace this undated token. Probably it is an error, or omission in description.

LAUNCESTON.
SHILLING.
7. O A castle within a circle; LAUNCESTON TOKEN. ONE SHILLING. 1811
 ℞. W. & G. PEARSE T. CHING H. NICOLS & J. PROCKTER within a circle, ISSUED TO FACILITATE TRADE
Boyne 107.
Boyne 46, 107, by an error, has NICHOLS instead of NICOLS. William and George Pearse were drapers of Newport, Thomas Ching, Chemist, Henry Nicols, Broad Street, and John Prockter, Silversmith, Southgate Street, Launceston.

STRATTON.
SHILLING.
8. O Arms as on North Cornwall no. 1.
 ℞ 12 within a wreath of olive; SHEPHARD. WATTS & CO. STRATTON. *R.*
Boyne 215.
John Shephard was a Farmer, and Watts & Co. the Postmasters.

9. ○ Arms (argent, per pale, a triple tower) of the city of Exeter, between two sprigs of olive; H.M. under; DEVONSHIRE SILVER TOKEN. *See* Devonshire no. 4.
℞ The same as last. R. *Halliday.*
Boyne 216.
For another token relating to Cornwall, see Devonshire no. 9.

10. ○ NORTH CORNWALL, the same as no. 1.
℞ DEVON AND CORNWALL in a circle; BARNSTAPLE * STRATTON * *Unknown.*
In Mr. Bowles' cabinet.

COUNTY.

PENNY.

COPPER.

11. ○ Arms, supporters, crest, and motto PRO REGE ET POPULO (for King and people); the foot of the right hand supporter is *between* the PO of POPULO
℞ PENNY PIECE in a circle, SUCCESS TO THE CORNISH MINES 1812 the P of PENNY lines with the *centre* of the second S in SUCCESS
Sharp 192, 1.

12. ○ Similar to last, but foot of supporter is *over* the O in POPULO
℞ Similar, but the P in PENNY lines with the *end* of S

13. ○ Similar, but the foot of supporter is *over* the *second* P of POPULO
℞ Similar, but the P lines to the *space* between S and T
Halliday.

DOLCOATH MINE.

14. ○ The same as last.
℞ CORNISH PENNY within a circle, PAYABLE IN CASH NOTES AT DOLCOATH MINE *Halliday.*
Sharp 192, 2.
Dolcoath Mine was situated at Camborne.

WEST WHEAL MINE.

15. ○ View of St. Michael's Mount; CORNISH MOUNT. ONE PENNY TOKEN.
℞ The Prince of Wales' feathers issuant from a coronet; motto, ICH DIEN (I serve), WEST WHEEL (*sic*) FORTUNE. ONE PENNY TOKEN. *R.r.*
Sharp 192, 4.
PLATE A, no. 8.

Sharp says Sir George Chetwynd had a specimen of this rare token in which the misspelling of WHEAL was "corrected by an indented A, formed by a punch." As this is not a variety of die it is omitted from formal description.

16. ○ View of St. Michael's Mount, with sea and vessels in the foreground, the nearest has *no* ropes between the mast and jib; legend, as before.

℞ Similar to last, but WHEAL instead of WHEEL and the I in ICH is *above* the end of the ribbon.

17. ○ Similar to last, but the nearer of the two vessels has *two* ropes between mast and jib, the flag on the castle is smaller.

℞ Similar to last, but the I in ICH is *below* the end of the ribbon. *Halliday.*

In consequence of its rich yield of ore the West Wheal Fortune Copper Mine was, during the great depression of 1807, one of the most prosperous in Cornwall. It was situated at Cudgvan, one mile from the present Marazion Road Station.

SCORRIER HOUSE.

18. ○ View of a pumping engine and winding machine, under 1811 in a circle; legend CORNISH * * PENNY * *

℞ A fish between blocks of tin in a circle; PAYABLE IN CASH NOTES AT SCORRIER HOUSE * *R*

Sharp 192, 6.

19. ○ As last.

℞ Similar, but legend FOR THE ACCOMMODATION OF THE COUNTY * ; the bottom block of tin lines to the *bow* of the D in ACCOMMODATION

Sharp 192, 7.

20. ○ Similar to last, but *hooks* attached to the drum of the machine instead of *rings*; the door is filled in with *brickwork*, whereas in the last it is *plain*.

℞ Similar, but the bottom block of tin lines to the *centre* of the D

21. ○ Similar, but the bottom block of tin lines to the *first* limb of D

22. Similar, but the summits of ground *straight* instead of *irregular*. *R*.

23. ○ Similar, but the window as well as the doorway is filled in with *brickwork*.

℞ Similar, but the bottom block of the tin lines to the *first* limb of A

24. ○ Similar, but *flat* tops to ones in date, whereas in all others they *slope*.

℞ Similar, but the bottom block of tin lines to the *second* O in ACCOMMODATION *R*. *Halliday.*

25. ⊙ Similar view of pumping engine, etc.; PAYABLE AT SCORRIER HOUSE upon a ribbon above; ex. ONE POUND NOTE FOR 240 TOKENS 1812

℞ The Prince of Wales' feathers issuant from a coronet and motto ICH DIEN (I serve) within a garter inscribed CORNISH PENNY

Halliday.

Sharp 192, 8.

26. ⊙ Similar to last, but a *plain rod* instead of a *chain* to lever.

℞ Laureate bust of George III to right, within a thick wreath of oak. R. *Halliday.*

Sharp 192, 9.

Scorrier House was near to Redruth, and in the occupation of John Williams.

PENZANCE.

TWO SHILLINGS.

TIN.

27. ⊙ A wheatsheaf in a circle. TWO SHILLINGS + TOKEN +

℞ TEA DEALER AND GROCER in a circle. SAMUEL HIGGS + PENZANCE +

28. ⊙ Similar, but reads ONE TOKEN + TWO SHILLINGS +

℞ Similar, but a circle of pellets, no inner legend. W · F · ROWE, GROCER · PENZANCE · (*M.* 9). *Halliday.*

CUMBERLAND.

WHITEHAVEN.

FARTHING.

COPPER.

1. O. A monogram *W B.* In an outer circle, PAYABLE AT WHITE HAVEN ⁙

℞. A ship under sail to right; in an outer circle, FARTHING TOKEN 1812 *Halliday.*

PLATE A, no. 9.

The token was issued by William Bragg, grocer, who was gazetted bankrupt Feb. 8, 1817.

2. O. A monogram *W K.* In an outer circle, PAYABLE AT WHITE HAVEN ⁙

℞. A tea canister; in an outer circle, FARTHING TOKEN 1812
R. *Halliday.*

The issuer of this farthing was William Kitchin, also a grocer.

DERBYSHIRE.

DERBY.

SHILLING.

SILVER.

1. ○ A griffin with wings displayed, gorged, issuant from a ducal coronet; legend, ONE SHILLING TOKEN. STERLING SILVER.
℞ FOR THE USE OF THE INN^S AT DERBY ASHBOURN CHESTERFIELD NOTTINGHAM LEICESTER LITCHFIELD (*sic*) BURTON &c The legend occupies the whole field. *R.r.*
PLATE A, no. 10.

2. Similar, but *with* a period after &c. *R.r.*
Boyne 60.

3. ○ West View of Peterborough Cathedral, SILVER XII TOKEN
℞ DERBY LEICESTER NORTHAMPTON AND RUTLAND LICENSED SHILLING SILVER TOKEN in a circle; legend, H. MORGAN LICENSED MANUFACTURER 12 RATHBONE PLACE LONDON. *R.r.*   *Halliday.*
Boyne, 61.

This obverse is similar to, but not the same as Peterborough, no. 3; the reverse is the same as Leicestershire, no. 1.

For other tokens relating to Derby, see Leicestershire, nos. 1, 2, 3 and 5.

DEVONSHIRE.
COUNTY.

SHILLINGS.

SILVER.

1. O View of Eddystone Lighthouse, ships at sea; *Value* ONE SHILLING. H. M on the rock, and H on the wall; the G in SHILLING is *below* the pennon from the mast.

℞ DEVON SILVER TOKEN. within a wreath of oak, H - M under.

Boyne, 62.

2. O Arms, vert, per fess, lamb and plough, chief, argent, a ship; crest a dove between sprigs of olive, H M under. SILVER TOKEN

℞ The same as last. *R.* *Halliday.*

PLATE A, no. 11.

3. O View of Eddystone Lighthouse, &c., as no. 1.

℞ ONE SHILLING TOKEN SOLD BY ROYAL LICENCE AT MORGAN'S * 12. RATHBONE PLACE LONDON displayed with various scroll ornaments. *R.*

4. O Arms, argent, per pale, a triple tower of the city of Exeter between sprigs of olive, H. M. under; DEVONSHIRE SILVER TOKEN.

℞ The same as last.

5. O The same as last.

℞ ONE SHILLING VALUE within an olive wreath. *Halliday.*

Boyne, 64.

6. O Arms as before, but the shield is *tinted*, between sprigs of oak and palm.

℞ ONE SHILLING VALUE between sprigs of olive, H. M. under.

7. Also a Proof in Copper. *R.*

8. O The same as last.

℞ The same as the obverse of no. 1, Eddystone Lighthouse, &c. *R.r.* *Halliday.*

9. O Arms, gules, a castle triple towered, but without sprigs at the sides; legend, ONE SHILLING and on a ribbon below; DEVONSHIRE

℞ DEVONSHIRE SOMERSETSHIRE AND CORNWAL (*sic*) SILVER TOKEN with Staffordshire knots above and below SOMERSETSHIRE AND CORNWAL *R.r.r.* *Halliday.*

PLATE I, no. 3.

10. Also in Copper.
In Mr. Bliss' cabinet.

"The Statesman," Sept. 18th, 1811, announced that "the Devonshire Bank has employed an artist in town to stamp near five thousand pounds worth of tokens for shillings and sixpences."

Holinshed, in his Chronicle of A.D. 1577, writing on the Silver Mines of Devonshire, says : " The Workmen of that County being not sufficiently numerous, or not sufficiently expert, three hundred and thirty-seven Miners were, in the Year 1296, brought from the Wapentake of the Peak in Derbyshire, who fined and cast into wedges, in the course of that year, 704 pounds three shillings and one pennyweight.

" In the next year 348 Miners were brought from the same place and to them were added.25 from Wales."

BARNSTAPLE.

SHILLING.

11. ☉ BARNSTAPLE TOKEN ONE SHILLING. 1811. The G in SHILLING lines to the centre of the E in TOKEN

℞ Arms (argent, a castle triple towered) of the Borough, between branches of palm and flowers.

PLATE L, no. 1.

12. Similar to last, but the G lines to the first limb of E in TOKEN
Boyne, 32.

13. ☉ ISSUED AT BARNSTAPLE. 14 NOVEMBER 1811 * BY MESS^RS JOS. EVANS JOHN BOWHAY MICH^L NOTT & R. GRIBBLE

℞ The plumes of the Prince of Wales, FOR CONVENIENCE OF CHANGE. in a circle ; DEVONSHIRE SILVER TOKEN FOR XII PENCE *
Halliday.

Boyne, 9.

For another Shilling of Barnstaple, see Stratton.

The names of the persons given on the token were the proprietors of the Barnstaple Bank.

SIXPENCE.

14. Similar to no. 11, but BARNSTAPLE TOKEN SIX PENCE. 1811.
Boyne, 8.

15. Similar to no. 13, but DEVONSHIRE SILVER TOKEN FOR VI PENCE
Halliday.

Boyne, 10.

EXETER.

SHILLING.

16. ☉ View of Eddystone lighthouse, similar to no. 1, but the G in SHILLING is *above* the pennon on mast; the initials H. M and H omitted.

℞ Arms, per pale, gules and azure; a triple tower and supporters of the city ; motto, SEMPER FIDELIS (always faithful) ; crest, a demi-lion holding an orb ; EXETER AND DEVON SILVER TOKEN R.
Halliday.

PLATE L, no. 2.

DEVONSHIRE. 41

17. O JOSEPH HICKS. * EXETER * ONE SHILLING TOKEN
℞ Similar to the obverse. *R.r.* *Unknown.*
This piece is generally badly struck. The issuer was a silversmith, of New Bridge, Exeter.

TEIGNMOUTH.

SHILLING.

18. O Crest, a demi-lion holding a lily; under the chaplet H M all within a garter, inscribed PAYABLE AT THE BANK Outer legend, ISSU'D. AT. TEIGNMOUTH. FOR. PUBLIC. ACCOMODATION (*sic*) 1811.

℞ FOR 20 OF. THESE TOKENS. WHICH COST. ME. EACH ONE. SHILLING I. PROMISE. TO. PAY. THE BEARER. A. I. £. BANK OF ENGLAND NOTE I. HOLLAND *R.*

PLATE L, no. 3.

19. O Similar to last, but with ID *under* the chaplet, and annulets on the garter as periods.

℞ Similar to last, but with small stars after ONE and before and after NOTE *R.r.r.*

20. Also in Copper. *Davies.*
In Mr. Bliss' cabinet.

COUNTY.

COPPER. TWOPENCE.

21. O View of a lighthouse; S. VIEW. OF. THE. EDYSTONE. LIGHTHOUSE. COMPLEATED. (*sic*) OC^R 9. 1759. BY. I. SMEATON. + Under, DEVONSHIRE PRIVATE TOKEN

℞ View of a lighthouse; VIEW. OF. THE. HIGH. LIGHTHOUSE. ON. THE. SPURN. POINT. COMPLEATED. (*sic*) AP. 7. 1777. Under the base line, W. UPCOTT. DES MAY. 1801. *R.r.*

Sharp 190, 1.

22. Also a Proof in Silver, which is in the *B. M.*   *Wyon.*

These dies were softened and repaired, and 24 impressions taken by the late W. J. Taylor.

W. Upcott was the famous book collector and antiquary.

"The *Edystone* lighthouse, built by Mr. *Winstanley* in the reign of King *William* III, took fire, and burnt all the timber work; but the stone work, 30 feet high, and founded on a rock, remained unhurt. Admiral *West*, at *Plymouth*, seeing the fire, sent out a boat, and took away the two men that had the care of the place."—*Historical Chronicle, Tuesday Dec.* 2, 1755.

"The store-vessel came into Plymouth from her moorings at the Edystone, with all the workmen on board, the lighthouse there being entirely compleated under the direction of that excellent mechanic, Mr. Smeaton, F.R.S., without the loss of one life, or any material accident."—*The Gentleman's Magazine, Oct. 9th,* 1759.

TAVISTOCK.

PENNY.

23. O A mining engine; DEVON MINES * 1811 * The chimney is emitting smoke to the *right*.

℞ The Prince of Wales' feathers issuant from a coronet; TAVISTOCK * PENNY TOKEN *

Sharp 193, 1.
PLATE A, no. 12.

24. Similar to last, but the chimney is emitting its smoke to the *left*.

25. Similar, but the chimney emitting much *less* smoke, and the windows of the building *not* filled in.   *R.*   *Wyon.*

DORSETSHIRE.
BLANDFORD.

SILVER. SHILLING.

1. ☉ The arms of the borough, argent, three lions passant gardant; BLAND FORD 1811.

℞ ONE SHILLING TOKEN. H. WARD. ✳ FOR PUBLIC ACCOMMODATION. *R.r.r.*

PLATE L, no. 4.

2. ☉ Arms as before, but within a garter; PAYABLE BY H. WARD BLANDFORD

℞ ONE SHILLING TOKEN in a circle. FOR PUBLIC ACCOMMODATION 1811. *Halliday.*

PLATE A, no. 13.

In 1806 a prize of fifteen guineas was awarded Henry Ward of Blandford, for a "New Striking-clock Movement," by which the whole train of wheels, used in common clocks, together with the barrel and weight are entirely superseded.

DORCHESTER.
SHILLING.

3. ☉ COX. MERLE &. PATTISON. DORCHESTER BANK ONE. SHILLING TOKEN PURE. SILVER displayed with various scroll ornaments.

℞ St. Dunstan standing and leading the Devil by the nose with a pair of pincers; between sprigs of olive, KNOW THYSELF On the ground, I. D. *R.r.* *Davies.*

PLATE A, no. 14.

The issuers of the token were bankers. Their London address was Cox, Merle & Pattison, 2, Cox's Court, Little Britain.

"St. Dunstan was born at Glastonbury, of which monastery he became Abbot, and died Archbishop of Canterbury in 988."—*Butler.*

The legend of St. Dunstan relates many miracles of him, the most popular of which is that St. Dunstan, as the fact really was, became expert in goldsmith's work; that while he was busied in making a chalice, the Devil annoyed him by his personal appearance, and tempted him; whereupon St. Dunstan suddenly seized the fiend by the nose with a pair of iron tongs, burning hot, and so held him while he roared and cried till the night was far spent.

There is an engraved portrait of St. Dunstan thus detaining the devil in bondage, with these lines, or lines, to that effect, beneath; they are quoted from memory:—

"St. Dunstan, as the story goes,
Once pulled the Devil by the nose
With red hot tongs, which made him roar,
That he was heard three miles or more."—*The Every-Day Book.*

POOLE.
SHILLING.

4. ☉ The arms of Poole, a dolphin, in chief three escallops, between sprigs of olive; TOWN AND COUNTY OF POOLE TOKEN. 1811.

℞ JAMES FERRIS. SILVERSMITH. POOLE. VALUE ONE SHILLING arranged in *two* straight lines, and *three* curved; two sprigs of olive below POOLE and a small ornament above.

Boyne 176.

5. ℺ The same as last.

℞ Similar to last, but there is *no* ornament above POOLE which is in a *straight* line; there are *four* leaves and *as many* berries on right-hand sprig, and *one* in the centre. *Halliday.*

6. ℺ Similar to last, but the berries on olive sprigs are much *larger*, more like annulets.

℞ Similar to last, but there are *five* leaves and *as many* berries on the right-hand sprig, the two last berries at the right are *nearly* side by side. *R.*

7. ℺ The same as last.

℞ Similar to last, but the two last berries at the right are *over* each other. *R.* *Unknown*

The issuer was a silversmith and watchmaker. He was declared bankrupt April 27th, 1816.

8. ℺ W. B. BEST within a garter inscribed PAYABLE BY Legend, ONE POUND NOTE FOR 20 TOKENS. 1812.

℞ Female seated on a bale, holding scales and cornucopia, a sword below; the initials K. S. under the figure. ONE SHILLING SILVER TOKEN. POOLE. *Made by Kempson & Son.*

Boyne 177.
See countermarked tokens of Dorset.

SIXPENCE.

9. ℺ Similar, but 40 TOKENS
℞ Similar to last, but SIX PENCE SILVER TOKEN. POOLE.
Made by Kempson.

PLATE A, no. 15.
William B. Best was a draper.

SHAFTESBURY.

SHILLING.

10. ℺ Arms of Shaftesbury, quarterly first and fourth argent, a fleur-de-lis, second and third azure, a leopard's head, DORSETSHIRE WILTSHIRE. & SHAFTESBURY. BANK TOKEN

℞ ONE SHILLING AT SHAFTESBURY OR S. LLOYDS BUCKLERSBURY LONDON Circular legend, FOR THE ACCOMMODATION OF THE PUBLIC. 1811 *R.*

Boyne 194.
Samuel Lloyd was an ironmonger in Barge Yard.

11. ℺ The same as last.

℞ A military bust to left (Nelson?), COMMERCIAL TOKEN I.B.X.R 1811 *R.r.r.* *Halliday.*

PLATE L, no. 5.
This piece is struck in brass.

DORSETSHIRE. 45

12. ○ Bust to left in naval uniform, COMMERCIAL TOKEN I.B.X.R 1811

℞ ONE SHILLING VALUE within an olive wreath. *R.r.*

13. The same in Brass. *R.r.*

14. ○ Arms similar to no. 10, but legend SHAFTESBURY BANK TOKEN HENDERSON & CO.

℞ A large XII within a wreath of laurel. *R.r.*

PLATE L, no. 6.

15. A Proof in Copper. *R.r.r.* *Halliday.*

16. ○ Arms as before between sprigs of olive, SHAFTESBURY BANK. LICENSED 14 MARCH 1811. The 14 is the same size as the figures in date; the point of shield is *under* the Y the centre bar of shield to left is above a leaf.

℞ DORSETSHIRE WILTSHIRE AND SHAFTESBURY BANK TOKEN *Value* ONE SHILLING A Staffordshire knot between *first* and *second* lines.

Boyne, 196.

17. Also in Copper. *R.r.r.*

18. ○ Similar to last, but the centre bar is *opposite* a leaf.

℞ Similar to last, but the word *and* in italics. *R.*

19. Similar, but the figures 14 *almost* as small as the letters in MARCH *R.* *Halliday.*

20. Similar to the preceding, but the Staffordshire knot is *omitted*. *R.r.r.*

21. ○ Similar, but the point of shield is *under* the R of BURY

℞ DORSETSHIRE WILTSHIRE *and* SHAFTESBURY BANK TOKEN VALUE ONE SHILLING FOR THE ACCOMMODATION OF THE PUBLIC. Ornament under ONE SHILLING *R.*

22. ○ Same as last.

℞ MAY TRADE THE PLOUGH & THE FLEECE FLOURISH IN ALL THE BRITISH ISLES SUCCESS TO AGRICULTURE & NAVIGATION. *Halliday.*

In Mr. Bliss' cabinet.
PLATE I, no. 5.

SIXPENCE.

23. ○ The arms as before, but no sprigs at the sides of the shield, SHAFTESBURY BANK. LICENSED 14 MARCH 1811. The 14 is the same size as the figures in date, and larger than the letters in MARCH

℞ DORSETSHIRE WILTSHIRE AND SHAFTESBURY BANK TOKEN *Value* SIXPENCE The top and bottom lines are *curved*, the last limb of N in TOKEN is under the foot of Y in SHAFTESBURY

Boyne, 197.

24. Similar to last, but the 14 is the *same size* as the letters in MARCH and the last limb of N in TOKEN is not *quite under* the foot of Y *Halliday.*

25. ○ Similar to last, but with FOR THE ACCOMMODATION OF THE PUBLIC added as an inner legend.
℞ Similar to last, but VALUE in Roman capitals. *R.r.*
PLATE L, no. 7.

THREEPENCE.

26. ○ HENDERSON & C^{O.} SHASTON BANK··TOKEN··
℞ A large 3 within an olive wreath. *R.r.r.* *Halliday.*
Boyne, 198.

SWANAGE.

TWOPENCE.

COPPER.

27. ○ SWANAGE FRIENDLY SOCIETY 1785
℞ VALUE TWO PENCE *R.r.* *Milton.*
PLATE J, no. 6.
This is of excellent workmanship.

DURHAM.

STOCKTON.

SHILLING.

SILVER.

1. O Arms (of Stockton) a castle over an anchor, STOCKTON. above; 1812 below. The anchor stock *extends* to the last embattlement of the tower, the cable loops quite *clear* of legend.

℞ SILVER TOKEN I SHIL^G Legend, CHRISTOPHER AND JENNETT a crosslet after JENNETT

2. O Similar, but the anchor stock *does not extend* to the last embattlement of the tower, the cable loops are larger, *nearly touching* the legend.

℞ As last. *Halliday.*

PLATE J, no. 7.

GATESHEAD.

FARTHING.

COPPER.

3. O JOHN HARROP GROCER & TEA-DEALER 1814 BRIDGE END GATES HEAD

℞ A tea cannister inscribed H G (Harrop Gateshead); legend, FINE TEAS * RAW & ROASTED COFFEE

4. Also in silver. *R.r.*

SOUTH SHIELDS.

5. O Bust to left FRANCIS. ROBINSON. STH SHIELDS

℞ A three-mast ship sailing to left SUCCESS TO THE COAL TRADE 1814. *R.* *Unknown.*

PLATE A, no. 16.

STOCKTON.

PENNY.

6. O View of a bridge; TEES above, 1813 below. CHRISTOPHER & JENNETT * STOCKTON * incuse on a broad rim.

℞ Figure of Britannia seated, BRITANNIA * ONE PENNY TOKEN * incuse on a broad rim. *P. Wyon.*

PLATE A, no. 17.

Christopher & Jennett were booksellers and printers.

ESSEX.
EPPING.
COPPER.

1. ○ A stag proper courant, under a tree.

℞ A star and garter inscribed, VALUE ONE SHILLING. In the centre $\frac{s}{1}$ Over the star a bugle horn; legend, EPPING ✱ ✱ FOREST ✱ E. SPENCE × DEALER × IN × COINS × LONDON × *R.r.* $17\frac{e}{\theta}$

PLATE I, no. 6.

2. Also with edge milled. *R.*
Atkins Ia.

3. Also with edge plain. *James.*
Sharp 2, no. 1.

WALTHAMSTOW.
PENNY, 1812.
TWENTY-THREE ACORNS.

4. ○ A lion statant gardant; ROLLING MILLS AT WALTHAMSTOW Ex. ONE PENNY 1812 The tip of the tail points to the *first* limb of the letter A and the 2 in date is under the first N in PENNY

℞ BRITISH COPPER COMPANY within a wreath of oak. Legend, SMELTING WORKS AT LANDORE ✱ There are *twenty-three* acorns; eleven to left and twelve to right.

PLATE A, no. 18.

There is a double obverse of this piece with one side incuse.

5. ○ Similar, but the tuft to tail points to the *centre* of A and the 2 in date is under the *first* limb of N

℞ Similar, the wreath has twelve acorns to left and eleven to right.

Sharp 193, 1.

TWENTY-TWO ACORNS.

6. ○ Similar, but tuft points to the *second* limb of A

℞ Similar, the wreath has *twenty-two* acorns, eleven on each side. *R.*

TWENTY-ONE ACORNS.

7. ○ Similar, but the tuft points *between* the letters W and A and the 2 in date is under E and N

℞ Similar, but the wreath has *twenty-one* acorns, ten to left and eleven to right.

8. ○ Similar to no. 1, but the tuft points to the *centre* of A and the 2 in date is under NN in PENNY

℞ Similar, but the wreath has eleven acorns to left and ten to right; the *second* acorn at the right nearly touching the star at the end of legend.

ESSEX.

Eighteen Acorns.

9. ☉ Similar, but the tuft points to the *first* limb of A

℞ Similar, but the wreath has *eighteen* acorns, eight to left and ten to right, and the 2 in date is under the E and N of PENNY *R.*

10. Similar, but the 2 in date is under the *first* limb of N in PENNY *all by P. Wyon.*

The British Copper Company was established in 1807 by subscription. Mr. Jones, of Lambeth, was the promoter.

11. ☉ A lion *passant gardant*, as no. 12, below, but legend and date as no. 4.

℞ Similar, but the wreath has *twenty-four* acorns, twelve to left and twelve to right. *P. Wyon.*

PLATE K, no. 7.

This pattern piece is of fine workmanship; and was presented by the artist to Sir George Chetwynd.

In Mr. Norman's cabinet.

1813.

Twenty-five Acorns.

12. ☉ A lion *passant gardant*, the same legend as before, but date 1813. The tuft of tail lines to the *second* limb of A, and the 3 in date is *under* the N in PENNY

℞ Similar to preceding, the wreath has *twenty-five* acorns, twelve to left and thirteen to right.

Twenty-four Acorns.

13. ☉ Similar, but the end of tail lines to the *centre* of A, and the 3 in date is under the *first* limb of N

℞ Similar, but there are *twenty-four* acorns in the wreath, twelve to the left and as many to the right.

Twenty-two Acorns.

14. ☉ Similar, but the end of tail lines to the *first* limb of A

℞ Similar, but wreath has *twenty-two* acorns, eleven on each side.

Nineteen Acorns.

15. ☉ Similar, but the end of tail lines to the *last* limb of A

℞ The wreath has *nineteen* acorns, eight to left and eleven to right. *R.*

16. ☉ Similar, but the ground line at the right points *between* the T and O, whereas it is *opposite* the letter O in all preceding.

℞ As last. *R.* *P. Wyon.*

The Rolling Mills were on the South-west of St. James's Street, between the River Lee and the present railway. The property was purchased by the East London Waterworks.

HALFPENNY, 1811.

Vincit Amor Patriæ.

17. ☉ Laureate bust to right; VINCIT AMOR PATRIÆ 1811 (the love of country exceeds everything); the laurel leaves point on either side *to* the o in AMOR

℞ Britannia seated, holding olive branch and trident, within a wreath of oak, with *fourteen* acorns, eight to left and six to right; there are ribbon ends to tie of wreath; the *centre and right* barbs of trident *touch* a leaf; B C C under the shield (British Copper Company).

Sharp 208, 3.

18. Similar, but a larger bust, and the point of drapery is *near* the Æ instead of *over* the last one in date.

19. ☉ Nearly as last, but the laurel points *more to* the o

℞ The wreath has *sixteen* acorns, seven left and nine right; the *centre* barb of trident *touches* a leaf, and the *right* of it is close to an acorn.

20. Similar, but the laurel *points to* the R

21. A rather smaller bust, laurel *points to* the o and R

22. ☉ Similar to last, but the laurel *points only* to the o

℞ The wreath has *fifteen* acorns, nine left and six right; the left and *centre* barbs of trident *touch* a leaf.

23. Similar bust, laurel *points between* the o and R

24. ☉ Similar, but the laurel *points to* the o The v points to end of ribbon *farthest* from neck.

℞ Wreath has *eighteen* acorns, nine on each side; the *right* barb of trident *touches* a leaf.

25. Similar, but the laurel *points to* the o and R .

26. Similar, but the v *points to end* of ribbon *nearest* the neck.

27. Similar, but the wreath has *sixteen* acorns, nine to left, seven to right; *left* and *centre* barbs of trident *touch* a leaf, the right is *under* an acorn.

28. Similar, the wreath has *sixteen* acorns, but eight on each side; the *left* barb *touches* a leaf. *all by T. Wyon.*

Brutus and Vincit Amor Patriæ.

29. ☉ Bust to left; BRUTUS
℞ Bust to right; VINCIT AMOR PATRIÆ *R.r.* *T. Wyon.*

Sharp 208, 4.

ESSEX.

BRUTUS.

30. O Similar to last.

℞ Britannia seated, &c.; the wreath has *eighteen* acorns, nine on either side; *right* barb of trident *touches* a leaf.

Sharp 208, 5.

31. Similar, but the wreath has *fifteen* acorns, eight left, seven right; *left* and *centre* barbs of trident *touch* a leaf.

32. Similar, but the wreath has *fourteen* acorns, eight left, six right; *right* barb *only touches* a leaf.

33. O Bust smaller than before, *with* a period after BRUTUS.

℞ The wreath has *twenty* acorns, eleven left, nine right; *all* the barbs of trident *nearly touch* a leaf. *T. Wyon.*

MERCURY. No date.

34. O Head of Mercury to left, wearing a *winged* petasus, a caduceus over the shoulder.

℞ Britannia seated, &c.; the wreath has *nineteen* acorns, ten left, nine right; *right* barb *touches* a leaf.

35. Similar, but the wreath has *eighteen* acorns, nine each side; the *centre* and *right* barbs *touch* a leaf.

Sharp 208, 6.

36. Similar, wreath has *eighteen* acorns, ten to left and eight to right; the *three* barbs each *touch* a leaf.

37. Similar, but the wreath has *nineteen* acorns, ten to left and nine to right. *Wyon.*

1813.

38. O A lion *passant gardant*; HALFPENNY 1813 The tuft of the tail points to the *first* limb of the *first* N

℞ Britannia seated within a wreath of oak; in her right hand an olive branch, in her left a trident; under the shield B C C The wreath contains *nineteen* acorns, ten to left and nine to right; the *centre* and *right* hand barb of the trident *touch* a leaf.

39. O Similar, but the lion's head *touches* the H and the tuft of tail points *between* the E and N

℞ Similar, but *eighteen* acorns in the wreath, ten to left and eight to right; the *left* and *centre* barb *touch* a leaf.

40. Similar to last, but the lion's tail *touches* the Y

41. Similar, but the tail points to the *first* limb of the *first* N and is again free from the letter Y *Wyon.*

1814.

42. ☉ A lion as before, tail points to *second* limb of the *first* N Dated 1814

℞ Similar, but with *eighteen* acorns, nine on each side; *no tie* to the wreath; the *right* hand barb *touches* an acorn.   R.   *Wyon.*

PLATE J, no. 8.

43. ☉ As last.

℞ An incuse impression of the obverse die.

In Mr. Norman's cabinet.

Sharp says these tokens were struck and issued by the British Copper Company, in Thames Street, London. The Company had smelting works at Walthamstow.

GLOUCESTERSHIRE.

CHELTENHAM.
SHILLING.
SILVER.

1. ○ View of St. Mary's Church in perspective, an avenue of trees; VALUE ONE SHILLING
℞ A POUND NOTE FOR 20 TOKENS GIVEN BY WILL^M BASTIN CHELTENHAM 1811

2. Also in tin. *R.r.r.* *Halliday.*
PLATE A, no. 19.

3. ○ PAYABLE BY MESS^{RS} J. & S. GRIFFITH CHELTENHAM OR AT NO. 2 RIVER S^T BATH in a circle. PAYABLE BY A. ONE POUND NOTE FOR 20 OF THESE TOKENS.
℞ The arms and crest of Bristol within a garter; inscribed DOLLAR SILVER Legend, SILVER TOKEN FOR XII PENCE *R.r.*
Unknown.

GLOUCESTER.
HALF CROWN.

4. ○ Arms of Gloucester, or, three chevrons gules, between ten torteaux, two sprigs of olive at the sides; GLOUCESTER TOKEN TWO SHILLINGS & SIXPENCE
℞ A POUND NOTE FOR EIGHT TOKENS GIVEN BY J. WHALLEY GLOUCESTER AND AT N^O 10 CHARLOTTE S^T FITZROY SQUARE LONDON
Halliday.
PLATE J, no. 9.

James Whalley traded as a banker and draper. His son became the representative of Peterborough in Parliament.

SHILLING.
WITH CREST.

5. ○ Arms of Gloucester between two sprigs of olive as before, crest a cap of maintenance; FOR XII PENCE *No period* in the legend, and the tassel is *between* the ones of value.
℞ View of Gloucester cathedral; GLOUCESTER. COUNTY. & CITY TOKEN. MDCCCXI.

6. Similar, but *a period* after each word in the legend on the obverse; and the tassel is *under* the last numeral of XII *Halliday.*
Boyne 91.

WITHOUT CREST.

7. O Arms of Gloucester between two sprigs of olive, GLOUCESTER CITY TOKEN ONE SHILLING   There are *thirteen* leaves in the olive branch at the right.

℞ PAYABLE ON DEMAND BY SAUNDERS & BUTT Legend, TO FACILITATE TRADE OCTOBER 20TH 1811

Boyne 92.

8. Similar, but the reverse is *dated* OCTOBER 25TH.

9. Similar to last, OCTOBER 25TH but with *twelve* leaves in olive branch at the right.

Saunders & Butt were chandlers.

10. O Arms of Gloucester between two sprigs of olive. GLOUCESTER TOKEN ONE SHILLING   On the *third* leaf at the right the letter H

℞ PAYABLE AT JA^S WHALLEY'S GLOUCESTER & AT N$^O_{TO}$ CHARLOTTE S^T FITZROY SQUARE LONDON. ^{S} in JA^S is under the *centre* of A in PAYABLE

Boyne 94.

11. Similar, but the ^{S} in JA^S is under the *first* limb of A in PAYABLE

12. O Arms of Gloucester between two sprigs of olive, GLOUCESTER CITY AND COUNTY

℞ MORGAN'S GLOUCESTER CITY & COUNTY SILVER MEDAL BY THE ROYAL AUTHORITY with a knot between the third and fourth line. *R.r.r.*

13. Also in copper, on a small flan the size of a sixpence. *R.r.*

Halliday.

CHELTENHAM.

PENNY.
COPPER.

14. O View of St. Mary's Church in perspective, an avenue of trees. Ex. VALUE ONE PENNY.

℞ A POUND NOTE FOR 240 TOKENS GIVEN BY JOHN BASTIN & C^O CHELTENHAM 1812   *R.r.*

PLATE K, no. 8.

John Bastin & Co. were tailors and drapers.

GLOUCESTERSHIRE. 55

15. O As last.
℞ Similar, but BY JOHN BISHOP & C°. *Halliday.*

Sharp 194, 2.

John Bishop advertised himself as tailor to H.R.H. the Prince Regent, and carried on business opposite the Plough Hotel, Cheltenham. He was declared bankrupt March 16, 1822.

SEDBURY.

PENNY.

16. O View of a mill with four chimneys emitting dense smoke. GENUINE BRITISH COPPER Ex. SEDBURY IRON WORKS

℞ ONE PENNY TOKEN within a mixed wreath of oak and laurel. H on the laurel leaf opposite N in TOKEN *Halliday.*

PLATE A, no. 20.

This reverse also occurs at Burton, Sheffield and Not Local.

HAMPSHIRE.

COUNTY.

SILVER.
SHILLING.

1. ○ Ships at sea, the sun rising   HAMPSHIRE TOKEN   At the left of ship, H.M   In the waves under the ship, at the *right* the letter P

℞ ISLE OF WIGHT PORTSMOUTH SOUTHAMPTON AND GOSPORT SHILLING SILVER TOKEN · Within an outer circle, H. MORGAN LICENSED MANUFACTURER 12 RATHBONE PLACE LONDON. *R.r. Patrick.*

Boyne 95.

2. ○ Arms of the county; gules, a rose surmounted by a crown. HAMPSHIRE SILVER TOKEN 1811   The *one* in date is *over* the first limb of R in SILVER   Point of shield is between the 8 and 1 of date.

℞ A sloop sailing. VALUE ONE SHILLING TO FACILITATE TRADE The top mast *touching the upright limb* of the E in ONE   The water line touches the T of TRADE

Boyne 96.

3. Also in copper.

4. Similar, but the mast is under the *extreme left* of the E   The water line touches the R

5. ○ Similar, but the point of the shield is over the 8 and the 1 is above the *centre* of R

℞ The mast similar to no. 2, but slightly more at the right, the water line as last.   *Unknown.*

SIXPENCE.

6. ○ Similar to preceding, but an ornament divides the legend; the point of shield is *between* the 8 and 1 of date; the figures of date *same size* as each other.

℞ Sloop sailing, VALUE SIXPENCE * TO FACILITATE TRADE.

Boyne, 97.

7. Also in copper.

8. Similar, but the point of shield is *over* the third numeral; the ones in date are *smaller* than the figure 8   *Unknown.*

ANDOVER.

SHILLING.

1811.

9. ⚬ The arms of the borough; argent, a lion under a tree. ANDOVER TOKEN FOR XII PENCE The point of shield lines with the *first* limb of K and the lion's foot is *half across* the trunk of the tree.

℞ PAYABLE BY W. S. &. I. WAKEFORD, 1811 within a wreath of oak. A *period* after the &. and I. The tops of ones *slope*. An acorn *under* the date, making *six* on the inside of wreath at the right. The P of PAYABLE *touches* a leaf.

PLATE J, no. 10.

10. Similar, but an acorn *over* the first A of PAYABLE *No* period after I and having *seven* acorns inside wreath at the right.

11. Also in copper.

12. Similar, but a leaf over the *first* A in PAYABLE

13. Similar, but with *eight* acorns in the inside of wreath.

14. Similar, but *a period* after I. and *nine* acorns in the inside of wreath.

15. ⚬ Similar, but point of shield *lines* with the centre of K and the lion's foot is only a *quarter across* the trunk of the tree.

℞ Similar, but a *period* after all initials, but *not* after & The tops of the ones in date are *flat*; there are only *four* acorns in the inside of wreath at the right, and *no* acorn under the date. R.

Boyne 2.

16. Also in copper. *R.r.* *Halliday.*

1812.

17. ⚬ Arms as before, point of shield lines with the *first* limb of K

℞ Similar, but *without* a period after I *Seven* acorns in inside of wreath, dated 1812

Boyne 3.

18. Also in copper.

19. Similar, but with *six* acorns in inside of wreath.

20. Similar, but *with* a period after I. *Halliday.*

William, Samuel, and Joseph Wakeford were bankers, who issued also bank notes. The bank closed in 1825. On April 20th, 1826, dividends were paid at the Star and Garter Hotel, Andover; and the final dividend at the same place on March 10th, 1827.

NEWPORT.

SHILLING.

21. O An antique ship in a circle; NEWPORT ISLE OF WIGHT 1811 The anchor *touches* the waves, there is a *break* in the flag near the mast, and the ones in date are *flat* topped.

℞ ONE SHILLING SILVER TOKEN in a circle. MAY PLENTY CROWN OUR HAPPY ISLE ✷ The terminal of the G in SHILLING lines to the *upright* limb of the first P in HAPPY

PLATE A, no. 21.

22. O Similar, but the flag is *severed* from the portion attached to the mast, and the anchor *does not touch* the water.

℞ Similar, but the terminal of the G lines to the *last* limb of A

Boyne 169.

23. O Similar, but the flag is *entire* and attached to the mast by its whole width; the anchor *touches* the water, the ones in date *slope*.

℞ Similar, but the terminal of the G lines to the *space* between PP in HAPPY. *Halliday.*

SIXPENCE.

24. O Similar to preceding.

℞ Beehive and bees in a circle; UNION TOKEN SIXPENCE

Boyne 170.

25. Also in Copper. *R.r.*

26. The same in Tin. *R.r.r.* *Halliday.*

The issuer of these tokens was Robert Bird Wilkins, ironmonger, etc.

Atkins, in "Tokens of the Eighteenth Century," under Newport, describes a halfpenny with the bust of Robert Bird Wilkins by Mainwaring. It was issued in large quantities, and even now is fairly common. The Newport silver pieces were also extensively circulated.

PORTSEA.

SHILLING.

27. O A crescent and star, the arms of Portsmouth; ACCOMMODATION OF TRADE 1811 The arms and legend divided by a band inscribed PORTSEA SILVER - TOKEN

℞ VALUE ONE SHILLING PAYABLE AT MESS^{RS} AVENELL & SIMMONDS QUEEN S^T PORTSEA *R.r.r.* *Unknown.*

PLATE L, no. 8.

William Avenell was a watchmaker. On July 30, 1814, Avenell was declared a bankrupt at the George Inn, Portsmouth.

PORTSMOUTH.

SHILLING.

28. O- PORTSMOUTH ACCOMMODATION. CHANGE A crescent and star in a circle.

℞ ONE SHILLING TOKEN within a garter inscribed DOLLAR SIL VER Outer legend, PAYABLE AT THE BULLION OFFICE 69 HIGH STREET 1811
Boyne 180.

29. O- The same as last.

℞ ISLE OF WIGHT, &c., as no. 1.
Boyne 181.

30. O- A crescent and star as before, but with an *eye* in the centre of the star; a garter inscribed PORTSMOUTH 1811 Legend, PAYABLE AT I. DUDLEYS

℞ XII PENCE in an olive wreath of *eleven* berries. SILVER TOKEN
Boyne 132.

31. Similar, but the crescent to left *nearly touches* the star, and the period omitted *between* I and D
PLATE J, no. 11.

32. O- Similar, but the tongue of garter *does not* touch the D in DUDLEYS which it *does* in the preceding.

℞ Similar to last, but the wreath has *seventeen* berries. *R.*
Halliday.

John Dudley was a goldsmith in the High Street.

33. O- A ship sailing; LET COMMERCE FLOURISH ISSUED BY I M STEPHENS 1811

℞ VALUE XII PENCE with olive sprigs under. PORTSMOUTH SILVER TOKEN *R.* *Unknown.*
Boyne 183.

I. M. Stephens was a jeweller. He was declared a bankrupt January 21st, 1815.—*London Gazette*.

ROMSEY.

SHILLING.

34. O- Arms, argent, a portcullis, between two sprigs of oak; H M under the shield; ROMSEY TOKEN. VALUE ONE SHILLING

℞ PAYABLE BY W. ADAMS 1812 within a wreath of oak; H. M below the wreath. (*See also* Suffolk no. 4.) *R.*
Boyne 188.

Boyne incorrectly describes this piece, as the date is 1812, not 1811. The issuer was not Webster Adams of Ipswich; the same die was probably used to save the cost of engraving a new one. W. Adams of Romsey was a rope manufacturer.

35. O The same as last.

℞ Ships at sea, etc., the sun rising; HAMPSHIRE TOKEN Similar to the obverse of no. 1. *R.r.*

36. O Similar to last, but ROMSEY TOKEN. VALUE + ONE SHILLING The initials H. M *omitted*.

℞ Ships at sea, the sun rising; WILLIAM LINTOTT & SONS. At the left P in the waves. *R.* *Patrick.*

Boyne 189.

The issuers of this token were merchants.

SOUTHAMPTON.

SHILLING.

37. O The arms of Hampshire, argent, a rose surmounted by a crown, between two sprigs of oak; SOUTHAMPTON TOKEN VALUE ONE SHILLING

℞ An antique ship; WILLIAM LOMER & SON *Unknown.*

Boyne 206.

The issuers were printers in the High Street. W. Lomer was declared a bankrupt on April 29th, 1822.

ANDOVER.

PENNY.

COPPER.

38. O The arms of Andover; ANDOVER TOKEN. FOR ONE PENNY. The ribs of the lion *are expressed.*

℞ PAYABLE BY W. S. & I. WAKEFORD 1812 within a wreath of oak.

PLATE A, no. 22.

39. Similar to last, but the lion's ribs *are not expressed.* *Halliday.*

Sharp 194, 1.

BASINGSTOKE.

40. O A spade and mattock in a wheelbarrow; JOHN PINKERTON VALUE ONE SHILLING

℞ A man in a barge sailing; BASINGSTOKE CANAL 1789

E A wreath of laurel. *Wyon.*

PLATE I, no. 7.

This token was current and paid as one shilling to the workmen during the cutting of the Canal. It differs from the general run of truck tickets in so far as it purports to be more of a general medium of exchange.

HEREFORDSHIRE.

COUNTY.

SILVER.
SHILLING.

1. O Arms of Hereford, three lions passant gardant, on a border azure, ten Scottish crosses, between sprigs of oak and palm; crest, a lion gardant holding a sword; there are *five* acorns in the oak sprig; HEREFORD COUNTY AND CITY TOKEN 1811

℞ PAYABLE IN CASH NOTES BY WAINWRIGHT & C? AND CARLESS & C? ONE SHILLING TOKEN displayed in six lines; the third and fifth being on scrolls.

PLATE A, no. 23.

2. Similar to last, but with *three* acorns only in the oak sprig. *R. Halliday.*

Wainwright & Co. were chemists and maltsters, and Carless & Co., drapers. T. Carless was declared bankrupt, Feb. 17, 1821, and B. Wainwright on November 22nd, 1822. In recognition of its loyalty, King Charles, in 1645, granted the addition of the border to the arms of the city.

HERTFORDSHIRE.

SAWBRIDGEWORTH.

PENNY.

COPPER.

1. O- Bust in very high relief; ROBERT o ORCHARD o SAWBRIDGE WORTH o o HERTS o o

℞ An open book lying at the foot of a tree; a church in the distance; ✷ SAWBRIDGEWORTH ✷ PENNY ✷ TOKEN ✷   Ex.: ✷ ✷ PAYABLE ✷ ✷ FEB^Y. XI ✷ 1801 ✷   *R.r.r.*   *James.*

Atkins 46, 1.

KENT.

FOLKESTONE.

SHILLING.

SILVER.

1. ⚬ The arms of the Cinque Ports, three lions passant gardant, as many hulls of ships; crest, a Royal crown; Inscribed on a ribbon below CINQ. PORT. TOKEN Legend, IOHN BOXER FOLKESTONE 1811

℞ ONE SHILLING VALUE within a wreath of olive. *Halliday.*

PLATE J, no. 12.

LANCASHIRE.

LIVERPOOL.

HALF A GUINEA.

COPPER.

1. O A phœnix issuant from flames; .THOS WILSON & CO · LIVERPOOL.
℞ LANCASHIRE TOKEN 1812 STANDARD 10 · 6 GOLD   *R.r.r.*
Halliday.
PLATE A, no. 24.
This is in copper. Research has failed to find its existence in the precious metal. The firm were merchants, carrying on business in Red Cross Street.

SHILLING.
SILVER.

2. O The arms of Liverpool argent, a bird (Liver) holding in the beak a sprig of laver; crest, ears of corn between two oak sprigs; THOS WILSON & CO. LIVERPOOL
℞ Female seated on a bale, holding scales and cornucopia; a sword rests against the bale; LANCASHIRE ONE SHILLING TOKEN 1812
Halliday.
Boyne 119.

MANCHESTER.

SHILLING.

3. O The arms of Manchester, gules, three bends or, between sprigs of oak and palm; MANCHESTER TOKEN. VALUE ONE SHILLING.
℞ View of a building; W. BALLANS TEA-DEALER MARKET-PLACE+
Boyne 138.

4. O The same as last.
℞ Similar to last, but Y and D on the base line of building; the date 1812. *added.* *R.r.r.*

5. O The same as last.
℞ View of same building; but legend, FOR PUBLIC ACCOMODATION. (*sic*) 1812   *Halliday.*
Boyne 139.

POULTON.

SHILLING.

6. O POULTEN TOKEN VALUE ONE SHILLING
℞ PAYABLE AT R. D HALLS in a circle. Legend ONE POUND NOTE FOR 20 TOKENS *R.*   *Unknown.*
Boyne 184.
The issuer was an ironmonger and grocer in the High Street.

LEICESTERSHIRE.

LEICESTER.

SHILLING.

SILVER.

1. ♆ The arms of Leicester, vert, a cinquefoil, between two sprigs of olive; ONE SHILLING SILVER TOKEN
℞ DERBY LEICESTER NORTHAMPTON AND RUTLAND LICENSED SHILLING SILVER TOKEN Legend, H. MORGAN LICENSED MANUFACTURER 12 RATHBONE PLACE LONDON.
PLATE A, no. 25.
A similar reverse will be found at Derby, no. 2.

2. ♆ The same as last.
℞ NOTTS DERBY LEICESTER NORTHAMPTON AND RUTLAND SHILLING SILVER TOKEN The outer legend similar to last, but the H. before MORGAN *omitted*. R.

3. ♆ The same as the reverse of no. 1, DERBY LEICESTER etc.
℞ The same as last, MORGAN LICENSED etc.
This token formed by the two reverses is very rare.

4. ♆ The same as no. 1. Arms of Leicester, &c.
℞ LEICESTER SILVER TOKEN ISSUED BY ROYAL LICENSE Legend, A. ONE. POUND. NOTE. WILL. BE. PAID· FOR 20 OF· THESE· AT· I. W & I. RAWSONS 1811 *R.r.* *Halliday.*
Boyne 114.

SIXPENCE.

5. ♆ Arms as before, but without the wreath of olive; SIX PENNY SILVER TOKEN
℞ DERBY LEICESTER AND RUTLAND SIX-PENNY TOKEN 1811. Legend, MORGAN LICENSED MAKER 12 RATHBONE PLACE LONDON
Boyne 113.

6. ♆ The same as last.
℞ Similar to no. 4 (RAWSONS), except in size and value. *R.r.r.*
Halliday.

For other tokens relating to Leicester, see Derbyshire.
Rawsons were cotton spinners and hosiery manufacturers in Churchgate.

K

LINCOLNSHIRE.

COUNTY.

SHILLING.

SILVER.
1. O A fleece suspended in a circle; LINCOLNSHIRE..+.., SILVER TOKEN..+..
℞ 12 PENCE 1811 within a wreath of oak.

Boyne 117.

2. O Arms azure, a fleece suspended; 1812 above. LINCOLNSHIRE SILVER TOKEN
℞ TWELVE PENCE an ornament above and below. FOR USE AND ACCOMODATION. (*sic*). *Halliday.*

Boyne 118.

ALFORD.

SHILLING.

3. O ALFORD SILVER TOKEN 12 PENCE in a circle; the second and third words on a ribbon in the centre, above the ribbon a dotted line. PAYABLE AT ELIZTH EMERTON & SON^S. + .

℞ A beehive with bees, 1811 in a circle; legend, INDUSTRY HAS ITS REWARD with palm branches below. R. *Halliday.*

Boyne 1.
The issuers of the token were drapers.

EPWORTH.

SHILLING.

4. O PAYABLE IN GOODS OR NOTES 1812. Legend, EPWORTH ISLE TOKEN. T. & W. READ. An ornament above PAYABLE

℞ View of a building (the Court house); ONE SHILLING. CURRENT VALUE A quatrefoil at bottom; the quatrefoil has the initials Y D & C° upon it. *Halliday.*

Boyne 78.

Thomas and William Read kept a general stores.
Numismatic Magazine, vol. VIII, p. 13, says : "There is a variety reading PAYADLE (*sic*) but I cannot trace it."

GAINSBOROUGH.

SHILLING.

5. ☉ Star, garter, and motto HONI SOIT QUI MAL Y PENSE (Let him be abashed who evil thinketh of it). Legend, JOHN GAMSON. GAINSBRO.

℞ Female seated on a bale, holding scales and cornucopia, a sword on the ground; the initials ẏ and D under the figure. ONE SHILLING TOKEN 1811. *R.r.* *Halliday.*

Boyne 87.

The issuer was a linen and woollen draper; on May 11, 1822, he was declared bankrupt.

6. ☉ A three-masted ship sailing; WILLIAM JERREMS. GAINSBRO.

℞ A windmill; ONE SHILLING SILVER TOKEN 1811 The top of window is *straight*, reaching to the *last* bar of sail, and there are *six* lines of brickwork on the building. *R.r.*

Boyne 88.

7. ☉ As last

℞ Similar, but the window is *arched*, the top reaching *between* the *fourth* and *fifth* bar of sail, and only *five* lines of brickwork are exhibited. *Unknown.*

See Notts. no. 1, for another token payable by W. Jerrems, who was a grocer.

8. ☉ A ship sailing under canvas; GAINSBRO TOKEN 1811

℞ A *near* view of a bridge; S. SANDARS above it in a circle. Legend, FOR TWELVE PENCE branches of olive under. *Halliday.*

9. ☉ The same as last.

℞ A *distant* view of a bridge in a circle; legend, FOR TWELVE PENCE Olive branches as last. *Halliday.*

PLATE A, no. 26.

Samuel Sandars was a corn merchant and maltster.

SIXPENCE.

10. ☉ SILVER TOKEN ISSUED BY MBRUMBY GAINSBURGH FOR VI PENCE

℞ A wheatsheaf. Below, 1812 Legend, TO ACCOMMODATE THE PUBLIC WITH SMALL CHANGE. *R.r.r.* *Halliday.*

PLATE B, no. 1.

This beautifully executed little piece is peculiar in so far that it is the only token where the initial forms a diphthong with the first letter of the surname. Martin Brumby made sail cloth for the Grimsby fishermen. He was declared bankrupt, Sep. 22, 1821.

HOLBEACH.

SHILLING.

11. ○ 1811 HOLBEACH AND LINCOLNSHIRE SILVER TOKEN H. M in a circle. Legend, A ONE POUND NOTE WILL BE PAID FOR 20 OF THESE BY R. B. HOFF+

℞ ONE SHILLING VALUE H. M within a thick wreath of oak. ISSUED BY ROYAL LICENCE *R.* *Halliday.*

Boyne 101.

Robert Beer Hoff the issuer carried on the business of a seedsman.

LINCOLN.

SHILLING.

12. ○ The arms of Lincoln argent, on a cross gules, a fleur-de-lys, between two sprigs of oak; LINCOLN SILVER TOKEN 1812

℞ MILLSON AND PRESTON within a garter, inscribed DOLLAR SILVER Legend, A ONE POUND NOTE WILL BE GIVEN FOR 20 OF THESE.

Boyne 115.

13. ○ Similar to last, but without the sprigs of oak and the cross is tinted gules and vert.

℞ Similar, but reads WILL BE PAID and H. M *added* under PRESTON   *Halliday.*

Boyne 116.

Millson and Preston were wine and spirit merchants.

14. ○ Shield of arms. First and fourth quarterly, or two fleur-de-lys, in the first and in the fourth a cross patée, second and third argent, three fleur-de-lys in the second, a lion rampant in the third, over all a cross gules; LINCOLN SILVER TOKEN

℞ ONE SHILLING TOKEN within a circle of dots. TO FACILITATE TRADE. An ornament at the bottom. *R.r.r.*   *Unknown.*

This reverse will be found also at London.

LOUTH.

SHILLING.

15. ○ LOUTH SHILLING TOKEN 1811   Legend, C. STOVIN & H CHAPMAN ..+..

℞ A fleece suspended. PAYABLE IN CASH NOTES.+. *R.*

Halliday.

Boyne 134.

Cornelius Stovin and Henry Chapman were drapers.

STAMFORD.

EIGHTEENPENCE.

16. ☾ A lion couchant, supporting the Royal standard, surmounted by a crown. Below, STAMFORD 1811

℞ SILVER 1s. 6ᴅ TOKEN Legend, PAYABLE IN CASH NOTES BY EDWᴅ & FRAˢ BUTT. *R.*

PLATE L, no. 9.

17. ☾ Similar to last, but the crown is *smaller*, and is *radiated*.

℞ The same as last. *R.* *Unknown.*

PLATE L, no. 10.

The issuers of this token were drapers.

MIDDLESEX.

LONDON.

EIGHTEENPENCE.

SILVER.

1. O View of a statue (Charles I) enclosed by railings with four lamps affixed. At the top of the pedestal at the left I and at the right D Legend, CHARING CROSS 1s. 6D.

℞ Large 18 within a wreath of oak; branches of wheat ears at top. LONDON SILVER TOKEN The ends of the tie in the oak wreath are over the *first* limbs of the L and E in SILVER R.

PLATE L, no. 11.

2. Similar, but the ends of the tie are over the *first* limb of L and the *last* limb of V IN SILVER R.

Boyne 120.

3. Also in Copper. R.r.r. *Davies.*

4. O LONDON SILVER TOKEN 1s. 6D. in a wreath of oak. MORGAN MAKER 12 RATHBONE PLACE LONDON

℞ DOLLAR SILVER TOKEN 1s. 6D. in similar wreath to obverse. H.M. under. *Halliday.*

Boyne 128.

"SILVER TOKENS AND SMALL CHANGE supplied to Regimental Paymasters, Manufacturers, Farmers, Shop and Inn Keepers, Clerks of Public Works, and all other Persons who require Change for their Business, or to pay Workmen."

"COUNTRY RESIDENTS may be accommodated, per COACH, with from Five Pounds worth to a large amount, weekly, by directing, with real Name, Occupation, and abode, to M &° Co. care of Mr. Heaton, No. 27, Clement's Lane, Strand, London, enclosing a remittance in Notes, or Good Bills. No letters admitted unless post paid."—*Star Newspaper, July 26th,* 1811.

This advertisement shows that Morgan at the time did not want his whereabouts known. It will be seen by the next announcement that he afterwards disclosed it, and that it was exhibited on some of the Tokens supplied.

"Local Tokens of Gold and Silver, invented and first made for Public Convenience, in March, 1811, by Messrs. Morgan and Co., Die Makers and Medallists, at their Licensed Token Manufactory, No. 12, Rathbone Place, Oxford Street, London, having been honoured with Legislative sanction and patronage, by Three successive Acts of parliament, continue to make to any design, for Companies and Individuals, at a short notice, in that superior style of execution which has obtained for M &° Co. during the last two years numerous and extensive orders for Bankers, Manufacturers and Shopkeepers, in almost every city and town throughout the United Kingdom. NB. Unpaid letters will not be admitted. Dies of numerous patterns ready engraved."—*The Star, London, June 24th,* 1813.

SHILLING.

5. O View of statue similar to No. 1, *with lamps* to railings CHARING CROSS

℞ The arms of London argent, first quarter a dagger erect, a cross gules, between two sprigs of olive; the shield at top is *curved.* ONE SHILLING SILVER TOKEN

Boyne 129.

From a Plate in the possession of the Author.

MIDDLESEX. 71

6. Also in Copper *R*. *Davies*.

7. O The same as last.
℞ A ONE POUND NOTE WILL BE PAID BY W^R JONES & C^O CHARING CROSS LONDON FOR 20 OF THESE *R.r.r.* *Davies*.
Boyne 125.

8. O A similar view of the statue and railings *without the lamps*. CHARING CROSS
℞ Arms of London as before, but shield at the top *straight*.
PLATE J, no. 13.

9. Also in Copper.

10. O The same as last.
℞ ONE SHILLING VALUE within a wreath of olive.
PLATE J, no. 14.

11. O The same as last.
℞ KNAPP & C^O ONE SHILLING between two sprigs of oak. H.M under. *R*.

12. Also in Copper. *R*.

13. O The same as last.
℞ SILVER * TWELVE PENNY TOKEN SOLD BY * MORGAN * 12 RATHBONE PLACE * LONDON * displayed with various ornaments. *R*.
Davies and Halliday.

This reverse also occurs at Cornwall, no. 3.

14. O A female *seated* holding a caduceus, her right arm leaning on a bale, supported by a cask, behind a ship. ENGLAND. IRELAND. SCOTLAND & WALES * LET COMMERCE FLOURISH
℞ LONDON TOKEN ONE SHILLING PAYABLE AT S. LLOYD'S BUCKLERSBURY 1811 The ones in date are *flat* topped.
Boyne 126.

This issuer's name also occurs on a Shaftesbury Bank Shilling (see Dorset). Samuel Lloyd was an ironmonger at 6, Barge Yard, Bucklersbury.

15. Also in Copper. *Halliday*.

16. O Similar, but the female is *standing* with her right foot on a globe. ENGLAND. IRELAND. SCOTLAND. AND. WALES * LET. COMMERCE. FLOURISH *R.r.* *Unknown*.
℞ Similar to last, but the ones in date *slope*.
PLATE B, no. 2.

17. ☉ LONDON TOKEN PAYABLE BY A ONE POUND NOTE FOR 20 OF THESE AT MORGANS 12 RATHBONE PLACE LONDON Legend, H. MORGAN LICENSED MANUFACTURER 12 RATHBONE PLACE LONDON.
℞ ONE SHILLING TOKEN—H.M within a wreath of oak. *R.r.r.*
Halliday.

18. ☉ As last.
℞ Arms and crest of Bristol within a garter, inscribed DOLLAR SILVER Legend, SILVER TOKEN FOR XII PENCE *R.r.r.* *Halliday.*
This reverse also occurs at Cheltenham and Mansfield.

19. ☉ ONE SHILLING LONDON SILVER TOKEN ISSUED BY ROYAL LICENCE in a circle. Legend, H. MORGAN LICENSED MANUFACTURER 12 RATHBONE PLACE LONDON.
℞ ONE SHILLING TOKEN—H.M within a wreath of oak. *Halliday.*

20. ☉ Arms emblematical of commerce and agriculture, between two sprigs of olive, crest, a dove with olive branch. SILVER TOKEN Under the wreath H M
℞ ONE SHILLING TOKEN SOLD BY ROYAL · LICENCE AT · MORGAN'S 12 · RATHBONE PLACE LONDON Scroll ornaments before and after SOLD BY and PLACE   *R.r.*
Boyne 132.
These arms also occur at Devonshire.

21. Similar, but with a *star* after MORGAN'S on the reverse. *R.r.*
22. ☉ The same as last.
℞ ONE SHILLING VALUE within a continuous olive wreath. *R.r.*
23. ☉ As last.
℞ SILVER ✷ TWELVE PENNY TOKEN SOLD ✷ BY MORGAN ✷ 12 RATHBONE PLACE ✷ LONDON ✷ with various scroll ornaments and an additional ornament between the *third* and *fourth* lines. *R.r.r.*

24. ☉ The same as last.
℞ KNAPP & C^O ONE SHILLING between sprigs of oak. H M under. *R.r.*

25. Also in Copper. *R.r.* *Halliday.*

26. A bottle inscribed N° 14 S^T MARTIN'S LANE LONDON with R W on the cork; PAYABLE AT R. WARRENS LIQUID BLACKING ..᾿+·· MANUFACTORY ..+··
℞ ONE SHILLING TOKEN 1811 an ornament above in a circle. Legend, ISSUED BY ROBERT WARREN LONDON *R.r.r.*

27. ☉ Same as last.
℞ Similar, but *without* the date and ornament. *Halliday.*
Boyne 133.

MIDDLESEX. 73

28. O Four hands joined ; LONDON YORK. SWANSEA AND LEEDS.
℞ ONE SHILLING TOKEN within a beaded circle. TO FACILITATE TRADE An ornament divides the outer legend. *R.r.r.* *Unknown.*
This reverse occurs at Lincoln.

SIXPENCE.

29. O View of a statue (Charles I) CHARING CROSS The top of the pedestal lines *to* the s in CROSS.
℞ Arms of London between two sprigs of olive. SIX-PENNY SILVER TOKEN The *corners* of shield cut off. *R.*
Boyne 122.

30. Also in copper. *R.*

31. O Similar, but Cupid supports *project* beyond the panels. CHARING CROSS The top of the pedestal lines *with* the o in CROSS
℞ Similar to last, but with *curved* line at top of shield.
PLATE B, no. 3.

32. Also in copper.

33. O The same as last.
℞ SIXPENNY TOKEN SOLD BY ROYAL LICENCE AT MORGAN'S · 12 · RATHBONE PLACE LONDON displayed with various scroll ornaments. *Halliday.*

34. O LONDON TOKEN FOR SIXPENCE PAYABLE AT S · LLOYD'S BUCKLESBURY 1811
℞ Female seated to right, holding a caduceus; a ship in the distance, ENGLAND. IRELAND. SCOTLAND & WALES. ✶ *Halliday.*
Boyne 127.

35. O Similar to last, but *without* FOR before SIXPENCE.
℞ Similar, but female *standing*, her right foot on a globe, ENGLAND IRELAND SCOTLAND AND WALES · *R.r.* *Unknown.*

36. O LONDON SIX-PENNY LICENSED SILVER TOKEN in a circle. MORGAN MAKER · 12 RATHBONE PLACE LONDON. ✶
℞ SIX PENNY TOKEN H.M in a wreath of oak.
Boyne 130.

37. Also in copper. *R.* *Halliday.*

38. O PAYABLE BY A 1£ NOTE FOR 40 OF THESE AT MORGANS TOKEN MANUFACTORY 12 RATHBONE PLACE LONDON
℞ The same as last.

39. ☉ Arms of London, &c., as on reverse of Charing Cross, with the *corners* of shield cut off.
℞ The same as last. *R.*
Boyne 131.

40. Also in copper. *R.* *Halliday.*

41. ☉ A ONE POUND NOTE WILL BE PAID BY WHALLEY. & C.º THAMES STREET LONDON FOR 40 OF THESE
℞ SIX PENNY TOKEN H.M within a wreath of oak. *R.* *Halliday.*

SIXPENCE.

COPPER.

42. ☉ The monogram *GH* 1800 The top of the 1 is *flat* and *no period* after date.
℞ SIX PENCE *R.r.* *Wyon.*

43. Also on an *octagonal* flan.
Boyne 31.

44. The same as last, but the top of the 1 *slopes* and a *period* after the date. *R.r.*

Pye states "these are circulated among the boys at Christ's Hospital," and Boyne adds "they had a limited circulation in the neighbourhood."
Similar Tokens were also issued for pence and halfpence.

THREE PENCE.

45. ☉ A bear gorged and chained; GOODMAN'S. FIELDS. BREW HOUSE. 1760
℞ THOMAS JORDAN AND CO. THREE PENCE. *R.r.*
Sharp 2, no. 1.

THREE HALFPENCE.

46. Similar, but THREE HALFPENCE *R.r.r.* *Unknown.*
Sharp 2, no. 2.

Both pieces are struck in brass.
The house of Jordan & Co. stood on the south side of the Minories.

PENNY.

47. ☉ Bust to right, on the truncation MILTON F Legend, ROBERT ORCHARD N.º 34 GREEK STREET CORNER OF CHURCH STREET SOHO LONDON ✱ Below the bust, 1803
℞ AND AT SAWBRIDGEWORTH HERTS MANUFACTURER OF CHOCOLATE & COCOA ON A NEW IMPROVED PRINCIPLE Legend, GROCER & TEA DEALER WHOLESALE RETAIL & FOR EXPORTATION *R.* *Milton.*
PLATE J, no. 15.

MIDDLESEX.

48. Also in silver. *R.r.r.*

Although no value is expressed, this piece is described as a token on the authority of the issuer's own advertisement, which is here reproduced :—

"A list of the Cabinets who have in their possession the Penny Token issued by me, Robert Orchard, Grocer &° Tea Dealer, No. 34, Greek Street, corner of Church Street, Soho, London. Engraved by Milton.

    Mr. Miller, Barnard's Inn, Holborn.
    Mr. Young, Ludgate Street.
    Mr. Rebello, Hackney.*
    Thomas Woodward, Esq., Bungay, Suffolk.
    Miss Banks, Soho Square.
    Mr. Miles, Tavistock Street, Convent Garden.
    Mr. Reeves, Lowestoft.
    British Museum.
    Mr. Hancock, Leather Lane, Holborn.
    James Bindley, Esq., First Commissioner of Stamp Office.
    Mr. James Conder, Ipswich.
    Mr. Madden, Hackney.
    Mr. Bauert, Altona.
    Mr. Warberg, Copenhagen.
    Mr. Milton, in Silver, Roll's Buildings, Fetter Lane. July 30, 1803."

* Rebello, who issued the artistic Hackney Penny, died in 1796. Orchard must therefore refer to one of his relations.

Mihell's caravan ticket, which states the office was established 1800, is ignored, there being no evidence to prove it existed at the token period. The name does not appear in the London Carriers' Directory of 1813.

HALFPENNY.
ELEPHANT.

49. O An elephant to left. statant, PIDOCK'S * * *EXHIBITION* Under the animal, JAMES

℞ An ape, with a stick in its left hand, THE WAN--DEROW 1801 PIDCOCK'S * GRAND. MENAGERIE. EXETER. CHANGE. LONDON *. *R.r.*

Atkins 310.

LION STATANT.

50. O A lion to right statant regardant, a dog on his back. LION AND DOG ·· 1801 ··

℞ A rhinoceros to left statant, chained. PIDCOCK EXETER CHANGE LONDON

Atkins 312.

This obverse is muled with the following reverses.

51. ℞ A zebra to right statant. PIDCOCK's *. GRAND · MANAGERIE · EXETER · CHANGE.

Atkins 313.

52. ℞ A two-headed cow to right statant. EXETER CHANGE ✠ STRAND LONDON ✠ *R.r.*

Atkins 314.

53. ℞ A kangaroo rampant regardant, THIS · KANGAROO'S · BIRTH · SEP · 10. 1800 A small J under the tail.

Atkins 315.

54. ℞ An ape, THE WAN--DEROW, etc., as no. 49.

Atkins 316.

LION COUCHANT GARDANT.

55. O A lion couchant gardant fondling a dog; PIDCOCK'S * GRAND. MENAGERIE. EXETER. CHANGE. LONDON *
℞ A cockatoo perched. ORANGE CRESTED COCKATOO 1801
Atkins 319.

WANDEROO, OR LONG-TAILED MONKEY.

56. O An ape, THE WAN--DEROW, etc., as no. 49.
℞ A two-headed cow to right statant, EXETER CHANGE ✥ STRAND LONDON ✥
Atkins 335.

57. O As last.
℞ A cockatoo, etc., as no. 55.
Atkins 339.

58. O As last.
℞ A crane to right. THE AFRICAN CROWN CRANE * PIDCOCKS EXIBITION * (sic)
PLATE I, no. 8.

KANGAROO.

59. O A kangaroo, as no. 53.
℞ A cockatoo, etc., as no. 55. R.
Atkins 338.

ZEBRA.

60. O A zebra, as no. 51.
℞ As last.
Atkins 332.

All by James of London; most of them manufactured by Lutwych of Birmingham.

"The grandest spectacle in the universe is now prepared at Pidcock's Royal Menagerie, Exeter Change, Strand, where a most uncommon collection of Foreign Beasts and Birds, many of them never before seen alive in Europe, are ready to entertain the wondering spectators. This affords an excellent opportunity for Ladies and Gentlemen to treat themselves with a view of some of the most beautiful and rare animals in creation. Amongst innumerable others are five noble African Lions, Tigers, Nylghaws, Beavers, Kangaroos, Grand Cassowary, Emus, Ostriches, &c. indeed such a numerous assemblage of living Birds and Beasts may not be found for a Century to come. This wonderfull collection is divided into three appartments, at one shilling each person, or the three rooms for two shillings and sixpence each person."—*The Morning Chronicle, London, May* 17, 1808.

An earlier advertisement, of Dec. 12, 1792, states: "A capital collection of wild beasts, so well secured, that the most timorous may approach them in safety."

The double-headed cow was advertised on Jan. 29th, 1791, "as BEING ALIVE and taking its sustenance with both mouths at the same time. To the Admiration of the Faculty, and the beholders in general; and it is the received opinion of John Hunter Esq. Professor of Anatomy, that She has two hearts."

The exhibition appears to have been taken to various parts of the country, as on April 21, 1798, the *Newcastle Chronicle* advertised that "there was on their way for Durham Races the grandest assemblage of chosen living rarities that ever travelled the kingdom in the age or memory of man. . . . Some of the marvels to be seen for the sum of one shilling." are given. A male Elephant, the largest ever seen in England, and its wonderful performances are described. A real Bengal Royal Male Tiger, the Pelican of the Wilderness, a Vulture from South America, a Nyl-ghau or horned horse, and other animals from the Pidcock Collection appear in this ornate advertisement.

Gilbert Pidcock died Feb. 1810, aged 67. About 1828 the animals were removed to the Surrey Zoological Gardens.

61. O- RATLEY DEALER IN COINS DUKES COURT S^T MARTINS LANE Before the C in COINS a small bust to right, T MILLAR (*sic*) BUNGAY in a small circle, and after S in COINS, in a similar circle, a shield of the Brewery and Block Company, of Southampton; outer legend, A GREAT VARIETY OF PROVINCIAL COINS & TRADESMENS TOKENS + 1801 +   *Wyon.*
℞ Blank.
PLATE J, no. 16.
This interesting piece is in lead, and probably unique. Ratley issued a fine token, popularly known as the "Tired Boy," after Henry Morland, which will be found described by Atkins at 347 Middlesex.

62. O- Two stockings crossed; PAYABLE AT ROMANIS'S 33 CHEAP SIDE 1814 An ornament divides the legend.
℞ A weaving frame; TRUTH STRENGTH & SPEED UNITED +
Halliday.
PLATE B, no. 4.
Robert Romanis was a wholesale and retail hosier, two doors west of Friday Street. He advertised as "Manufacturer to the Honorable East India Company."

63. O- Bust to right; R. WARREN. THE INVENTOR OF JAPAN LIQUID BLACKING.
℞ A bottle inscribed N^O 14 S^T MARTINS LANE LONDON with R. W on the stopper. ROBERT WARRENS. LIQUID BLACKING MANUFAC TORY.   *Halliday.*
Sharp 209, 9.
It has been stated that Charles Dickens was employed by Robert Warren, but this is an error. In the life of the eminent novelist, by John Forster, it is recorded that young Dickens worked for James Warren, blacking manufacturer, 13, Suffolk Street, Charing Cross. Robert Warren was in no way connected with the latter in business.

64. O- A swan with two necks; PAYABLE AT THE MAIL COACH OFFICE LAD-LANE LONDON   Under LONDON W · W
℞ A mail coach and horses; SPEED, REGULARITY & SECURITY
Halliday.
PLATE B, no. 5.
This was a famous posting-house. The *Sun*, Aug. 6, 1794, has an advertisement: "Swan with two necks, Lad Lane. By command of their Lordships, His Majesty's Postmaster General. The Royal Mail Coach to Weymouth," &c., &c.—*The Sun, London, Aug.* 6, 1794.
The swan with two necks is a corruption of the swan with two nicks, *i.e.* nicks in the beak: a sign that the bird was owned by the king, whose mark was two nicks. They were so marked on the Monday following Midsummer-day.—*Vide Burn, no.* 984, *London Traders, Tavern Tokens.*
W. Wilson was the proprietor of the tavern when the token was issued.

65. O- A building, inscribed over the door NEW AUCTION MART Legend, HALFPENNY PAYABLE AT THE OLD STOCK EXCHANGE IN BANK NOTES ESTABLISHED 1811
℞ SALES OF ESTATES, HOUSES, MANUFACTURED GOODS, AND MISCELLANEOUS PROPERTY, SPEEDILY EFFECTED WITHOUT RISK. PUBLIC AUCTIONS EVERY DAY AT 12. PRIVATE ORDERS FOR ALL KINDS OF GOODS PUNCTUALLY EXECUTED. within an inner circle; outer legend, THOMAS WOOD. BROKER, AUCTIONEER & GENERAL AGENT.
Sharp 209, 10.
Early this morning (Tuesday, April 23rd, 1816) a fire broke out in a bed-room of the

Coffee-house over the Old Stock Exchange, at the corner of Swithins (Sweetings) Alley, close to the north-east corner of the Royal Exchange. The fire soon communicated to every part of the building, in which, at the bottom, were an Auction Mart, and a large Wine-company, and above stairs the Coffee-house and several counting houses, all of which are entirely consumed."—*Gentleman's Magazine for May*, 1816.

The word ESTABLISHED on the token has led many to doubt if it was struck in 1811, but the report quoted above clearly proves its existence at the token period.

On Jany. 5th, 1809, Mr. Shuttleworth, of 17, Austin Friars, advertised in the *Morning Chronicle* that he would sell at Garraway's, the Old Stock Exchange, which was contiguous to the north-east corner of the Royal Exchange, occupying the angle formed by Threadneedle Street and Sweeting's Alley.

T. Wood, auctioneer, of Bartholomew Lane, was declared a bankrupt on Dec. 8th, 1813.—*Star, Dec. 9th*, 1813.

FARTHING.

66. O ROBERT ORCHARD GROCER & TEA DEALER N° 34 GREEK S^T SOHO LONDON WHOLESALE & RETAIL 1803

℞ A Chinaman standing beween bales and casks, a ship in the distance, MAKER OF CHOCOLATE & COCOA ON A NEW PRINCIPLE Under the figure FARTHING

PLATE B, no. 6.

67. O As last.

℞ View of a building, ROBERT · ORCHARD · TEA · WAREHOUSE · CORNER OF CHURCH ST. AND. AT SAW BRIDGEWORTH HARTS (*sic*).

PLATE B, no. 7.

68. O Bust to right, ROBERT ORCHARD GROCER & TEA DEALER N: 34 GREEK ST: CORNER CHURCH . ST. SOHO LONDON 1804

℞ As last, except that the A in HARTS has been altered to E

Milton.

Atkins 763.

PIDCOCK.

LION.

69. O A lion couchant regardant fondling a dog, EXETER CHANGE LONDON PIDCOCK

℞ A beaver to left ; THE BEAVER 1801

Atkins 769.

70. O As last.

℞ A wandroo holding a stick ; THE WANDEROW 1801

Atkins 770.

WANDEROO.

71. O As reverse last ; WANDEROW etc.

℞ A pelican to left ; PIDCOCK EXETER CHANGE LONDON.

Atkins 773.

BEAVER.

72. ⚬ A beaver to right; THE BEAVER 1801
    ℞ A cockatoo; EXETER CHANGE STRAND LONDON   *R.r.*
    Atkins 771.

73. ⚬ As last.
    ℞ A pelican to right; PIDCOCK EXETER CHANGE LONDON.
    Atkins 772.

Pidcock was succeeded by Polito early in the nineteenth century. He was followed by Cross, and the animals were finally removed in 1828. Two years afterwards Exeter Change was taken down.

NORFOLK.
COUNTY.
SHILLING.
SILVER.

1. ℺ NORFOLK SUFFOLK AND ESSEX SILVER TOKEN FOR ONE SHILLING with scrolls on either side.
℞ View of Eddystone Lighthouse and ships at sea; VALUE ONE SHILLING *R.r.*
Boyne 171.

2. ℺ The same as last.
℞ ONE SHILLING TOKEN H.M within a wreath of oak. *R.r.r.*

3. ℺ The same as last.
℞ Shield, arms of agriculture; crest, a dove, etc.; as London, no. 20. *R.r.r.*   *Halliday.*

ATTLEBOROUGH.
TWO SHILLINGS.

4. ℺ Arms perpure on a bend or, an escutcheon perfess three crosses; supporters and helmet of the Duke of Norfolk; motto on a ribbon SOLA VIRTUS INVICTA (Virtue alone is invincible); crest, a lion statant gardant; ATTLEBURGH TOKEN. TWO SHILLINGS. H on the ground at the *right*.
℞ A female standing, an olive branch in her right hand, a fish in her left; WILLIAM PARSON & SON OCT^R 11. 1811 H on the ground at the *left*. *R.r.*   *Halliday.*
Boyne 31.

5. ℺ Arms, argent, a castle triple towered; under a lion passant gardant, between laurel and palm branches; legend as last; H on the first *palm* blade.
℞ The same as last. *R.r.r.*   *Halliday.*

The issuers were grocers. Mr. Parsons was declared bankrupt on April 27th, 1816.—*London Gazette.*

SHILLING.

6. ℺ PAYABLE AT WM. RF. & RK Above a Staffordshire knot; ATTLEBOROUGH
℞ I SHILLING within a radiated circle; FOR THE USE OF TRADE 1811 *R.*   *Halliday.*
Boyne, 4.
This token was issued by William Muskett, Richard Francis, both clockmakers, and Robert Kiddell, shoemaker, draper and grocer.—*Numismatic Magazine.*

NORFOLK. 81

DISS.
SHILLING.

7. O Arms argent, nine bars wavy azure; crest, an anchor. PAYABLE AT * MUSKETT & SONS *
℞ 12 PENCE within an oak wreath. DISS TOKEN MDCCCXI   *R.r.*
Halliday.
PLATE B, no. 8.
For similar arms and crest see North Lopham.

LYNN.
EIGHTEENPENCE.

8. O The arms of Lynn, azure, three conger eels' heads, in the mouth of each a cross crosslet, within a garter inscribed DOLLAR SILVER   Crest, a pelican in her piety. A 1$£$ NOTE AND 1^S WILL BE PAID FOR 14 OF THESE BY I HEDLEY LYNN ✠ OR AT H. MORGANS TOKEN AND BULLION OFFICE LONDON
℞ DOLLAR SILVER TOKEN 1s. 6d.   In a wreath below H. M   The same as London, no. 4.   *R.r.*   *Halliday.*
PLATE L, no. 12.

9. Also in copper.   *R.r.*   *Halliday.*

SHILLING.

10. O SILVER TOKEN STAMP OFFICE KINGS LYNN 1811 in a circle. FOR THE ACCOMMODATION OF TRADE +
℞ ONE SHILLING VALUE H.M in a wreath of oak; legend, ISSUED BY ROYAL LICENSE   *R.*   *Halliday.*
Boyne 136.
For another shilling payable at Lynn see Mansfield, Nottinghamshire, no. 1.

SIXPENCE.

11. O A ONE POUND NOTE WILL BE PAID BY I HEDLEY STAMP OFFICE LYNN FOR 40 OF THESE 1811
℞ SIX PENNY TOKEN H. M in a wreath of oak.   *Halliday.*
PLATE B, no. 9.
Besides being the postmaster, Isaquey Hedley was a bookseller.

NORTH LOPHAM.
SHILLING.

12. O Arms and crest, similar to Diss; PAYABLE AT ⁂ S. PORTER'S NORTH LOPHAM *
℞ 1 SHILLING in a radiated circle. FOR THE USE OF TRADE
R.r.   *Halliday.*
PLATE L, no. 13.
The issuer, Samuel Porter, was a banker. He was declared bankrupt on Jan. 10th, 1826.

M

YARMOUTH.
SHILLING.

13. ○ The arms of Yarmouth; three demi-lions conjoined with as many demi-herrings, gules and azure, within a wreath of oak. NORFOLK AND SUFFOLK TOKEN ONE ✶ SHILLING ✶ There is *one* acorn at the corner of shield at the left.

℞ Arms of Bury St. Edmunds, azure, three crowns, two and one, each over sceptres in saltire, between branches of olive and palm; 1811 under. PAYABLE AT J. HUNTON'S YARMOUTH & AT BLYTH & Cº BURY. The top outside olive leaf is *under* the U in HUNTON'S

PLATE B, no. 10.

14. ○ Similar to last; there are *two* acorns at the left hand corner of shield.

℞ Similar to last, but the olive leaf *points* to the *foot* of the H in HUNTON'S *Halliday.*

Boyne 229.

John Blythe & Co. were mercers in the Butter Market, Bury St. Edmunds. The firm was noted for Suffolk hemp goods.—*Vide Golding* 89, I.

John Hunton was a linen draper in the Market Place, Yarmouth. After the issue of the token he migrated to London, where he was in business as a mercer, at 21, Bishopsgate Street Without, but resided at Low Leyton, in Essex.

He became involved in speculation, and lost a considerable sum in Spanish bonds.

Hunton was found guilty and condemned to death for forgery on bills of exchange. He was one of the last to suffer capital punishment for the crime of forgery. A petition was presented to the Home Secretary praying his reprieve, and among the names who signed was M. N. Rothschild. "The Times" advocated clemency without avail, as Hunton was executed at Newgate with *three* others on Dec. 8th, 1828.—"*Camden Pelham's Chronicles of Crime,*" *Times Newspaper.*

15. ○ The arms of Yarmouth within a garter inscribed PAYABLE. BY. F. R. REYNOLDS. YARMOUTH

℞ Arms, dexter three crosslets, and as many in sinister, in the bend argent, a lion rampant, over two batons in saltire, within a garter inscribed NORFOLK TOKEN FOR XII PENCE. Under the shield 1811 *Halliday.*

PLATE J, no. 18.

16. ○ The same as last.

℞ A castle. Under 1811 Crest, a hand holding baton, in a garter inscribed as last. *R.r.* *Halliday.*

PLATE B, no. 11.

Frederick Riddell Reynolds was an attorney, who likewise carried on the business of a brewer and merchant, King Street, Yarmouth. He issued promissory notes for five shillings.

N.M. 1893.

We read of a successful capture of some of these tokens :—

"The Yarmouth coach was robbed, a few nights since, of silver tokens, to the amount of £19 17s. of one shilling each, out of a box containing the same description of tokens to the amount of £100. The coach goes from the White Horse, Fetter Lane, and changes coaches at Ipswich, where the coach becomes a Mail; the box was there discovered to have been broken and shattered, and when it reached the gentleman at Yarmouth to whom it was directed, tokens to the above amount were discovered to be missing. A guard has been in custody for several days on suspicion of being concerned in the robbery; two or three witnesses were examined, but they not being able to prove anything against him, he was discharged."—*The Evening Sun, London, Nov.* 22*nd,* 1811.

NORWICH.

TWOPENNY PIECE.
COPPER.

17. ○ Arms of the city, a castle triple towered, base a lion passant gardant gules; NORWICH TWO PENNY PIECE FOR CHANGE NOT PROFIT.

℞ NORWICH on a ribbon, a shuttle above, legend ROB.^T BLAKE. COTTON & BOMBAZINE MANUFACTURER.

PLATE B, no. 12.

18. Also in silver. *R.r.r.* *Halliday.*

This is in the British Museum.
Robert Blake's works were in Higham Street.

PENNY.

19. ○ View of a castle; NORWICH CASTLE

℞ Two sheep in a meadow; BARKER, WOOLLEN DRAPER 1811

PLATE B, no. 13.

20. Also in silver. *R.r.* *P. Wyon.*

Samuel Barker was a linen and woollen draper who had a shop in London Lane.

HALFPENNY.
With Crest.

21. ○ The figure of Hope supporting a shield inscribed DUNHAM & YALLOP GOLDSMITH'S NORWICH

℞ Arms of the city, crest Prince of Wales' plumes and motto, ICH DIEN (I serve) REGENCY 1811 On a label below, RELIEF IN DISTRESS The top bar of shield lines with the *first* limb of N

Sharp 209, 1.

22. ○ Similar, but *with* a period after NORWICH.

℞ Similar to last, but the top bar of shield lines with the *second* limb of N *T. Wyon.*

Without Crest.

23. ○ Britannia standing helmeted, a lion at her side; NEWTON SILVERSMTH AND JEWELLER The centre plume on helmet *touches* the small H The lion's tail touches the *first* letter of legend.

℞ Arms of the city as before, but crest *omitted*; NORWICH MDCCCXI The portcullis to the castle *is not* seen.

Sharp 209, 2.

24. ○ Similar to last, but the plume is larger, and forms three *distinct* feathers; the lion's tail *is quite clear* of the letter N

℞ Similar to last, but the portcullis to the castle is *expressed.*
R.r.r.

25. Also in Silver. *R.r.r.*

26. Similar, but the plume is much smaller; at the left it *nearly touches* the M

27. Similar, but the feathers forming the plume are *all the same size.*

28. Similar, but the plume has a long *sweeping* curve.

Newton's silversmith's shop was in London Street.

TUNSTEAD AND HAPPING.
PENNY.

29. O A wheat sheaf; PAYABLE AT THE CORPORATION HOUSE. ℞ ONE PENNY TOKEN within a circle. TUNSTEAD & HAPPING. 1812.

Sharp 195, 2.

HALFPENNY.

30. O Similar to last, but HALF PENNY TOKEN *Halliday.*

PLATE B, no. 14.

The Corporation House was a workhouse in the Parish of Smallburgh. It is still in existence, and situated three miles from Stalham railway station.

WROXHAM.
THREEPENCE.

31. O A wheelbarrow with mattock and spade laid across it; TO. PAY. WORKMEN. AND. PROMOTE. AGRICULTURE ✠ Under the wheelbarrow, MARLE · PIT TOKEN

℞ 3 PENCE PAYABLE AT WROXHAM Outer legend, D. COLLYER. PROPRIETOR · 1797. *Milton.*

PLATE J, no. 17.

The issuer of the token was the Rev. Daniel Collyer, who afterwards accepted a living in Kent.

NORTHAMPTONSHIRE.

PETERBOROUGH.

TWO SHILLINGS.
SILVER.

1. O Arms, gules, two keys in saltire, a crosslet in the angles within a garter inscribed, DOLLAR SILVER. Legend, PETERBOROUGH TOKEN PAYABLE BY GEORGE GRIFFIN

℞ SILVER TOKEN 2 SHILL 1812 within a wreath of oak. H.M under. *R.r.*

PLATE L, no. 14.

2. Also in Copper. *R.r.* *Halliday.*

EIGHTEENPENCE.

3. O The west front of Peterborough Cathedral; SILVER TOKEN 1811 within a circle of pellets.

℞ FOR EIGHTEEN PENCE within a wreath of olive. PETERBOROUGH BANK TOKEN COLE & C° in a circle of pellets.

Boyne 174.

4. Also in Copper. *R.r.*

SHILLING.

5. O Similar to last.
℞ FOR XII PENCE Otherwise as last. *R.r.*

PLATE B, no. 15.

6. Also in Copper. *R.r.* *Halliday.*

See Derbyshire, no. 2, for another shilling token with view of Peterborough Cathedral. Cole & Co. were one of the principal city bankers; their London Agents, Glyn & Co., 12 Birchin Lane.

NORTHUMBERLAND.

NEWCASTLE-ON-TYNE.

HALF CROWN.
SILVER.

1. ☉ Arms, three castles, two over one, gules, and supporters of Newcastle; *Motto*, FORTITER DEFENDIT TRIUMPHANS (Triumphing it bravely defends). Crest, a lion holding a standard issuant from a castle; PAYABLE BY JOHN ROBERTSON. NEWCASTLE ON TYNE.

℞ Female seated on a bale, with spear and cornucopia; a ship in the distance; NORTHUMBERLAND & DURHAM XXX PENCE TOKEN 1811 On the ground, P. WYON F.

PLATE B, no. 16.

EIGHTEENPENCE.

2. ☉ Similar to last, but the motto *omitted*.

℞ Similar to last, but *without* the artist's name, and reads 18$^{\underline{D}}$ TOKEN   *R.r.r.*

PLATE L, no. 15.

3. Also in Copper.   *R.r.r.*   *P. Wyon.*
Both obverse and reverse have a broad toothed border.

SHILLING.

4. ☉ View of a coal staith with a ship laying to, in a circle. BERWICK MAIN COLLIERY + 1811 +

℞ ONE SHILLING PAYABLE AT NEWCASTLE ON TYNE AND LONDON · + ·   *R.*

Boyne 160.

5. Similar to last, but the name *spelled* BEWICKE   *Halliday.*
Boyne 159.

Samuel Cook, the inventor of a self-acting plane to convey coals from the mines to the Tyne, was part proprietor of this colliery when the tokens were issued.

6. ☉ Arms, supporters, etc., as on no. 2; NORTHUMBERLAND AND DURHAM 1812

℞ Britannia seated with her attributes, a ship in the distance; BRITISH ONE SHILLING TOKEN MDCCCXII
Boyne 168.

7. Also in Copper.   *R.r.r.*

In the *Gentleman's Magazine*, 1815, p. 305, John Bell, the issuer of the farthing tokens, says: "This was done by a person at Shields to pay off amongst the common people as a Robertson's token, and appeared to be made of worse silver."

8. ☉ Arms, etc., as before; PAYABLE BY ALEX^R KELTY NEWCASTLE ON TYNE

℞ View of a colliery; NORTHUMBERLAND & DURHAM 12^D TOKEN 1812

PLATE B, no. 17.

Boyne, by an error in dating this token 1811, caused much search to be made in vain.

NORTHUMBERLAND. 87

9. ○ Also in Copper. *R.r.r.* *Halliday.*

On p. 592 John Bell again says: "There was another pair of dies sunk prior to this (differently executed), but very few impressions struck from them, being found too large for circulation."

10. ○ Arms, etc., as no. 2; PAYABLE BY JOHN ROBERTSON. NEWCASTLE ON TYNE·

℞ Female seated, etc., as on no. 2; NORTHUMBERLAND & DURHAM 12$\underline{D}$ TOKEN 1811   The spear *is under* the N   A small W on the ground.

Boyne 164.

11. ○ Similar to last, but IOHN *instead* of JOHN and a border of dots *added*.

℞ Similar to last, but the spear points *between* the N and D A border of dots as on the obverse.

12. Similar to last, but the spear is *under* the N the small W on the ground *omitted*, and *without* the hyphen under the small D

13. ○ Similar, but the tail of the left hand supporter *approaches* nearly to the legend, whilst that on the right *points* more upwards in the direction of the T

℞ Similar, but the W is again *on* the ground.

SIXPENCE.

14. ○ Arms, etc. as on no. 2; PAYABLE BY IOHN ROBERTSON NEWCASTLE ON TYNE

℞ Female seated, etc. as before; NORTHUMBERLAND & DURHAM 6^D TOKEN 1811   *No initial* on ground.

Boyne 166.

15. ○ Also in Copper on a large flan. *P. Wyon.*

Boyne 167.

The movement of the times as reproduced below will be read with interest.

CAUTION
To the Public againſt taking Local Silver Tokens.

Newcastle, Nov. 26, 1811.

"Mr. John Robertson, Silver Smith, Dean Street, hav-
"ing, by public Advertiſement, announced his Intention
"of iſſuing Silver Tokens, for general Circulation, as Shillings
"and Sixpences, in this Town and the adjoining Counties,—We,
"the Underſigned, think it neceſſary to inform the Public, that we
"will not receive, in Payment, any Tokens which may be iſſued,
"either by the ſaid Mr. John Robertson, or by any other INdivi-
"dual whatever."

[Here follow the signatures of 118 names of individuals or firms.]

"N.B.   We have Authority to ſay, that all Local TOKEN[S] will
"be refuſed in Payments by the regular Bankers in Newcaſtle."

S. HODGSON, PRiNter, Newcastle.

IN Consequence of a Report which has been circulated, that J. Robertson does not hold himself responsible for the Tokens issued by him, he begs Leave to inform the Public that such Report is groundless, and that he conceives himself as much responsible to the Public upon the Tokens issued by him, as if they were promissory Notes payable on Demand.

In Answer to a most malicious Advertisement which appeared in the Tyne Mercury of this Week, stating, that various local Tokens issued in this Neighbourhood had been assayed, and found on an Average not to exceed in Value from 8d. to 8½ each,—J. Robertson begs Leave to assure the Public, that the Statement contained in that Advertisement is a gross Misrepresentation, and calculated to mislead the Public. Perhaps no two of J. Robertson's Tokens are exactly of the same Weight, but any twenty of them, taken promiscuously, will average in real Value from 10d. to 10½. each.

Newcastle, May 1, 1812.

S. Hodgson, Printer, Newcastle.

John Robertson, silversmith, was declared bankrupt, Feb. 20, 1821.—*London Gazette.*

PENNY.

COPPER.

16. ☌ View of a coal staith with a ship laying to, in a circle. BEWICKE MAIN COLLIERY + 1811 +

℞ ONE PENNY PAYABLE AT in a circle. NEWCASTLE ON TYNE AND LONDON . + ·

PLATE B, no. 18.

17. Also in Silver. *R.r.r.* *Halliday.*

BEWICKE MAIN COLLIERY and WORKS, DURHAM, TO BE SOLD BY AUCTION, BY MR. MUNN,

At the Auction Mart (London) on Thursday the 26th instant, at Twelve, by Direction of the Assignees of Harrison, Cooke and Co. with the concurrence of the Mortgagees, in one Lot.—*Star Newspaper, September 17th,* 1811.

FARTHING.

18. ☌ The arms of Newcastle on Tyne. JOHN BELL. BOOKSELLER. QUAY.

℞ A double-fronted shop; BELL over the door. Under 1815. *R.r.*

Batty 613.

19. ☌ As last.

℞ NEWCASTLE. TOKEN. 1815· *R.r.*

Batty 619.

20. ☌ As last.

℞ A barge sailing. *R.r.*

Batty 620.

21. ☌ As last.

℞ ROBERT. OLIVER. DRAPER ... QUAY ... NEWCASTLE. 1815. *R.r.*

Batty 618.

22. O A double-fronted shop; BELL over the door. Under 1815.
℞ FARTHING YOUNGEST SON OF. FORTUNE. *R.r.*
Batty 616.

23. O As last.
℞ ROBERT · OLIVER · DRAPER...QUAY...NEWCASTLE. 1815. *R.r.*
Batty 617.

24. O As last.
℞ A PRODDY in a circle of pellets. *R.r.*
Batty 615.

25. O ROBERT · OLIVER · DRAPER ... QUAY .. NEWCASTLE. 1815.
℞ NEWCASTLE. TOKEN. 1815.
In the British Museum.

26. O As last.
℞ A PRODDY in a circle of pellets. *R.r.*

27. O A Turk's head.
℞ As last.
In the British Museum.

28. O As last.
℞ COALY TYNE. *R.r.*
Batty 622.

29. O A barge sailing.
℞ COALY TYNE.
In Mr. Norman's cabinet.

30. O NEWCASTLE TOKEN. 1815.
℞ FARTHING YOUNGEST SON OF. FORTUNE. *R.r.*
Batty 621.

31. O As last.
℞ A barge sailing. *Unknown.*
In the British Museum.

These are all in white metal, and those numbered to Batty were purchased by that gentleman of the executors of John Bell, who was an antiquary and collector. He was declared bankrupt on Nov. 1st, 1817.

32. O A rose spray.
℞ $\frac{1}{4}$ TOKEN 1812. An ornament under.
In Mr. Macfadyen's cabinet.

This is in white metal, and of fine workmanship. It is located in consequence of its similarity in make and material to Bell's tokens, and is with a Newcastle-on-Tyne collector.

33. O A tobacco plant in bloom; GENUINET✱OBACCO & SNUFF✱
The bottom leaf at the right points to A in TOBACCO
℞ JOHN ELLIOTT 1814 TOBACCONIST QUAY-SIDE NEWCASTLE

34. Similar, but the bottom leaf at the right points to B

35. Also in Silver. *R.r.*

36. Similar, but *with* a period after NEWCASTLE.

37. Also a proof in Brass. *R.r.*
This is in the British Museum.

38. Similar, but with the date *omitted*. *Halliday.*
PLATE B, no. 19.

John Davidson, who was in a similar business to Elliott's, issued in the second decade of the century an advertisement of farthing size, but as no value or date is expressed it is omitted.

D. T. BATTY.
From a Photograph in the possession of Wm. Norman.

NOTTINGHAMSHIRE.

MANSFIELD.

SHILLING.

SILVER.

1. ☌ PAYABLE BY E. DAWSON MANSFIELD W. JERREMS GAINSBOROUGH I. HEDLEY LYNN NORFOLK & H. MORGAN LONDON 1812 in a circle. Legend, A POUND NOTE WILL BE PAID FOR 20 OF THESE+.

℞ The arms, crest, etc., similar to Bristol, within a garter inscribed DOLLAR SILVER   Legend, SILVER TOKEN FOR XII PENCE   *R.r.r.*

Boyne 140.

This reverse also occurs at Cheltenham.
Edward Dawson was the Mansfield postmaster.

2. ☌ Beehive and bees. C & G. STANTON. HANCOCK. WAKEFIELD & C^O & W^M ELLIS. MANSFIELD

℞ Female seated on a bale, with scales and cornucopia. ONE SHILLING SILVER TOKEN 1812   The initials Y & D *under* the hilt of the sword; a small H on the *left corner* of the bale.   *R.*

PLATE B, NO. 20.

3. Similar to last, but the initials Y & D are near the *end* of the sword. The H on the bale is *omitted*.   *Halliday.*

Boyne 141.

Charles and George Stanton, and Hancock, Wakefield & Co., were cotton manufacturers; William Ellis a draper and woollen salesman.

NEWARK.

SHILLING.

4. ☌ View of a building. TOWN HALL NEWARK SILVER TOKEN FOR ONE SHILLING 1811   The head of the figure on the pediment is *under* the E in TOKEN

℞ T. STANSALL CHA^S MOOR RICH^D FISHER W^M FILLINGHAM W^M READETT AND T. WILSON   Legend, · THE CURRENT VALUE. PAYABLE IN CASH NOTES.

Boyne 158.

5. Similar to last, but there is *no* period after T in the first line of the reverse, *nor* between THE and PAYABLE in the *outer* legend.

PLATE B, NO. 21.

6. Similar, but *no* period between VALUE and NOTES   The line W^M FILLINGHAM is *above* the S in NOTES

7. ○ Similar, but the head of the figure is *under* the K in TOKEN
℞ Similar, but reads T STANZAIL CHA^N MOORE RICH^N FISHER W^R FILLINGHAM W^R READETT AND F WILSON   *R.*
This singular piece is a counterfeit.

8. ○ As last.
℞ Similar to no. 5, but the T of first line *intersects* the C of CURRENT   *R.*   *Halliday.*

Thomas Stansall was a grocer, Charles Moor a chemist, Richard Fisher and William Fillingham drapers, William Readett grocer, and Thomas Wilson a brazier.

ARNOLD.

FIVE SHILLINGS.
COPPER.

9. ○ A fleece suspended from an apple tree; DAVISON AND HAWKSLEY
℞ The Roman fasces with the axe, a spear and cap of liberty in saltire; ARNOLD WORKS 1791 * A-CROWN *   *R.r.*
PLATE K, no. 10.

TWO SHILLINGS AND SIXPENCE.
10. Similar, except in size and value; * HALVE A CROWN *   *R.r.*
Boyne 13.

ONE SHILLING.
11. Similar, except in size and value; * ONE SHILLING *   *R.*
Boyne 14.

SIXPENCE.
12. Similar, except in size and value * SIX PENCE *   *Wyon.*
Boyne 15.

A few of these pieces were gilt and silver-plated. Boyne says: "In the M.S. Catalogue the Arnold Works are said to be a mill for spinning wool at Nottingham." These mills for the manufacture of worsted were situated near the Qean, Nottingham. They were destroyed by fire in January, 1791. This probably accounts for the scarcity of the tokens, especially those of the higher values.

NEWARK.

PENNY.
13. ○ View of a castle and the river, 1811 under. Legend, NEWARK TOKEN FOR ONE PENNY +   A small H at the left.
℞ T. STANSALL CHARLES MOOR RICH^D FISHER W^M FILLINGHAM W^M READETT T. WILSON and, in a circular legend, THE CURRENT VALUE. PAYABLE IN CASH NOTES. The M in FILLINGHAM is *below* the S in NOTES.
Sharp 195, 1.

14. Similar to last, but the M is the *above* S in NOTES. *R. Halliday.*

NOTTINGHAM.

15. ☉ W.ᴹ BAKER NOTTINGHAM An ornament between BAKER and NOTTINGHAM Legend, A POUND NOTE FOR 240 TOKENS. 1813.
℞ ONE PENNY TOKEN within a wreath of oak and laurel. *R.*
Turnpenny.
Sharp 195, 5.
The issuer was a hosier in Fletchergate.

16. ☉ A *distant* view of Nottingham Castle; ONE PENNY TOKEN Ex. 1812
℞ The arms of the borough in a circle; PAYABLE BY J. M. FELLOWES · A POUND NOTE FOR 240. The top of the cross is under BY
Sharp 195, 2.

17. Similar, but the top of the cross is under J.

18. ☉ Similar to last, but *dated* 1813
℞ Similar, but the *period* between A and PAYABLE *omitted*.
P. Wyon.

19. ☉ A *near* view of the castle; ONE PENNY TOKEN Ex. NOTTINGHAM 1813 A scroll before and after NOTTINGHAM
℞ As last. *R.r.* *P. Wyon.*
Sharp 195, 3.

20. ☉ A *still nearer* view of the castle; NOTTINGHAM PENNY. Ex. TOKEN 1813
℞ Similar, but point of crown in line with the *first limb* of the second A in PAYABLE instead of to the *centre* of that letter. *P. Wyon.*
PLATE B, no. 22.

J. M. Fellows & Co. were bankers at Nottingham; their agents in London being Taylor, Hanbury & Co.

SHROPSHIRE.

DAWLEY.

SHILLING.

SILVER.

1. O SELLS CHAINS FOR PITS CRANES &c. OF BEST HORSE-NAIL IRON AT 5D. PER LB. in an inner circle; legend, GILBERT GILPIN DAWLEY SHROPSHIRE.

℞ A wild boar at speed; PAYS THE BEARER A SHILLING 1811
R.r. *Halliday.*

HALFPENNY.
COPPER.

2. O Same as last.

℞ Similar to last, but legend, PAYS THE BEARER A HALFPENNY 1811 *Halliday.*

PLATE B, no. 23.

This is in the British Museum.

The Mechanics' Section of the Society of Arts, in 1805, awarded the silver medal and thirty guineas to Gilbert Gilpin for "an improved crane and flexible chain."—*Vide Randall, Appendix to Life of John Wilkinson.*

Gilpin, before commencing business, was employed by John Wilkinson, the great ironmaster. He died in 1827, and Palmer says " was buried in Wrexham Churchyard, where his tomb may yet be seen."

HALESOWEN.

PENNY.

3. O A mounted yeoman at speed; GOD SAVE THE KING 1813 A small H on the ground at the right.

℞ View of a church (St. Mary's) PENNY TOKEN. PAYABLE AT THE WORKHOUSE HALESOWEN. A small H on the base line at the left.
Halliday.

PLATE B, no. 24.

Sharp says Sir George Chetwynd had "a variety," but advanced collectors have failed to find it.

The following inscription is placed over the door of the workhouse :—"The ground on which this building was erected, the garden hereunto belonging, together with 3 houses next adjoining, were given by Sir Thomas Lyttelton, Baronet, to the parish of Halesowen, for the accommodation of the poor, in the year of our Lord 1730."—*Angell's History of Halesowen.*

The church is remarkable for its beautiful spire. King John (Tanner says, ann. reg. 16) gave the manor and advowson of the church to Peter de Rupibus, Bishop of Winchester, for the endowment of an abbey for canons of the Premonstratension order, which seems to have been begun and finished at the charges of the Crown, though the bishops of Winchester had the patronage.

SOMERSETSHIRE.

BATH.

FOUR SHILLINGS.

SILVER.

1. O Arms, a chief two lions passant, on the base argent a lion rampant, holding an oak tree; supporters, Commerce and Justice; motto, on a riband below, TO FACILITATE TRADE Justice holding scales as crest; legend, BATH TOKEN FOUR SHILLINGS The right foot of Justice points *between* T and R in TRADE Her left foot is *over* A in the same word.

℞ A POUND NOTE GIVEN FOR FIVE OF THESE TOKENS C. CULVER HOUSE. I. ORCHARD AND J. PHIPPS within an inner circle; legend, MARGARETS BUILDINGS BATH The name, CULVERHOUSE is in line with the S of BUILDINGS *R.r.*

PLATE I, no. 9.

2. Also in Copper. *R.r.r.*

Boyne 12.

3. O As last.

℞ Similar to last, but ORCHARD is in line with the S of BUILDINGS *R.r.r.*

4. O Similar to last, but the right foot of Justice is *over* the R in TRADE, her left *spans* A and D of TRADE

℞ A POUND NOT GIVEN FOR FIVE TOKENS BY C. CULVERHOUSE I. ORCHARD AND J. PHIPPS No inner circle. *R.r.r.*

Boyne 13.

5. Similar, but I. instead of J. PHIPPS *R.r.r.*   Halliday.

6. O As last.

℞ A fleece suspended; SHIPS COLONIES & COMMERCE 1811 *R.r.r.*   Halliday and P. Wyon.

PLATE L, no. 16.

7. Also in Copper. *R.r.r.*

This reverse will be found on the Not Local Three Shilling Piece.

Charles Culverhouse was a baker, No. 5, Margaret's Buildings; Isaac Orchard, auctioneer and upholsterer, No. 6; J. Phipps, shoemaker, No. 2, all in Margaret's Buildings, which was a street near to the Royal Crescent.

The advertisement copied below indicates that the tokens were in circulation in 1815.

"Decr. 29th, 1814.
BATH TOKENS

Messrs. Culverhouse Orchard and Phipps, respectfully inform the Holders of their Tokens that they continue to exchange them for Notes in quantities of not less than One Pound, agreeably to their original engagements with the Public at No. 6 Margarets Buildings every day in the present week, between the hours of Eleven and Four, and afterwards on Saturdays only, between the same hours."—*Bath Chronicle, Dec. 29th,* 1814.

8. ○ Arms, argent in chief, two bars wavy, azure; in base a battlemented wall loopholed, over all a sword erect; supporters, dexter, a lion rampant, sinister a bear contourne, both resting on a base of rough stones; crest, hands clenched; BATH TOKEN + FOUR SHILLINGS + Under the arms, 1811 The lion's head *touches* the B in BATH The left hand cuff lines to the *first limb* of H The tops of ones in date are *flat*.

℞ A POUND NOTE FOR 5 TOKENS GIVEN BY S. WHITCHURCH AND W^M DORE A Staffordshire knot below, *nearly touching* the legend, *commencing* at W and *terminating* at O in DORE

9. Similar, but the Staffordshire knot *commences* at M and *terminates* at the R and is *farther* from the legend.

10. Similar, but the lion's head is *quite free* of the B in BATH The left cuff lines *between* T and H The tops of the ones in date *slope*, and the last numeral *touches* the base line. *R.*

11. Similar, but the left cuff lines to the *first limb* of H
PLATE C, no. 1, obverse only illustrated.

12. Also in Copper. *R.r.r.*

13. ○ Similar, but the left cuff lines *between the limbs* of H The tops of ones in date are *flat*, the figures in date *distant* from the base line.

℞ Similar, but the knot *commences* at the *last* limb of M and terminates at the *first* limb of R in DORE *R.*
Boyne 16.

14. ○ BATH TOKEN 1811 within a *wreath of oak;* legend, FOUR SHILLINGS The tops of the ones in date *slope*.

℞ As last. *R.r.r.* *All by P. Wyon.*
PLATE C, no. 1, obverse only illustrated.

Samuel Whitchurch and William Dore were tradesmen at 26 and 24, Market Place; the former being an ironmonger, and the latter a hatter. William Dore became promoter and partner in the Bath City Bank. The sign of the Golden Fleece which was suspended over William Dore's hat shop is now in the possession of Mr. Sydney Sydenham of Bath. The popularity of the issue of the tokens was beyond question, as will be seen from the subjoined notices.

"The Four Shilling pieces issued by the two public-spirited tradesmen of this City Whitchurch & Dore) have been subjected to chemical analysis by Drs. Chichester and Wilkinson, and they are found to be equal in purity to Portuguese dollars, from which they are probably made, the proportion of alloy which they contain being 11 per cent. of copper.

Sterling Silver is worth 6s. 4d. per oz., and one of these tokens weighs 10 dwts., and would sell as old silver for more than 3s.

The small profit the issuers may receive, is duly merited by the advantage derived by the public from the circulation of these tokens in the absence of the legal coin of the realm."
—*Bath Chronicle, Nov. 28th,* 1811.

"To Messrs. Whitchurch and Dore.
Bath, 24th January, 1812.
Gentlemen,
We beg leave to return you our sincere thanks for the very seasonable relief which your Silver Tokens have afforded us at a time when we (in common with our Fellow-Citizens) were labouring under the greatest inconvenience for want of small change.

SOMERSETSHIRE.

" While your respectability at once dissipated any apprehension of loss, your public spirit has impressed us with gratitude; we therefore earnestly hope that you will not withhold such further supplies as the necessity of the case may require.

" We are, Gentlemen, yours, etc.

W. Kemp	Wm. May	James Taylor
Jas. Evill and Son	Sheppard and Trinder	R. M. Payne
Evill and Newell	Stephen Leedham	Moger and Nicholson
John Daniel	H. Godwin	B. Shaw and Son
Edward Gibbons	John Barnard	Sam Hallett
Evill and Godwin	Geo. Barnard	Henry Griffith "
S. and W. Slack		

—*Bath Chronicle, Thursday, Jan.* 30, 1812.

These signatures represented the principal traders of Bath at the time, such as Jewellers, Auctioneers, Booksellers, Grocers, Linen and Woollen Drapers, Merchants and others.

PROVINCIAL TOKENS.

" Whitchurch and Dore beg to inform their friends and the public that they purpose to continue to take, in exchange for goods at their respective Shops, so long as the wisdom of Parliament may permit such Local Coin to be circulated, the following Tokens: viz. those issued by the Marlborough Bank; the Bristol, Andover and Gloucester Tokens; the Frome Tokens, of one and two shillings each, also the tokens which have been issued by their neighbours in Bath;—With respect to their *own* Tokens, as their promise is exhibited in very legible characters on the face of every one of them, Whitchurch and Dore have only to say that they hold themselves in readiness to perform *that promise* whenever it shall be required of them.

" Market Place, Bath, 9th May, 1812."—*Bath Chronicle, May* 14*th*, 1812.

Décr. 22nd, 1814.

WHITCHURCH AND DORE TOKENS.

" Whereas the Act of Parliament restricts the payment of and for Local Silver Tokens to the original issuers of such Tokens, after the 19th inst.

" Messrs. Whitchurch and Dore hereby give notice that their Tokens will be received and paid by themselves only on this day and in future at the Shop of the said Mr. Whitchurch in the Market Place.

" Bath, 20th Dec., 1814."—*Bath Chronicle, Dec.* 22*nd*, 1814.

TWO SHILLINGS.

15. ⊙ Arms and supporters; motto, TO FACILITATE TRADE   Justice holding scales as crest; legend, BATH TOKEN TWO SHILLINGS

℞ A POUND NOTE GIVEN FOR TEN TOKENS BY C. CULVERHOUSE I. ORCHARD AND J. PHIPPS   *Halliday.*

PLATE C, no. 2.

SHILLING.

16. ⊙ Similar, but BATH TOKEN ONE SHILLING 1812

℞ A POUND NOTE GIVEN FOR 20 OF THESE OUR TOKENS C. CULVERHOUSE I. ORCHARD AND J. PHIPPS   Legend, MARGARETS BUILDINGS BATH   *Periods* after initials. *R.*

Boyne 15.

17. Similar, but *without* the periods after C I and J   *R.r. Halliday.*

The tokens were advertised as follows:—

" Base and Spurious Twelvepenny Tokens having for some time incommoded the Public, and it being now discovered that the only Bristol Tokens which freely circulated in this city have been basely imitated to a great extent, we have at length been induced to accede to the presseing solicitations of our friends, and thus announce to the public that they may now be supplied with Silver Shilling Bath Tokens of weight and purity equal, if not superior, to any yet issued.

"As our aim has hitherto been, so it will continue to be, to satisfy the public mind, and supply them with necessary change of intrinsic worth, as near their nominal value as can possibly be done without suffering loss by the issue; and the Tokens thus issued will be readily exchanged for Bank Notes in any quantity, at either of our houses.—CHARLES CULVERHOUSE, ISAAC ORCHARD, JAMES PHIPPS."
—*Bath Chronicle, Feb.* 27, 1812.

Another advertisement shows the reputation of the tokens in 1812:—

"Sydney Gardens, Vauxhall, Bath. In honour of His Majesty's Birthday. On Thursday, June 4th, 1812, will be A Grand Gala.

"To prevent the great inconvenience and delay to the Company at the Gate, and more particular from the present *scarcity of change*, parties are requested to previously provide themselves with tickets.

"N.B.—No tokens taken but those of Messrs. Garratt &* Co., Bristol; Messrs. Whitchurch &* Dore, and Messrs. Culverhouse, Orchard &* Phipps, Bath."
—*Keene's Bath Journal, June 1st,* 1812.

BRISTOL.

SHILLING.

WITHOUT SUPPORTERS.

18. O Arms, argent, a ship, issuant from a castle, of the city of Bristol; crest, arms in saltire, in one hand a serpent *nowed*, in the other a pair of scales; no legend.

℞ BRISTOL SILVER TOKEN. 12 in a circle. FOR NECESSARY CHANGE. 1811

PLATE L, no. 17.

19. Also in Copper. *R.r.* *Halliday.*

An early notice of the token:—

"A society in Bristol are now issuing twelve penny Silver tokens to remedy the inconvenience arising from the scarcity of change. They are said to be of equal fineness with the silver issues of the Bank of England, and have the Bristol arms on one side, and on the other 'For necessary change, Bristol Silver Token. 12 (pence) 1811.'"
—*Bath Chronicle, August 8th,* 1811.

WITH SUPPORTERS.

20. O Arms of Bristol, with supporters, and helmeted; crest as last; ONE SHILLING TOKEN GENUINE DOLLAR SILVER 3^{DWT} NOV^R 1. 1811

℞ ISSUED BY E· BRYAN BRISTOL within a floral wreath. SOMERSET WILTS DEVON. GLOUCESTERSHIRE. NORTH AND SOUTH WALES. AND BRISTOL TOKEN. *Unknown.*

Boyne 32.

E. Bryan adopted a similar method of advertisement as other issuers:—

"A REMEDY FOR THE SCARCITY OF CHANGE.

"The public are respectfully informed that in consequence of the impositions practised by the putting into circulation Tokens of light weight and inferior metal, and particularly by the recent unprincipled imitation of such as from their respectability had procured free circulation, a New Shilling Token of genuine Dollar silver, and intrinsically worth about eleven-pence farthing, exclusive of the manufacturing, has within these few days been issued by E. Bryan, City Printing-Office, Corn Street, Bristol; intended for circulation in the counties of Somerset, Wilts, Gloucester and in North and South Wales:—The public may rest assured, that the above Token is of the value and quality stated. Individuals, companies or communities can be supplied to any amount.

"No discount whatever can be allowed, but if ordered in quantities, they will be sent carriage free, and insured."—*Bath Chronicle, December 12th,* 1811.

Bristol Commercial Token Bank Company.

August 12.

21. O. Arms and crest of the city of Bristol without supporters, within a garter inscribed VIRTUTE ET INDUSTRIA (By Virtue and Industry); legend, BRISTOL TOKEN FOR XII PENCE The tail of the snake in crest *touches* the N of TOKEN The flag on mainmast reaches the *centre* of the flag on left tower, a *portion* of the flag staff and a *corner* of the flag is *seen* on the tower at the right.

℞ PAYABLE BY MESS^{RS} FRA^S GARRATT W^M TERRELL EDW^D BIRD LAN^T BECK & FRAN^S H. GRIGG. in a circle; legend, ISSUED IN BRISTOL AUG^T 12. 1811. TO FACILITATE TRADE. The F in FRA^S lines *to the foot* of T in TO and the final T in GARRATT points *between* D and E in TRADE ·

Boyne 34.

22. O. Similar to last, but the tail of the snake *does not touch* the N in TOKEN and the tower at the right is *without* the staff, the corner of the flag is *seen* as in last.

℞ Similar, but the F in FRA^S lines *between* T and O of TO The last T in GARRATT points to the *first limb* of E in TRADE. *R.*

23. O. Similar, but the tower at the right is *without* the staff *and* flag.

℞ Similar, but the last T in GARRATT points *between* D and E in TRADE. *R.*

24. O. Similar, but the tower at the right shows a *portion* of the staff and the *corner* of the flag as in no. 21.

℞ Similar, but there is *no period* after GRIGG the F lines to the *foot* of T in TO and the last T in GARRATT points to the *first limb* of E in TRADE. *R.*

<small>The outer legend of this reverse is tinted or, and known as the "frosted border" variety. Mr. Bowles is in possession of the reverse die.</small>

25. O. Similar, but the flag on the tower at the left *floats clear* above the flag on the mainmast and *nearly all* the flag on the tower at the right is *seen*.

℞ Similar, but F in FRA^S lines *between* the T and O of TO the final T in GARRATT points *between* D and E in TRADE. as no. 23. *R.r.*

26. O. Similar, but the tail of the snake in crest *touches* the N in TOKEN The staff is *omitted* on the tower at the right, the corner of flag is *exhibited*.

℞ Similar, but F lines to the *foot* of T in TO as in no. 21. *R.r.*

All by Halliday.

100   *NINETEENTH CENTURY TOKEN COINAGE.*

27. O- Arms, etc. as before ; the tail of snake *does not touch* the N of TOKEN   The flag on the mainmast reaches to the *centre* of the flag on the left tower.

℞. Similar, but reads PAYABLE BY MESS^{RS} FRA^S CARRATT (*sic*) W^M FERRELL (*sic*) EDW^D BIRD LAN^R (*sic*) BECK & FRAN^S H. GRIGG. The F in FRA^S lines between T and O of TO and the final T in GARRATT points *between* D and E of TRADE.

28. Also in brass.   *Unknown.*
    The last two are contemporary forgeries, and very rare.

AUGUST 22ND.

29. O- Arms and crest of the City of Bristol within a garter inscribed VIRTUTE ET INDUSTRIA   The tail of snake in crest does *not touch* the N of TOKEN   Legend, BRISTOL TOKEN FOR XII PENCE   The flag on the mainmast reaches the *centre* of the flag on the left tower.

℞. PAYABLE BY MESS^{RS} FRA^N GARRATT W^R TERRELL EDW^D BIRD LAM^T BECK & FRAN^N H. GRIGG   Legend, TO FACILITATE TRADE. ISSUED IN BRISTOL AUG^T 22 1811   The F in FRA^N lines to the foot of T in TO R.   *Unknown.*

30. O- Similar, but the flag on the left tower floats clear above the one on the mainmast ; the tail of the snake in crest *touches* the N in TOKEN

℞. Similar, but reads PAYABLE BY MESS^{RS} FRA^N GARRETT (*sic*) W^R TERRAIL EDM^D BIRD LAM^T BECK & FRAN^N H. GREGG (*sic*) in a circle. Legend, TO FACILITATE TRADE. ISSUED IN BRISTOL AUG^T 22 1811. R.
                    Boyne 35.

31. Same as last in copper ; the reverse is silver plated. *R.r.*

32. Same as last in copper, on a larger flan (*M.* 8), not plated. *R.r.*   *Unknown.*

The last three are contemporary forgeries, but all are rare.
   Francis Garratt, Bristol Buildings, and 9, Cathay, was a grocer ; William Terrell, 17, The Black, a rope maker ; Edward Bird, silversmith, Launcelot Beck, haberdasher, both of Clare Street, and Francis Hore Grigg, 34, High Street, haberdasher.
   Garratt & Co. are said to have issued Silver Shilling Tokens to the amount of £27,000.
             —*Bath Journal, Nov. 11th,* 1811. *See Official Balance Sheet.*

" Bristol, 17th Feb. 1812.
IMPORTANT CAUTION.
We, the undersigned, hereby caution the public against a spurious Imitation of our Twelve-penny and Sixpenny Tokens, differing, however, in the names on the reverse, which in the Base Tokens are all *erroneously spelt*, as will be perceived in the specimens subjoined.

ORIGINAL TOKEN.	RATHBONE-PLACE TOKEN.
Payable	Payable
By Messrs	By Messrs
Fras Garratt	Frans Garrett
Wm. Terrell	Wr Terrail
Edwd Bird	Edmd Bird
Lant Beck &	Lamt Beck &
Frans H	Frann H
Grigg.	Gregg

SOMERSETSHIRE. 101

"Considering it an imperious duty which we owe to the public and ourselves to trace the authors of this *infamous deception*, we have succeeded in ascertaining that it has been carried into effect by the *well-known* Mr. H. Morgan, No. 12, Rathbone-place, and A. B., No. 35, Cock Lane, Snow-Hill, London, and that the new coinage he has produced is of inferior value to his *former tokens*, said to be issued by *Royal License*, and which fortunately for the community, have been long since detected, and the circulation stopped.

"We have with equal certainty ascertained *Mr. Morgan's Resident Agent in Bristol*, whose name we for the present for-bear announcing, in the hope that this public notice will so effectually put the public and the parties on their guard, as to render further measures unnecessary.

                Francis Garratt   Wm Terrell
                Edward Bird   Launcelot Beck
                Francis H Grigg."

                                          —Bath Chronicle, Feb. 27th, 1812.

TOKEN BANK NOTE.

The note in the plate on the other side is the only one at present known.

It was obtained by Mr. Bowles from a descendant of William Terrell, one of the partners in the Token Bank.

The building, illustrated at the left of the note was built in 1811, in Corn Street, is still in existence, shows the same elevation, and is known as the "Commercial Rooms."

Mr. Bowles has since secured from a descendant of Francis H. Grigg, another of the partners, an *unissued* Five Pound Note of the same Token Bank, which is believed to be unique, and of which the following is a copy:

```
                             COMMERCIAL
         No. ...       BRISTOL TOKEN COMPANY.                  £ FIVE
         View of          I Promise to pay the Bearer
         Commercial     the sum of FIVE POUNDS, on Demand.       The
         Rooms,       at Mefsrs Willm Storrs Fry & Sons, Bankers in London.  Arms of
         Bristol.       Value received the.... day of .... 181... No. ...   Bristol.
                        For Garratt, Terrell, Bird, Beck & Grigg
                      Entd ...
                     FIVE POUNDS
```
(left margin: FG. WT. EB. LB & FHG. BRISTOL)

This Token Bank also issued Bankers' drafts on London; a blank of which is here given:

```
       £         No.         Bristol            181
                         COMMERCIAL
                    BRISTOL TOKEN COMPANY
             Established August 12th 1811 to facilitate Trade
          .   .   . after  .  .  . pay  .  .  .  .  .  .  .  .  .  .
          or order   .  .  .  .  .  .  .  .  .  .  .  .  .  .  .  .
                           value received as advised
                    For Garratt, Terrell, Bird, Beck & Grigg
           To
              Messrs Willm Storrs Fry & Sons,
                 Bankers,
                    London.
```
(left margin: FG. WT. EB. LB & FHG. BRISTOL)

Subsequent to the circulation of the tokens, a statement of account was published, showing the enormous number issued, at a loss of £5,588 10s. 2d. It is generally supposed that silver tokens produced great profits to the issuers; considering the cost of silver and the light weight of the tokens, but it will be seen that in this instance, such was not the case:

GARRATT, TERRELL, & COMPANY'S ACCOUNT CURRENT.

Dr.	Tokens.		Contra.	Cr.
1812.	To cost of 85,332 oz. Silver which made £32,000 of Tokens at 6s. 0½d. per oz. . . .	£25,777 13 6	1812 Nov. By cash received for 28,600 oz. Silver, at 5s. 11d. per oz. . . .	£8,460 16 8
	To cost of making 640,000 Tokens at £4 per thousand. . .	2,560 0 0	1814 Dec. By amount of Tokens now paid 28,600 oz. worth 5s. 2d. per oz. .	7,388 6 8
			By amount now out 26,000 oz. at 5s. per oz.	6,500 0 0
			By Interest during circulation	400 0 0
			By Loss	5,588 10 2
		£28,337 13 6		£28,337 13 6

January 2d, 1815.   The above is a true statement.

— Garratt,
Wm. Terrell,
Edw. Bird,
Lant. Beck,
F. H. Grigg.

The following printed notices speak for themselves:

TOKENS.
REDCLIFF - PARISH.
Public Notice.

Messrs. Garratt & Co. having publicly declared that after the 2nd of November, they will not give for their Tokens, the value for which they were issued by them: We, the undersigned, have determined that we will not receive them in payment for more than
Nine Pence each,
After this Day.

S. & J. Fitchew.	Purnells & Co.
James Clark.	John Simpkin.
John R. Grant.	Heny. Gwyther.
William Frost.	William Puke.
John Clark	John B. Cross.
E. B. Willmot.	Robt. Rowland.
Steph. Doughty.	Thomas W. Hall.
John B. Jacques.	Thomas Lane.
Samuel Lucas.	Petr. Peace Jun.
Brookman & Son.	G. A. Hogarth.

Richard White.
Bristol, 31st October 1812.
T. Lane, Printer, Redcliff-Street, Bristol.

TOKENS.

At a meeting convened to take into consideration the issue of Garratt & Co's. Tokens, it was unanimously Resolved, (as they will not be paid after Monday morning next) not to take them after this present day Saturday, Oct. 31, 1812.
Castle-Street   Stephen Biss, St. Philips.
William Major, Printer, St John's Steps, Bristol

From an Original in the possession of H. B. Bowles.

SOMERSETSHIRE. 103

BRISTOL, MONDAY, NOV. 2, 1812.
" GARRATT & Co. Engage to pay the Tokens Issued by them until the 25th of March, 1813.
Evans & Grabham, Printers, Mercury Office, 34, Broad-Street.

"No. 22, High-Street, Nov. 15, 1814.
" To the Tradesmen of Bristol.
" With a view to relieve the inconvenience felt by the Public at large (but more especially by the labouring classes) in consequence of the sudden stoppage of the old copper currency, WM. RINGER was induced to write a letter to the Honourable Commissioners of His Majesty's Mint, Tower, London, to inquire of them whether any REAL cause existed for such stoppage: In reply he received a letter on Saturday last, 12th inst. (which he will be happy to shew to any Gentleman who will call on him any day before 9 in the morning, or after 4 in the afternoon) stating that it was the intention of Government to withdraw the Old Halfpence from circulation, for which purpose the Mint Office was now open to receive them, under certain restrictions and limitations to be stated on personal application at said office, on certain days named. W. R. immediately wrote to a Friend in London to procure for him the necessary particulars, which he expects to receive by to-morrow's post, and whilst upon this information, he is content to receive Old Tower Halfpence in payment for Stockings, he begs leave most earnestly to invite his fellow Tradesmen to follow his example in their respective articles of Sale, and thereby rid the city of an Evil, which it will be their own fault if they ever suffer to exist again, at the same time assuring them, that any information he may receive on the subject shall be quite at their service
"Good Old Tower Halfpence taken for Stockings between the Hours of Nine in the Morning and Four in the Afternoon
Major, Printer John's Steps"
It will be seen by this important announcement how unpopular were the old Tower halfpence, and the keenness with which some tradesmen took advantage of the discredited copper currency to dispose of their wares.

NO DATE.

33. O- The arms and crest of the City of Bristol within a garter inscribed VIRTUTE ET INDUSTRIA Legend, BRISTOL TOKEN FOR · XII PENCE
℞ PAYABLE BY A ONE POUND NOTE FOR 20 OF THESE AT P. ROSE'S STATIONER BRISTOL. Legend, H. MORGAN LICENSED · MANUFACTURER 12 RATHBONE PLACE LONDON *R.r.r.*

34. O- The arms and crest of the City of Bristol within a garter inscribed VIRTUTE ET INDUSTRIA Legend, BRISTOL TOKEN XII PENCE The tail of snake in crest *touches* the N of TOKEN. The flagstaff on the mainmast is *under* the T in ET
℞ BRISTOL SHILLING SILVER TOKEN. ISSU'D BY ROYAL LICENCE Legend, H. MORGAN LICENSED MANUFACTURER 12 RATHBONE PLACE LONDON. *Halliday.*
Boyne 37.

35. O- Similar, but the tail of snake in crest *does not touch* the N in TOKEN and PENCE in the legend *reads* PENSE The flagstaff is *under* the scale pan between the arms.
℞ As last.

36. O- As last.
℞ Similar, but ISSUED *instead* of ISSU'D in the legend. *R.*
Unknown.

37. ☉ Prince of Wales' plumes and motto, ICH DIEN issuant from a coronet above a drum, inscribed $\mathcal{G}\ \mathcal{R}$ Cannon, flintlock, trumpet, and flags, with an ornament below.

℞ BRISTOL SHILLING TOKEN ISSU'D BY ROYAL LICENCE Legend, H. MORGAN LICENSED MANUFACTURER 12 RATHBONE PLACE LONDON. *R.r.r.* *Halliday.*

JULY 12TH.

38. ☉ The arms and crest of the city of Bristol within a garter, inscribed VIRTUTE ET INDUSTRIA Legend, BRISTOL MEDAL THE XII OF JULY

℞ BRISTOL AND WELCH PRINCIPALITY SILVER MEDAL F. GARRATT & F^S HORE GRIGG Legend, PROSPERITY TO WALES & THE CITY OF BRISTOL. *R.r.*

39. ☉ As last.

℞ As last, with the *addition* of the words ISSUED BY *R.r.r.*

40. ☉ As last.

℞ Similar, but *reads* BRISTOL AND WELCH PRINCIPALITY SILVER MEDAL FR GARRATT LAM^T BECK & F^S HORE GRIGG *R.r.r.*

41. ☉ As last.

℞ BRISTOL AND WELCH PRINCIPALITY SILVER MEDAL ISSUED BY ROYAL LICENCE Legend, PROSPERITY TO WALES & THE CITY OF BRISTOL *R.r.*

SEPTEMBER 5TH.

42. ☉ As last.

℞ WALES AND BRISTOL in a circle. Legend, MERTHYR ✶ 5TH SEP 1811 ✶ *R.r.r.* *Unknown.*

BRISTOL BRIDGE.

43. ☉ A bridge of three arches. BRISTOL & WILTSHIRE TOKEN 1811 The tops of the ones in date are *flat.*

℞ VALUE 12 PENCE in a radiated star. PAYABLE BY NIBLOCK & LATHAM. AT THEIR WAREHOUSE. BRIDGE S^T & TROWBRIDGE The point of star at the right lines with the *terminal* of E in WAREHOUSE ·

PLATE C, no. 3.

44. ☉ Similar to last, but the tops of the ones in date *slope,* and there are *projections* on either side between the pillars and the lamps.

℞ Similar, but the point of star lines with the *first limb* of E. *R.* *Halliday.*

J. Niblock and R. S. Latham, Mercers, Bath, were declared bankrupts, Nov. 30, 1821. Boyne 39.

SOMERSETSHIRE.

WITH SUPPORTERS, SEPTEMBER 6TH.

45. O. Arms of the city of Bristol, with supporters, and helmeted; crest as before. LET TRADE & COMMERCE FLOURISH. BRISTOL ISSUED BY W. SHEPPARD · EXCHANGE · SEP^T 6 1811 The tops of the ones in date are *flat*.

℞ VALUE 12 PENCE in a wreath of oak. SOMERSETSHIRE WILTSHIRE GLOUCESTERSHIRE SOUTH WALES AND BRISTOL TOKEN There are *two* acorns above the intersection of the wreath. *Halliday.*

Boyne, 41.

46. O. Similar to last, but SHEPHARD *instead* of SHEPPARD and the tops of the ones in date *slope*.

℞ Similar, but with *one* acorn above the intersection of the wreath. R. *Unknown.*

William Sheppard was a bookseller, and Lottery Office keeper, in Corn Street.
—*Numismatic Magazine, vol. VIII, p.* 66.

The following form of advertisement was resorted to by W. Sheppard, to call attention both to the tokens and his business :—

Advt.   SCARCITY OF CHANGE.

"Wm. Sheppard, Bookseller, Stationer and Dealer in Patent Medicines, &c. opposite the Exchange, Bristol, in consequence of the distressing scarcity of Change, has procured a quantity of Silver Tokens with which he will accommodate his Friends and Customers in the Country on their remitting, post paid, cash notes for the quantity they may want. At the same time, orders in the line of his business, will be duly attended to."

"Bristol, September, 1811."—*Bath Chronicle, Sept.* 26*th,* 1811.
The issuer of this token was declared bankrupt, April 11th, 1818.

BRISTOL QUAY.

47. O. A three-masted ship sailing. VALUE ONE SHILLING FOR THE ARMY &^{C} ✱

℞ N^O 37 QUAY BRISTOL   Legend, PAYABLE AT GOVERNMENT STORES R TRIPP & C^O 1811 R.

PLATE C, no. 4.

48. O. As last.

℞ As last, but R TRIPP & C^O 1811 *omitted*. R.   *Halliday.*

Robert Tripp and Co. were tailors and accoutrement makers. They also had stores in Duke Street. R. Tripp was gazetted bankrupt June 10, 1817.

SIXPENCE.

ARMS AND SUPPORTERS.

49. O. Arms, crest, etc. as on the shilling. BRISTOL SIXPENNY TOKEN · TO FACILITATE TRADE · 1811 .

℞ 6^D within a floral wreath. GENUINE DOLLAR SILVER ISSUED BY E BRYAN.

50. O. Same as last.

℞ Similar, but *with a period* after E. in E. BRYAN. *Unknown.*

Boyne 33.

P

WITHOUT SUPPORTERS, AUG^T 12.

51. O Arms and crest of the city of Bristol within a garter inscribed VIRTUTE ET INDUSTRIA Legend, BRISTOL TOKEN FOR VI PENCE

℞ PAYABLE BY MESS^{RS} FRA^S GARRATT W^M TERRELL EDW^D BIRD LAM^T BECK & FRAN^S H GRIGG. in a circle. TO FACILITATE TRADE. ISSUED IN BRISTOL AUG^T 12. 1811. *Halliday.*

PLATE C, no. 5.

AUG^T 22.

52. O Similar, but the corner of the flag is *not seen* on the tower at the right as in last.

℞ Similar to last, but *reads* PAYABLE BY MESS^{RS} FRA^N GARRATT W^R TERRELL EDW^N BIRD LAM^T BECK & FRA^N (*sic*) H GRIGG Dated AUG^T 22 1811. R.

53. O As last.

℞ Similar to last, but *reads* PAYABLE BY MESS^{RS} FRA^N GARRETT W^R TERRAIL EDM^D BIRD LAM^T BECK & FRAN^N H. GREGG. (*sic*).
Unknown.

NO DATE.

54. O As last.

℞ BRISTOL SILVER SIX-PENNY TOKEN ISSUED BY ROYAL LICENCE in a circle. MORGAN LICENSED MAKER 12 RATHBONE PLACE LONDON.

Boyne 38.

55. O Similar, but the corner of the flag *is seen*.

℞ PAYABLE AT MORGANS WAREHOUSE FOR BUCK & DOE SKINS CASTLE S^T BRISTOL in a circle. A 1£ NOTE WILL BE PAID FOR 40 OF THESE. *R.r.* *Halliday.*

JULY 6TH.

56. O Arms and crest of the city of Bristol within a garter inscribed VIRTUTE ET INDUSTRIA Legend, BRISTOL MEDAL THE VI OF JULY

℞ BRISTOL & SOUTH WALES SILVER MEDAL ISSUED BY F GARRATT & F^S HORE GRIGG in a circle. PROSPERITY TO WALES & THE CITY OF BRISTOL. *R.r.r.* *Unknown.*

JULY 12TH.

57. O Arms and crest of the city of Bristol within a garter inscribed VIRTUTE ET INDUSTRIA Legend, BRISTOL MEDAL THE XII OF JULY

℞ BRISTOL & WELCH PRINCIPALITY SILVER MEDAL ISSUED BY ROYAL LICENSE Legend, PROSPERITY TO WALES & THE CITY OF BRISTOL+
Unknown.

In the cabinet of Sir William Henry Wills, Bart., M.P.

Bristol Bridge.

58. O A bridge of three arches; BRISTOL & WILTSHIRE TOKEN 1811
℞ VALUE 6 PENCE in a radiated star.   PAYABLE BY. NIBLOCK &
LATHAM. AT THEIR WAREHOUSE BRIDGES (sic) & TROWBRIDGE   R.

59. O As last.
℞ Similar to last, but reads BRIDGE S^T *Halliday.*
PLATE B, no. 25.

Niblock, in 1795, issued two halfpenny tokens. The Bristol Bridge, with a quaint reverse, where two men are standing, one of whom says, "I want to buy some cheap bargains," to which the other replies, "Then go to Niblock's, Bridge Street." The second token has on the obverse a case of merchandise with the legend GENERAL COMMISSION & PUBLIC SALE ROOM. Same address.
Vide Atkins 178, 86 and 89.

WITH SUPPORTERS.

60. O Arms, supporters and crest of the city of Bristol; SEP^T 6 1811 under. BRISTOL PAYABLE BY W. SHEPPARD. EXCHANGE
℞ 6 PENCE in a radiated star; SOMERSETSHIRE WILTSHIRE GLOUCESTERSHIRE SOUTH WALES AND BRISTOL TOKEN   *Unknown.*
Boyne 42.

WITHOUT SHIELD.

61. O 6 PENCE in a radiated star; R. TRIPP & C^O BRISTOL 1811
℞ PAYABLE BY ONE DOLLAR FOR 10 TOKENS & 2^d OR 20 TOKENS FOR 2 DOLLARS & 4^d AND 40 FOR A ONE POUND NOTE.   *R.*
Unknown.
Boyne 44.

The following notices are taken from a collection of broadsides, etc., relating to Bristol, in the possession of Mr. G. E. Weare, Weston-super-Mare:—

"BRISTOL TOKENS."

"As the time limited for payment of the *Bristol Tokens* will expire on Tuesday next, Nov. 3rd, *We*, the undersigned, do hereby call a *Meeting* (of the traders and others of this City, who feel interested) to be held at the *Rummer Tavern*, All Saints Lane, this present Tuesday evening, at Six o'clock, to consider of, and adopt some plan to prevent a recurrence of the late inconvenience for want of change.

Bristol,
October 27, 1812.

Joseph Hall.
Tuckett & Sons.
John Thomas & Son.
Hugh Taylor.
James Edwards.

"T. Lane, Printer, 59, Redcliff Street, Bristol."

The notice below shows the invective of the period by those who were opposed to tokens of any kind:—

"PARTNERS WANTED.

"A Mechanic who can procure *nearly two hundred pounds!!!* wishes to join *one* or *two persons*, who can each advance a like sum, to embark with him in a *speculation* which will produce *without any risk to them* a profit of at least *Two hundred per cent!!!!* and in which *no credit or responsibility* is at all necessary.

"For particulars address, *post paid*, to *Mister Fudge, Humbug-Row*, Bristol.

"N.B.—To save trouble the *speculation* is to *glut* the City with *Silver Tokens*, following up by a plentiful issue of Bank-Notes, of considerably *less value*; and it may be worth a future consideration to issue *Copper* and *Brass Tokens*, which the *Partnership* would find particularly profitable from their possessing such an *ample stock of the latter article.*

"Evans & Graham, Printers, 34, Brood Street, Bristol."

It appears from a perusal of other broadsides and cuttings from contemporary Bristol newspapers in Mr. Wear's collection that twenty-one firms or individual tradesmen who were carrying on business in Redcliff parish, in the city of Bristol, gave public notice to the effect that Messrs. Garratt & Co. having publicly declared that after the 2nd of November they (Garratt & Co.) would not give for their tokens the value for which they were issued by them, the tradesmen referred to would not receive them in payment for more than 9d. each. On the other hand, twenty-two firms or individual tradesmen issued a manifesto, in which they offered to take the tokens for their full value " until this City shall be more effectually supplied with Government Coin," the signatories testifying their belief that the tokens " have been of essential service to this City, and that the discontinuance of them would very materially affect its trade, and reduce its inhabitants *to as great distress as was experienced prior to their being issued.*"

The correspondents who wrote to the editors—or, rather as was the custom in the period, " To the Printer "—approached the matter from various standpoints, both favourable and unfavourable, alike to the principle of the issue of tokens and to those who issued them. One correspondent gives what he alleged to be the question of pure silver in the tokens as follows:—

Worth.

Tokens marked Garratt, Terrell, Bird and Grigg, contain $57\frac{3}{4}$ grains of pure silver . . . . $9\frac{1}{2}$ fractions
Tokens marked Bryan . . . . $9\frac{1}{4}$ „
  „   „   Sheppard . . . . 9 „
  „   „   Tripp's 6d. tokens . . . . . . $4\frac{1}{2}$ „

It was stated that the Bristol tokens were made of dollar-silver, without any additional alloy; that all the attendant expenses as to the coinage, carriage, insurance, etc., are on an average one penny each token. It was also stated that the Birmingham manufacturer charged one half profit; upon each token the issuers have a fraction more than one penny; this profit was acquired at a very considerable risk. One of the writers alleges that Messrs. Garratt & Co. had their shilling tokens made at the nett cost of 129 shillings per gross, independent of carriage and insurance to and from Birmingham. It was also alleged that dollar silver had advanced in price from 5s. 11d. per ounce to 6s. 6d. per ounce; that there was a strong probability that by March, 1813, the prices would have so far advanced "that the public might have preferred rubbing the tokens plain, and hoarding them as good, passable *Tower-Shillings.*"

CHARD.

SHILLINGS.

62. ☌ CHARD SOMERSET 1811 in an olive wreath.

℞ 1 within a radiated garter inscribed SHILLING   Legend, ISSUED. FOR. THE. BENEFIT + OF · TRADE +   *R.*

PLATE L, no. 18.

63. ☌ Similar, but *reads* CHARD SOMERSET SEPT.^R 1811

℞ As last. *R.r.*

Boyne 47.

64. Also in Copper. *R.r.r.*   *Halliday.*

FROME SELWOOD.

TWO SHILLINGS.

65. ☌ Full faced bust (Edward I) crowned; FROME SELWOOD TOKEN FOR 2 SHILLINGS

℞ AT MESS^{RS} WILLOUGHBY & SONS and a sugar loaf upon a cross radiated A ONE POUND NOTE GIVEN FOR 10 TOKENS 1812   *R.r.*

Halliday.

PLATE C, no. 6.

SHILLING.

66. ☾ Similar to last, but TOKEN FOR 12 PENCE

℞ AT MESS^{RS} WILLOUGHBY M^{RS} SINKINS H. RYALL W. SPARKS W. GERARD GRIFFITH & GOUGH. upon a cross radiated. A ONE POUND NOTE GIVEN FOR 20 TOKENS 1811 *Halliday.*

Boyne 85.

"According to the Norman Survey King Edward held Frome."

Willoughby & Sons were grocers; Mrs. Jane Sinkins, draper, in the Market Place; Henry Ryall, grocer, in Catherine Hill; William Sparks and William Gerard, grocers, Market Place; Griffith & Gough, grocers, Stoney Street.—*Numismatic Mag. no.* 156.

TAUNTON.

SHILLING.

67. ☾ In a shield a crown surmounted by a cherub; PAYABLE AT JOHN BLUETTS 1811

℞ VALUE XII PENCE within a wreath of oak. TAUNTON TOKEN *R.r.r.* *Unknown.*

PLATE L, no. 19.

John Bluett was a wine and spirit merchant.

BATH.

PENNY.

COPPER.

68. ☾ A fleece suspended from a ribbon; BATH TOKEN 1811 The *left* foreleg is over the *first* one in date, the ones are in a *straight* line, and *slightly pointed* at the tops, the tail *falls below* the hock.

℞ A POUND NOTE FOR 240 TOKENS GIVEN BY S. T. WHITCHURCH AND W. DORE The T in TOKENS is *over* the N in GIVEN *R.*

Sharp 196, 1.

69. Similar, but the T in TOKEN is over the *space* between GIVEN and BY

70. Similar, but the left foot of the fleece *nearly touches* the *first* one in date; the ones are *flat. R.*

71. Similar, but the date is in a *curved* line and farther from the legs of the fleece; the ones are *pointed.*

72. Similar to last, but the first one in date is *between* the forelegs; the ones in date are *more pointed* than the last.

PLATE C, no. 7.

73. ○ Similar, but the first one in date is *under* the *right* foreleg; the tail *does not fall* below the hock; the ones in date *slope*.

℞ Similar, but the T of TOKENS is above the *last* limb of N in GIVEN   *P. Wyon.*

ARMS AND SUPPORTERS.

74. ○ Arms and supporters of the City; Crest, hands clenched; BATH PENNY+++ TOKEN+++ 1811

℞ A POUND NOTE FOR 240 TOKENS GIVEN BY S_ WHITCHURCH AND W. DORE   *R*.   *P. Wyon.*

Sharp 196, 2.

BRISTOL.

PENNY.

ARMS AND CREST.
COPPER.

75. ○ Bust to right, robed, laureated (George III); ONE PENNY TOKEN 1811   Tops of ones *slope*, and the last numeral in date *nearly touches* the robe.

℞ Arms, helmeted, with supporters; CIVITAS BRISTOL   Crest, arms crossed, snake and scales; the outer scale pan extends to the *elbow* of the arm, the waves under the ship are formed by *three pairs of thin* lines, and there are *five stays* from ship to castle; the snake *has* a forked tongue.

Sharp 196, 3.

76. Similar, but the last numeral in date *does not touch* the robe.
PLATE C, no. 8.

77. Similar to last, but the outer scale pan extends to the *muscle* of the arm; the waves under the ship are formed of *three thick* lines; there are *no stays* from ship to castle; the snake is *without* a tongue.

78. Similar to last, but with only *a slight slant* to the tops of the ones.

79. ○ Similar, but the tops of the ones in date are *flat*.

℞ Similar; the snake *with* a tongue, but *no* fork.   *R*.

80. Similar, but there is only *one stay* from ship to castle, and the towers are *without* flags.   *Halliday.*

SOMERSETSHIRE. 111

Bristol Brass & Copper Company.

Portcullis perpendicular.

81. ○ Arms and crest of the city; VIRTUTE ET INDUSTRIA 1811 The mast next the castle is the *shorter* of the two; there are *four* stays, and the doorway under portcullis is *filled in* with *perpendicular* lines.

℞ ℬ ℬ & COPPER C̲O̱ ONE PENNY. PAYABLE AT BRISTOL SWAN SEA & LONDON. The downstroke of the ℬ is under the *second* N and very short; ℬ ℬ in *solid* lines.

Sharp 196, 5.

82. ○ As last.
℞ Similar, but the monogram ℬ ℬ is *outlined*.

Portcullis plain.

83. ○ Similar, but there are *five* stays from ship to castle; the doorway under portcullis is *plain*.

℞ Similar, but the downstroke of ℬ extends *above* the curve of the letter, and is under the Y in PAYABLE The monogram in *solid* lines.

Portcullis horizontal.

84. ○ Similar, but the tops of the two masts equal; *six* stays from ship to castle, and the doorway under the portcullis is filled in with *horizontal* lines.
℞ As last.

85. ○ Similar, but *five* stays from ship to castle; the two loop-holes above the doorway are *filled-in with brickwork*, showing *faintly*.

℞ Similar, but the downstroke of the ℬ extends above the curve, and is under the *second* N The monogram ℬ ℬ is *outlined*.

86. ○ Similar, but the top of the two masts *equal* in height, and the two loopholes above the doorway are *plain*.
℞ As last.

87. ○ Similar, but the two loopholes above the doorway are filled in with *brickwork*, showing *faintly*.
℞ Similar to last, but ℬ ℬ *solid*.

Ship Sailing.

88. O A ship, with *five* port-holes, sailing under topsails, in a circle; PATENT SHEATHING NAIL MANUFACTORY. BRISTOL. The mainmast points *between* the I and N of SHEATHING

℞ ONE PENNY TOKEN in a circle. PAYABLE AT BRISTOL AND LONDON 1811 *Flat* tops to ones in date.

Sharp 196, 8.

89. O As last.

℞ Similar, but the tops of ones in date *slope*.

90. O Similar, but the mainmast points to the *centre* of N in SHEATHING *Six* port-holes to ship.

℞ As last.

91. O Similar, but the mainmast points to the *first limb* of N in SHEATHING

℞ As last. *Halliday.*

With Boat at Stern. 1811.

92. O Ship under sail with boat at stern, in a circle. PATENT SHEATHING NAIL MANUFACTORY BRISTOL *Ten* port-holes to ship.

℞ PENNY TOKEN in a circle. PAYABLE AT BRISTOL AND LONDON. 1811 The tops of ones in date are *flat*. *Halliday.*

93. O As last.

℞ PENNY TOKEN in a circle. PAYABLE BY, S. GUPPY; BRISTOL 1811 *No period* after BRISTOL Ones in date *slope*.

PLATE C, no. 9.

94. O As last.

℞ Similar, but *with a period* after BRISTOL.

95. O Similar to last, but with *nine* port-holes to ship.

℞ Similar to last, but PAYABLE, BY; S. GUPPY BRISTOL. 1811.

Sharp 196, 7.

1813.

96. O A ship sailing to right fully rigged, no *inner* circle PATENT SHEATHING NAIL MANUFACTORY. BRISTOL. under the ship 1813

℞ ONE PENNY TOKEN in a circle. PAYABLE BY S. GUPPY AT BRISTOL AND LONDON + *Halliday.*

In the cabinet of Sir William Henry Wills, Bart.

Samuel Guppy traded at 34, Queen Square, Bristol, and 22, Dowgate Hill, London.

SOMERSETSHIRE.

BRISTOL AND SOUTH WALES.

WITH PORTCULLIS.

97. ○ Arms of the city of Bristol within a garter, crest above; VIRTUTE ET INDUSTRIA. 1811. There are *seven stays* at the right of the main-mast, the bowsprit *touches* the edge of the garter, *flat* tops to ones in date, and the portcullis is formed of *two horizontal* and *two perpendicular* lines.

℞ Prince of Wales' plume encircled by a coronet; motto ICH DIEN on a ribbon. ONE PENNY TOKEN. BRISTOL & SOUTH WALES. The I in ICH lines to R in BRISTOL *R.*

Sharp 196, 9.

98. ○ Similar, but there are *six stays* from the mainmast, and the tops of the ones in date *slope*; the portcullis is formed of *two horizontal* and *three perpendicular* lines; H under the right tower.

℞ Similar, but I in ICH lines with I in BRISTOL

PLATE C, no. 10.

99. ○ Similar, but the H under the tower *omitted*.

℞ Similar, but the I in ICH lines to the *space* between I and S in BRISTOL

100. ○ Similar, but with *five stays* from the mainmast; the bowsprit does *not touch* the edge of the garter; the portcullis is formed of *one horizontal* and *three perpendicular* lines.

℞ As last.

101. ○ Similar, but there are *no stays* above the top sails at the left.

℞ Similar, but the I in ICH lines to the I in BRISTOL The B at the top is *disjointed*.

102. Similar, but with *seven stays* from the main-mast; H under the tower. *Halliday.*

WITHOUT PORTCULLIS.

103. ○ Similar, but with *six stays* at the right of main-mast, and stays above the top sails at the left; there is *no* portcullis; the tag of the garter is *above* the date instead of *between* the 8 and the 1 No H under the tower. *R.*

℞ As no. 99.

PLATE C, no. 10.

104. ○ Similar, but with only *three stays* from the main-mast, and there are *no stays* from the sails to flags at the left; tag of garter is *between* the 8 and 1 of date. *R.* *Halliday.*

℞ As no. 101.

Phœnix Glass Works.

105. O A phœnix issuant from flames, within a wreath of oak and laurel.

℞ ONE PENNY TOKEN in a circle surrounded by an oak wreath. *R.* *Halliday.*

Batty 1069.

Issued by "Rickets, Evans & Co., Phœnix Glass Company, Temple Gate without Bristol."

Bristol Brass and Copper Company.

HALFPENNY.

106. O Arms and crest; VIRTUTE ET INDUSTRIA 1811 The hand holding the scales is under the I in INDUSTRIA

℞ *B B* & COPPER *C⁰* HALFPENNY. PAYABLE AT BRISTOL SWANSEA & LONDON.

Sharp 210, 1.

107. O Similar, but the hand holding the scales is under the N

℞ Similar, but the downstroke of *B* at the right *projects above* the curve of the letter.

PLATE C, no. 11.

108. O Similar, but the hand holding the scales is under the *space* between the I and N

℞ Similar, but the downstroke of *B does not project* above the curve of the letter.

109. O As last.

℞ Similar, but the *B* at the right is *outlined.* *Halliday,*

SHIP TO LEFT. 1811.

110. O A ship sailing to left, under topsails, PATENT SHEATHING NAIL MANUFACTORY. BRISTOL. The pennant reaches the *centre* of A and only *one* lift to sprit-sail.

℞ HALF PENNY TOKEN in a circle. PAYABLE AT BRISTOL AND LONDON 1811 *Scarcely* any tops to ones in date; the P of PENNY lines just *below* the E in PAYABLE.

Sharp 210, 2.

111. O Similar, but the pennant *barely* reaches the A

℞ Similar, but the P of PENNY lines to the end of L

112. Similar, but the pennant *only* reaches the T There are *two* lifts to sprit-sail, and the ship *shows* its stern.

113. ○ Similar, but the pennant *approaches the* T and follows the circle to A The stern *not seen*.

℞ Similar, but the P of PENNY lines with the *end* of E and the tops of ones in date *slope*.

114. ○ As last.

℞ Similar, but the P of PENNY lines with the *centre* of E

115. ○ Similar, but the pennant reaches the *second limb* of A Only *one* lift to sprit-sail.

℞ Similar, but with *scarcely* any top to ones of date; the top of PENNY lines with the *centre* of L   *Halliday.*

SHIP TO RIGHT.

116. ○ Similar, but the pennant only reaches to the *first limb* of H The ship sailing to the right shows its stern.

℞ HALF PENNY TOKEN in a circle. PAYABLE AT BRISTOL AND LONDON 1811 Ones in date *flat*; the top of PENNY lines *just below* the L in PAYABLE   *Halliday.*

SHIP TO LEFT WITH BOAT AT STERN.

117. ○ A ship under sail to left, with a *boat* at stern; PATENT SHEATHING NAIL MANUFACTORY BRISTOL.

℞ HALF PENNY TOKEN in a circle. PAYABLE AT BRISTOL AND LONDON 1811

1812.

118. ○ A ship under sail with a *boat* at stern, as last.

℞ HALF PENNY TOKEN in a circle. PAYABLE BY S. GUPPY. BRISTOL & LONDON. 1812.   *Halliday.*

FARTHING.

SHIP TO RIGHT.

119. ○ A ship under topsails sailing to the right, the stern not *seen*, in a circle. PATENT SHEATHING NAIL MANUFACTORY BRISTOL

℞ FAR-THING TOKEN in a circle. PAYABLE AT BRISTOL & LONDON 1811.

PLATE C, no. 12.

120. Also in Silver. *R.r.r.*   *Halliday.*

. Mr. Weare, of Weston-super-Mare, has in his collection a Notice which was posted on the hoardings at Bristol during the time when the tokens were in full circulation, and which by his kindness is here copied:—

"Let Trade and Commerce
FLOURISH !
COPPER
TOKENS!!!

"Reports having been industriously circulated in this city, that the currency of COPPER TOKENS has been stopped, which has a tendency greatly to injure the RETAIL TRADERS; THE PUBLIC ARE RESPECTFULLY INFORMED, THAT NO SUCH STOPPAGE HAS TAKEN PLACE, On the contrary, they have free circulation, and the said *Report* is only the result of idle *Chit-Chat*. The Author of this, a tradesman and a Citizen, is convinced, that the greater majority of his *Fellow Citizens* are of his opinion, and would much rather take them than so much bad old copper, now in circulation.

With respect to their not being made payable, he begs leave to observe, *they are far preferable to some* WHITE *ones* for payment, *you have a bit of paper of their own coining* tendered you, *which*, intrinsically, is not worth *half a farthing*, and should you not like that, you must pocket your Tokens, and be off. So much for being made payable ;—but give me the COPPER TOKENS, which are *not made payable*, but are *valuable*, and will pass everywhere.
A TRADESMAN."

Major, Printer, John's Steps.

TAUNTON.

PENNY.

121. ☊ A workman at a forge; TAUNTON PENNY TOKEN

℞ A POUND NOTE FOR 240 TOKENS   Legend, PAYABLE AT MESS$^{RS}_{..}$ COX'S. IRON FOUNDRY.   *P. Wyon.*

PLATE C, no. 13.

WIVELISCOMBE.

THREEPENNY PIECE.

122. ☊ A female seated on a beehive with spear and olive branch; a sheep behind her; a ship in the distance; Ex. 1814 The whole within a circle; THREE PENNY TOKEN +·WIVELISCOMBE +

℞ A POUND NOTE GIVEN + FOR 80 TOKENS + BY JN^O FEATHER STONE   R.   *Halliday.*

Sharp 190, 1.

123. ☊ Similar to last.

℞ A POUND NOTE GIVEN + FOR 80 TOKENS + BY R. NORTH & C^O
R.   *Halliday.*

Sharp 190, 2.

TWOPENNY PIECE.

124. ○ A female seated on a beehive with spear and olive branch; an ox by her side; in a circle, TWO PENNY TOKEN. WIVELISCOMBE.

℞ A POUND NOTE GIVEN. FOR 120 TOKENS BY W. TEMLETT &. J. CLARKE. *R.* *Halliday.*

PLATE I, no. 10.

PENNY.

125. ○ Similar, but ONE PENNY TOKEN. WIVELISCOMBE.

℞ A POUND NOTE GIVEN. FOR 240 TOKENS BY W. TEMLETT. &. J. CLARKE. *R.* *Halliday.*

Sharp 197, 12.

This is one of the exceptions where the legend is made to read intelligibly, by not describing the centre arrangement first.

STAFFORDSHIRE.

BILSTON.

SHILLING.

SILVER.

1. ○ The arms of Stafford; a castle between four lions, passant guardant, and one on the ground; BILSTON SILVER TOKEN ONE SHILLING A circular line above the castle.

℞ PAYABLE BY RUSHBURY AND WOOLLEY 1811 in a circle. ONE POUND NOTE FOR 20 TOKENS *R.r.*

PLATE C, no. 14.

2. ○ Similar, but *without* the circular line above the castle.

℞ Similar to last, but COMMERCIAL CHANGE 1811 inscribed on a garter *added* to the legend. *Halliday.*

Boyne 18.

SIXPENCE.

3. ○ As last, except in size; SIX PENCE
℞ As last, but ONE POUND NOTE FOR 40 TOKENS *Halliday.*

Boyne 8.

Rushbury and Woolley were military ornament manufacturers. Edward Woolley patented an improvement for making screws Nov. 18, 1818.

FAZELEY.

HALF CROWN.

4. ○ Arms of the Harding Family; or, on a bend azure, three martlets, a sinister canton of the second, rose between two fleur-de-lys, within palm branches; FAZELEY SILVER TOKEN MDCCCXII

℞ HALF CROWN TOKEN between four sprigs of palm. PAYABLE BY PEELS HARDING & COM^{PY}. + . + . *R.r.* *Halliday.*

Boyne 75.

The issuers were bankers and cotton spinners. The first Sir Robert Peel, Bart., was a partner in the business of the Tamworth Old Bank. Their London agents were Dorrien, Magens and Mello, who demanded the Mint authorities to strike from their bullion the shilling of 1798.—vide *Grueber, pp.* 149, 858.

SHILLING.

5. ○ Arms of the Harding family; FAZELEY SILVER TOKEN 1ST OCTOBER 1811 *in a* radiated border.

℞ ONE SHILLING within a thick wreath of oak. *R.r.r.*

This is an artist's proof struck in brass, and the only specimen known with SHILLING fully displayed.

STAFFORDSHIRE.

Eleven Acorns.

6. O. Similar to last, but *with* a fine toothed border.

℞. Similar, but ONE SHILL^G within a wreath of oak, *eleven* acorns at the left, *not* counting the one over the tie, the letter H is on the *fourth* centre leaf at the *left*.

7. O. Similar, but PAYABLE BY P. H & C^O FAZELEY SILVER TOKEN 1ST OCTOBER 1811. The left corner of shield is *between* the B and L of PAYABLE

℞. Similar, but a figure 5 is on the *fifth* leaf at the *right*.
Boyne 76.

Ten Acorns.

8. O. Similar, but the *left* corner of the shield is under the *bow* of B in PAYABLE

℞. Similar, but with *ten* acorns at the left.

9. Also in copper. *R.r.*

10. O. Arms as before; FAZELEY SILVER TOKEN 1811 Legend, PAYABLE BY PEEL^S HARDING & C^O.

℞. As last. *Halliday*.
Plate C, no. 15.

Sixpence.

11. O. Arms of the Harding family; FAZELEY SILVER TOKEN 1811 PAYABLE BY PEEL^S HARDING & C^O

℞. 6 PENCE within a wreath; the *centre limb* of the last E in PENCE *is clear* of the top and bottom limbs of that letter. The H and figure 5 *omitted*.
Boyne 78.

12. O. Similar, but the *centre limb touches* the top and bottom limbs of the letter E in PENCE *Halliday*.

STAFFORD.

Shilling.

13. O. A building (The Shire Hall); STAFFORD TOKEN FOR TWELVE PENCE 1811 Tiles are *seen* on the roof; the eaves of the building at the right lines *with* the foot of L - A Staffordshire knot below.

℞. The arms of Stafford; a castle and four lions; *J.C.* under. The *right*-hand corner of tower lines *between* the paws of the lion.
Boyne 207.

14. O. Similar, but the tiles on the roof are *not expressed*, and the eaves lines *between* the E and L

℞. Similar, but the lion's paw *nearly touches* the tower.
Halliday.

COUNTY.

PENNY.

COPPER.

15. O̵ Laureate bust to right (George III) STAFFORDSHIRE PENNY TOKEN The nose of the effigy points to the *first limb* of E in STAFFORDSHIRE.

℞ Female figure seated, holding palm and olive branches, a shield at her side; COMMERCE 1811 The *centre* blade of palm points to the *last* E in COMMERCE The shield is *not* tinted. R. *Halliday.*

Sharp 197, 3.

16. O̵ Similar to last, but the nose lines with the *last limb* of the second R in STAFFORDSHIRE

℞ Similar, but the *centre* palm blade points to the letter C

17. O̵ Similar, but the effigy has an *aquiline* nose.

18. O̵ Similar to last, but with P on the bust; and the nose in line with the *first limb* of the R

℞ Female figure seated, holding palm and olive branches, a shield at her side; COMMERCE 1811 A ship in the distance; there is a P *between* the figure and the shield, which *is tinted.* R.

1814.

19. O̵ Similar to last, but centre leaf of laurel points *between* the R and D whereas before it pointed to the *last limb* of R The P *omitted* from the bust.

℞ Similar, but dated 1814 *No* ship, and the P does *not* appear.

Sharp 197, 4.

NO DATE.

20. O̵ Similar, but the circle of pellets *as in the last omitted.*

℞ Female seated, holding palm branch and cornucopia; a ship in the distance; COMMERCE R. *Patrick.*

Sharp 197, 5.

21. O̵ Bust unlaureated to right (George III); STAFFORDSHIRE PENNY TOKEN Under the bust 1811 the first numeral is over the *centre* of the Y in PENNY

℞ TO FACILITATE TRADE within a wreath of oak; an acorn above T in TO on the *inside* of wreath.

Sharp 197, 1.

22. O̵ Similar, with an acorn above the T and O of TO

23. O̵ Similar, but the first numeral in date is over the *last limb* of the Y A flaw at the *left* of ST in STAFFORDSHIRE

℞ As no. 21. *Turnpenny.*

STAFFORDSHIRE. 121

MULE 1812.

24. ○ Similar to no. 19, bust laureated.

℞ View of mining engine and machinery; PAYABLE AT SCORRIER HOUSE ONE POUND NOTE FOR 240 TOKENS 1812
Halliday and Patrick.
Sharp 197, 6.

MULE, NO DATE.

25. ○ As last.

℞ View of a building; PAYABLE AT THE EXCHANGE BURTON
R.r. *Patrick.*

This building represents the old Royal Exchange, London, which was destroyed by fire in 1838.—*Bazaar Articles.*

1811.

26. ○ Laureate bust to right, date 1811 under. STAFFORDSHIRE ONE PENNY TOKEN

℞ PAYABLE BY H. BAYLIS. BIRMINGHAM. W-HAMPTON. & BILSTON. within a wreath of oak. *P. Wyon.*
Sharp 197, 2.

HALFPENNY.

27. ○ Laureate bust to right; STAFFORDSHIRE HALF-PENNY TOKEN

℞ Female figure seated holding palm and olive branches, a shield at her side. COMMERCE 1814 ℞. *Halliday.*
PLATE C, no. 16.

BILSTON.

From a Silver Medal in the possession of the Author.

TWOPENNY PIECE.

28. ○ View of iron furnaces and engine house PRIEST FIELD FURNACES 1811 T.H on the ground at the *right*; a *small* emission of smoke from the chimney.

℞ TWO PENCE PAYABLE AT BILSTON S. FEREDAY BRADLEY BILSTON & PRIESTFIELD · COLLIERIES & IRON WORKS ·
PLATE C, no. 17.

29. Similar, but the chimney is emitting *dense* smoke, and the T.H is *omitted*. *Halliday.*
Sharp 191, 2.

Sir Edward Thomason, in his Memoirs, p. 45, records that Samuel Fereday was the greatest ironmaster in the world; that he, Thomason, manufactured over two million copper tokens for him; that he employed nearly 5,000 persons, and every Friday, during the period of striking, Fereday sent a carriage to Thomason's works for the tokens with which to pay his numerous workpeople. Fereday resided at Ettingshall Park, and was the principal in the firm of Fereday &* Co., Bankers, Bilston.

30. O Bust, unlaureated, to right, robed (George III) ONE POUND NOTE FOR 120 TOKENS 1811 The shoulder lines *between* O and N in ONE

℞ View of the Exchange; PAYABLE BY RUSHBURY & WOOLLEY BILSTON
Sharp 191, 1.

31. Similar, but *larger* bust, the shoulder lines *with* the O in ONE
Halliday.

PENNY.

32. O Bee hive and bees within a square; ONE POUND NOTE FOR 240 TOKENS · 1813 ·

℞ Three cannon balls within a circle; PAYABLE BY JAMES ATHERTON. BILSTON. *Halliday.*
Sharp 198, 18.

James Atherton was an iron founder, and made cannon balls for the Government.

JOHN OF GAUNT, 1811.

33. O Crowned bust to left of John of Gaunt; ONE POUND NOTE FOR 240 TOKENS 1811 The point of crown lines to the *first* limb of N in NOTE and the figures 240 are the *same size* as the letters in the legend.

℞ A horseman at speed; PAYABLE BY EDWARD BEEBEE BILSTON *No period* after BY or BEEBEE
PLATE C, no. 18.

34. O Similar, but point of the crown lines to the *last* limb of N in NOTE and the 4 is *larger* than the other figures. *R.r.*
℞ As last.

1812.

35. O Similar, but dated 1812.
℞ Similar, but *a period* after BY. and BEEBEE.
Sharp 198, 15.

36. O Similar, but *a period* after TOKENS.
℞ Similar, but *without a period* after BY or BEEBEE *R.r.*
Turnpenny.
Sharp 198, 16.

Edward Beebee carried on business as a stone mason in High Street, Bilston.—*Bazaar Articles.*

STAFFORDSHIRE. 123

IRON WORKS.

37. O View of iron furnaces and engine house, PRIEST FIELD FURNACES 1811 The engine chimney emits only a *small* quantity of smoke.

℞ ONE PENNY PAYABLE AT BILSTON Between sprigs of palm, the monogram 𝒮𝓕 Legend, BRADLEY BILSTON & PRIESTFIELD. COLLIERIES & IRON WORKS.
Sharp 198, 20.

38. O Same as last.

℞ ONE PENNY PAYABLE AT BILSTON S. FEREDAY with a double line beneath. BRADLEY BILSTON & PRIESTFIELD · COLLIERIES & IRON WORKS. The T of AT is over the *centre* of N in BILSTON
Sharp 198, 19.

39. O Similar to last, but the chimney is emitting *more* smoke.

℞ Similar, but the T of AT is over the *last limb* of N in BILSTON
Sharp 198, 22.

40. O As last.

℞ Similar to last, but the I of BILSTON is *under* the Y of PAYABLE *instead* of under the A   R.

41. O Similar to last, the first one of date is *between* the two limbs of R

℞ Similar, but the T of AT is over the *centre* of N and the I of BILSTON is under the *space* between A and Y of PAYABLE

42. O Similar to last, but the chimney emitting *still more* smoke, H on the ground at the left; the first one of date is under the *upright* limb of R

℞ As last.   R.   *Halliday.*

DOUBLE INSCRIPTION, WITH PERIOD AFTER DATE.

43. O ONE PENNY PAYABLE BY in a circle; legend A POUND NOTE FOR 240 TOKENS · The P of PENNY lines to the *centre* of U in POUND and the N in ONE is *under* the E in NOTE

℞ SAMUEL FEREDAY BILSTON 1812. the first one in date is *under* the I and L of BILSTON
Sharp 198, 17.

44. O Similar, but the period under the O is at the *left* of that letter.

℞ Similar, but the first one in date is under the *first limb* of L

45. O Similar, but the P of PENNY lines to the *end* of O. The N in ONE is *under* the T and E of NOTE

℞ Similar, but the B of BILSTON is *under* the F and E *instead* of the F of FEREDAY

46. ⊙ As last.

℞ Similar, but the period is at the *right* of the O in BILSTON

47. ⊙ Similar, but the top of P lines to the *first limb* of U

℞ Similar, but the S in BILSTON is *under* the E in FEREDAY *instead* of at the *left* of that letter.

48. ⊙ Similar, but the N in ONE is under the T in NOTE and there is a *crosslet* to the figure 4

℞ Similar, but the first one of date is under the *first limb* of L and the period is under the *centre* of O in BILSTON   *Halliday.*

NO PERIOD AFTER DATE.

49. ⊙ Similar, but P in PENNY lines *between* the O and U of POUND and the N in ONE is *under* the E in NOTE

℞ Similar, but the period after 1812 *omitted*.

50. ⊙ Similar, but the P lines to the *centre* of U in POUND

℞ Similar, but the A in FEREDAY is *under* the L in SAMUEL whereas previously it was *under* the *space* between the E and L
   Halliday.

S. Fereday, Ettingshall Park, Staffordshire, Ironmaster, was declared bankrupt Feb. 19, 1821.

BUST OF GEORGE III.

51. ⊙ Bust to right, robed, unlaureated (George III); ONE POUND NOTE FOR 240 TOKENS 1811   The nose of the effigy lines to the O in TOKENS

℞ View of a building; PAYABLE BY RUSHBURY & WOOLLEY BILSTON   The *attennæ* or horns of the grasshopper *touch* the *first limb* of the B in RUSHBURY and, BILSTON is in a *straight* line.
   Sharp 198, 13.

52. Similar, but the point of bust is *midway* between the S and date, whereas in the former it is much nearer the *last numeral*.

53. Similar, but the nose *points* to the T in TOKENS

54. Similar, but the horns of the grasshopper *touch* the *last limb* of H in RUSHBURY

55. Similar, but the horns of the grasshopper *touch* the H and B of RUSHBURY   *Halliday.*

DATE ON OBVERSE AND REVERSE.

56. ⊙ Bust to right; ONE POUND NOTE FOR 240 TOKENS 1811

℞ View of a building; the date 1811 under. BILSTON is in a *curved* line. PAYABLE · BY ·· RUSHBURY ·· & · WOOLLEY
   Note the punctuation in the reverse legend.

57. Similar, but the point of bust *near* the S instead of *midway* between that letter and the *last* numeral in date. R.   *Halliday.*

STAFFORDSHIRE.

No Date under Bust.

58. O Bust to right; ONE POUND NOTE FOR 240 TOKENS *No date under the bust.*
℞ As last. *Halliday.*

No Period after BILSTON.

59. O Laureate bust to the right, draped and armoured; ONE PENNY TOKEN 1811
℞ View of a building; PAYABLE AT BILSTON Under the building, ROYAL EXCHANGE The top of the building at the right lines to the *second* limb of A in PAYABLE The summit of the weather vane is seen *above* the grasshopper. R. *Turnpenny.*
Sharp 198, 12.

60. O Bust draped, to the right, *not* laureated; ONE PENNY TOKEN 1811 The last numeral in date *touches* the bust.
℞ Similar, but the grasshopper is *on* the summit of the vane. R. *Halliday.*
Sharp 197, 7.

BUST (ROBED WITH ERMINE).

61. O Similar to last, but the bust is robed with ermine, the letters smaller, and the date quite *clear* of the bust. The nose of the effigy *points* to the N in TOKEN
℞ Similar, but the top of building lines to the *foot* of the Y The final E in EXCHANGE terminates *with* the base line of the building.

62. O Similar, but the nose *points* to the E in TOKEN
℞ Similar, but EXCHANGE extends *beyond* the line of the building; the top of building at the left lines *between* A and Y in PAYABLE

63. O Similar, but the dots on the robe are very *prominent.*
℞ Similar, but the top of building lines to the *foot* of Y

64. O Similar, but the nose of the effigy *points* to the N and the spots on the robe are *small.*
℞ Similar, but the top of building lines *between* the A and, EXCHANGE *does not reach* to the end of the base line of the building.

65. O Similar, but the nose of the effigy *points* to the E
℞ Similar, but the top of building lines to the *last limb* of A The grasshopper *nearly touches* the T in AT and, EXCHANGE *extends* beyond the base line.

66. O Similar, but the nose points between E and N There are pellets on the robe instead of small spots. The figures in date *very large.*

℞ Similar, but the top of the building lines to the *first limb* of A R. *Halliday.*

A Period after BILSTON.

67. O Bust as before, the legend in *smaller* letters; the nose of the effigy *points* to the E The last I in date is under the *centre* of the robe.

℞ Similar, but the top of building at the left lines to the *foot* of the Y and there *is a period* after BILSTON. EXCHANGE terminates *with* the base line.

68. O Similar, but the nose points *between* the E and N and the 8 in date is under the *centre* of the robe; the last numeral is *nearer* the bust.

℞ Similar, but the top of building lines *between* the A and Y The grasshopper in this is *much smaller* than in any others.

69. O Similar, but the nose *points* to the N The second I in date is under the *centre* of the robe.

℞ Similar, but the top of building lines to the *foot* of the Y

70. O Similar, but the *second* and *third* figures of date are under the *centre* of the robe.

℞ Similar, but the top of the building lines to the *first limb* of A and EXCHANGE does *not extend* to the end of the base line.

71. O Similar, but the nose points to the E and the *third* figure of date is under the *centre* of the robe.

℞ Similar, but the top of the building at the left lines *between* the A and Y and EXCHANGE *terminates* with the base line. *Halliday.*

HALFPENNY.

72. O ONE HALF PENNY PAYABLE BY in a circle. A ONE POUND NOTE FOR 480 TOKENS.

℞ SAMUEL FEREDAY BILSTON 1812.

Sharp 319, 2.

73. A Proof with a *broad* toothed border. R. *Halliday.*

PLATE C, no. 19.

BURSLEM.

PENNY.

74. ℴ ONE PENNY TOKEN in a circle. FOR PUBLIC ACCOMMODATION . . * . .

℞ ONE POUND NOTE FOR 240 TOKENS 1813 in a circle. PAYABLE BY I & R RILEY AND MACHIN & C° BURSLEM   *P. Wyon.*
Sharp 198, 3.

John and Richard Riley were earthenware manufacturers, and Machin & Co. colour makers, in Hill Street.

Riley's Semi-China, within a belt and buckle, is found on blue willow pattern.—*Vide Chaffers' Marks and Monograms on Pottery and Porcelain*, 10th ed., 1903, *p.* 630.

BURTON.

PENNY.

75. ℴ View of a building (Bond End Mill); PAYABLE BY JAMES PARDOE BURTON 1814.

℞ ONE PENNY TOKEN in a *thin* wreath of oak and laurel, a border of *pellets.*
Sharp 198, 24.

The issuer was a tape and cotton manufacturer.

76. ℴ As last.

℞ ONE PENNY TOKEN within a *thick* wreath of oak, a *serrated* border. *R.*   *Turnpenny.*

See Sedbury, Gloucestershire, for a similar reverse.

MULES.

77. ℴ As last.

℞ Druid's bust to left; PENNY TOKEN. PURE COPPER PREFERABLE TO PAPER. *R.r.*

78. ℴ View of the Royal Exchange; PAYABLE AT THE EXCHANGE BURTON

℞ As last.   *Turnpenny and Wyon.*
Sharp 199, 25.

79. ℴ As last.

℞ ONE PENNY TOKEN within a thin wreath of oak and laurel. H on the leaf *opposite* N in TOKEN   *R. Turnpenny and Halliday.*

80. ℴ As last.

℞ Prince of Wales' crest, encircled by a coronet, and motto ICH DIEN on a ribbon. TO FACILITATE TRADE . * . Under the plume 1813 *R.*   *Turnpenny and Halliday.*

CHEADLE.

PENNY.

81. O TOKEN 1812 in a circle. CHEADLE COPPER & BRASS COMPANY
. ＊ . The T of TOKEN *lines with* the C in COPPER

℞ ONE PENNY in a circle. PAYABLE IN LONDON CHEADLE AND NEATH · The Y of PENNY lines with the *last limb* of A in AND

82. Similar, but the Y of PENNY lines to the *centre* of N in AND

83. O Similar, but the T of TOKEN is *between* the E and C

℞ Similar, but the Y of PENNY lines *with the first limb* of N in AND
P. Wyon.
Sharp 199, 26.

This famous Company was founded by Patten in 1717. The smelting works were built at Bank Quay, near Warrington, and the Brass Mills erected soon afterwards at Cheadle. The River Churnet supplied the power for the wire mills. The works were subsequently removed to Neath Abbey, South Wales.

DARLASTON.

PENNY.

84. O ONE PENNY PAYABLE BY in a circle. A ONE POUND NOTE FOR 240 TOKENS. The Y of PENNY lines to the figure 2 in 240

℞ JOB WILKES DARLASTON 1812 The ones in date are *curved*. R.

85. Similar, but the Y in PENNY lines to the figure 4 R.
Sharp 199, 27.

86. Similar, but dated 1813 and the ones in date are *straight*. R.
Unknown.
Sharp 199, 28.

These are almost invariably struck over some other token.

Job Wilkes was a gun lock maker in Bilston Street, Darlaston. The house occupied by him when the token was struck is now the "Bradford Arms."

LICHFIELD.

TWOPENCE.

87. O View of a factory and river with trees at the sides ; JOHN HENRICKSON LEMMONSLY MILL NEAR LITCHFIELD (*sic*) ＊ Ex. TWO-PENNY TOKEN On the ground at the right, H

℞ Arms of the city of Lichfield between oak branches crossed beneath a lion's head ; landscape, trees and view of cathedral and castle ; bodies and limbs of three men on the ground, all proper, with crowns and swords dispersed over the field. ONE POUND NOTE FOR 120 TOKENS R.
Halliday.
PLATE D, no. 1.

The issuer resided in Dam Street, in this city.

PENNY.

88. ○ Similar, but ONE-PENNY TOKEN   The H on the ground is omitted.   R.
℞ Similar, but 240 TOKENS   *Halliday.*
Sharp 199, 29.

NEWCASTLE-UNDER-LYME.

89. ○ A bale of cotton inscribed with the initial T within an oval wreath of laurel ; PAYABLE AT THE COTTON WORKS NEWCASTLE. Legend, ONE POUND NOTE FOR 240 TOKENS
℞ ONE PENNY TOKEN in a circle. FOR PUBLIC ACCOMMODATION 1813   *Sheriff.*
Sharp 199, 30.
" Issued by John Harrison Thompson, the proprietor."—*Bazaar Articles.*

PERRY BARR.

90. ○ A wheatsheaf ; PAYABLE BY W^M BOOTH PERRY BARR   The wheatsheaf is under the Y of BY and the ground lines with the P of PAYABLE
℞ PENNY TOKEN in a circle. STAFFORDSHIRE✢1811✢   The ones in date are formed by fine strokes, and there is a *flaw* over the N in TOKEN   *R.r.*   *Patrick.*

PLATE D, no. 2.

" William Booth, 'near to the House of Queslet,' it is said, struck the Perry Barr token as a cover for his forgeries, for which he was found guilty and executed at Stafford on August 15, 1812.

" It may be of interest to know that when Booth was arrested a specimen of this token was found in the farmhouse at Perry Barr, and handed to the late Mr. Hamper, a magistrate of Warwickshire."—*Token Coinage of Warwickshire*, 802.

EXECUTION OF BOOTH FOR FORGING BANK NOTES AT STAFFORD.

" On Sat. Aug. 15, about 12 o'clock, William Booth was brought upon the scaffold to suffer the punishment due to his crimes ; he acknowledged the justice of his sentence. A most distressing occurrence took place at the time of his execution, the rope slipping, he fell to the ground and many people thought he was dead, but the unfortunate man got up and fell on his knees, praying for mercy for his misdeeds. The assistants then prepared the scaffold again, but owing to a mistake the drop remained fast, when Booth gave the signal for it to fall, and it was not until much force had been applied that the drop fell. The number of people who attended was not so numerous as was expected, but all appeared much shocked at the sufferings of the poor malefactor."—*The Star, Aug.* 20, 1812.

91. ○ Similar, but the wheatsheaf is under BY and the ground lines with the P of PERRY
℞ Similar, but the ones in date are formed of *thick* strokes and the *flaw is absent* from over the N in TOKEN   *Unknown.*

A modern copy of good workmanship ; it is described so that collectors may easily identify the genuine token.

POTTERIES.

PENNY.

92. ○ A kiln, at the right a workman laden with pottery; STAF FORDSHIRE POTTERY 1813
℞ ONE PENNY TOKEN in a circle. Legend FOR PUBLIC ACCOM MODATION·· ✶ ·· *R.* *Halliday.*
PLATE D, no. 3.

RUGELEY.

TWOPENCE.

93. ○ A wheel with machinery; DOUBLE BLOWING ENGINES FOR FOUNDRIES MADE BY E· BARKER RUGELY Below, TWO PENNY TOKEN
℞ A hydraulic blowing machine; STREET'S SINGLE PATENT BLOWING ENGINES FOR SMITHS · 1815 *R.r.* *Halliday.*
PLATE D, no. 4.

PENNY.

94. ○ ONE PENNY PAYABLE BY in a circle. ONE POUND NOTE FOR 240 TOKENS✶
℞ EDWARD BARKER RUGELEY *Halliday.*
Sharp 200, 33.

STAFFORD.

SHORT GATEWAY.

95. ○ The arms of the town, a castle and four lions statant gardant; STAFFORD above; 1801 below; the embattlement of the centre tower at the left is under the A and F of STAFFORD The apex of the arch to the doorway reaches to the *eighth* course of the masonry.

℞ The monogram 𝑊 𝐻 A crosslet at each side; above, PENNY Below, a Staffordshire knot in *solid* lines; the end of the tie at·the right is *under* the bow of the knot. *P. Wyon.*
Sharp 200, 35.

E, PAYABLE BY HORTON AND COMPANY.++. *R.*

LONG GATEWAY.

96. ○ Similar to last, but the embattlement of the central tower at the left is under the *first limb* of F and the apex of the arch is built to the *ninth* line of masonry.

℞ Similar to last, but the knot is *outlined* and the end of the tie at the right *intersects* the bow of the knot; from which a flaw extends to the *edge* of the token.
E, As last. *P. Wyon.*
PLATE D, no. 5.

STAFFORDSHIRE.

97. O. Similar, but dated 1803

℞. Similar, but the end of the tie at the right is *over* the bow of the knot, and there is *no flaw* in the die.

E, As last.   *P. Wyon.*

Sharp 200, 37.

The Stafford-knot was a charge on the banner of Sir Henry de Stafford. Horton & Co. were boot manufacturers, one of the principals occupied a high public position in the town.

STAFFORD AND STAFFORDSHIRE.

98. O. ONE PENNY in a circle. STAFFORD & STAFFORDSHIRE *

℞. TOKEN 1811 in a circle. FLINT COPPER COMPANY A rose ornament below. *R.r.*

WALSALL.

THE BEAR AND RAGGED STAFF.

99. O. Bear and ragged staff; PAYABLE BY FLETCHER & SHARRATT The bear's ears are *under* the E in FLETCHER

℞. WALSALL TOKEN ONE PENNY 1811 in a wreath of oak.; the centre acorn has a *long* stem, and an acorn *touches* the W in WALSALL.

Sharp 200, 38.

100. Similar, but the bear's ears are *under* the H

101. Similar, but the acorn is *above* the W in WALSALL

102. Similar, but the centre acorn has a *short stem.*

103. Similar, but the centre acorn has *no stem*, and an acorn *nearly* touches the L in WALSALL whereas in the last it is *distant* from it.

104. O. Similar, but the bear's ears are under the *last limb* of H and the *centre* of E

℞. Similar, but the centre acorn has a *short stem.*

105. Similar, but the ears *point* to the *first limbs* of H and E The centre acorn has *no stem* at the junction of the wreath. *R.*

Turnpenny.

WALSALL CHURCH.

106. O. View of St. Matthew's Church; W T F under. PAYABLE BY FLETCHER & SHARRATT

℞. WALSALL TOKEN ONE PENNY 1811 in a wreath of oak; the *centre* acorn has a *short stem. R.*   *Turnpenny.*

PLATE D, no. 6.

DRUID'S HEAD.

107. ℞ A druid's head; PAYABLE BY JOSEPH PARKER. The hood points to the E in PAYABLE

℞ WALSALL TOKEN ONE PENNY 1811 in a wreath of oak; there are *three* acorns, with *long stems* on the inside of the wreath at the left; the first acorn is *under* the P of PENNY

Sharp 200, 42.

108. ℞ Similar, but the head of the Druid is *shorter*, the hood points to the L in PAYABLE and the first fold of the hood commences under the Y in BY

℞ Similar, but the first acorn is at the *left* of P in PENNY

P. Wyon.

109. ℞ Similar, but there is a *border* to the hood, which points to the E in PAYABLE The first fold commences under the *space* between the Y and J

℞ Similar, but with an acorn on a *short stem* at the *right*, close to the *last* L in WALSALL and the first acorn at the left *turns from* the I in date.

110. ℞ Similar, but the head has a Roman nose, and the first fold of the hood is under the J

℞ Similar, but the first acorn at the left *inclines to* the I in date.

111. ℞ Similar, but the head has a Grecian nose, the hood points to the L and the first fold commences under the Y in BY

℞ As last.

112. ℞ Similar, but the first fold of the hood commences under the B in BY

℞ Similar, but the *centre* acorn *omitted*, and the two inside acorns at the right have *long stems*. R.

113. ℞ Similar, but the head points to the E and the first fold commences under the *space* between Y and J

℞ As last. *Unknown.*

DOUBLE OBVERSE.

114. ℞ Bust and legend as before; the first fold of the hood commences under the Y in BY

℞ Similar to the obverse, but the first fold of the hood commences under BY

This double obverse is in Mr. Norman's cabinet.

The decline of the latter pieces, both in workmanship and specific gravity, seems to intimate that they were forgeries of the time.

Joseph Parker was a locksmith.

STAFFORDSHIRE. 133

HALFPENNY.

115. O Bear and ragged staff; PAYABLE BY FLETCHER & SHARRATT
℞ WALSALL HALFPENNY TOKEN 1811 in a wreath of oak.
Turnpenny.
PLATE D, no. 7.

WEDNESBURY.

PENNY.

116. O Bust to right robed (George III). ONE PENNY TOKEN 1812
℞ View of a building; ROYAL EXCHANGE under. Legend,
FOR PUBLIC ACCOMMODATION *Halliday.*
Sharp 200, 43.

This token was issued by Abel Round, a maltster of Wednesbury.

HALFPENNY.

117. Similar to last, but HALFPENNY TOKEN 1812 *Halliday.*
PLATE D, no. 8.

WEST BROMWICH AND COSELEY.

PENNY.

118. O PENNY TOKEN 1812 in a circle. WEST BROMWICH & COSÉLEY
℞ IN CASH NOTES in a circle. PAYABLE BY JAMES COOKSEY.
Halliday.
Sharp 200, 44.

James Cooksey was a nail manufacturer.

WEST BROMWICH, OLDBURY, TIPTON & BRIERLEY.

PENNY.

119. O PENNY TOKEN 1811 in a circle. WEST-BROMWICH · OLDBURY ·
TIPTON & BRIERLY ✶ The N in TOKEN lines to the *centre* of N in
TIPTON
℞ A POUND NOTE FOR 240 · PAYABLE AT WEST-BROMWICH · BY
W · WHITEHOUSE & C°. The 4 is at the *left* of the N in NOTE
Sharp 201, 45.

120. O Similar, but the N in TOKEN lines to the *centre* of &
℞ As last.

121. O As last.
℞ Similar, but the 4 points to the *right* of O in NOTE

122. O Similar, but the N in TOKEN lines *between* & and the N in
TIPTON
℞ As last. *Halliday.*

Whitehouse & Co. were canal carriers, and their London House was at the Axe, Aldermanbury.

WITHYMOOR.

PENNY.

123. ○ Interior of a forge ; on a label above, WITHYMOOR SCYTHE WORKS   Ex. ONE PENNY 1813. *No brickwork* at the right of the forge.

℞ Agricultural tools in a circle ; crossed spades under ; ONE POUND NOTE FOR 240 TOKENS · PAYABLE BY JA͇S GRIFFIN & SON͇S   The B in BY is under the 2

PLATE D, no. 9.

124. ○ Similar to last, but dated 1814   There *is brickwork* at the right of the forge.

℞ Similar, but the B in BY is *under* the 4   *Sherriff*.

Sharp 201, 47.

WOLVERHAMPTON.

There were no issuers of Nineteenth Century Tokens in this town. They were extensively circulated there. Fereday's and Rushbury & Wooley's, being the principal.

"At a meeting of the inhabitants of Wolverhampton, on Thursday last, they resolved —'That the great influx of silver and copper tokens, issued by individuals, companies and corporations, is becoming a serious public grievance,' and they agree with each other to discontinue the receiving of them in payment."—*Worcester Herald, Jan.* 1812.

From an Original Pen and Ink Sketch in the possession of Wm. Norman.

SUFFOLK.

IPSWICH.

SHILLING.

SILVER.

1. O The Prince of Wales's plume and motto; ICH DIEN A drum, inscribed 𝒢 𝓡 (George the King) and implements of war; I D on the ground.

℞ 1811 IPSWICH SHILLING SILVER TOKEN H.M in a circle. Legend, A ONE POUND NOTE WILL BE PAID FOR 20 OF THESE BY W ADAMS. The S of SHILLING *lines* with the E of NOTE *R.r.*
Boyne 104.

2. O As last.

℞ Similar, but the s *lines* with the o of NOTE and a *cross* after ADAMS+ *R.r.* *Davies.*
Webster Adams was a pipe-maker in Currer's Lane.

3. O As last.

℞ SILVER TOKEN TO CONVENIENCE THE ARMY AND THE PUBLIC *Value* ONE SHILLING Scrolls at the *sides* of TO and AND *R. Davies.*

4. O The arms of Ipswich, a lion rampant gardant, three demi-hulks in a garter inscribed, DOLLAR · SILVER · Crest a demi-lion; IPSWICH TOKEN FOR XII PENCE

℞ PAYABLE BY W· ADAMS 1812 in a wreath of oak; H M under.
Boyne 105.

5. Also in Copper. *R.r,* *Halliday.*
See Hampshire, no. 34.

6. O The same as last.

℞ PAYABLE AT CLAYTON AND HYDE'S in a circle. ACCOMMODATION CHANGE 1811 *R.r.* *Halliday.*
Boyne 106.

This reverse is also used for a Shoreham token.

NEEDHAM MARKET.

SHILLING.

7. O SILVER TOKEN STAMP OFFICE NEEDHAM 1811 H·M in a circle. Legend, A ONE POUND NOTE WILL BE PAID FOR 20 OF THESE BY J. STEWARD×

℞ ONE SHILLING VALUE H·M in a wreath of oak. ISSUED BY ROYAL LICENCE *R.r.* *Halliday.*
Boyne 157.

This reverse is also used for a Holbeach and a Lynn token.

WOODBRIDGE.

EIGHTEENPENCE.

8. ○ Figure of Justice standing; FOR THE ACCOMMODATION OF TRADE 1811
℞ SILVER TOKEN VALUE 1s. 6d. H M in a wreath of oak. PAYABLE AT STUDD & MATHEWS'S WOODBRIDGE · + ·

PLATE L, NO. 20.

9. Also in copper. *R.r.* *Halliday.*

Boyne 226.

The issuers were grocers and drapers.

SHILLING.

10. ○ VALUE ONE SHILLING PAYABLE AT W SIZERS WOODBRIDGE in a circle.
℞ WOODBRIDGE SILVER TOKEN 1811 in a circle. Legend, FOR THE ACCOMMODATION · OF · TRADE *R.* *Wyon.*

Boyne 225.

William Sizer, who issued the token, was a grocer and excise officer.

BENHALL.

COPPER.

HALFPENNY.

11. ○ IOHN SHUCKFORD WADE in a circle.
℞ BENHALL SUFFOLK 1765. in a circle. *R.* *Halliday.*

Golding 91, 1.

"Mr. Wade had a fine estate at Benhall; he was a large farmer and osier grower. Mr. Wade was also a shipowner at Aldeburgh, where he was buried 4. April, 1839. The date on the token is the year of his birth.

The token was probably issued for a halfpenny, for paying the wages of his Work people, about the year 1811, as it is very similar to the pieces struck at that time."—*Golding's Coinage of Suffolk.*

J. S. Wade, the issuer, "was awarded a prize for planting fifteen acres with upwards of 12,000 sets of osiers per acre, which it was certified on reputable authority are now in a thriving state and fit for basket making."—*Monthly Magazine, April* 1, 1807.

GLEMHAM.

12. ○ GLEMHAM SUFFOLK 1732 in a circle.
℞ 1812 FRANCIS WADE · * · in a circle. *R.* *Halliday.*

PLATE J, NO. 19.

The date on this hitherto unpublished piece confirms Mr. Golding's assumption as to the date of the issue of the younger brother John's token.

SUFFOLK.

HOXNE.

TWOPENCE.

13. ☾ A trooper leaning at the side of his horse, in a circle. LOYAL YEOMAN PRO REGE LEGE ET PATRIA (For King, Law and Country).
℞ I PROMISE TO PAY TO THE HON:^BLE GEO: YEOMAN OR BEARER THE SUM OF TWO-PENCE ON THE PERFECT ESTABLISHMENT OF PEACE & UNANIMITY FOR KING LORDS. AND COMMONS. John Bull
Outer legend, OLD ENGLAND. 2: MARCH 1798. ENT.^D JA.^S LOYAL.
R.r.r. *Wyon.*

Atkins 360, 1.

This piece was engraved by the same artist as the Penny and Halfpenny of Hoxne, the motto of which is PRO ARIS ET FOCIS (for our altars and our homes), indicating a different school of thought prevalent in the stormy days of the French revolutionary period. The tokens were all made at Peter Kempson's workshop, Birmingham.

LOWESTOFT.

PENNY.

14. ☾ Female seated on a rock, resting her arm on an anchor, a ship in the distance; SUCCESS TO THE LOWESTOFT FISHERIES 1811
℞ ONE PENNY TOKEN   Legend, NON SIBI SED PATRIÆ. (Not for himself, but for his country). PAYABLE AT I CHASTON'S LOWESTOFT.
P. Wyon.

Sharp 201, 1.

15. ☾ The same as last.
℞ Similar, but an inner circle added; a scroll ornament above. ONE PENNY TOKEN   A sprig of laurel below.   *P. Wyon.*

PLATE D, no. 10.

John Chaston was a draper and bank agent.

SURREY.

GODALMING.

SHILLING.

SILVER.
1. O- In the centre XII   Legend, GODALMING * TOKEN · *
℞ A woolsack, inscribed 1811   Legend, PRO BONO * PUBLICO. *
(For the Public good). *R.r.r.*
PLATE L, no. 21.

SIXPENCE.

2. Similar to last, except in size and value, VI   *R.r.r.   Unknown.*
The issuers of these tokens were probably Moline & Co., bankers.

RIPLEY.

SIXPENCE.

3. O- In script characters *JCS*   Legend, RIPLEY SIXPENCE
℞ 6   No inner circle. . .   *Unknown.*
This is in tin.
In Mr. Bowles' cabinet.

WEYBRIDGE.

SHILLING.

4. O- A barrel in a circle; I BUNN & C^{O} WEYBRIDGE IRON WORKS.
℞ ONE SHILLING TOKEN   On a band azure, DOWGATE WHARF
LICENSED   *P. Wyon.*
PLATE D, no. 11.

PENNY.

COPPER.
5. O- View of mills and water wheel; WEYBRIDGE MILLS.
℞ ONE PENNY PAYABLE AT WEYBRIDGE I BUNN & C^{O} 1812   Legend,
HOOP & IRON WAREHOUSE. DOWGATE WHARF.   *P. Wyon.*
PLATE D, no. 12.
The issuers were Bunn & Johnson of Dowgate Wharf, Upper Thames Street.

LONDON ROAD.

FARTHING.

6. O- Laureated head to right (George IV); I KING· LONDON ROAD
1821
℞ Two pipes in saltire; TOBACCONIST 1821   *Halliday.*
Waters 49.
Issued by John King, 10, London Road, Southwark.

RICHMOND.

FARTHING.

7. O INNOCENT VIRTUOSO RICHMOND SURREY Ornaments under RICHMOND and above SURREY
℞ TOBACCONIST & PURVEYOR * OF FOREIGN SNUFFS 1821
Unknown.

Waters 53.

Robert Innocent, George Street, Richmond, was also a dealer in curios.

WALWORTH.

FARTHING.

8. O JAMES BEAN 1814 TOBACCONIST NO 1 • BLACK PRINCE ROW WALWORTH ROAD SURRY (*sic*)
℞ GENUINE TOBACCO & SNUFF WHOLESALE & RETAIL *R.*
Unknown.

Waters 47.

Black Prince Row was on the left side at the commencement of the Walworth Road, opposite the famous Elephant and Castle. There is still a Black Prince Court in the immediate neighbourhood.

SUSSEX.

BRIGHTON.

SHILLING.

SILVER.

1. ☦ SILVER TOKEN J· B PHILLIPSON CHEMIST BRIGHTON with various ornaments, within a wreath of olive.

℞ ONE SHILLING PAYABLE BY R· PHILLIPSON DRUGGIST CHICHESTER with various ornaments, within a wreath of olive. *R.* *Halliday.*

Boyne 20.

J. Bradshaw Phillipson conducted the business at Brighton, and his brother, Robert, at Chichester.

CHICHESTER.

CROWN.

2. ☦ Two hands clenched, UNION TOKEN FIVE SHILLINGS MDCCCXI The final s of SHILLINGS is the *same size* as the other letters.

℞ PAYABLE AT H^y COMPER'S OR B· CHARGES CHICHESTER within a wreath of oak, a Staffordshire knot between the *fifth* and *sixth* lines; the R of CHICHESTER is *between* E and S of CHARGES *R.r.*

3. ☦ Similar to last, but the final s of SHILLING^s is *smaller.*

℞ Similar, but the R is *under* the s of CHARGES *R.r.* *Halliday.*

Henry Comper was a draper, and Benjamin Charge a harness maker.

HALF CROWN.

4. ☦ Similar to last, but value 2 SHILL & 6^D.

℞ Similar to last, but reads PAYABLE AT H^y. COMPER'S OR B. CHARGE'S CHICHESTER The top of the small Y in H^y is *above* the final limb of H *R.r.*

Boyne 51.

5. ☦ As last.

℞ Similar, but the top of the small Y is *level with* the final limb of H *R.r.* *Halliday.*

PLATE L, no. 22.

ONE SHILLING.

6. Similar, but reads ONE SHILLING No *wreath* on the reverse. *R.* *Halliday.*

PLATE D, no. 13.

7. ☦ A view of the Market Cross; CHICHESTER ACCOMMODATION XII PENCE The base line of the building commences *at* the X of XII

℞ PAYABLE AT B & J. CAFFIN'S J. REDMAN'S W. HALSTEAD'S AND C. SHIPHAM'S 1811

PLATE J, no. 20.

8. Similar, but the base line commences *near* to the *first* C in CHICHESTER *R.*   *Unknown.*

9. O Arms, a triple towered castle, over the entrance a shield guttu-de-poix in chief, indented a lion passant gardant; CHICHESTER SILVER TOKEN · 1811

℞ PAYABLE BY T· DALLY & C⁰ 1$\underline{S}$ in a circle. Legend, COMMERCIAL * CHANGE * inscribed on a band, *vert.*   *P. Wyon.*

PLATE E, no. 1.

10. O The same as last.

℞ XII PENCE in the centre. Legend, COMMERCIAL CHANGE *R.*

P. Wyon

Boyne 55.

Thomas Dally & Co. were drapers in East Street, who, in 1794, issued a halfpenny token: obverse, bust, of Queen Elizabeth; reverse, the Chichester cross. On the edge is PAYABLE AT DALLYS CHICHESTER × It was the work of Thomas Wyon, and 5 cwt. were struck.—*Vide Atkins* 197, 14.

SIXPENCE.

11. Hands in grip, etc. Similar to the shilling no. 6, excepting in size and value; SIX PENCE *R.*   *Halliday.*

Boyne 53.

12. A castle, etc. Similar to the shilling no. 9, excepting in size and value. 6$\underline{D}$ *P. Wyon.*

Boyne 56.

ROWFANT.

SHILLING.

13. O A farmer with horses ploughing; HENRY HUNT ROWFANT HOUSE SUSSEX On the ground at the right Y & D

℞ ONE SHILLING 1811 in a circle. Legend, TOKEN IN EXCHANGE FOR · LABOUR · *R.r.*   *Halliday.*

PLATE L, no. 23.

Henry Hunt was a farmer in the Parish of Worth, one mile from Rowfant.

SHOREHAM.

SHILLING.

14. O View of a church with tower and weather vane; SHOREHAM · TOKEN XII · PENCE

℞ PAYABLE AT CLAYTON AND HIDE'S in a circle. Legend, ACCOMMODATION CHANGE 1811 *R.r.*

PLATE L, no. 24.

15. Similar view, but *with* an *inner circle added;* legend, etc., as before, but reads PENSE (*sic*). *R.r.*

PLATE L, no. 25.

This reverse also occurs on an Ipswich token.

Thomas Clayton and John Hyde were grocers at Shoreham.

STEYNING.

SHILLING.

16. O SILVER SHILLING TOKEN PAYABLE AT S GATEIS OR I CHEESMANS STEYNING SUSSEX in a circle. Legend, ISSUED BY ROYAL LICENCE FOR THE CONVENIENCE OF TRADE · 1811

℞ A beehive and bees, within a hop and barley wreath. H· M under the hive. *R.*

Boyne 211.

17. Similar, but the *first* issuer's name GATE'S (*sic*) *instead* of GATEIS *R.r.* *Halliday.*

Samuel Gateis kept the Three Tuns Inn, and John Cheesman was a draper. These tradesmen issued the token jointly.

From a unique tinted Print in the possession of the Author.

WARWICKSHIRE.

BEDWORTH.

SHILLING.

SILVER.

1. ☻ A crest ; out of crescent two dragons' heads addorsed ; FOR THE CONVENIENCE OF CHANGE· ISSUED OCT^R 25· 1811·
   ℞ ONE SHILLING TOKEN PAYABLE AT BEDWORTH-MILL ✶ *Wyon.*

PLATE K, no. 12.

Bedworth Mill is one of the oldest in the county, and is now used as a silk mill. It is at present in the occupation of Mr. A. E. Jagger.

Henry Poynty Lane, the issuer of the token, carried on business as a wool comber, or "garsy comber." The motive power was obtained from the finest water wheel of its day, which stands in its original position, although in a somewhat dilapidated state. The crest of Henry Poynty Lane was two eagles' heads addorsed, issuant from a crescent.

BIRMINGHAM.

TWO SHILLINGS AND SIXPENCE.

THE OVERSEERS.

2. ☻ West view of a building; BIRMINGHAM TOKEN Ex. 2s 6D MDCCCXI There is a *side wicket* in addition to the central entrance.

℞ The arms of Birmingham; quarterly first, and fourth azure, a bend of nine lozenges or, second and third per pale indented, gules. ONE POUND NOTE FOR EIGHT TOKENS PAYABLE AT THE WORKHOUSE *R.r.r.*   *Wyon.*

PLATE D, no. 14.

It is said that a variety of this piece exists where the value 2s. 6D. is above the building, divided by the tower. At this period Birmingham was much inconvenienced for the want of silver coin, as will be seen from the efforts of the overseers.

"A Deputation of the Overseers of Birmingham waited upon the Chancellor of the Exchequer (Spencer Perceval) a few days since, and having represented the extreme distress of the town for the want of small change, obtained three thousand pounds in dollars, which arrived, and a further sum of £6000, in 3s. and 1/6 pieces is expected."—*Star Newspaper, July* 11*th*, 1811.

WRIGHT'S.

3. ☻ A Chinaman, in his hand a palm branch, standing between a canister, vase, and a chest labelled FINE TEA All surrounded by a band inscribed TWO SHILLINGS AND SIXPENCE· Legend, PAYABLE BY EDWARD WRIGHT BIRMINGHAM

℞ Shield of arms. WARWICKSHIRE SILVER TOKEN POUND NOTE FOR EIGHT 1811 *R.r.r.*

Boyne 23.

4. ℞ As last.

℞ As last, but the P in POUND is *between* the limbs of the R in WARWICK whereas in the former it is *under* the last limb of that letter. *R.r.r.* *Halliday.*

PLATE L, no. 26.

The arms are those of the de Birminghams, who were lords of the manor.

Edward Wright carried on business as a mercer and a grocer at 33, Bull Street, the corner of the Minories.

THE OVERSEERS.

SHILLING, 1811.

5. ℞ West view of a building. BIRMINGHAM TOKEN ONE SHILLING Under the building 1811 The eaves of the building at the left lines *between* B and I in BIRMINGHAM and the I in date is *over* the S in SHILLING

℞ The arms of Birmingham. ONE POUND NOTE FOR 20 TOKENS PAYABLE AT THE WORKHOUSE The centre bar of shield at the right lines to the *space* between S and E in WORKHOUSE

Boyne 21.

6. ℞ As last.

℞ As last, but the centre bar lines to *centre* of E in WORKHOUSE

7. ℞ As last, but the eaves *opposite* to I in BIRMINGHAM and the first numeral in date is over the S and H in SHILLING

℞ As last, but the bar in centre of shield lines *above* the E

8. ℞ As last.

℞ Similar, but the bar lines to the *centre* of E

9. ℞ Similar, but eaves lines to the bow of B The first numeral of date is at the *left* of S

℞ Similar, but the centre bar is in line with the *first* limb of E

10. ℞ As last.

℞ Similar, but the bar lines to the *terminal* of E

11. ℞ Similar, but the eaves *opposite* to I in BIRMINGHAM and the upright *rabbets* in window are *omitted.*

℞ Similar, but the bar lines to *centre* of E

12. ℞ As last.

℞ Similar, but centre bar lines to *terminal* of E   *Wyon.*

13. ℞ Similar, but the eaves opposite to the space *between* B and I of BIRMINGHAM The first numeral in date is at the *left* of S in SHILLING The vane is *without its summit.*

℞ Similar, but the bar lines to the *centre* of E   *R.*

WARWICKSHIRE.

14. O Similar, but the eaves opposite the I The N in TOKEN *nearly touches* the wall, and the *first numeral* in date is over the S in SHILLING There are *no upright rabbets* to the windows.
℞ Similar, but *without* the horizontal centre bar. *Unknown.*

<small>The two last are in copper, and forgeries of the time. Both are rare, the last especially so.</small>

1812.

15. O Similar to the preceding, but *without the wicket* at the left, and dated 1812 The pavement is *longer* than the wall.
℞ Similar to the preceding, but the centre bar of shield lines with the *first limb* of E

16. Similar, but the centre bar of shield lines to the *centre* of E

17. O Similar, but the pavement is *shorter* than the wall.
℞ As last. *Willets.*

SIXPENCE, 1811.

18. O Similar to last, but dated 1811 and the *wicket* is at the left, as on the shillings of this date.
℞ Similar to preceding, but ONE POUND NOTE FOR 40 TOKENS The centre bar lines with the *first limb* of E *Wyon.*

<small>In Mr. Bowles' cabinet.</small>

1812.

19. O Similar, but dated 1812 and the wicket *omitted*.
℞ As last.

<small>Boyne 22.</small>

20. O As last.
℞ Similar, but line of shield to *centre* of E R. *Willets.*

<small>PLATE L, no. 27.</small>

WILLEY.

THREE SHILLINGS AND SIXPENCE.

21. O Bust to right, IOHN WILKINSON IRON MASTER ·
℞ A two-mast barge under sail FINE SILVER 1788 WILLEY Ė, SNEDSHILL BERSHAM BRADLEY R.

<small>PLATE L, no. 11.</small>

22. Also a proof in copper. *R.r.r.*

<small>This is in the British Museum.</small>

23. As last, but edge PAYABLE IN ANGLESEA· LONDON OR LIVERPOOL· X· *R.r.r.* *Hancock.*

This piece was current for three shillings and sixpence. Pye says only 100 were struck.
Mr. A. N. Palmer, in an excellent little work on "John Wilkinson and the old Bersham Iron Works," illustrates a one guinea Brymbo Iron Works Note, issued in 1814, with the promissory of the Trustees of the late John Wilkinson. The halfpenny tokens of this celebrated ironmaster had a very extensive circulation in Wales, Staffordshire and Warwickshire. Many tons of them were made at Soho. The varieties of die are very numerous.
John Wilkinson died at Hadley, Shropshire, on July 14th, 1808, aged 80 years.

TWO SHILLINGS AND SIXPENCE.

COPPER.

24. O· A female seated, her right hand extending *alms* to an old man, her left supports a child kneeling; a boy is *at the side* of the man.

℞ In script characters *BWH* (Birmingham Workhouse) above the monogram 1788 Legend, TWO SHILLINGS AND SIXPENCE·
Dixon.

Boyne 21.
See Countermarked Section no. 43.

TWO SHILLINGS.

25. The same as last, but AND SIXPENCE partly obliterated by a puncheon.

These pieces are occasionally met with, and there can be no doubt but what they were altered by order to pass for two shillings.

ONE SHILLING.

26. O· A beehive and bees. INDUSTRY HAS ITS SURE REWARD
℞ 1799   1·S *R.r.* *Wyon.*

Atkins 202, 4.

These were the earliest tokens issued by the overseers of the poor of Birmingham, and although in copper were circulated and honoured at their face value.
Boyne and other authors have been under the impression that the Two Shillings and Sixpence existed in Silver and Brass, but this is an error, as some were heavily Silver plated and Copper gilt.
See also Warwickshire Countermarks for other Workhouse Tokens.
The overseers, in 1808, also issued paper money for Five Pounds, One Pound, Five Shillings and Two Shillings and Sixpence. The author has in his possession (formerly the property of R. L. Grew) an original Workhouse Note for Five Shillings in leather, signed T. Saddington and Jas. Welch. The notes differ from other paper money, as they are mostly issued on "Account of the Town" or "Parish" of Birmingham; clearly indicating that the Overseers, at that time, provided, at least, a part of the currency.

COUNTY.

PENNY.

27. O· Laureated bust (George III) to right. WARWICKSHIRE 1813
℞ Britannia seated on a rock to left, a spear in her left hand, in her right a laurel branch; the Union shield at her side. ONE PENNY TOKEN *R.* *Halliday.*

Sharp 201, 1.

From the Original Copper-plate in the possession of the Author.

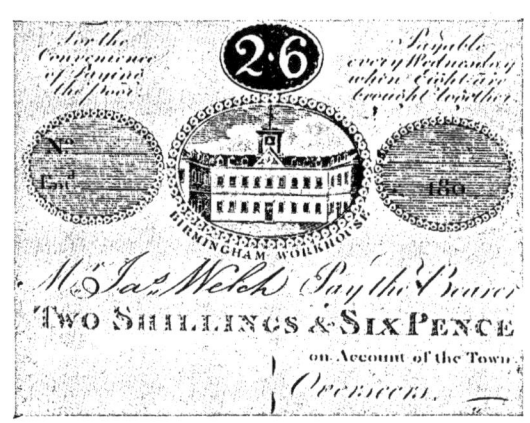

The Birmingham Overseers.
SIXPENCE.

28. ☉ West view of a building, showing centre tower and weather vane. Legend, BIRMINGHAM SIX PENCE 1813 On the pavement w There is *no side wicket*.

℞ The arms of Birmingham. Legend, ONE POUND NOTE FOR 40 TOKENS PAYABLE AT THE WORKHOUSE (*Size M.* 13¾). *R.r.r.*
PLATE D, no. 15. *Willets.*

The specific gravity of this token varies slightly. The author has weighed, except one, all the known pieces: the lightest was 5 ozs. 3 dwts., and the heaviest 5 ozs. 7 dwts. The diameter is Mionnet 13¾ in all cases.

There are seven known specimens. Recently one was bequeathed to the Birmingham Museum; until which it was believed that only six were struck. This is the only Nineteenth Century Sixpenny token in copper containing equivalent metal value. The Birmingham overseers, at a time when copper was comparatively cheap and silver dear, thought by this means a currency could be circulated on economical lines, but its excessive weight was an insurmountable obstacle.

29. A copy of last without the w on the pavement.
weight 4 *ozs.* 8½ *dwts.* (*M.* 13).
30. The same on a thin flan, but with a fine corded rim.
weight 1 *oz.* 1½ *dwts.*
31. The same in gold. *weight* 1 *oz.* 5½ *dwts.*
32. The same in silver. *weight* 5 *ozs.* 7½ *dwts.*
33. The same in silver on a thin flan. *weight* 1 *oz.* 5½ *dwts.*
Unknown.

Of these copies, there were six perfect specimens struck as 29; a similar number, on a thin flan as 30; one example in gold as 31; and one each as 32 and 33 in silver. The dies have been destroyed.

THREEPENNY PIECE.

34. ☉ West view of the Workhouse. BIRMINGHAM THREE PENCE 1813 The 1 in date is over the *space* between the two last letters in THREE and there is a w on the pavement, but no *side wicket*.

℞ Arms as before. ONE POUND NOTE FOR 80 TOKENS PAYABLE AT THE WORKHOUSE The second O in WORKHOUSE is over the O in TOKENS

Sharp 190, 1.

35. O. Similar to last, but the first numeral of date is over the *first* E in THREE

℞ Similar, but the second O in WORKHOUSE is over the K in TOKENS *R.r.* *Willets.*

"The old workhouse was erected in 1733; enlarged 1766, and further extended in 1779. It stood in Lichfield Street, just below the Assize Courts, and was demolished in 1853."— *Token Coinage of Warwickshire.*

PENNY.
1811.

36. O. West view of the Workhouse showing central entrance and *side wicket.* BIRMINGHAM above, 1811 below.

℞ The arms of Birmingham. Legend ONE PENNY TOKEN *R.r.*
Wyon.

PLATE E, no. 2.
This is a pattern penny, and is found with milled and plain edges.

1812.

37. O. A larger view of the same building *without* the side *wicket*, W on the pavement. BIRMINGHAM ONE PENNY Under the building 1812 The *summit* of the weather vane is under the *first* limb of N in BIRMINGHAM

℞ The arms of Birmingham. ONE POUND NOTE PAYABLE AT THE WORKHOUSE FOR 240 TOKENS. The second A in PAYABLE is under the O of POUND and the 4 is at the *left* of the *first* O of WORK HOUSE

Sharp 202, 4.

38. Similar to last, but the A is under the *space* between the O and U The 4 is under the *centre* of the W in WORKHOUSE *R.*

39. O. Similar to last, but the *summit* of the vane is under the *centre* of the N in BIRMINGHAM

℞ Similar to last, but the centre of shield is above the space between R and K in WORKHOUSE Prior to this it is *over* the R

40. O. As last.

℞ Similar, but the A is under the O in POUND The *centre* of shield is over the R The 4 under the *space* between the W and O in WORKHOUSE *R.*

41. Similar, but the 4 is under the commencement of the *first* O in WORKHOUSE *Willets.*

1813.

42. O. Similar, but dated 1813 The summit of the vane is under the *first limb* of N and the W on the pavement is *omitted.*

℞ Similar to last, but the H in THE is over the O in FOR

Sharp 202, 6.

43. O Similar, but the summit of vane is under the *centre* of N
℞ Similar, but the 4 is *under* the W and the H in THE is over R in FOR *Willets.*

1814.

44. O Similar, but dated 1814 The W *again* on the pavement.
℞ Similar, but the H in THE is over O in FOR
Sharp. 202, 7.

45. O As last.
℞ Similar, but the H in THE is over O *and* R in FOR   *R.r.*
Willets.

GIBSON.

46. O View of the Mills (metal rolling and wire drawing). *Ex*, 1812.
℞ THOMAS GIBSON BRADFORD S? MILLS BIRMINGHAM Legend, A POUND NOTE FOR 240 TOKENS ·· ✶ ··   *Halliday.*
PLATE E, no. 3.

These works still exist as metal making and rolling mills, Cooper, Goode & Company, Limited, are the occupiers.

THOMASON.

47. O Bust to left (Thomason) within a wreath of oak.
℞ TOKEN FOR ONE PENNY 1811 The top of the ones in date are *flat. R.r.*
Sharp 206, 18.

48. O Similar to last, but the tops of the ones *slope. R.r. Halliday.*
PLATE E, no. 4.

This bust, Sharp describes as that of an "eminent Birmingham manufacturer and distinguished patron of the arts."

"It is believed to be that of the late Mr. Boulton, son of Matthew Boulton, founder of the Soho Mint."—*Note by Benjamin Nightingale, of Addenda, to Sharp.*

Nightingale fell into an excusable error as Matthew Boulton and Sir Edward Thomason were both regarded as "distinguished patrons of the arts." In his Memoirs, p. 45 (1811, the date of the token) Sir Edward says : "I remember presenting to many gentlemen, who were then collectors of tokens, one of each of those which I executed as they came out ; among the rest, to my esteemed friend, John Johnstone, M.D., and received from him the following note :—

"Dr. John Johnstone begs that Mr. Thomason will accept his thanks for his obliging and handsome present of a set of tokens, which he values highly as a specimen of the ingenuity of one of his townsmen, and the more as containing a very *good likeness on one of the tokens of Mr. Thomason himself.**—*Temple Row, Dec.* 4, 1811."

Sir Edward died on the 29th ult., at his residence in Warwick, in the 80th year of his age, deservedly and deeply lamented. He was an eminent medallist and manufacturer of bronzes at Birmingham, and received the honour of Knighthood, 27th June, 1832, for being instrumental in improving the Arts and Manufactures of England. He was likewise a Knight of the Red Eagle of Prussia, of Francis I, of Merit, of the Order of the Lion of the Netherlands, of Isabel the Catholic of Spain, of the Sun and Lion of Persia, etc., and acted for upwards of twenty years as Vice-Consul for seven of the Continental Powers. His name is known in literature by his "Autobiography during half a century."

Sir Edward was married to a daughter of Samuel Glover, Esq., of Abercarne.—*The Illustrated London News, June 9th,* 1849.

* The italics are my own.—W. J. D.

BIRMINGHAM AND NEATH.

Tops of Ones slope.

49. O. A crown in a circle. BIRMINGHAM AND NEATH · 1811 · The tops of the ones *slope* a little.

℞. ONE PENNY in a circle. CROWN COPPER COMPANY · +‡+ · The top of P in PENNY is above the *last limb* of W in CROWN

Sharp 202, 15.

Flat topped Ones in date.

50. O. Similar, but the tops of the ones in date are *flat*.

℞. Similar, but the P of PENNY lines with the *centre* of W

51. Similar, but the P lines with the *first limb* of W

52. Similar to last, but the *centre* jewel on the band of the crown is *diamond* shaped, whereas in all others it is *oblong*. R.

53. O. Similar, but the cross does *not touch* the orb, the centre jewel as in no. 49.

℞. Similar, but the top of P lines to the *space between* W and N in CROWN.

Tops of Ones slope.

54. O. Similar, but the tops of ones *slope*.

℞. Similar, but top of PENNY lines to *centre* of W R.

55. Similar, but the top of PENNY lines to *last limb* of W Halliday.

The Crown Copper Company established copper smelting works at Neath in 1803. The offices were in the Minories, and subsequently at 36, Cannon Street, Birmingham.

Risca payable in Birmingham.

56. O. Range of furnaces, the smoke emitting to *right* from *eleven* chimneys. RISCA above; COPPER WORKS below. Under the furnaces 1811

℞. ONE PENNY TOKEN in a circle. BIRMINGHAM · UNION COPPER COMPANY · *R.r.r.* *Halliday.*

57. O. Range of furnaces as before, dense smoke emitting from *ten* chimneys to *left*; under 1811 in a circle. RISCA ✻ UNION COPPER COMPANY ✻

℞. ONE PENNY TOKEN in a circle. PAYABLE IN BIRMINGHAM ·· ⁒ ··

Sharp 202, 10.

58. Similar to last, but smoke not so *dense* from the chimneys; a *flaw* under the I of RISCA and at the *end* of building opposite the Y will identify this piece.

59. Similar to last, but much *less* smoke and *without* the *flaws*.

SQUARE CUFFS.

60. O- Hands clenched, 1811 under in a circle; a line of pellets above the hands. Legend, BIRMINGHAM AND RISCA ✶ COPPER COM PANY ✶ The corner of the cuff points to the R in RISCA and the cuffs are *square*.
℞ ONE PENNY TOKEN in a circle. Legend, PAYABLE IN BIRMING HAM ·· ⸪ ·· *Halliday.*

Sharp 202, 8.

PAYABLE IN CASH NOTES.

61. O- Similar to last, but the corner of cuff points to the S in RISCA
℞ ONE PENNY TOKEN in a circle. PAYABLE AT BIRMINGHAM · IN CASH NOTES · The top of PENNY lines with the *centre* of the *first* A in PAYABLE

Sharp 202, 9.

62. Similar, but the P of PENNY lines to the *foot* of Y

63. O- Similar, but the corner of cuff at the left points *to* the I in RISCA R.
℞ As last.

ROUND CUFFS.

64. O- Similar, but the cuffs are *round*.
℞ As last.

"In consequence of the commercial success of the Copper Companies, a new one was formed under the style of the Birmingham and Risca Union Copper Company. Their smelting works were erected near Newport, Mons. Competition consequently became very keen, which led to a trade arrangement by which the Union Company was dissolved."
—*Modern Birmingham, p.* 46, *by Charles Pye,* 1818.

UNION COPPER COMPANY.

FLAT TOPPED ONES.

65. O- Hands clenched; an ornament above, and 1812 below, in a circle. Legend, UNION COPPER COMPANY · BIRMINGHAM · The centre of the cuff lines *with* the N in COMPANY · The tops of ones in date are *flat*.
℞ ONE PENNY TOKEN in a circle. Legend, PAYABLE IN CASH NOTES ·· ✶ ·· The top of the Y in PENNY lines *with* the *last limb* of N in NOTES ·

Sharp 202, 12.

66. Similar, but the cuff lines *between* A and N of COMPANY ·
Halliday.

Ones in Date slope.

67. Similar, but the ones in date *slope*; and, ONE PENNY TOKEN in *smaller* letters.

68. Similar, but the Y in PENNY lines with the *centre* of N in NOTES.

69. Similar, but the Y lines to the *top* of the O in NOTES.

70. ☉ Similar, but centre of the cuff lines *with* the *first limb* of N in COMPANY.
℞ Similar, but the top of the Y lines to the *centre* of N in NOTES.

71. Similar, but the top of the Y lines to the *last limb* of the N

72. Similar, but the Y lines to the *top* of O in NOTES.

73. ☉ Similar, but the cuff *between* A and N of COMPANY.
℞ As last. *Halliday.*

For Public Accommodation.

74. ☉ Similar, but the tops of the ones in date are *flat*, and the centre of cuff lines with the *first limb* of N in COMPANY.
℞ ONE PENNY TOKEN in a circle. Legend, FOR PUBLIC ACCOMMODATION ·· * ·· The top of the Y in PENNY lines to the *centre* of D in ACCOMMODATION.

Sharp 202, 13.

75. Similar, but centre of cuff lines to the *centre* of N

76. Similar, but centre of cuff lines *between* A and N of COMPANY.

77. Similar, but the top of the Y lines to the *bow* of D   *Halliday.*

Birmingham and Sheffield, 1811.

Flat Ones in Date.

78. ☉ ONE PENNY in a circle. Legend, BIRMINGHAM AND SHEFFIELD.
℞ TOKEN 1811 in a circle. Legend, COPPER COMPANY divided by an ornament; the tops of the ones in date are *flat*. R. *Halliday.*

79. ☉ As last.
℞ Similar, but the N in TOKEN lines to the *first limb* of A instead of to its *second*. R.r.

1812.

80. Similar, but dated 1812 The top of the Y of PENNY lines with the *first limb* of E in SHEFFIELD.

Sharp 202, 16.

81. Similar, but the top of the Y lines to the *centre* of E

82. Similar, but the top of the Y lines to the *first limb* of F

THE ONES IN DATE SLOPE.

83. O Similar, but the top of the Y lines to the *centre* of E
℞ Similar, but the tops of the ones in date *slope*. R.

84. Similar, but the tops of the ones in date *slightly* slope.
Halliday.

Made for sale for manufacturers of Birmingham and Sheffield, with which to pay wages. There never was a Copper Company of the name indicated on the tokens.

BIRMINGHAM AND SOUTH WALES.

NO PERIOD BEFORE OR AFTER DATE.

85. O Prince of Wales' plumes encircled by a coronet; motto, ICH DIEN all in a circle. Legend, BIRMINGHAM & SOUTH WALES · 1812 · The tops of ones *slope, no period* before or after date.

℞ A horse in a circle. COPPER TOKEN ONE PENNY The horse's ear points to *centre* of E in COPPER R.

Sharp 203, 19.

86. O Similar, but the tops of ones *flat*, and the terminal of & is *curved*.

℞ Similar, but horse's ear points to *first* limb of E in COPPER

A PERIOD BEFORE AND AFTER DATE.

87. Similar to last, but *with* a period before and after date.

88. Similar, but the horse's ear points to the *centre* of E

89. Similar, but the horse's ear points to the *end* of E

90. O Similar, but on a much smaller flan; the *terminal* of the & is *flat* on the top; the date in much *smaller* figures.

℞ Similar, but the horse's ear points *between* the E and R of COPPER *Halliday.*

91. O Similar, but the tops of the ones in date *slope*, and the terminal of the & is *curved*.

℞ Similar, but the horse's ear points to the centre of E in COPPER

This is another instance where the tokens were made for sale, as no firm or company existed as pretended in the legend.

Rose Copper Company.

Flat Tops to Ones in Date.

92. O ONE PENNY in a circle. Legend, BIRMINGHAM AND SWANSEA· The top of PENNY lines *between* the W and A in SWANSEA·
℞ TOKEN 1811 in a circle. ROSE COPPER COMPANY A rose ornament at bottom. The tops of the ones are *flat*, and the top of TOKEN lines with the *centre* of M in COMPANY   R.

Sharp 202, 14.

93. O Similar, but top of PENNY lines to *last limb* of W in SWANSEA·
℞ Similar, but TOKEN lines to *last limb* of M in COMPANY

The Tops of Ones Slope.

94. O Similar, but PENNY lines *between* W and A in SWANSEA·
℞ Similar, but the ones in date *slope*.

95. Similar, but top of TOKEN lines with the *centre* of M in COMPANY

96. Similar, but tops of ones do not *slope as much*.

97. Similar, but top of PENNY lines with *centre* of A in SWANSEA·

Halliday.

1812.

98. O A lion supporting a shield bearing a rose, thistle and shamrock, in a circle. BIRMINGHAM AND SWANSEA 1812
℞ A rose spray in a circle. COPPER TOKEN + ONE PENNY +

Halliday.

PLATE E, no. 5.

The Rose Copper Company, formed in 1793, conducted the Birmingham agency at its warehouse in Cherry Street. The famous Matthew Boulton was one of its shareholders.

Birmingham and Warwickshire, 1811.

99. O ONE PENNY in a circle. BIRMINGHAM & WARWICKSHIRE ✱ The top of PENNY lines with the *first limb* of S
℞ TOKEN 1811 in a circle. FLINT COPPER COMPANY A rose ornament below.

Sharp 203, 21.

100. Similar, but the top of PENNY lines with the *centre* of K

Halliday.

These were imitations of the Rose Copper Company's tokens of 1811, made for sale.

1812.

101. ℞ A crown with *thirteen* pearls on the arch of the crown, six to left, seven to right, in a circle. BIRMINGHAM & WARWICKSHIRE · The band of the crown at the bottom lines with the s in SHIRE ·

℞ ONE PENNY 1812 in a circle. FOR GENERAL CIRCULATION · * · The top of PENNY lines with the *centre* of the first E in GENERAL

Sharp 203, 20.

102. ℞ Similar to last, but the top of cross is *under* the w which before was *between* & and w   The band of crown lines with the H of SHIRE ·

℞ Similar, but PENNY lines with the *first limb* of E

103. Similar to last, but the shape of the & different, being *flat* at the top, and there are *fifteen* pearls, seven to left and eight to right, on arch of crown. The band lines to the s of SHIRE ·

104. Similar, but the & at the top turns *downward;* there are *thirteen* pearls, six to the left and seven to the right. The band lines to the H in SHIRE · R.

105. Similar, but the crown has *fourteen* pearls, seven on each side. There is a B (Birmingham) inscribed on each side of the orb under the arch of the crown, and a B on each section of the cross.
Halliday.

These pieces, also made for sale, were a colourable imitation of the genuine Crown Copper Company's tokens of Birmingham and Neath.

HALFPENNY.

106. ℞ HALF PENNY in a circle. BIRMINGHAM AND SWANSEA · The top of the H in HALF lines to the *centre* of G

℞ TOKEN 1811 in a circle. COPPER COMPANY An ornament under. The T in TOKEN is in line with the *second* P in COPPER
Halliday.

This piece is presumed to be unique. The omission of ROSE from the reverse legend probably caused its rejection.

FLAT-TOPPED ONES IN DATE.

107. ℞ As last.

℞ TOKEN 1811 in a circle. ROSE COPPER COMPANY The top of T in line with the *bow* of the C in COPPER and the tops of the ones are *nearly flat*.

Sharp 210, 1.

108. Similar, but the T in line with the *last limb* of E in ROSE

109. ℞ Similar, but the H in HALF lines to the *space* between the N and G in BIRMINGHAM

℞ As last.

TOPS OF ONES IN DATE SLOPE.

110. ○ Similar, but the top of H in HALF lines to the *centre* of G
℞ Similar, but the tops of the ones in date *slope*; the last numeral is under the *space* between E and N of TOKEN

111. Similar, but the top of T lines to the *centre* of the *space* between ROSE COPPER

112. Similar, but the top of H lines to the *centre* of the *space* between N and G in BIRMINGHAM   *Halliday.*

The Copper Companies were :
1. The Birmingham Mining and Copper Company, formed in the year 1790, who issued halfpenny tokens in 1791 and the two following years. These are described by Atkins on pp. 210-213. They were art productions by the famous Wyon (Thomas). The tokens were, as in the nineteenth century, extensively counterfeited. Imitations were also issued in the name of bogus companies, called Birmingham Company, and the Metal and Copper Company.
2. The Rose Copper Company, established 1793.
3. The Crown Copper Company, formed 1803.
4. The Union Copper Company, which sprung into existence about 1807.

As will be seen, all these companies resorted to the issue of tokens as a ready means of disposing of the metal they produced. Without exception these bodies gave as near as they could intrinsic value in their token coinage, and, although it was the means by which they disposed of copper by the ton, the issues were popular, as an honest and ready exchange in the coinage of the period, and were appreciated by the public.

SIR ORIGINAL.

From a Block the property of SPINK & SON.

113. ○ Bust to right with wig. SIR ORIGINAL At the right I. G. H
℞ THIS IS MY WORK JOHN GREGORY HANCOCK AGED 7 YEARS 1800   *Ex.* INDUSTRY PRODUCETH WEALTH   *R.r.*
Batty 2322.

114. The same in brass. *R.r.r.*

SHAKESPEARE.

115. ○ Bust to left. W. SHAKE SPEARE In small letters under the bust I · G · Hancock aged 7 y's
℞ As last. *R.r.*
Batty 2321.

116. Also in brass. *R.r.*

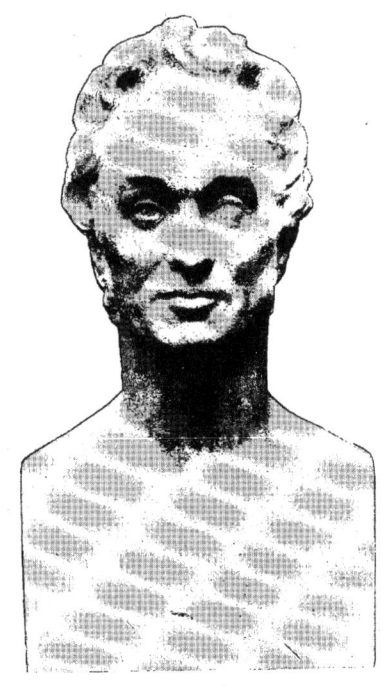

CHARLES PYE.

From a Bust in the possession of J. Macmillan.

WARWICKSHIRE. 157

117. O As last.
℞ As no. 112, but reads PRODUSETH (*sic*) R.*r.r.*

Norman's sale 316, July 14th, 1903.

Strictly speaking, these specious tokens belong to the eighteenth century, but, as they were struck too late to be included in *Conder*, and are not described in *Atkins*, they are admitted.

Pye tells us that "doubts having been expressed as to the *bonâ fides* of this work being that of young Hancock, induced his father to make an affidavit that they were entirely engraved by his son; and the gentlemen for whom they were made declare they were perfectly convinced of the truth of this affidavit."

"It is to be regretted that the subsequent career of this precocious boy is unknown. It is, indeed, beyond comprehension that all attempts should fail to trace what became of the remarkable son of so distinguished an artist."—*The Token Coinage of Warwickshire*.

It has recently been observed by Mr. Hamer that, as I. G. Hancock, jun., was born June 24th, 1791, he would be at least 8 years and six months old at the beginning of 1800; so that either a mistake was made in reference to the age or the date, or perhaps in reference to both.

COVENTRY.

PENNY.

118. O Bust in profile to left with antique dress. PHILEMON HOLLAND · M· D· Under the bust, DIED 1636 AGED 85·
℞ View of an interior. *Ex.* FREE SCHOOL COVENTRY
E. PENNY TOKEN PAYABLE BY E· W· PERCY COVENTRY ×

PLATE E, no. 6.
Thirty-six impressions.

119. Also in Silver.

Six impressions.

120. O Blank.
℞ As last, but a trial piece *before letters;* struck in tin. R.*r.*

121. O Similar, but HOLLOND (*sic*), and the legend under the bust omitted.
℞ Unfinished.
E. Plain.

Atkins 205, 22.

"This is also a trial piece in tin, of which six impressions were struck."—*Vide Pye* 4, *XV**

122. O As 118.
℞ Similar to 118, but two boys detected by the schoolmaster playing at marbles. 1801
E. As 118.

Atkins 205, 23.

"Only six impressions were struck when the die broke."—*Pye* 5, *XV.**

123. ☉ As last.

℞ An open book resting against two others, lettered BRITANNIA CYROPÆDIA · The first page of the open book is inscribed :

With one Sole Pen	(on the other),	*A Pen it was*
I wrote this Book	.	*When I it took*
Made of a		*A Pen I*
gray Goose-Quill		*leave it Still.*

By the book is an inkstand with a quill pen in it. Ex. 1801 · I· G· H
E As 118.

PLATE J, no. 21, reverse only illustrated.

Eighteen impressions were struck and the dies destroyed.

124. ☉ As last.

℞ As last, but a trial piece before letter struck in tin.

Hancock.

125. ☉ Blank.

℞ As last.

"Four unfinished Proofs in Tin."—*Vide Pye* 6, *XV**.

Philemon Holland was appointed, in 1608, usher of the Free School. In 1612, presented with the Freedom of the City, and appointed master in 1628. Holland was the first translator of Camden ; and the "Romanes Histories" MS. he claimed to have written throughout with one pen. "A monumental pen," says Fretton, "which he solemnly kept, and which, ultimately, was enclosed in silver by a lady of his acquaintance."—*The Token Coinage of Warwickshire.*

HANCOCK'S WORKSHOP AT THE SOHO MINT.
From a Trial Piece in the Possession of the Author.

Birmingham 9th April 1798

I was duly honour'd with your Letter of the [...]
consider myself oblig'd to you for your patronage
[...]ins you mention, have long been very scarce,
[...]ne none are to be met with, but in the possession
[...]ollectors, the last Southampton that has been
[...]y knowledge, was sold for more than five Guineas,
[...] a commission to offer that sum for it, & it was
I presume you have seen my former publication
[...]cial Coins, if not, Mr Nichols can shew it you,
[...] objection to selling the originals from which
[...] engrav'd, if you or any other person is inclin'd
[...]em all together, they are in general in high
[...]on, the two you mention cannot be surpass'd by
[...], the price I have fix'd upon them is fifty Guineas,
[...] impressions to accompany them by way of
[...] the Dollar you was so obliging to delineate, is
[...]ave not seen, but it is not calculated for this
[...], or wou'd have been oblig'd to you for the loan of

Your obedient Servant
Chas Pye

WILTSHIRE.

MARLBOROUGH.

SHILLING.

SILVER.

1. ☉ One Shilling 1811 in a circle. Legend, Marlborough Old Bank Token
℞ King Gosling Tanner & Griffiths in a circle. For Neceffary Change *R.*
PLATE L, no. 28.

2. ☉ Four hands joined in a circle. KING · GOSLING · TANNER & GRIFFITHS + The centre of the cuff lines to the o in GOSLING ·
℞ ONE SHILLING TOKEN 1811 in a circle. Legend, MARLBOROUGH + OLD · BANK +
Boyne 144.

3. Similar, but the centre of the cuff lines to the s in GOSLING · *R.*

4. ☉ As last.
℞ Similar to last, but with a *circular* inscription ONE · SHILLING + TOKEN + and the date *omitted. R.r.* *Halliday.*
Boyne 145.

SIXPENCE.

5. ☉ Similar to last, excepting in size.
℞ SIXPENCE TOKEN 1811 with a Staffordshire knot above, in a circle. MARLBOROUGH OLD - BANK *Halliday.*
Boyne 146.

The London agents of this bank were Spooner, Attwood & Co., 27, Gracechurch Street, London, and New Street, Birmingham.

STAVERTON.

HALF CROWN.

6. ☉ View of mills over a river, with a clock tower on the centre mill. Legend, STAVERTON FACTORY · NEAR BRADFORD · WILTSHIRE ·
℞ 2 6 1811 between palm branches. Legend, PROSPERITY TO THE WOOLLEN MANUFACTORY ···:··· *R.r.r.* *T. Wyon.*
Boyne 210.

160   NINETEENTH CENTURY TOKEN COINAGE.

From the top of an Invoice in the possession of A. W. WATERS.

PENNY.

COPPER.

7. ☉ View of mills over a river, with a clock tower on the centre mill. Legend, STAVERTON FACTORY · NEAR BRADFORD · WILTSHIRE · on the ground at the right, T W   The summit of the weather vane is under the *centre* of the N in STAVERTON

℞. A fleece suspended from a ribbon. Legend, ONE PENNY TOKEN 1811   The tail of the fleece *falls below* the hock. *R.r.*

Sharp 203, 1.

8. ☉ Similar to last, but *without* the periods in the legend; the T W on the ground *omitted*, and the summit of the vane is under the *first limb* of the N in STAVERTON

℞. Similar to last, but the tail *does not extend below* the hock of the fleece. *R.r.*   *T. Wyon.*

PLATE E, no. 7.

These mills, which were between Trowbridge and Bradford, were partly destroyed by fire early in the nineteenth century. The experiments of manufacturing cloth in this part of the country were of an enterprising character, but, unfortunately, brought several occupiers to grief. John Cooper & Co. were the proprietors of the mills when the tokens were issued. The mills are now adapted for milk condensing. There is a tablet on the present buildings to commemorate the date of the fire. For this information the author is indebted to Lord Edmond Fitzmaurice.

The Bath Chronicle, April 15*th*, 1813, says :—" The creditors who have proved their debts under a Commission of Bankrupt, awarded and issued against John Jones, late of Staverton, in the County of Wilts, clothier, banker, dealer and chapman, are requested to attend a meeting to be held at John's Coffee House, Cornhill, London, on Thursday the 22d day of April, inst., at twelve o'clock at noon."

WORCESTERSHIRE.

COUNTY AND CITY.

SHILLING.

SILVER.

1. O Arms, sable and gules, a castle argent; three pears in canton sinister, between olive and palm branches. The motto CIVITAS IN BELLO IN PACE FIDELIS (A city in war and in peace faithful) on a ribbon below. WORCESTER COUNTY & CITY TOKEN *

℞ VALUE ONE SHILL: in a wreath of oak and acorns. TO FACILITATE TRADE 1811 *Halliday.*

PLATE E, no. 8.

Issued by the Directors of the House of Industry, and Overseers of the Poor.

BEWDLEY.

TWO SHILLINGS AND SIXPENCE.

COPPER.

2. O TWO SHILLINGS AND SIXPENCE N° Legend, STANLEY COLLIERY NEAR BEWDLEY I & B THOMPSON

℞ WE PROMISE TO PAY THE BEARER ON DEMAND A ONE POUND NOTE FOR EIGHT OF THESE PIECES *Unknown.*

PLATE K, no. 13.

In Mr. Norman's cabinet.

This Colliery, situated ten miles from Stourport, was sold by auction on Dec. 9th, 1822.

DUDLEY.

PENNY.

3. O Figure of Justice standing between a cask inscribed RESPON SIBILITY and a bale. DUDLEY & BIRMINGHAM TOKEN ONE PENNY 1811 On the ground at the left, H The ones in date *slope.*

℞ RICHARD WALLIS BIRMINGHAM T & I · BADGER DUDLEY Legend, A POUND NOTE FOR 240 TOKENS with an ornament below. The last letter in BIRMINGHAM is quite *clear* of the O and K in TOKEN The whole surrounded on obverse and reverse by an Etruscan border.

Sharp 203, 1.

4. Similar, but the last letter in BIRMINGHAM *touches* the O and K of TOKEN

5. O Similar, but the ones in date have *flat* tops.

℞ Similar, but the final M of BIRMINGHAM lines with the top of the O in TOKEN instead of its *centre.* R.

6. ○ Similar, but ones in date *slope*.
℞ Similar, but the issuers' initials are T & J ·

7. ○ An anvil pointing to the *left*; the date 1812 under in a circle. The ones in date *slope*. Legend, DUDLEY ONE PENNY TOKEN
℞ A vice, JAMᔆ WILKINSON VICE MAKER in a circle. A POUND NOTE FOR 240 TOKENS +
Sharp 203, 2.

8. ○ Similar, but the anvil points to the *right*, and the tops of the ones in date are *flat*.
℞ As last. *Halliday.*

LYE.

9. ○ Bust to left (George III) 1811 under. A small H *on the shoulder.* NAIL & TRACE MANUFACTORY The tops of ones in date *slope*.
℞ ONE PENNY TOKEN between palm and olive branches. PAYABLE BY J · FORREST & Cº LYE FORGE · + · H on the *second* palm blade; there are *six* berries in the olive branch. *Halliday.*
Sharp 203, 3.

10. ○ Similar, but *without* the small H on the *shoulder*; the tops of ones in date are *flat*.
℞ Similar, but there are *no* berries in the olive branch, and the H on the palm branch *omitted*. *Unknown.*
Probably a forgery of the time.

11. ○ A tree in a circle. SPADE, SHOVEL, TRACE & CHAIN MANUFACTORY · 1811 · On the trunk of the tree H
℞ ONE PENNY TOKEN in a circle. PAYABLE AT THE LYE WAREHOUSE BY T. WOOD & Cº *Halliday.*
PLATE E, no. 9.

REDDITCH.

12. ○ Prince of Wales' plumes encircled by a coronet. REDDITCH TOKEN + ONE PENNY + The quills of the feathers are *straight*.
℞ PAYABLE BY W · BARTLEET & W · HEMMING Legend, A POUND NOTE FOR 240 TOKENS - 1813 - An ornament above the date.
Sharp 204, 5.

WORCESTERSHIRE. 163

13. O- Similar to last, but the quills of the feathers are *curved*, and the one at the right is over the *centre* of E in PENNY instead of its *first limb*. R. *Halliday*.

Both the issuers were needle manufacturers, but at separate establishments.

WORCESTER 1811.

14. O- Arms of the city. CIVITAS IN BELLO IN PACE FIDELIS ·· x^x_xx ·· The lower bar of shield is in line *with* the A in CIVITAS

℞ VALUE ONE PENNY between palm and olive branches. WORCESTER CITY AND COUNTY TOKEN · 1811 · There are *six* berries in the olive branch, the tops of ones in date *slope*.

Sharp 204, 6.

15. Similar, but the tops of ones in date are *flat*. R.

16. Similar, but with *seventeen* berries in the olive branch; the ones in date *slope*.

17. O- Similar, but the lower bar of shield lines *between* A and S in CIVITAS

℞ Similar, but with only *six* berries in the olive branch; the tops of ones in date are *flat*.

18. Similar, but with *seven* berries on olive branch.

19. Similar, but *nineteen* berries on olive branch.

20. O- Similar, but the lower bar of shield is in line with the S in CIVITAS

℞ Similar, but there are *six* berries on olive branch. The first two blades of palm on the inside are *unequal* in length; the second *nearly touching* the foot of the Y in PENNY

21. Similar, but the two blades of palm under N and Y are *nearly equal* in length.

22. O- Similar, but lower bar of shield lines *above* the S in CIVITAS

℞ Similar, but with *seven* berries on olive branch, and the tops of ones are *pointed*.

23. Similar, but tops of the ones in date are *flat*.

1814.

24. O- Similar, but lower bar of shield lines *to* S in CIVITAS

℞ Similar, but *twenty-one* leaves on olive branch, and dated 1814

25. ○ Similar, but lower bar of shield lines *between* A and S in CIVITAS
℞ Similar, but with *eighteen* leaves on the olive branch.
Unknown.

This is a forgery of the period.
William Cotton, in his *Tokens of Worcestershire*, quotes :—
"In the *Worcester Herald* of November 16th, 1811, the following advertisement, referring to these tokens, appears :
"'THE DIRECTORS of the HOUSE OF INDUSTRY finding the demand for their TOKENS greater than they at first calculated upon, and that many disappointments have occurred in consequence thereof, have now provided a sufficient quantity to supply the public with any amount. They likewise beg to state, that as the Advantage arising from issuing these tokens, independent of the convenience of the trading Interest, will be applied in aid of the Poor Rates, they trust they will meet due encouragement from every class.
"'N.B.—These Tokens will be regularly exchanged at any time for Bank Notes at their office in Friar's Street, and they presume to add, that their Responsibility must have a preference to the issue of any Individual.'
"In the same year, October 12th, we read :
"'It is with much satisfaction we learn, that in order to relieve the public inconvenience so universally felt from the want of small change in this city and neighbourhood, the Directors of our House of Industry, at the earnest solicitations of many respectable tradesmen and others, have resolved to circulate CARD TOKENS of 2s. 6d. each, to which their responsibility will be attached, and consequently that of the united parishes ; by which, the principal objection hitherto made on the subject of similar issues, will be obviated.'"

26. ○ Arms as before, within a *double* circle. JOHN KNAPP JUNIOR · WORCESTER ·
℞ ONE PENNY 1812 in a circle. FOR GENERAL CIRCULATION *R.r.*
Sharp 204, 7.

27. Similar, but ONE PENNY in a circle. PAYABLE IN CASH NOTES · 1813 ·
Halliday.
Sharp 204.

John Knapp Junior was a glover.

HALFPENNY.

28. ○ VALUE HALF PENNY between palm and olive branches. WORCESTER CITY AND COUNTY TOKEN · 1811 · The third blade of palm points to the *centre* of the F in HALF
℞ Arms as before. CIVITAS IN BELLO IN PACE FIDELIS ·· ×ˣ× ··
Sharp 211, 1.

29. Similar, but the third blade of palm points to the *foot* of F

30. ○ Arms as before. JOHN KNAPP JUNIOR · WORCESTER ·
℞ HALFPENNY in a circle. TO FACILITATE TRADE · 1813 ·
Sharp 211, 2.

31. Similar, but *without* the period after WORCESTER *R.*

32. Similar, but VIGORNIA *substituted* for WORCESTER · *Halliday.*

WORCESTERSHIRE. 165

FARTHING.

33. O Arms as before. JOHN KNAPP JUNIOR · WORCESTER ·
℞ ONE FARTHING in a circle. TO FACILITATE TRADE · 1813 ·
PLATE E, no. 10.

34. Similar to last, but VIGORNIA · *substituted* for WORCESTER ·
Halliday.

TWO SHILLINGS.

PORCELAIN.
35. O I Promise to pay the Bearer on demand two Shillings. W Davis At the China Factory.
℞ W P C (Worcester Porcelain Company) in raised letters. *R.r.r.*
Cotton 50.

ONE SHILLING.

36. Similar, except in size and value One Shilling. *R.r.r.*
Cotton 51.

SIXPENCE.

37. Similar, except in size and value Sixpence. *R.r.r.*

About the year 1760, tokens were issued by the proprietors of the Worcester Porcelain Company about the same size as the coins of the value represented. There is a set of these Porcelain Tokens in the British Museum and in Sir A. W. Franks's collection (R. W. Binns, quoted by W. Chaffers, " *Marks and Monograms on Pottery and Porcelain,*" 10th ed., 1903, *p.* 756).

The issuer of these tokens was one of the principal founders of the Worcester Porcelain Industry in 1751.

The house taken for the Company's Works was a famous one, being the residence of Sir William Windsor, *temp.* Henry VII.

The building now forms part of Dent's glove factory.

YORKSHIRE.
COUNTY.
SHILLING.
SILVER.

1. O A fleece suspended. FOR PUBLIC ACCOMMODATION
R VALUE ONE SHILLING. A scroll ornament between ONE and SHILLING within a garter, tinted or. YORKSHIRE WEST RIDING TOKEN 18 11 The date divided by the tag of the garter. *Halliday.*
Boyne 235.

BARNSLEY.
SHILLING.

2. O The arms of Leeds between sprigs of palm and oak. Crest, a star within an oval. WILLIAM HORSFALL · BARNSLEY ·
R Female seated on a bale, holding scales and cornucopia. ONE SHILLING SILVER TOKEN 1812. *R.r.r.* *Halliday.*
PLATE M, no. 1.

This reverse occurs again on a Sheffield token. Until recently the firm was carrying on business as Horsfall & Co., and is now in existence as a limited company.

BRADFORD.
SHILLING.

3. O Arms, gules a chevron between three bugle horns, stringed, two and one, within a wreath. Crest, a boar's head. JAMES LAY COCK · BRADFORD ·
R Justice standing between a bale, labelled Y & D and a cask inscribed WINE & SPIRITS Legend, ONE SHILLING TOKEN 1812
Halliday.
PLATE K, no. 14.

James, subsequently to the issue of the token, took his brother Thomas as a partner, who was a dealer in oils. The firm was declared bankrupt April 4th, 1815. Dividend paid Nov. 22, 1817.—*London Gazette.*

BRIDLINGTON.
SHILLING.

4. O B B B in the field, one over two. BRIDLINGTON 1811.
R ONE SHILLING SILVER TOKEN Legend, COOK & HARWOOD
Unknown.
Boyne 27.

5. O A shield with $_B^{BB}$ in a wreath of olive. Legend, COOK AND HARWOOD 1812 Scroll ornaments on either side of date
R 12 in large figures inscribed, TWELVE PENNY the letters incuse. Legend, BRIDLINGTON SILVER TOKEN
Boyne 28.

Leeds 22 April 1848.

Dear Sir,

I forgot to mention in my last that in the 2nd Vol of the Grammont memoirs, is an portrait of Comte A Hamilton, which please inlay & let it face Title page to Vol. 2.

We have just had a 3 days Sale here, some prime things amongst them, & fetc the best lots fair prices, some Manuscript Her visitations by Camden & Dethick &c, fetched 10£ to 15£ per Vol. — Also Coins so so, but so so, I got however 3 fine Conquerors found in the neighbourhood of the late owner a clergyman — North Riding Yorks. full face crowned inner circle, or sword a sceptre Rev a cross two of York, & one MAINT an uncertain mint perhaps.

With kind regards
Yours truly
Wm Boyne

Mr J H Burn

From the Original in the possession of the Author.

YORKSHIRE.

6. ℞ Arms of the Priory of Bridlington. A ship between B B B within palm and olive branches. BRIDLINGTON QUAY 1811
℞ ONE SHILLING SILVER TOKEN Legend, JAMES STEPHENSON · + · + ·
Wyon.

Boyne 29.

DONCASTER.

SHILLING.

7. ℞ The cross of Otho de Tilli, BIRKINSHAW · DONCASTER ·
℞ Figure of Justice standing by a bale, inscribed Y & D A ship in the distance to right. Legend, ONE SHILLING SILVER TOKEN 1812
Halliday.

PLATE J, no. 22.

Birkinshaw was a pawnbroker carrying on business near to the Castle Hotel.

OTHO DE TILLI.

"One of the most interesting antiquities of this town" (Doncaster) "is the cross of *Ote de Tilli*. It is a cylindrical column eighteen feet in height, with four half cylinders of smaller diameter attached to it. Each column was originally surmounted by a cross pattée raised on a slender shaft. The Puritanical zeal of some soldiers of the Earl of Manchester in the Civil Wars urged them to pull down the crosses, and the whole pillar might soon have perished had not William Patterson, who was Mayor in 1678, interested himself in its preservation.

"The original position of this cross was at the beginning of Hallgate, but when that part of the town was improved, in 1793, it was removed to its present site, or rather a facsimile of it with a vane instead of the crosses was erected. Around the cross, at about the height of seven feet, is an inscription in the Langobardic character.

ICEST EST LA CRVICE OTE D TILLI A KI ALME DEY FACE MERCI — AMEN."

—*Extract from Allan's* "*History of the County of York,*" 1831, *vol. III, p.* 94.

"Ote or Otho de Tille is a name which often presents itself in the records of the affairs of this neighbourhood. He lived in the reigns of Stephen and Henry II and was seneschal or steward of Conningsborough under Hameline Earl of Warren."

8. ℞ A lion holding a standard, the crest of the town of Doncaster. The pennant is inscribed DON Legend, MIRFIN AND PARKER · DONCASTER ·
℞ Female seated on a bale to right, with scales and cornucopia; on the ground a sword; a ship in the distance at the right. The initials Y & D under. Legend, ONE SHILLING SILVER TOKEN 1812 The D is over the *first* 1 in date. H on the bale.

Boyne 68.

9. Similar to last, but the D in Y & D is over the *second* 1 in date, the H is *omitted. R.*

10. Similar, but the D is over the *space* between 1 and 2 in date.
Halliday.

SIXPENCE.

11. ℞ Similar to last except in size; the pennant is inscribed DO *instead* of DON
℞ Similar, but *without* the sword on the ground. Legend, SIX-PENCE SILVER TOKEN · 1812 ·
Halliday.

PLATE E, no. 11.

HULL.

EIGHTEENPENCE.

12. O The arms of Hull; azure, three coronets in pale between olive branches. HULL 1811 There are *six* berries in the right and *four* in the left wreath; the tooth of the border does *not touch* the second limb of U in HULL

℞ 1s. 6D in the centre, with a rose spray above and below. RUDSTON · AND PRESTON · *R.*

Boyne 102.
A radiated border on both obverse and reverse.

13. Similar, but a tooth of the border *touches* the second limb of U

14. Similar, but *five* berries on *each side* of the wreath, the border tooth is again *free* of the U in HULL

15. Similar, but there are *five* berries in the wreath at the right and *four* at the left.

16. Similar, but *six* berries at the right and *five* at the left.
Unknown.

SIXPENCE.

17. Similar to preceding, excepting in size and value. 6ᴰ *Four* berries at the right and *six* on the left of wreath. *Unknown.*
Boyne 46.

LEEDS.

SHILLING. 1811.

18. O Arms between palm and olive branches; azure, a fleece suspended on a chief, or; three mullets of five points. (Boyne says the tints are wrongly depicted). Crest, a star within an oval. Legend, JOHN SMALPAGE & S · LUMB · LEEDS ·

℞ A female seated on a bale with scales and cornucopia, a ship in the distance, a sword on the ground with Y & D above it. Legend, ONE SHILLING SILVER TOKEN 1811 The ship lines *above* the E in ONE
Boyne 108.

19. O Similar, but the nose and hind legs of the fleece are on *one line* in the shield.

℞ Similar, but the ship lines *with* E and the D of Y & D *touches* the sword.

20. Similar, but the D is *between* the dress and sword, the hilt extends to the *end* of the bale, the sword *points* to Y in Y & D

21. Similar, but the nose of the fleece is on the *line above* that on which the hind legs *rest*.

22. Similar, but the hilt of sword *does not* extend to the *end* of the bale.

23. ○ Similar, but the nose and legs of the fleece are *on one line*.
℞ Similar, but the point of sword extends *beyond* the Y There *is grass* over the hilt.

24. Similar, but the D is *between* dress and sword; and *no grass* over the hilt.

25. Similar, but the D *touches* the bale.

26. ○ Similar, but the nose of the fleece is on the *line above* that on which the hind legs *rest*.
℞ Similar, but the D *touches* the sword.

27. Similar, but the hilt *nearly* to the *end* of the bale, the point of sword *extends beyond* the Y in Y & D
PLATE E, no. 12.

28. ○ Similar, but the nose of the fleece is *on one line*.
℞ Similar, but the D is *between* the dress and sword; and there *is grass* over the hilt. *Halliday.*

The varieties of die are tending to make this otherwise common token scarce.

1812.

29. Similar to preceding, but dated 1812. *Halliday.*
Boyne 109.

Boyne informs us, John Smalpage was a tailor and draper; when called upon to meet the repayment of the tokens he was financially embarrassed, but Beckett & Co., Bankers, enabled him to tide over the difficulty for a time. Smalpage's place of business was at 22, Briggate, and S. Lumb was a cloth-dresser in Meadow Lane. J. Smalpage was subsequently (Sep. 15, 1821) declared bankrupt.

ARMS AND SUPPORTERS.

30. ○ Arms as before, but with crowned owls as supporters; crest, two maces in saltire; no legend.
℞ ONE SHILLING SILVER TOKEN PAYABLE AT THE LEEDS WORK HOUSE · 1812 · *Halliday.*
PLATE K, no. 15.

SIXPENCE.

31. Similar to 29, except in size and value. SIX-PENCE SILVER TOKEN 1812
Boyne 110.

SCARBOROUGH.

SHILLING.

32. O- The arms of Scarborough; an antique ship, a castle towered, with a star between the ship and castle; no legend.
℞ ONE SHILLING SILVER TOKEN 1811 in a circle. LORD & MARSHALL ✳ SCARBOROUGH ✳ *Halliday.*
Boyne 191.

33. O- Similar arms, but within a garter. Motto, HONI SOIT QUI MAL Y PENSE. Legend, THE CURRENT VALUE IN CASH NOTES divided by a quatrefoil labelled Y & D
℞ Similar to last, but dated 1812 *Halliday.*
PLATE E, no. 13.

SIXPENCE.

34. O- Similar to last, but Y & D omitted, and *a period* instead of a *quatrefoil* divides the legend.
℞ Similar, but SIX PENCE *Periods* divide the legend *instead of stars.* *Halliday.*

Lord and Marshall were hardware merchants.

SHEFFIELD.

HALF GUINEA.
GOLD.

35. O- A Phœnix issuant from the flames. YOUNGE, WILSONS & YOUNGE · SHEFFIELD · in a fine toothed border.
℞ STANDARD GOLD 10 · 6 Legend, YORKSHIRE TOKEN 1812 in a similar border. *R.r.r.* *Halliday.*
PLATE M, no. 2.

HALF CROWN.
SILVER.

36. O- The arms of Sheffield, eight arrows in saltire banded between two pheons, oak and palm branches at the sides; crest, a cherub. YOUNGE & DEAKIN · SHEFFIELD ·
℞ Female to left seated on a bale with scales and cornucopia; the bale is inscribed Y & D A sword *on the ground.* TWO SHILLINGS & SIX PENCE SILVER TOKEN 1812 A small H to the left, under the robe. *R.* *Halliday.*
PLATE M, no. 3.

"A public meeting of the inhabitants of Sheffield was called last week to consider the propriety of issuing a local silver coinage; when it was resolved that pieces of the denomination of 2s. 6d. and 1s. be stamped and sent into circulation to an amount not exceeding 10,000£. and not less than 5,000£."—*Bath Chronicle, Oct. 24th,* 1811.

YORKSHIRE.

EIGHTEENPENCE.

37. O Similar to last, but the arms are not on a shield; a wreath of olive encircles the arms and crest. S & C · YOUNGE & C^O SHEFFIELD ·

℞ Female, etc. as before, but the sword *leans* against the bale. ONE SHILLING & SIXPENCE TOKEN 1812 There are *no initials* on the ground. *R.r.*

38. Also in Copper. *R.r.r.* *Halliday.*

SHILLING, 1811.
NO WREATH TO SHIELD, FLAT TOPS TO ONES IN DATE.

39. O Similar to last, but *without* the wreath YOUNGE & DEAKIN· SHEFFIELD ·

℞ Similar to last, but ONE SHILLING SILVER TOKEN 1811 *Grass* above the sword hilt, and the tops of ones in date are *flat*. Y & D on the ground. The point of sword *extends beyond* the Y and nearly touches the edge of the ground.

Boyne, 200.

40. Similar, but *no grass* above the sword hilt, the point of sword is *under* the Y

41. Similar, but the point of sword *extends beyond* the Y and the hilt to the *extreme edge* of the bale.

TOPS OF ONES IN DATE SLOPE.

42. Similar, but the tops of the ones in date *slope*, and point of the sword *extends beyond* the Y in Y & D

43. Similar, but *grass* over the hilt. A small H on the ground at the right.

44. Similar, but the point of the sword is *under* the Y The H on the ground is *omitted*.

PLATE E, no. 14.

45. Similar, but the point of the sword has *four* blades of *grass* above it.

46. Similar, but the point of the sword is *midway* between Y and & *No grass* above the hilt. *all by Halliday.*

1812.

47. O As no. 39.

℞ Similar, but dated 1812 No wreath to shield. The tops of the ones are *flat*, the point of the sword is *under* the & of Y & D

Halliday.

This is the same reverse as the Leeds Shilling of 1812.
In Mr. Bliss' cabinet.

WREATH TO SHIELD.

48. ○ Arms in a wreath of olive; crest, a cherub. S & C · YOUNGE & C°. SHEFFIELD ·

℞ Similar to last, but the sword *rests* against the bale; the initials Y & D *omitted.* The base of the letters are *square*, and there are *four* blades of grass at end of sword.

Boyne 202.

49. Similar, but with *three* blades of grass at end of sword.

50. A close copy, but the base of the letters *scolloped*, and *four* blades of grass at end of sword. *Halliday.*

OVERSEERS OF THE POOR.

51. ○ Arms as before, but *without* the wreath. SHEFFIELD 1811 A *pellet* between the arrow barbs.

℞ ONE SHILLING TOKEN Legend, OVERSEERS OF THE POOR A quatrefoil labelled Y & D with two periods on either side divides the legend. The terminal of the second limb of N in TOKEN lines to the *last limb* of R in POOR

Boyne 204.

52. Similar, but the terminal of the second limb of N lines *between the limbs* of R

53. Similar, but *without* the *pellet* between the arrow barbs.
Halliday.

PLATE E, no. 15.

SIXPENCE.

54. ○ Arms *without* the wreath. YOUNGE & DEAKIN · SHEFFIELD ·

℞ Similar to preceding except in size. SIX-PENCE SILVER TOKEN 1811 There is *no sword* by the seated figure.

Boyne 201.

THIRSK.

SHILLING.

55. ○ Arms azure, a cross patonce argent. THIRSK 1812 The legend is divided on each side by a quatrefoil.

℞ SILVER TOKEN in a circle. Legend, THIRSK ASSOCIATION ONE SHILLING

Boyne 221.

Boyne says the arms should have been tinted sable and gold.
For SCURR countermark see Countermarked Tokens of Yorkshire.
Richard Scurr, clock and watch maker, Thirsk, was declared bankrupt June 28th, 1817.—*London Gazette.*

YORKSHIRE. 173

WHITBY.

SHILLING.

56. ☉ Arms of Whitby Abbey, argent, three shells (ammonite), two over one. WHITBY ASSOCIATION · 1811 ·

℞ SILVER TOKEN ONE SHILLING   A quatrefoil inscribed Y & D under SHILLING   *Halliday.*

YORK.

SHILLING.

57. ☉ Arms of the city, quarterly argent, on a cross gules, five lions passant gardant, between olive and palm branches. Legend, YORK 1811 There are *four* berries in the olive branch; on the *second* palm blade at the right of the last numeral in date, the letter Y (YORK) The bottom horizontal line of the cross at the left, lines to the *third* berry from the top of the branch, which is *without* a stem.

℞ CATTLE AND BARBER An ornament above and below. Legend, ONE SHILLING SILVER TOKEN The *top* of the B in BARBER lines to the top of S in SILVER The centre of the rose in the upper ornament is under the *last* limb of H in SHILLING

Boyne 233.

58. Similar, but the third berry from the top *has* a stem.

59. Also in Copper, but the Y is *omitted*; the 8 in date is *not joined* in the centre. *R.*

60. ☉ Similar, but with Y on the *first* blade at the *right* of the last numeral, the 8 in date *properly* formed.

℞ Similar, but the B in BARBER lines *above* the S in SILVER The rose is between H and I in SHILLING

61. ☉ Similar, but the Y on the palm is *omitted.* The bottom horizontal line of cross lines *between* the *second* and *third* berry from the top of the olive branch; the third berry is *without* its stem.

℞ Similar, but the B in BARBER lines *just below* the top of S in SILVER and the centre rose in the ornament is under the *first* I in SHILLING

BOTTOM LINE OF CROSS OPPOSITE A BERRY.

62. ☉ Similar, but the letter Y is on the first palm blade *over* the *last* numeral in date. The line of cross opposite the *third* berry.

℞ Similar, but the centre rose of the ornament is under the *space* between the H and I in SHILLING

63. ☉ Similar, but the Y is on the *second* palm blade at the right of the last numeral in date. The third berry *has* a stem.

℞ Similar, but the centre rose is under the *first* I in SHILLING the B in BARBER lines *between* S and I in SILVER *R.*

64. ♂ Similar, but the *third* berry from the top is *without a stem,* the Y on the *second* palm blade is also at the right of the *last* numeral in date.

℞ Similar, but the centre rose is under the *last* limb of H the top of B in BARBER is in line with the *bottom* of the S in SILVER

PLATE E, no. 16.

65. ♂ Similar, but the third berry from the top *has* a stem.
℞ As last. *R.*

66. ♂ Similar, but in Copper, the third berry from the top is *without* a stem.
℞ Similar, but the centre of the ornament is *between* the H and I of SHILLING   *R.*

67. ♂ Similar, but the olive branch has only *three* berries, the *second* or the one opposite the cross *has* a stem.
℞ Similar, but the centre of the rose is under the space *between* H and I of SHILLING   *Halliday.*

WITH ORNAMENTS AT SIDE OF SHIELD.

68. ♂ Similar, but an ornament *added* on either side ; there are *nine* berries in the wreath.
℞ CATTLE · AND BARBER · ONE SHILLING   SILVER TOKEN · the *bottom* of B in BARBER lines to the *terminal* of the S in SILVER the centre of the rose is under the H in SHILLING   *R.*

69. ♂ Similar, but the cross is *not tinted*, a period after YORK ·
℞ As last.   *R.*
Boyne 232.

70. ♂ As last.
℞ Similar, but the bottom of the B lines *to* the I in SILVER The rose is *under* the H and I of SHILLING   *R.*   *Unknown.*

SIXPENCE.

71. ♂ Similar to the Shillings with the cross *tinted*; the stem of the palm is *over* the first one in date, and the letter Y is *omitted.*
℞ Similar, but legend SIX PENCE SILVER TOKEN   The top of B in BARBER lines to the *centre* of the S in SILVER
Boyne 234.

72. ♂ As last.
℞ Similar, but the top of B lines to the *bottom* of S in SILVER

73. ♂ Similar, but the stem of the palm is *between* the first two numerals in the date.
℞ As last.

YORKSHIRE.

74. ○ As last.

℞ Similar, but the top of the B in BARBER lines to the *centre* of S in SILVER *Halliday.*

Cattle and Barber were goldsmiths and jewellers in Coney Street, York.

"An issue of silver tokens has been made by Messrs. Cattle and Barber of York. These tokens are of the value of Shillings and Sixpences, and are finished in a neat style, bearing on one side the arms of the City of York, and on the other, their value, with the names of the issuers."—*Chronicle, Oct.* 12, 1811.

BARNSLEY.

PENNY.

COPPER.

75. ○ A weaver working a loom, no legend; the sley board *touches* the weaver's head at the *left*, and the cloth turns *under* the piece beam; the end of the piece beam is *seen* opposite to the knee of the weaver at the *right*.

℞ PENNY TOKEN in a circle. Legend PAYABLE AT JACKSON & LISTERS WAREHOUSE✶ BARNSLEY✶ The upright of the P is over the *upright limb* of the T in TOKEN and NN in PENNY are *without* their terminals.

76. ○ Similar, but the sley board *touches* the weaver's head in the *centre*, the cloth *longer*, the piece beam is *not seen* at the right of the weaver.

℞ Similar to last, but NN in PENNY are *correctly* formed.

PLATE E, no. 17.

77. ○ Similar, but the sley board *touches* the weaver's head at the *right*, the piece beam is *seen* at the *right* of the weaver, the *end* of the cloth is *pointed*.

℞ Similar, but the upright of the P is over the *commencement* of the T in TOKEN

78. ○ Similar, but the sley board *passes through* the weaver's head at the *right*, and is *connected* to the sley of the loom, *no* cloth is *seen* at the *left* of the weaver.

℞ As last. *R.* *Halliday.*

Sharp 204, 1.

Jackson & Listers were linen manufacturers and bleachers.

BEVERLEY.

THREEPENCE.

79. ○ The arms of Beverley, in chief argent, a beaver, three wavies azure. Legend, THE BEVERLEY NEW FRIENDLY SOCIETY ESTABLISHED 1789.

℞ THOMAS LECK FATHER Legend, THREE PENNY TOKEN 1813 *Wyon.*

PLATE K, no. 16.

The Beverley Brotherly Society, under the auspices of John Gould, Father, issued a very fine piece, the size of a penny, in the eighteenth century.—*Vide Batty* 629.

DONCASTER.

80. O Justice standing with scales and sword between bale and cask BIRKINSHAW ∴ DONCASTER ∴ On the ground V & D at the left of the figure.
℞ ONE PENNY TOKEN 1812 within a wreath of oak. *Halliday.*
PLATE E, no. 18.

BRADFORD WORKHOUSE.

See the Countermarked Tokens of Yorkshire.

HULL.

PENNY.

81. O A view of lead works. Under 1812 There are *four* small chimneys emitting smoke; and a stack or tall chimney which exhibits a very *small quantity* of smoke.
WORKS ℞ ONE PENNY HULL LEAD WORKS with an ornament under
PICARD Legend PAYABLE IN BANK OF ENG? OR HULL NOTES BY I. K.
NOTES The *last limb* of the second N in PENNY is under the N in NOTES
Sharp 204, 4.

82. O As last.
℞ Similar, but the *last limb* of the second N in PENNY is under the O in NOTES
PLATE E, no. 19.

83. O Similar, but with a *little more* smoke to the stack, and a *thinner* volume from the smallest chimney.
℞ As last.

84. O Similar, but there is *no* smoke exhibited from the small chimney *next* the stack.
℞ Similar, but the *last limb* of the second N in PENNY is under the N in NOTES

85. O Similar, but *still more* smoke from the stack, and the small one emits a *thick* volume at the left, H on the ground.
℞ As last.

86. O Similar, but the stack emits a *large* volume of smoke, there is a *key stone* over the centre of the archway; at the left H on the wall and H on the ground.
℞ Similar, but the *last limb* of the second N in PENNY is under the *last limb* of the N in NOTES

From a Photograph in the possession of W. Sykes.

YORKSHIRE.

87. ○ Similar, but the smoke issuing from the small chimney is *upright*, and *clear* of the stack, which previously it *touched*; the *keystone* over the centre of the archway *omitted*, as also are the initials on the wall and ground.
℞ As last.

88. ○ Similar, but *less* smoke from the stack and small chimney; a *keystone* over the archway.
℞ HULL LEAD WORKS An ornament above and below. Legend ONE PENNY · PAYABLE BY I · K · PICARD ·

89. ○ Similar, but the stack emits *much less* smoke.
℞ As last. *Halliday.*
Sharp 204, 3.

DOUBLE INSCRIPTION.

90. ○ HULL PENNY 1812 Legend, ONE POUND NOTE FOR 240 OF THESE TOKENS ·
℞ PAYABLE BY I · K · PICARD AT HIS LEAD WORKS IN HULL OR AT 124 UPPER THAMES STREET LONDON · * · *Halliday.*
Sharp 204, 5.

91. ○ As last.
℞ Similar, but the name instead of I · K · PICARD is J · R · PRICHARD and 184 UPPER THAMES STREET LONDON · * · R.r. *Halliday.*

This token was probably the first prepared, the mis-spelling of the name necessitated a new reverse die.

WELLINGTON.

92. ○ Bust to left (Wellington) unlaureated, in military uniform. VIMIERA · TALAVERA · BUSACO · BADAJOZ · SALAMANCA + The star of the most noble order of the garter *does not* appear on the bust.
℞ A mounted Cossack to right with musket and lance. COSSACK PENNY TOKEN *Halliday.*
PLATE F, no. 1.

This token is one of Halliday's finest productions, and is scarce, in consequence of its popularity with the American token collectors.

1813.

93. ○ Bust to left, similar to last, but *with* the noble star *on the* breast. VIMIERA · TALAVERA · BADAJOZ · SALAMANCA · VITTORIA ·
℞ A female seated to left; in her right hand an olive branch, in her left a trident, at her side the union shield; in the distance a ship. ONE PENNY TOKEN 1813
Sharp 207, 21.

NO DATE.

94. Similar, but without the date. R. *Halliday.*
Sharp 207, 24.

A A

HALFPENNY.

95. O. A lion sejant, the dexter paw on a shield gules, within a bordure a fleur-de-lys (the crest of the Picard family) ESSE· QUAM· VIDERI (to be rather than seem to be.)

℞ HULL HALF PENNY 1812 Legend, PAYABLE BY I · K · PICARD· LEAD WORKS HULL · The Y in PENNY lines to the *last limb* of R in WORKS
Halliday.

Sharp 211, 2.

96. O. Similar, but there are *no periods* in the legend.
℞ As last.

Sharp 211, 1.

97. Similar, but the Y in PENNY lines to the *first limb* of R in WORKS

98. Similar, but the Y in PENNY lines to the O in WORKS *Halliday.*

"John Kirby Picard's works were situated at the west end of the south side of the Queen's Dock. For some time prior to entering into the business of his father, Picard practised as an attorney-at-law in Trinity House-lane, and eventually became a barrister, and was chosen as a Deputy-Recorder of Hull. He was a man of considerable wealth, and in 1811 was solicited to stand as a candidate for the office of Member of Parliament for Hull, but declined in a letter dated 4th March, 1811, written from Summergangs House, Holderness-road, Hull. Picard became greatly reduced in circumstances, and died in 1843."—*W. Sykes's Hull Coins and Tokens.*

Mr. Sykes' information in the latter part of the paragraph is corroborated by the *London Gazette*, of Feb. 13, 1827, which announced that J. K. Pickard, white lead merchant, Russell Street, Covent Garden, had been declared bankrupt.

WELLINGTON'S BATTLES.

99. O. Bust laureated to left, in military uniform. HISPANIAM ET LVSITANIAM RESTITVIT WELLINGTON · (Wellington restored Spain and Portugal.) In the wreath there are *four* berries, *one* button on coat.

℞ CUIDAD (*sic*) RODRIGO JAN · 19 · 1812 · BADAJOZ APRIL 2· 1812 · SALAMANCA JULY 22 1812 &C. &C. &C. In an outer circle, VIMIERA AUG 21 · 1808 · TALAVERA JULY 28 · 1809 · ALMEIDA MAY 5 · 1811 ·

100. The same in Gold.

In the author's copy of Sharp, formerly the property of Robert, brother of William Boyne, at p. 212, the following note appears : "Head of Wellington ℞ Inscription on his battles 1812. A proof of this in gold was sold at Younge & Co.'s sale Sheffield in 1867."

101. The same in Silver.

102. Similar, but *with periods* after JULY · 22 · and 1812 · in the *seventh* line of the reverse.

103. The same in Silver.

104. Similar, but *two* berries in the wreath.

105. ○ Similar, but *without* the button on the coat.

℞ Similar, but *with periods* after JULY 22 · and 1812 · in the *seventh* line.

106. ○ Similar, but the button *again* on the coat, letters of legend *smaller*. Tip of wreath points to M in LVSITANIAM whereas in the others it is under the *second* A

℞ Similar, but *no period* after 1812 in *fifth* and *seventh* lines.

107. Similar, but &c. &c. &c. *omitted* and MADRID AUG 12 · 1812 · *substituted*.

108. Similar, but with *three* berries in the wreath. A *long* stalk *projecting* from the end of the *third* leaf.

109. Similar, but there are *no berries* in the wreath.

110. Similar, but button on coat *very large*, tie of wreath *hangs below* collar.

111. Similar, but *no* button on coat.

112. ○ Similar, but the button *again* on the coat, *four* berries in wreath. *Periods* after JULY · 22 · and 1812 ·

℞ Similar, but *without* a period after JAN

113. Similar, but *three* berries in the wreath.

114. ○ Similar, but with *four* berries in the wreath.

℞ CIUDAD instead of CUIDAD and *periods* after JAN · and AUG · R.

115. Similar, but *without* the periods after JAN and AUG

116. ○ Similar, but there are *no* berries in the wreath.

℞ SALAMANCA JULY 22 · 1812 · MADRID AUG 12 · 1812 · S^T SEBASTIAN SEPT 8 · 1813 · PAMPLUNO OCT 31 · 1813 · surrounded by CUIDAD RODRIGO JAN 19 · 1812 ⁖ BADAJOZ APRIL 2 · 1812 · The whole within an inner circle. The outer legend as before. R.

Halliday.

Extract from MS. on the Local Coinage of Kingston-upon-Hull, by John Richardson, dated on cover 1848, but evidently not finished until a much later period.

"SUMMERGANGS HOUSE, once the residence of J. K. Picard, and then pronounced upon the united judgement of 4 Nobles, 2 Marquises, and 2 Earls, the most gentlemanly and prettiest place of its size between Hull and London, . . . and when the Head of the Chancery Bar came to spend a few days of retirement with me J. K. P. at this house he expressed precisely the same opinion upon it as did the other Noble Lds. Hastings and Warwick, etc., etc.

"His business and pleasure as a rich man often calling him to London, and having an extensive acquaintance with the Nobility, Judges of the Land, and the Leading men in Parliament and the fashionable world, he was tempted to enter into the gambling dissipations of the period. At this time the French Armies in Spain and Portugal, under the command of Napoleon Buonaparte's Generals, were being beaten in a succession of Battles by Arthur, Duke of Wellington, and the idea struck Picard that he would issue a Token with the names of the Battles, and their dates, on one side and a profile of Wellington on the other, and as he gained fresh victories, he issued new Tokens with the additional battles, until at length, instead of having one list of victories in a circle round and in the centre of the token, he was obliged to add another circle with victories and dates. At one of the meetings where gaming was going on, some of these tokens were exhibited by him, and as Wellington was then the idol of the British people and the intimate friend of the Prince Regent, afterwards George 4th, the circumstance was mentioned to the Prince Regent, who invited him to Court, to exhibit his Tokens. Before he had an audience of Royalty he ordered several to be struck off in Silver, containing all the victories of Wellington to that date. The date of the last victory on these silver Tokens will therefore enable us to judge at what time, or nearly so, he went to Court.

"The author, in personal interviews with J. K. Picard, received from him the substance of the paragraphs relating to this Token, and also the Penny and Halfpenny Tokens, called the Lead Mill Tokens as related before. Picard at that time lived in Pemberton Street, Holderness Ward."

In the *Advertiser*, of August 14th, 1813, is the following notice respecting his Copper Tokens.

COPPER TOKENS.

"Some imitations of my Wellington Tokens being in circulation, without either the name of the person who issues them, or any pledge for repayment, I feel it due to the public and myself, immediately to call in all my Tokens bearing the name and likeness of Lord Wellington. I therefore request that they may be presented here, on or before the 7th of September next, between nine and ten o'clock in the morning on each day, when a clerk will be in attendance to receive them, and deliver Hull or Bank of England notes in exchange. After which day I cannot hold myself responsible for any of the above description. *BUT ALL the Copper Tokens with my name on them, I shall continue issuing*, so long as they may be of use to the Public, and *for the repayment* of THEM shall always hold myself responsible."

Lead Works, Hull, Aug. 13th, 1813.   J. K. PICARD.

John Picard established the Lead Works, which were on the Dockside, in the latter part of the eighteenth century, later John Smith joined the business, but when the tokens were issued the proprietor of the Mills was John Kirby Picard.

"In 1812, the English army, then in Spain, were distressed for the want of small change.

"I was applied to through Mr. J. K. Picard, of the great Lead Works, Hull, who, I understood, was appointed the agent, to obtain a peculiar coinage to pass in Spain for the value of one penny English; and which coinage was not to interfere with the coinage of the English Government, or with that of the Spanish Government.

"It was resolved then to have on the obverse the head of Wellington, and on the reverse the following victories: Battle of Vimiera, Passage of the Douro, Battle of Talavera, Lines of Torres Vedres, Battle of Albuera, Capture of Badajos, Battle of Salamanca.

"To make a good likeness of Lord Wellington for this coin, Mrs. Wellesley Pole* sent me a wax profile from Saville Row, Jan. 1812.

"I made upwards of two millions of these pieces in copper, which passed current with the army."—*The Memoirs of Sir Edward Thomason, p.* 48.

* The wife of William Wellesley Pole, who was appointed Master of the Royal Mint, on the 30th September, 1814.

KEIGHLEY.
See the Countermarked Tokens of Yorkshire.

LEEDS.
FARTHING.

117. O Arms, gules, a lion rampant between three acorns; no legend.

℞ A pair of scales. LEEDS 1812   *R.r.*
Boyne (Yorkshire Tokens) 37, 20.

Boyne says: "This was issued by William Jackson, tobacconist, at the time tobacco was sold at a penny three farthings the half-ounce." The writer of the *Bazaar Articles* adds "and also a tea dealer carrying on business at Lower Head Row, Sheffield."

118. Similar, but dated 1817   *Halliday.*
PLATE F, no. 2.

From a Plate in the possession of the Author.

MALTON.

FARTHING.

119. ☉ MALTON 1815
℞ ESTO JUSTUS (Be just). *Unknown.*

The issuer of this token, in adopting the motto, inferred that it was of just weight, and therefore the public were served. All efforts to trace the name of the issuer have failed.

SHEFFIELD.

PENNY.

120. ☉ Bust (George III) draped and laureated. FOR PUBLIC ACCOMMODATION SHEFFIELD On the shoulder H The nose of the effigy lines *to* the D in ACCOMMODATION and there are *two* projecting laurel leaves in the wreath.

℞ Britannia seated to left, with her attributes; a ship in the distance. ONE PENNY TOKEN 1812 The centre barb of trident is under the *foot* of the T and there are *six* leaves in the olive branch held by Britannia. *Halliday.*

Sharp 205, 8.

The issuer of this token is not known.

121. ☉ Similar, but the H on the shoulder is *omitted*, and there is *one* projecting laurel leaf in the wreath.

℞ Similar, but the centre barb of trident is under the O and there are *nine* leaves in the olive branch. R. *Unknown.*

A forgery of the time.

WORKHOUSE, 1812.

122. ☉ West view of the workhouse. OVERSEERS OF THE POOR· 1812· The eaves of the building at the left lines *between* the R and S of OVERSEERS The base line at the right lines to the *first limb* of R in POOR·

℞ Justice standing, with scales and olive branch, on a pedestal. SHEFFIELD PENNY TOKEN On the corner of the base at the right, H

Sharp 205, 9.

123. ☉ Similar, but the eaves of the building at the left lines to the *last limb* of the R in OVERSEERS The base line at the right is *below* the R in POOR·

℞ As last.

124. ⊙ Similar, but the eaves lines to the *centre* of the R in OVER SEERS and the base lines to the *centre* of the R in POOR·
℞ As last.

125. ⊙ As last.
℞ Similar, but the H on the base line is *omitted*. R. Halliday.

1813.

126. ⊙ A view of a building and legend as before, but dated 1813. The eaves of the building at the left lines *between* the R and S of OVERSEERS The base line of the building at the right is *opposite* the *first limb* of R in POOR· The centre bar to the door is *extended* to the masonry, and there is only *one* rail projecting on either side of the building.
℞ Justice standing, legend as before, with H on the base at the right; the first laurel leaf at the bottom is *partly hidden* by the arm of the figure.

PLATE K, no. 17.

127. ⊙ Similar, but the centre bar to the doorway *extends only* to the cross bar.
℞ Similar, but the first laurel leaf is *fully exhibited*.

128. ⊙ Similar, but the eaves lines to the *last limb* of the R in OVERSEERS The centre bar *extends* to the masonry, and there are *two* rails projecting on either side of the building.
℞ As last.

129. ⊙ As last, but the base line is opposite the *last limb* of the R in POOR· Only *one* rail projects on either side of the building, and *no cross bars* to the gate.
℞ Similar, but the first laurel leaf *partly hidden* by the arm of the figure; the left foot *does not* come to the edge of the pedestal as previously, the H on the pedestal is *omitted*.

130. ⊙ Similar, but only *four* perpendicular bars to the gate, the long one is *omitted*.
℞ Similar, but the first laurel leaf is *exhibited*, and the H *again appears* on the pedestal.

131. ⊙ Similar, but the eaves lines to the *centre* of the R *six* perpendicular bars, the base line is *between* the limbs of the R in POOR· and the bar in the centre *extends* to the top of the door; *two* projecting rails on either side of the building.
℞ Similar, but the H on the pedestal *omitted*.

132. ⊙ As last.
℞ Similar, but the letter V is on the pedestal at the right.

YORKSHIRE.

133. ◯ Similar, but the base line of the building is *opposite* the *last limb* of R in POOR.

℞ Similar, but *without* the initial on the pedestal.

1815.

134. ◯ View of Sheffield Workhouse, and legend as before, but dated 1815. The eaves at the left in line with the S of OVERSEERS The base line of the building is *opposite* the *last limb* of R in POOR.

℞ Similar to preceding, but Y & D·on the pedestal at the left, the first leaf of laurel is *partly hidden* by the arm of Justice.

135. ◯ Similar to last, but the eaves lines between the R and S of OVERSEERS and the base line of the building *touches* the *first limb* of R in POOR.

℞ Similar to last, but the first laurel leaf is fully *exhibited*.
Halliday.

The Westbar Pump stands on the site of the old Workhouse represented on the token.

136. ◯ A female standing, similar to preceding reverse, but between laurel and palm branches; the legend is *omitted*, and there is *no* initial on the pedestal.

℞ ONE PENNY TOKEN within a mixed wreath of oak and laurel. H on the laurel leaf opposite the N in TOKEN *R. Halliday.*

This reverse occurs at Burton and Not Local.

SHIELD OF THE TOWN TRUST.

137. ◯ Arms as described on the Half Crown, but without the oak and palm branches; under the arms, SHEFFIELD Legend, PAYABLE AT S· HOBSON & SON'S· BUTTON MANUFACTURERS·

℞ Britannia seated to the left, with her attributes, a ship in the distance; under the shield H Legend, ONE PENNY TOKEN 1812 Incuse on a raised band.

Sharp 205, 6.

138. ◯ As last.

℞ Similar to last, but dated 1813. *Halliday.*

Sharp 205, 7.

This token is of similar design to the Soho Penny by Küchler of 1797.

PHŒNIX IRON WORKS.

LONG CANNON.

139. ◯ View of Iron Mills; under, a pyramid of cannon balls, one, two and three between two cannons. Legend, PHŒNIX IRON-WORKS SHEFFIELD The lips of the cannon at the right, line to *end* of the small door in the wall.

℞ Justice standing with her attributes, between a corded bale and a cask labelled S J & C° A crowbar and two chisels on the ground. Legend, ONE PENNY TOKEN 1813 The hilt of the sword *touches* the centre cord of the bale, the right-hand beam of the scales line to the *foot* of the T in TOKEN

PLATE F, no. 3.

SHORT CANNON.

140. O Similar, but the lip of the cannon at the right lines to the *centre* of the small door in the wall which is *barred*, whereas in the last it is *plain*.

℞ Similar, but the hilt of the sword is *over* the centre of the corded square on the bale *near* to the robe of Justice, the right-hand beam of scales lines *to* the O of TOKEN *Halliday.*

Sharp 205, 15.

These works are still carried on at Furnace Hill. The proprietors who issued the token were Longden & Gregory, afterwards Longden, Walker & Co. The present occupiers of the works Longden & Co.

ROSCOE MILLS, 1812.

141. O View of a range of mills showing *fourteen* chimneys, a weather vane and flagstaff. Legend, ROSCOE PLACE SHEFFIELD On the ground at the right H There is an emission of smoke from *four* chimneys.

℞ Female seated to left on a bale labelled Y & D In her right hand a pair of scales, in her left a cornucopia of fruit; a sword on the ground and a ship in the distance. Legend, ONE PENNY TOKEN 1812 The point of sword is over the *centre* of the 8 in date

Sharp 205, 12.

142. Similar to last, but with an emission of smoke from *five* chimneys.

143. O Similar, but with an emission of smoke from *nine* chimneys, and the flagstaff *displays* its flag.

℞ Similar, but *without* the Y & D on the bale; the scale balance is *exhibited*, whereas in the last it is *not seen;* the point of sword is over the *space* between the *two first* numerals of date.

Halliday.

1813.

144. O Similar, but with an emission of smoke from *five* chimneys, and the flagstaff is *without* a flag.

℞ Similar, but dated 1813 On the bale Y & D The point of sword is over the *centre* of the 8 in date.

Sharp 205, 13.

145. O Similar, but with an emission of smoke from *seven* chimneys.

℞ As last.

146. O As last.

℞ Similar, but the cross bar at the hilt of the sword is *smaller* and *does not extend* to the base line; which it *does* in the last.

YORKSHIRE.

147. ○ Similar, but with an emission of smoke from *eight* chimneys.

℞ Similar to last, but the point of sword is *over* the *bow* of the 8 in date at the right. *Halliday.*

Shaw, Jobson & Co. were the issuers of the tokens. In 1887 the works were carried on by Barker & Sylvester; the patterns of their stove grate business were afterwards purchased by H. E. Hoole. The building has since been dismantled to make room for City improvements, but two streets newly made are named Roscoe Road and Jobson Road.

From a medal block in the possession of the author.

HALFPENNY.

148. ○ Bust of Lord Nelson to left in naval uniform. On the ribbon of the order of the garter, a medal. Legend, ENGLAND EXPECTS EVERY MAN TO DO HIS DUTY. There is *a band* of braid on the collar of the coat.

℞ 1811 PAYABLE AT N.º 18 NORFOLK ROW SHEFFIELD Legend, HALFPENNY · TOKEN A bird (the domestic cock) under SHEFFIELD

149. ○ Similar to last, but *with* w on the medal, and there are *two bands* of braid on the collar.

℞ As last.

PLATE F, no. 4.

150. ○ As last.

℞ A man-of-war sailing under canvas to right. Legend, BRITISH NAVAL HALPPENNY (*sic*) 1812 *T. Wyon.*

Sharp 211, 4.

ROSCOE MILL.

151. O View of factory warehouses, with gateway and office entrances. Legend, ROSCOE PLACE · SHEFFIELD · On the base line of the building at the left Y & D Also under the base line the Y & D is repeated.

℞ A female seated on a corded case, labelled S J & C⁰ In her right hand a pair of scales, in her left a cornucopia of fruit; a ship in the distance. There is *no sword* on the ground. Legend, HALFPENNY TOKEN 1812   *Halliday*.
PLATE F, no. 5.

Younge & Deakin were merchants and button manufacturers, in Union Street, Sheffield. The dies for the tokens, and their production, were the work of Thomas Halliday and Sir Edward Thomason, of Birmingham. It is evident that there was an understanding that the initials of Younge & Deakin were to be punched on the dies. The initials on token no. 151 are those of Shaw, Jobson & Co., who, at the time, occupied Roscoe Works.

SOWERBY BRIDGE.

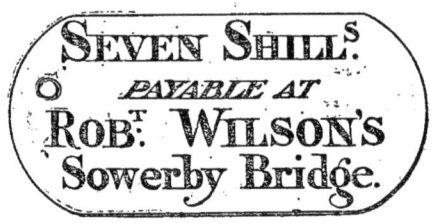

COPPER.
152. O SEVEN SHILL⁵ PAYABLE AT ROB.ᵀ WILSON'S SOWERBY BRIDGE ·
℞ N⁰ *R.r.r.*

YORK.

FARTHING.

153. O A cupid-arm, in the hand an olive branch. Legend, PEACE AND ALLIANCE ·
℞ YORK FARTHING 1814   *Unknown*.
PLATE F, no. 6.

WALES.

BRECKNOCKSHIRE.

BRECKNOCK.

SHILLING.

SILVER.

1. ℺ Arms (of Brecknock). A robe corded and tasselled. BRECK NOCK SILVER TOKEN FOR XII PENCE The T of TOKEN is over the centre of the robe.

℞ FOR ALL PARTS OF THE KINGDOM in three curved lines. A scroll ornament under KINGDOM Legend, PAYABLE AT GEORGE NORTHS GENERAL WAGGON WAREHOUSE The S in PARTS *lines to* the G in WAGGON and is quite *free* of that letter.

PLATE K, no. 18.

2. ℺ Similar to last, but T and O of TOKEN are over the centre of the robe.

℞ Similar to last, but the S in PARTS *intersects* the A in WAGGON

Halliday.

In Mr. Bowles' cabinet.

George North was a carrier between Brecknock and London; his house of call, the George Coach Office, Snow Hill, Holborn.

CARMARTHENSHIRE.

CARMARTHEN.

SILVER.
SHILLING.

1. O Crest, a crowing cock between sprigs of laurel. Legend, MORRIS & SONS On the *first* laurel leaf at the left H There are *three* berries in the olive branch at the right.

℞ CARMARTHEN TOKEN XII PENCE 1811 with a sprig of palm on either side.

PLATE K, no. 19.

2. O Similar to last, but there are *four* berries in the wreath at the right.

℞ As last. *R.r.* *Halliday.*

Boyne 45.

The crest was that of the Morris family. The issuers were bankers; their London agents, Foster, Lubbocks & Clarke.

3. O The script capital *W* in a beaded circle. Legend, CARMARTHEN BANK 1811

℞ XII within a band, which is inscribed TWELVE PENCE Legend, ROBERT WATERS & ROBERT WATERS · + · *R.r.* *Unknown.*

Boyne 46.

This bank stopped payment in 1863. The name of the firm then was Waters, Jones & Co.; the London agents, Barclay & Co.

PENNY.

COPPER.

4. O Arms argent, a castle triple towered; a chough (jackdaw) on each of the side towers, between ostrich feathers; base, a lion passant gardant, all in a circle. Legend, CARMARTHEN + PENNY + The horizontal bars of the gateway are fixed to reach the *centre*, the windows are *not* filled in.

℞ A cask within a wreath of oak. PAYABLE BY W· GRIFFITHS & Co 1812 There are *twenty-eight* leaves in the wreath at the left.

Sharp 192, 2.

5. O As last.

℞ Similar, but with *twenty-four* leaves in the wreath at the left.

6. O Similar, but the gateway is barred to the *top*.

℞ As last.

7. ☉ Similar, but the windows are *also barred*, the birds are *larger*.
℞ Similar, but with *twenty-seven* leaves in the wreath at the left. *R.*

PLATE F, no. 7.

8. ☉ Similar to last, but the *third* window at the right *only* barred, and the birds are *smaller.*

℞ PAYABLE BY WILL^M MOSS CARMARTHEN – SWANSEA · – AND AT JACOB & HALSE LONDON 1813 within a wreath of oak and acorns.

Halliday.

Sharp 192, 1.

Sharp incorrectly described the token JACOBS & HALSE.

William Moss was an ironmonger, and Jacob & Halse were factors, 1, Crescent, Jewin Street. The firm last named dissolved partnership on Jan. 8, 1823.

DENBIGHSHIRE.

GLANCLYDWEDOG.

PENNY.

COPPER

1. O View of a mill showing a *bell* at the end of the higher building. Legend, GLANCLYWEDOG FACTORY   Under the building 1813
℞ ONE PENNY TOKEN in a circle. Legend, ONE POUND NOTE FOR 240 TOKENS · *Halliday.*

PLATE F, no. 8.

FLINTSHIRE.

SHILLING.

SILVER.
1. O. Arms, sable, two keys in saltire. Crest, the Prince of Wales' plumes; the ribbon inscribed IC DIEN (*sic*) FLINTSHIRE BANK AUGUST 12 · 1811

℞ BANK TOKEN Under, in script capitals, *J O S & O* Above, a Staffordshire knot. Legend, FLINTSHIRE ONE SHILLING The top of the *J* does *not extend* beyond the K in BANK The commencement of *&* *touches* the *O*
.Boyne 79.

2. Similar, but the top of the *J* *extends beyond* the K The commencement of *&* does *not touch* the *O*

3. Similar, but the *J O S & O* omitted, and a Staffordshire knot above and below BANK TOKEN The end of the lower knot points to the A in BANK
Boyne 80.

4. Similar, but the end of the knot points to the O in ONE R.
Halliday.

SIXPENCE.

5. O Arms, crest and motto, as on the shilling. A similar legend, but there is no period after 12
℞ Similar to no 1, but value SIXPENCE
Boyne 81.

6. Similar to no. 3, but value SIXPENCE
PLATE F, no. 9.

"The Holywell and Flintshire Bank has issued silver tokens of shillings and sixpences, to the standard of the dollar. The device on one side is the County arms, and the Prince of Wales' crest, bearing the date of the 12th of August, 1811 :—on the reverse 'Flintshire Bank Token,' with the value."—*Bath Chronicle, Sept. 14th,* 1811.
Oakley & Company were the bankers, and their London agents, Ramsbottom & Co.

FLINT.

PENNY.

COPPER
7. O View of mills showing *eight* chimneys, mast and rigging of a vessel laying to by a crane. Legend, FLINT LEAD WORKS 1813 The *first* and *fifth* chimneys from the left do not emit smoke, the third is built from the *ground*, there are *seven* stays to the masts.

℞ ONE PENNY TOKEN in a circle. Legend, ONE POUND NOTE FOR 240 TOKENS · The top of P in PENNY lines to the *last* limb of N in POUND The figure 4 is *without* a crosslet.
PLATE F, no. 10.

8. Similar, but the top of P lines to the *centre* of the N in POUND

9. Similar, but the top of P lines to the *first limb* of N   R.

Sharp 193, 1.

10. ☌ Similar, but the *fifth* chimney from the left is the *only one* which does not emit smoke, and the third is built over with *brickwork* at the bottom; there are *eight* stays to the masts.

℞ Similar, but the top of P lines to the *second limb* of U and the figure 4 *has* a crosslet.

11. Similar, but the top of P lines to the *first* limb of U

12. ☌ Similar, but with *six* stays to the masts, and *shrouds* added. There is *no* emission of smoke from the *first* and *fourth* chimneys from the left. The third chimney built to the ground. The summit of the mast *touches* the first limb of R in WORKS

℞ Similar, but the top of P in PENNY lines to the *last limb* of the N in POUND   The figure 4 is *without* a crosslet.   R.

13. Similar, but the *third* chimney from the left is built over with *brickwork* at the bottom; the *first* and *fifth* chimneys *do not* emit smoke.

14. Similar to last, the *fifth* chimney from the left is the only one which does *not* emit smoke; the summit of the mast does not *quite* touch the *first limb* of R

15. Similar, but there are *ten* chimneys, the fourth, sixth and ninth from the left *do not* emit smoke, the summit of the mast only reaches the *last limb* of R in WORKS   *All by Halliday.*

These lead smelting mills had been long established when the tokens were issued. The writer of the *Bazaar* articles says: "In fact there is said to be no safety in attempting to limit their antiquity.... The works passed into the hands of Roskell, Tipton and Co.; by which firm, or their successors (Roskell, Williamson and Co.) we believe the token was issued. The Flint Lead Works are now absorbed in the more extensive Alkali Works of Muspratt Bros. and Huntley."

GLAMORGANSHIRE.

MERTHYR TYDVIL.

SILVER.   SHILLING.

1. ☉ View of a foundry with *six* windows, smoking chimneys, an elevator at the right, all in a circle, surrounded by a laurel wreath. No legend.
℞ MERTHYR 5TH SEP. 1811 Ornaments divide the legend. The ones in date *slope* R.
PLATE F, no. 11.

2. Also in Copper. *R.r.*

3. ☉ Similar, but with an *additional* window in the foundry.
℞ Similar, but the ones in the date are *flat*. *R.r.*

4. ☉ Similar, but the laurel wreath is *omitted*.
℞ As no. 1.
In the Murdoch collection of tokens.

5. ☉ View of a foundry, similar to no. 1.
℞ WALES AND BRISTOL in a circle. Legend, MERTHYR 5TH SEP Ornaments divide the legend. *R.*

6. ☉ Similar, but the smoke from the centre chimney *meets* the smoke from the one at the left.
℞ Similar, but the letters of the legend are *larger*, the W in WALES is *below* the M in MERTHYR whereas in the last it was in *line* with the *first limb* of that letter. *R.r.* Halliday.

7. ☉ The Prince of Wales' plumes. MERTHYR SILVER TOKEN FOR 12 PENCE Legend, TO FACILITATE TRADE CHANGE BEING SCARCE 1811 The tops of the ones in date are *flat*.
℞ BY MORG^N. LEWIS MORG^N. MORGAN DAVID WILLIAMS W^M. WILLIAMS. MERTHYR TIDVIL A sprig of palm over MERTHYR TIDVIL Legend, A POUND NOTE GIVEN FOR 20 OF THESE SILVER TOKENS ... *Both* letters of BY are under the figures 20
PLATE K, no. 20.

8. ☉ Similar, but the ones in date *slope*.
℞ Similar, but Y in BY is under O of 20 and only *seven* blades in the palm spray *instead* of *eight*. *R.r.r.* Halliday.

C C

NEATH.

SHILLING.

9. ☉ An embattled tower between buildings, flag posts at the sides, H H on the ground ; all within a circle. Legend, PAYABLE AT H · REES'S & D · MORGAN'S The first flag post at the left is supported by *two* stays.

℞ 12 PENCE 1811 in a circle. Legend, NEATH SILVER TOKEN

Boyne 154.

10. ☉ Similar, but there is only *one* stay to the first flag post at the left.

℞ As last.

11. Similar, but *without* the inner circle on the reverse. R.

Boyne 155.

12. ☉ Similar, but the roof line of the building at the left lines *between* L and E in PAYABLE instead of *to* the L

℞ As last. R.

13. ☉ Similar, but *without* the flag posts at the right. Legend, S? WALES & NEATH SILVER MEDAL *

℞ 12 MARCH 1811 Legend, NEATH SILVER MEDAL R.r.

Morgan was declared bankrupt April 22, 1826, and paid dividend December 6th, 1827. He was an ironmonger.

SIXPENCE.

14. ☉ A tower as no. 7. PAYABLE AT H REES'S & D· MORGAN'S · On the ground H H

℞ SIX PENCE within an olive wreath. Legend, NEATH SILVER TOKEN

PLATE F, no. 12.

15. ☉ As last.

℞ 12 MARCH 1811 *Halliday.*

This is in brass, and in Mr. Bliss' cabinet.

SWANSEA.

SHILLING.

16. ☉ View of Swansea Castle, showing a *flagstaff* on each tower, houses at the sides. No legend.

℞ PAYABLE AT S· PADLEYS & I· ANDREWS[S] within a laurel wreath. Legend, SWANSEA SILVER TOKEN FOR XII PENCE *Halliday.*

Boyne 217.

Sylvanus Padley, wine and spirit merchant in the Strand, was one of the principal inhabitants of Swansea, and occupied several public positions.

17. ○ Similar view of Swansea Castle; but the tall tower shows a *weather vane*, and the houses at the sides are *omitted*. SWANSEA TOKEN FOR XII PENCE · MDCCCXI ·

℞ A key suspended from a knotted ribbon. PAYABLE BY· JOHN VOSS DRAPER &c. *Halliday.*
Boyne 218.

The design of this piece was taken from John Voss's token of the eighteenth century, by Thomas Wyon; illustrated in Pye 46, 1, and described by Conder 36, 2. In that instance, as was the custom, the edge is inscribed PAYABLE ON DEMAND whereas in this, as is the case in most of the silver tokens of the nineteenth century, the pledge is inscribed on the face of the coin. Ten cwt. of the halfpenny tokens were issued. John Voss, of the *Golden Key*, circulated a large quantity of his silver shillings.

PENNY.

COPPER.

18. ○ ONE PENNY A star above and below in a circle. Legend, NANTRHYDNŶVILAS AIR FURNACE Cº.·

℞ 1813 A star ornament above and below in a circle. Legend, PAYABLE AT SWANSEA & MORRISTON · The ornament over the date is under the s and E in SWANSEA
Sharp 194, 1.

19. Similar, but the ornament over the date is under the N and S in SWANSEA and the figure 3 is *smaller*. R. *Turnpenny.*

The writer of the *Bazaar* articles informs us that the Air Furnace Company was established by the Bevans of Morriston, near Swansea, for the purpose of profitably utilising the slag thrown out of the smelting works at Landore.

20. ○ ONE PENNY TOKEN A quatrefoil above and below. Legend, SWANSEA AND SOUTH WALES · 1813 ·

℞ BY L· W· DILLWYN T· BEVINGTON AND J· BEVINGTON An ornament under the *second* BEVINGTON Legend, PAYABLE AT THE CAMBRIAN POTTERY SWANSEA + *Halliday.*
Sharp 194, 2.

The Cambrian Pottery was on the river Tawe, where the North Dock now is.

The Cambrian Potteries were erected in the Strand, Swansea, and pottery first made there in 1780. In 1802 L. W. Dillwyn became sole proprietor.

The opaque porcelain at these potteries "delineated natural history, birds, butterflies and flowers. The ware became remarkable for its beautiful and truthful paintings."

A plate, painted in wild roses, in the South Kensington Museum, is marked Dillwyn & Co.

Mr. Richard Drane, of Cardiff, says "there were two Bevingtons, Quakers; one was part proprietor of the works, and the other commercial representative or traveller."

A trident is one of the marks found on Cambrian pottery.

Chaffers says "The name of Bevington is occasionally found on pieces of recent manufacture, but we have no information respecting him."—*Marks and Monograms on Pottery and Porcelain*, 10th ed., 1903, *p.* 929.

The Swansea penny, issued by Dillwyn and T. & J. Bevington, shows conclusively that the latter were potters as early as 1813.

MONMOUTHSHIRE.

ABERCARNE.

SHILLING.

COPPER.

1. O ONE SHILLING N⁰ – Legend, ABERCARNE IRON WORKS SAMUEL GLOVER

℞ I PROMISE TO PAY THE BEARER ON DEMAND A ONE POUND NOTE FOR TWENTY OF THESE PIECES   *Unknown.*

PLATE K, no. 9.

In Mr. Norman's cabinet.

This County was in the Principality of Wales until 1535.

MONTGOMERYSHIRE.

WELSHPOOL.

SHILLING.

SILVER.

1. O 1813   Legend, MONTGOMERYSHIRE ONE SHILLING
℞ R· GRIFFITHS CORNER SHOP W · POOL   Legend, ONE POUND NOTE FOR 20 TOKENS   *R.r.r.*   *Unknown.*
PLATE M, no. 4.

The issuer was also a County banker. He was declared bankrupt on November 12th, 1816.—*London Gazette.*

PEMBROKESHIRE.

HAVERFORDWEST,

SHILLING.

SILVER.

1. O A castle triple towered; issuant from the centre, a herald with a cavalry bugle. On each of the side towers, a flagstaff and flag. HAVERFORD WEST SILVER TOKEN FOR 12 PENCE 1811 ····₀₀····
℞ PAYABLE AT MESS^{RS} THOMAS & PHILLIPS DAVID JARDINE JOHN LLOYD & W & J· PHILLIPS Not in a circle. Legend, ONE POUND NOTE FOR 20 TOKENS· *Halliday.*
PLATE F, no. 13.

The issuers of this token were the principal tradesmen, who formed a private company to supply the public with necessary change.

SCOTLAND.

AYRSHIRE.

TWO SHILLINGS AND SIXPENCE.

SILVER.

1. ○ Bust to right, GEORGIVS· P· S· C· D· 1799 (Georgius Princeps Senescallus Scotiæ Cornubia Dux.) Under the bust, *Milton*

℞ Arms. The order of St. George; and motto, Honi soit qui Mal y Pense surrounded by four shields, crowned. First, England and Scotland impaled, difference by a label of three points; second, France; third, Ireland; fourth, Hanover; between each the Prince of Wales' plumes. Legend, BR· L· PR· E REG· SC· PR ET· SEN COR· DUX (Brunsvicensis Lunenburgensis. Princeps; et Regni Scotiæ Princeps et Senescallus. Cornubia Dux.)

Boyne 24, 16.

2. Also in Gold.
3. Also in Copper.
4. Also in White Metal. *R.r.*

ONE SHILLING AND SIXPENCE.

5. Similar to no. 1, except in size, but with *Milton F* under the bust.

6. Also in Gold.
7. Also in Copper.
8. Also in White Metal.
9. ○ A Trial Piece, of the obverse of no. 5, in White Metal, *without* the artist's name, and in a circle *instead* of a toothed border. ℞ Blank. *R.r.r.* *Milton.*

PLATE I, no. 13.

10. Similar to no. 5, but the apex of the Hanoverian shield is over the I of HONI *instead* of over the *space* between HONI SOIT *R.*

This is generally found in copper, and recognised by eighteenth century token collectors as a halfpenny.

MULES.

The obverse of no. 5 is muled with the following reverses of Eighteenth Century Tokens.

11. A female seated, in her right hand a garland, her left resting on a shield charged with St. Andrew and his cross, a thistle at the right. SCOTIA REDIVIVA At the left M on the ground. *Ex.* 17 €ℱ 97

PLATE·I, no. 14. *Milton.*

Davis' Sale, Sotheby, Wilkinson & Hodge, March 14, 1901, no. 578.
This reverse die was engraved for Colonel Fullarton, who issued the Wallace Halfpenny Token, *vide Atkins* 299, I.

12. A female standing, holding her robes in her right hand, dropping with her left herbs into a still, a plant at the right. HYGEIA PREPARING VELNOS' VEGETABLE SYRUP✷ In the exergue, P· *R.r.*

Milton and Ponthon.

PLATE I, no. 15.

SHILLING.

13. O Similar to no. 1 except in size, and *Milton ℱ* under the bust omitted.

℞ Similar, but legend reads REGNI SCOTIÆ SENES CALLVS *R.r.r.*

PLATE I, no. 12.

SIXPENCE.

14. Similar to no. 1, except in size, and *M.* under the bust. *R.r.r.*

Boyne 25, 19.

15. Also in Gold.

16. Also in Copper.

17 Also in White Metal.

The gold impressions were in the Murdoch Collection, and sold in the Scottish Series, lot 373, by Sotheby Wilkinson & Hodge, on the 13th of May, 1903. The degree of rarity applies to original specimens.

The original half crown and eighteenpence may be identified by the absence of the flaw under the bust. The restrikes are on thick instead of thin flans. The illustrations on Plate I are from originals. Subsequently to the restriking by Matthew Young, the dies were taken to the late W. J. Taylor, who supplied the tokens to order as required, and those in gold are of yet more recent striking.

Sharp says : "The dies for this rare token were made for COLONEL FULLARTON, afterwards Governor of Trinidad, under the direction of Mr. Young; the object not being mentioned at the time by COLONEL FULLARTON, but it afterwards appeared the coins were intended for circulation as shilling tokens in SCOTLAND, the sanction of the PRINCE OF WALES having been previously obtained. The late SIR JOSEPH BANKS happening to see the dies whilst in the possession of MILTON, was so struck by the resemblance of the design to the National silver coin, and the illegality of the Royal Arms being thus assumed by the PRINCE upon a piece intended to be current, that he cautioned the artist against further proceeding, since he might be liable to a charge little short of High Treason. In consequence, the project was abandoned, only a few proofs being struck, and those in copper."

Sir George Chetwynd, quoting this, states : "for the same purpose dies were prepared for the striking of shillings smaller than those for the halfpenny, which they resemble in every other respect, except the legend of the reverses. A few pieces were struck in Silver for presents. Dies were also prepared for half crowns and sixpences exactly like the halfpenny, size only excepted. It does not appear that any impressions, except a very few in soft metal, were taken off at the time ; but afterwards there were some struck in silver from the dies which were in Mr. Young's possession."

BERWICKSHIRE.

DUNS.

FARTHING.

LEAD.
1. O GRAY TOBACCONIST
   ℞ DUNSE 1813   *Unknown.*
   In the British Museum.

2. O ECCLES 1813
   ℞ blank   *R.r.r.*
   Neumann 24923.

EDINBURGHSHIRE.

EDINBURGH.

LEAD.
FARTHING.

1. O W. BEGG 139 COWGATE
   ℞ ONE FARTHING 1813   *R.r.*
   PLATE K, no. 21.

2. O J. BROWN L^N M^K. (Lawn Market)
   ℞ FARTHING 1805   *R.r.*
   Neumann 24839.

3. O Wm CALDER EDINBURGH
   ℞ TEAS & SPIRITS 1806   *R.r.*
   Neumann 24840.

4. O S. P. CHRISTIE TOBACCONIST
   ℞ ROYAL EXCHANGE 1812   *R.r.*
   Neumann 24843.

5. O A star.   A D. DOUGLASS EDIN^R
   ℞ Two pipes in saltire.   TOBACCONIST LAUN (*sic*) MARKET.   *R.r.*

6. O MENELAWS WEST BOW 1805
   ℞ TEA AND SPIRIT WAREHOUSE   *R.r.*
   Neumann 24863.

7. O D. PURDIE WEIGH HOUSE
   ℞ EDINR. 1806   *R.r.*

COPPER.

8. O ALEX ROBB TIN SMITH * CANNON GATE *
   ℞ PAYABLE AT 289   Palm branches below.   *R.r.*
   Batty 1238.
   This is found in copper and lead.

9. O JOHN STEELE'S TIN & OIL SHOP
   ℞ PAYABLE 224 * CANON GATE *   *R.r.*
   Atkins 321, 112.

LEAD.

10. O An ancient gateway in a shield; crest, an anchor.   NISI DOMINUS FRUSTRA. (It is vain without the Lord.)
    ℞ J. T.   B. C 1821.   *R.r.*
    This piece is oval, and in white metal. *Nisi dominus frustra*, motto of Inglis Edinburgh.

11. ○ J. WILL
    ℞ COWGATE HEAD 1806 *R.r.*
    Neumann 24883.

12. ○ A jug within a circle. J THOM + CHINA MERCHANT ·
    ℞ COWGATE FARTHING *R.r.*
    Atkins 321, 116.

13. ○ ALEX^R WISE· F·
    ℞ EDIN^R 1806 *R.r.*   *Unknown.*
    Neumann 24885.

DALKEITH.
FARTHING.
LEAD.
14. ○ J. MILLER DALKEITH
    ℞ 1806 *R.r.*
    Neumann 24832.

15. ○ A & J SCOTT DALKEITH 1812
    ℞ TEAS SPIRITS & WINES *R.r.*
    PLATE K, no. 22.

16. ○ JA^S WHITE DALKEITH·
    ℞ 1806 *R.r.*
    Batty 1153.

ESKMILLS.
FARTHING.
LEAD.
17. ○ WIL^m JAKSON· PAPIN·
    ℞ ESK MILL 1812 *R.r.*
    Neumann 24889.

LEITH.
FARTHING.
LEAD.
18. ○ JOHN EGGO
    ℞ LEITH 1806 *R.r.*
    Neumann 24898.

COPPER.
19. ○ LEITH Wm CHRISTIE   An ornament above and below LEITH
    ℞ ONE FARTHING 1819
    PLATE F, no. 15.

LEAD.
20. ○ A· MCEWEN
    ℞ WATER OF LEITH 1806 *R.r.*
    Neumann 24860.

21. O W MILLER 1806
    ℞ LEITH FARTHING· *R.r.*
    Atkins 323, 139.

22. O W MILLER· SENIOR:
    ℞ LEITH· 1806 *R.r.*
    Atkins 323, 140.
    The two last are found in copper and lead.

23. O JAS· POLLOCK
    ℞ LEITH + 1806 *R.r.*

24. O R WILSON· TOBACCONIST 1812
    ℞ NORTH LEITH *R.r.*
    Neumann 24915.

MUSSELBURGH.

FARTHING.

LEAD.
25. O 1805 MUSSELBURGH
    ℞ COWANS FARTHING *R.r.*

26. O T· THOMSON MUSSEL^{GH}
    ℞ FARTHING 1805 *R.r.*
    Neumann 24892.

27. O *W Gray*
    ℞ 1805 A scroll above and below the date.
    PLATE I, no. 17.

28. O M & S
    ℞ 1806
    The last two are in Mr. Fletcher's cabinet.

FIFESHIRE.

DUNFERMLINE.

FARTHING.
COPPER.
1. O J. KIRK · ✳ - MERCH^T HIGH — STREET ✳   An ornament below MERCH^T.
   ℞ DUNFERMLINE ✳ FARTHING ✳ 1817   *R.r.*

LIMEKILNS.

FARTHING.
LEAD.
2. O PAYABLE· AT· R· MAILLERS · · · ·.LIMEKILNS·
   ℞ ONE FARTHING 1819   *R.r.*

3. O As last.
   ℞ GROCER· & SHIP CHANDLER·   An ornament above and below SHIP

FORFARSHIRE.

DUNDEE.

SHILLING.
SILVER.

1. ☊ An armed Highlander. FROM THE HEATH = COVERED MOUNTAINS OF SCOTIA WE COME Below, in a sunk oval, the arms and motto, DEI DONUM (The gift of God) of Dundee. The end of the sword points to A in MOUNTAINS
    ☋ View of a ruin. DUNDEE SHILLING PAY^{LE} BY J. WRIGHT JUN Over the ruin the date 1797 *Ex.* BROUGHTY CASTLE *R.r.*
PLATE M, no. 5.

2. Also in Copper.

3. ☊ As last.
    ℞ View of the Cross. DUNDEE SILVER MEDAL PRICE ONE SHILLING At the sides of the Cross, W DES Under, CROSS TAKEN DOWN 1777 *R.r.r.*

4. Also in Copper. *R.r.r.*
    Norman's sale, 419, Sotheby, Wilkinson & Hodge, July 15th, 1903.

5. Similar to last, but the end of the sword points to the T in MOUNTAINS *R.r.*
PLATE I, no. 16.

6. Also in Copper. *R.r.*   *Wyon.*

James Wright, of Dundee, was a famous collector, and was ardent in his efforts to obtain issuers of eighteenth century tokens. He wrote the preface for James Conder, and, in an able article, under the *nom de plume* of "Civis," in the *Gentleman's Magazine*, 1796, said : "Excepting the Coins of the Romans, there has nothing occurred parallel to these within so short a period, since the eras of the independent State of Greece, when almost every City had its distinct Coinage."

BRECHIN.

HALFPENNY.
COPPER.

7. ☊ West view of a mill showing a water wheel. EAST MILL BRECHIN 1801
    ℞ West view of a church. PAYABLE BY SMITH AND WILSON Under the building, CHURCH
PLATE F, no. 16.

8. ☊ As last.
    ℞ Similar to last, but the legend omitted, except CHURCH
    E. PAYABLE BY SMITH AND WILSON + + +   *Willets.*

Atkins 294, 5.
Smith & Wilson were flax-spinners.

HADDINGTONSHIRE.

PRESTONPANS.

FARTHING.
LEAD.
1. O G · NIMMO · PRESTON · PANS · 1813 ·
℞ GROCER · AND · TOBACCONIST · *R.r.*

INVERNESS-SHIRE.

BRACTEATE TOKENS OF THE HIGHLANDS.

TWOPENCE.

BRASS.

1. I'LL PAY 2· PENCE G : BEVERLY   A crown above, a thistle below, all within a border of pellets. *R.r.r.*
PLATE N, no. 1.

2. I PROMISE TO PAY ON DEMAND 2 PENCE G BEVERLY in a cable circle. *R.r.r.*
PLATE N, no. 2.

3. I Promiſe to Pay on demand twopence fter IN? GRAY 1758 in a circle. *R.r.*
PLATE N, no. 3.

4. ANGUS M^C DONELL WILLIAM FRASER   Four stars above ANGUS   Outer legend, WE PROMISE TO· PAY· Y^E BEARER ON DEMAND 2 Pence all within an oval. *R.r.*
PLATE N, no. 4.

"William Fraser was a merchant in Fort William, in 1744, thereafter vintner in Inverness."—*Inverness-shire Antiquarian Notes, by C. Fraser Mackintosh, F.S.A.*

5. I Promiſe to Pay on demand 2 pence W M^C Intosh∗ in a circle. *R.r.*
PLATE N, no. 5.

6. I Promiſe to PAY on demand two Pence fter ALEX· M^C PHERSON 1761 in a circle.
PLATE N, no. 6.

In Mr. Fletcher's cabinet.
In the manuscript catalogue of the Banks Collection in the British Museum, it is noted that this token was received as currency at Fort William in 1787.

7. I PROMISE TO PAY ON DEMAND 2 PENCE D Mr VICAR in a cable circle. *R.r.*
PLATE N, no. 7.

"Duncan Mc Vicar was appointed barrack master at Fort Augustus in 1768."— *C. Fraser Mackintosh, F.S.A.*

8. I'LL PAY 2 PENCE A· STEWART   Three castles above and three pellets, two over one, below. *R.*
PLATE N, no. 8.

9. The same as last, struck on a thick flan in white metal.

In the British Museum.
The Banks manuscript catalogue in the British Museum notes that the tokens of A. Stewart were received as currency at Port Augustus in 1789.

LANARKSHIRE.

GLASGOW.

PENNY.

COPPER.

1. ☌ View of a building showing front warehouses with gateway, a factory at the left; there are *nine* chimneys PHŒNIX IRON-WORKS GLASGOW   Under the base line Y & D   There is no smoke seen from the *second* chimney from the right end of the building.

℞ Justice standing between a corded case and a cask, labelled between the first and second hoops, S and between the second and third, S· J & C°   The figure of Justice has in her right hand a sword; in her left, a pair of scales; *three* chisels by a crowbar, on the ground, coins by the case ONE PENNY TOKEN 1813   The point of the sword is under the *last limb* of the *first* N in PENNY   The left foot of the figure is over the *second* one in date.

PLATE F, no. 17.

2. ☌ Similar, but smoke is emitted from *all the nine* chimneys; the *fourth* from the end of the building at the right is under the *space* between R and K in WORKS

℞ Similar to last, but the initials on the cask are *omitted*; the hilt of the sword does *not touch* the case, *two* chisels by the crowbar.

Sharp 228, 1.

3. ☌ As last.

℞ Similar, but the hilt of the sword *again touches* the case, the foot of the figure points to the *last* numeral of date, only *one* chisel by the crowbar.

4. ☌ Similar, but the *fourth* chimney from the right end of the building is under the *first limb* of K in WORKS

℞ As last.

5. ☌ As last.

℞ Similar, but the point of sword is under the *centre* of the first N in PENNY and there are *two* chisels by the crowbar, the position of the left foot as on no. 1.   *Halliday.*

The writer of the Bazaar Articles, says " The Phœnix Iron Works appear to have been established in Glasgow at the commencement of the present (nineteenth) century by Thomas Edington .... the works are still actively carried on ... The Phœnix Iron Foundry is situate at 94, Garsube Road (corner of Anne Street), Glasgow."

FARTHING.

6. ◯ D BONE & C° & PAYABLE AT GLASGOW
℞ 1806 ? The last numeral *detrited*.
In Mr. Norman's cabinet.

7. ◯ JOHN Mᶜ MILLAN & Cᵒ. –1816–
℞ TOBACCONIST + GLASGOW·+ *R*. *Unknown.*

CALTON.

FARTHING.

8. ◯ A pair of scales, HENRY REID + 1815 CALTON +
℞ TEAS· SPIRITS WINES· & GROCERIES· *Unknown.*
PLATE F, no. 14.

9. ◯ Similar, but BARROWFIELD ROAD added to the *legend* and the date *omitted*.
℞ As last. *R*.
Atkins 320, 102.

10. ◯ A pair of scales with two ornaments H · REID · BARROW · FIELD CALTON·
℞ As last. *R*.
Atkins 320, 103.

"These tokens are wrongly attributed by Mr. Atkins to Edinburgh."—*Lionel L. Fletcher, Spink's Circular, Jan.* 1903.

HAMILTON.

FARTHING.

11 ◯ HAMILTON RETAILERS TOKEN
℞ ONE· FARTHING 1814 *Unknown.*
PLATE K, no. 23.

PEEBLESHIRE.

FARTHING.

LEAD.

1. O ROB.ᵀ FRAZER · PEEBLES · 1813 ·
   ℞ Three fishes in fess TEA AND SPIRIT · DEALER ·   *Unknown.*
   In Mr. Fletcher's cabinet.

Scotland was famous for its farthing tokens. There are described in Atkins' *Tokens of the Eighteenth Century*, no less than 136, but he says "some of them may belong to the nineteenth century." Probably many of them do, but to recognise these where no value or date is expressed, would open a wide door for the inclusion of many doubtful pieces.

IRELAND.

Co. DUBLIN.

DUBLIN.

SHILLING.

SILVER.

1. O. A female robed and seated to left on a rock, supporting on her left shoulder a caduceus, her right hand pointing to a merchant vessel; on the prow, I (Ireland). *Ex.* The *countermark*, a harp crowned. No legend.

℞. FOR ONE BRITISH SHILLING 1804 Above the word FOR a small countermark of Hibernia. Legend, SOLD BY CLARK WEST AND C° *R*.

PLATE M, no. 6.

2. The same in copper, but *without* the countermarks on obverse and reverse. *R.*

3. O. Similar, but with COMMERCE *above* the seated figure.
℞. Similar, but the date is *omitted*. *R.r.r.* *Hancock.*

Boyne 6.

The countermarks are similar to those of the Dublin Assay Office of the time, but without the letters. Aq. Smith says " Clarke and West, wholesale goldsmiths and jewellers, resided at No. 9, Capel Street, in 1804. This long established firm is now represented by Messrs. West and Son, 18 and 19, College Green."

4. O. A robed female figure seated to right on a mound, holding the model of a ship. Legend, CONFIDENCE AUGMENTS THE VALUE Under the figure an oval, inscribed *J B C°* (Irish Bullion Company)

℞. FOR ONE BRITISH SHILLING D 2. 16 G. (2 dwts. 16 grains). Legend, SOLD BY THE IRISH BULLION C°. Hall marks on either side of D 2. 16 G. The O in ONE lines to the B in BY *R.r.*

5. Similar, but without the countermarks. *R.r.*

PLATE M, no. 7.

6. Similar to no. 4, but the D and G^s and the period after ONE *omitted*, the O in ONE lines to the *space* between BY *R.r.* *Hancock.*

PLATE M, no. 8.

These three tokens were made at Peter Kempson's manufactory, Birmingham. Aq. Smith was under the impression that this reverse was the same as no. 4, but the die worn from repeated lapping; this is not so, as will be seen on reference to the illustration of both the reverses in plate M.

From a Plate in the possession of the Author.

DUBLIN.

7. ○ A tripod altar with burning incense, entwined by a serpent, olive branches at the left, and a celestial globe at the right. 2 DWT 20 GS STERLING   Legend, PUBLIC HAPPINESS 1804

℞ A female figure supporting a crown, above a cippus inscribed, HEALTH TO THE KING   Legend, PRO BONO PUBLICO

Boyne 23, 8.

8. ○ As last.

℞ Similar, but legend reads, PROBONO PUBLICO and, KING on the cippus in much larger letters.

PLATE F, no. 18.

"So great is the scarcity of silver in Dublin that it is customary to pay 10d. for change of a £1. note."—*Bath Chronicle*, Sep. 24, 1812.

The state of the silver coinage in Ireland was worse in 1804 than in 1812, when this announcement was made.

PENNY.

COPPER.

9. ○ Hibernia seated to left, a harp at her side, PAYABLE AT THE PAWNBROKERS OFFICE BISHOT ST

℞ The monogram *W F B & Co*   Above the monogram, PENNY   Below, 1804   Legend, LICENCED BY ACT OF PARLIAMENT TOKEN   *Mossop.*

Atkins 3.

The initials are those of W. F. Bently & Company, trading as indicated on the token.

10. ○ Bust to left laureated, on the shoulder I PARKES   Legend, WELLINGTON & VICTORY 1814

℞ A robed female seated to left on a rock, with spear and olive branch, a shield, bearing the Irish harp at her side, a ship in the distance EDW^D BEWLEY 1816   On the ground I P F·   *Parkes.*

Sharp 238, 2.

The issuer was a grocer at 35, South Earl Street.

ROLLING MILLS.

11. ○ View of the interior of a rolling mill showing two men at work, and a large fly-wheel; ONE PENNY TOKEN   In the exergue, J· HILLES DUBLIN   The last cog in the wheel is *clear* of the man's head at the right.

℞ A sprig of shamrocks, PAYABLE IN BANK OF IRELAND NOTES· 1813

Sharp 237, 1.

12. Similar, but without the period after J and the corner of the last cog in the wheel is *hidden* by the man's head.   R.   *Halliday.*

Sharp 237, 2.

PLATE F, no. 19.

James Hilles, wholesale iron merchant, Abbey Street, was free of the six and ten per cent. duty in the Customs House, Dublin.—*Wilson's Dublin Directory*, 1799.

CREST A COCK.

13. ○ Crest, a cock upon a wreath in a circle, MERCHANTS above; STORES below. Legend, FOR THE USE OF HIS OWN ESTABLISHMENT· 1813· The O of OF is over the *centre* of the M in MERCHANTS

℞ TOKEN in a circle. JAMES'S above, STREET below. Legend, EDWARD STEPHENS'S DUBLIN The second T in STREET is over the *last* limb of the N in DUBLIN The ceriphs or tops of the ones in date point to the *left*. *R.r.*

PLATE F, no. 20.

14. ○ Similar, but *both* letters of OF are over the M in MERCHANTS

℞ Similar, but the T is over the *centre* of the N in DUBLIN

Halliday.

15. ○ Similar, but the ceriphs to the ones in date point to the *right*.

℞ Similar, but JAMES'S *omitted* from above. Under the circle JAMES'S STREET *Halliday.*

Sharp 264, 2.

16. ○ Crest, a cock, a much larger bird, *without* the inner circle. Legend, FOR THE USE OF HIS OWN ESTABLISHMENT · 1813 ·

℞ A harp of *nine* strings surmounted by a royal crown. E · STEPHENS · DUBLIN *R.r.r.*

Sharp 264, 1.

This rare piece is from a pattern by Halliday, and was rejected in favour of the bird in a circle, with the additional legend.

WELLINGTON AND ERIN GO BRAGH.

BUST TO LEFT, 1813.

17. ○ Bust to left *laureated*, in military uniform. WELLINGTON & ERIN GO BRAGH (Ireland for ever) 1813 The projecting laurel leaf points to the & There is a *button* on the epaulet strap.

℞ A harp of *nine* strings surmounted by a royal crown. E · STEPHENS · DUBLIN· The arch of the crown is decorated with *nineteen* pearls.

PLATE F, no. 21.

18. Similar, but the projecting laurel leaf points to the N in WELLINGTON

Sharp 238, 1.

19. The same in silver *R.r.r.*

This was in the possession of Aq. Smith, and described in a note at the end of his silver tokens in 1855.

20. Similar, but the top of the cross is *directly under* the upright limb of P in STEPHENS· whereas in the former it is *slightly* at the right. *R.r.r.*

This is in tin, *vide* Davis' sale, 796, March 15th, 1901.

DUBLIN.

21. ☉ Similar, but the bust *unlaureated*.
℞ Similar, but there are *twenty-three pearls* in the arch of the crown. *R.r.* *Halliday.*
PLATE I, no. 22.

1814.

22 ☉ Similar to last, but the bust laureated, dated 1814 The *button* on the epaulet strap *omitted*, the star is over the 8 in date.
℞ As last.

23. Similar, but the centre laurel leaf points to the & the button *again* on the epaulet strap, the star is over 1 and 8 of date.

24. Similar, but the star is over 8 and 1 of date.

1816.

25. ☉ A draped laureated bust with long *flowing* hair. WELLINGTON & ERIN GO BRAGH On the shoulder P
℞ A harp of *ten* strings, surmounted by a royal crown. EDW^D STEPHENS 1816 *Parkes.*
PLATE F, no. 22.

26. ☉ Bust laureated, after the *antique*. I PARKES on the shoulder; the top centre laurel leaf points *to* & and the end of ribbon to the H in BRAGH
℞ Similar to last, but the harp has *nine* strings; the top of cross on the crown is under the *upright* limb of E in STEPHENS

27. ☉ Similar, but the centre laurel leaf points *between* & and E in ERIN and the end of ribbon to G in BRAGH
℞ As last.

28. ☉ As last.
℞ Similar, but the harp has *eight* strings; the top of cross is under the *space* between T and E in STEPHENS

29. ☉ Similar, but I PARKES F on the shoulder.
℞ Similar, but with *nine* strings to the harp; the right corner scroll projection lines to the S in STEPHENS

30. ☉ As last.
℞ Similar, but the harp has *eight* strings, the corner scroll projection lines to the N in STEPHENS

31. ☉ Similar, but the end of ribbon points to the H in BRAGH
℞ Similar, but the harp has *nine* strings. *Parkes.*

32. ☉ Similar, bust to left laureated with bare neck. I PARKES F on the shoulder; over the head, WELLINGTON Under, ERIN GO BRAGH
℞ Similar to last, a harp with *nine* strings, etc.

33. ○ As last.
℞ Similar to last, but the harp has *eight* strings.   *Parkes.*
PLATE F, no. 23.

Edwin Stephens was a corn factor and proprietor of the Merchants Stores, 30, West Cole Alley, and one of the few citizens free of custom duty.—*Wilson's Directory*, 1799.

BUST TO RIGHT.
1818.

34. ○ A laureated and draped bust to the right. WELLINGTON & ERIN GO BRAGH
℞ A harp of *eight* strings surmounted by a royal crown. IRELAND 1818 *R.*   *Wyon.*

1822.

35. ○ Similar to last, but the bust has *long* flowing hair. Legend, WELLINGTON ERIN GO BRAGH
℞ Similar, but dated 1822, and the harp has *ten* strings.

36. ○ As last.
℞ A robed female figure seated; a trident in her left hand, in her right a laurel sprig, at her side the union shield, a ship in the distance. Above, HIBERNIA   *Ex.* 1822   *Unknown.*

GEORGE III.

1800.

37. ○ A laureated and draped bust to right (George III) *with long* flowing hair. ONE PENNY TOKEN The projecting laurel leaf points to the *centre* of the second N in PENNY
℞ A female seated *to right*; in her left hand a sprig of shamrock, her right hand resting on a shield. IRELAND 1800 *R.*
Unknown.

This is a forgery of the time, and the figure intended for Britannia is peculiar, as she is seated to the right. There can be no doubt that the token was struck much later than the date indicated. Mr. Fletcher has a specimen *post-dated* 1827.

1814.

38. ○ Similar to last, but the projecting laurel leaf points to the *first limb* of the second N in PENNY
℞ A harp of *ten* strings surmounted by a royal crown. IRELAND 1814 The tops of the ones in date are *flat*. *R.r.*

39. ○ Similar, but the bust is *without* the *long* flowing hair; W on the shoulder; a *period* after the legend.
℞ Similar to last, but the ones in date *slope*.   *R.r.*   *Wyon.*

DUBLIN. 217

1819.

40. ○ Bust to right, *with long* flowing hair, laureated and draped. ONE PENNY TOKEN. The top leaf of laurel points to the Y in PENNY
℞ A harp of *nine* strings surmounted by a royal crown. IRELAND 1819 *Küchler.*

1820.

41. ○ Similar, but *without* the period after the legend; the top leaf of laurel points to the *first limb* of the second N in PENNY
℞ Similar, but dated 1820

42. ○ Similar, but the top leaf of laurel points to the *centre* of the second N in PENNY
℞ As last. *Küchler.*
This is struck on a thinner flan.

BUST TO RIGHT.
St. Patrick Apostle.

1806.

43. ○ Bust to right crowned with a wreath of shamrock. S^T PATRICK APOS 432
℞ A harp of *nine* strings surmounted by a royal crown. IRELAND 1806 *R.* *Parkes.*

PLATE G, no. 1.

This is struck over J. Hilles' Penny of 1813. Others are found struck over various tokens of later make.

Referring to the difficulty of recognisng some of the Irish busts, the writer of the *Bazaar Articles* suggests the appropriate legend: "Whose image and Superscription hath it."

1818.

44. ○ Bust laureated to right (George III). LUKE· XX : CHAP· XXV : VER· (And he said unto them, Render therefore unto Cesar the things which be Cesar's).
℞ A harp of *eight* strings surmounted by a royal crown. IRELAND 1818

1821.

45. ○ As last.
℞ Similar, but dated 1821

1822.

46. ○ As last.
℞ A female figure seated to left; a trident in her left hand, in her right an olive branch, the union shield at her side, a ship in the distance. HIBERNIA 1822 *P. Wyon.*

BUST TO LEFT.

ST. PATRICK.

1815.

47. O Bust unlaureated to left, a cross on the breast. sᵀ PATRICK APOS 432

℞ A robed female figure seated; in her left hand a spear, in her right an olive branch, a shield at her side bearing a harp; in the distance a ship. HIBERNIA 1815 *R.* *Parkes.*

These were made at a later date, as they are found struck over Stephens' tokens of 1818. The figures on the tokens represent the year A.D. 432, when it was supposed the Patron Saint of Ireland commenced his mission to convert the pagan Irish to Christianity.

GEORGE PRINCE REGENT.

1818.

48. O Bust (Prince of Wales) laureated to left, on the shoulder W Legend, LUKE XX : CHAP · XXV : VER · Under the bust E· STEPHENS·

℞ A harp with *eight* strings surmounted by a royal crown IRELAND 1818

PLATE G, no. 2.

1822.

49. O As last.

℞ As 46 ; female seated with trident, etc. Legend, HIBERNIA 1822

DOUBLE OBVERSE.

50. O As last.

℞ As no. 44 ; bust to right (George III) LUKE etc. *R.r.*
P. Wyon.

EDMUND BURKE.

1806.

51. O Bust to left unlaureated, P on the shoulder ONE POUND VALUE FOR 240

℞ A harp of *nine* strings surmounted by a royal crown IRELAND 1806

This was engraved at a later period than that indicated, as specimens are found struck over tokens of a later date.

1815.

52. O As last.

℞ As 47 ; female with spear, etc. HIBERNIA 1815 *Parkes.*

DANIEL O'CONNELL.

53. O A large laureated bust to left, IRELANDS ADVOCATE

℞ A harp of *nine* strings surmounted by a royal crown ; three leaves of shamrock on the sound board, MAY OUR FRIENDS PROSPER
Parkes.

PLATE G, no. 3.

WITHOUT BUSTS.

54. ○ A harp of *nine* strings, surmounted by a royal crown. HIBERNIA 1805
℞ ONE PENNY in a circle. Legend, FOR PUBLIC ACCOMMODATION
Wyon.

DOUBLE REVERSE.

55. ○ A harp of *nine* strings, surmounted by a royal crown, IRELAND 1806 The cross on the crown *does not* touch the orb.
℞ Similar to the obverse, but dated 1805.
Some of the tokens without issuers' names, were also circulated in England.

HALFPENNY.

56. ○ Hibernia seated to left, her right hand resting on her knee, her left supporting a harp. PAYABLE AT THE PAWNBROKERS OFFICE BISHOP S^T The head of the figure is under F and A of PAWNBROKERS A *flaw* runs through the die from B in PAYABLE to T in THE
℞ W J B & C^O Under the monogram 1804 Legend, LICENCED BY ACT OF PARLIAMENT * * * *R.r.r.*
Sharp 238, 2.
The obverse die failed, which necessitated a new one.

57. ○ Similar to last, but the head of the figure is under the A and W of PAWNBROKERS and *without* the *flaw* in the die.
℞ As last. *Mossop.*
PLATE G, no. 4.

58. ○ View of the interior of a rolling mill, showing two men working, and a fly-wheel. HALFPENNY TOKEN above. *Ex.* J. HILLES DUBLIN
℞ A sprig of shamrocks, PAYABLE IN BANK OF IRELAND NOTES 1813 *Halliday.*
Sharp 238, 3.

59. ○ Hibernia seated to right supporting a harp in her right hand, and a cornucopia in her left, HALFPENNY PAYABLE AT Under the figure: MDCCCIII
℞ A ship sailing under canvas, THE WAREHOUSE OF NEVILL & C^O DUBLIN *R.r.r.* *Mossop.*
PLATE M, no. 9.
Brent Nevill, Sheriff's Peer, was a merchant at 52, Abbey Street. He was exempt from Custom dues.

Wellington:

1805.

60. ○ Unlaureated and undraped bust to left. FIELD MARSHAL WELLINGTON

℞ A harp of *nine* strings surmounted by a royal crown. HIBERNIA 1805 *R.* *Unknown.*

1816.

61. ○ A laureated bust to left in military uniform. THE ILLUSTRIOUS WELLINGTON

℞ A harp of *eight* strings surmounted by a royal crown. WATERLOO HALFPENNY 1816 *Halliday.*

George III.

1814.

62. ○ Laureated and draped bust to right. HALFPENNY TOKEN The centre laurel leaf *points* to the Y in HALFPENNY

℞ A harp of *ten* strings surmounted by a royal crown. IRELAND 1814 *R.* *Unknown.*

1819.

63. ○ Similar, but the centre laurel leaf is *under* the *second* N in HALFPENNY

℞ A harp with *nine* strings. IRELAND 1819 The scroll of the harp at the right lines to the *first limb* of the N and the cross *touches* the L in IRELAND

64. ○ As last.

℞ Similar, but the scroll of the harp at the right lines *to* the *centre* of the N and the cross is *quite clear* of the L *R.* *Küchler.*

The two last tokens, and the pennies of similar design described under nos. 40, 41 and 42, resemble the 1805 regal coinage of Ireland, manufactured at the Soho Mint and engraved by Küchler. This eminent artist, besides engraving the dies for the regal coinage of 1797-1807, and the tokens made at Soho for the Bank of England and Bank of Ireland, was perhaps the finest commemorative medal designer this Country has had. Unfortunately, he had a dispute with Matthew Boulton a short time before the death of the great inventor, which lead to a separation after many years of service. At the time of the quarrel, Küchler was engaged on a medallion of Boulton, which afterwards was finished by Pidgeon, who received £300 for the work. Küchler, at one time carried on business at Bride Court, Fleet Street, as a medal engraver. He died in comparative poverty, and rests in Handsworth Churchyard; where there is no stone to perpetuate his memory.

65. ○ Laureated and draped bust to right. LUKE· XX· CHAP· XXV : VER·

℞ A harp of *eight* strings surmounted by a royal crown. IRELAND 1821 *Küchler.*

St. Patrick, Apostle.

66. ○ An unlaureated draped bust to right, a cross on the breast. s^T PATRICK : APOSTLE 432 + The cross is suspended by a *chain*.

℞ A harp of *nine* strings surmounted by a royal crown. IRELAND 1806 *R.r.*

67. ○ Similar, but legend s^T PATRICK APOS 432 On the shoulder P The cross is connected to the rosary or necklet by a *loop* instead of a *chain*.

℞ As last. *R.* *Parkes.*

PLATE G, no. 5.

The last two pieces and the penny of similar design, although dated 1806, were struck at a later period.

68. ○ A large laureated bust to right. HALFPENNY TOKEN

℞ Hibernia seated to left, supporting a harp of *eight* strings. HIBERNICUS 1820 *Parkes.*

Without Busts.

69. ○ Hibernia seated to left; her right hand supporting a harp of *eight* strings, her left resting on her knee. HIBERNIA 1804 The harp points to the letter A

℞ FOR THE CONVENIENCE OF TRADE No inner circle.

Sharp 138, 5.

70. ○ Similar, but the harp points to the letter I

℞ A ship sailing under canvas. FOR THE CONVENIENCE OF TRADE * *R.* *Mossop.*

Sharp 238, 5.

71. ○ Hibernia seated to left; supporting in her left hand a harp of *six* strings, her right resting on her knee. Under the harp a shamrock. ONE HALFPENNY TOKEN · 1820

℞ A ship sailing under canvas. TRADE AND NAVIGATION · *Unknown.*

72. ○ A beehive and bees. FROM INDUSTRY ABUNDANCE FLOWS·

℞ A harp of *nine* strings surmounted by a Royal crown. To the left of the crown E and to the right Mc Legend, ONE HALFPENNY TOKEN 1819 *R.r.*

73. Also in Silver. *R.r.r.* *Mossop.*

74. ○ Britannia seated with her usual attributes; a ship in the distance. HALFPENNY

℞ A harp of *nine* strings surmounted by a Royal crown. THE UNION 1801 *Küchler.*

PLATE G, no. 6.

75. ○ Hibernia seated supporting a harp of *nine* strings.

℞ A harp of *eleven* strings surmounted by a royal crown HIBERNICUS 1830 *Unknown.*

This was struck at an earlier period, although dated 1830.

ORDS.

76. ○ A laureated bust to left. GEORGE ORDS TOKEN
℞ A harp of *seven* strings surmounted by a Royal crown.
IRELAND 1834 *Unknown.*
Although this token is dated 1834, it has every appearance of having been struck during the token period.

PANTHEON.

77. ○ West view of a building. Under, 1802
℞ PANTHEON Legend, PAYABLE AT THE PHUSITECHNIKON *A flaw* appears at the P in PANTHEON
Atkins 432, 140.

78. Similar to last, but the last letter in PANTHEON *extends beyond* E in THE whereas in the last it is *in line* with the circular legend. There is *no flaw* by the letter P. *P. Wyon.*
A very similar token was issued in 1799, but the entrance to the Pantheon has plain instead of panelled doors.
The writer of the *Bazaar Articles* states that the issuer of the token was William Binns, an ironmonger, at the Pantheon, 25, Stephen's Green, which was a stores for the sale of a variety of articles.

1820.

79. ○ A laureated and armoured bust to left. No legend. The ribbon from the wreath *rests* on the shoulder-piece.
℞ A harp of *ten* strings, 1820 The scroll of the harp is over the space *between* 8 and 2 of date.

80. Similar, but the harp has *nine* strings, the scroll of the harp is *over* the 2 in date.

81. Similar, but the scroll is *over* the 8 in date.

82. ○ Similar, but the ribbon falls below the shoulder-piece.
℞ Similar to last, but the scroll is over the 1 and 8 in date.
Unknown.

These tokens are of rude execution, in brass or yellow metal, and resemble the imitation regal money circulated during the reign of George III. They are included for the same reason as the 1812 Not Local pieces, to show the debased token issues or forgeries of the period. Breton says there are 25 minute varieties.

83. Also in Copper, dated 1825 *R.r.*
Probably struck 1820.

SWORDS.

84. ○ Hibernia seated to left holding a harp of *six* strings. FINGALL ✶ HALFPENNY ✶ 1804 ✶
℞ *W H Cº* PAYABLE AT SWORDS OR DUBLIN *R. Mossop.*
Atkins 345, 168.

85. Similar, but legend reads FOR THE GOOD OF THE PUBLICK ✶ 1804 ✶ *R.* *Mossop.*

86. Also in Silver, on a thin flan. *R.r.r.* *weight 2 dwts. 19 grs.*
Boyne 22, 7.
Fingall is a district, and Swords a town, both in County Dublin.

Co. GALWAY.

MENLOUGH.

SIXPENCE.

COPPER.

1. O A leopard passant gardant, within a garter inscribed VIRTUS SOLA NOBILITAT· (Virtue alone ennobles.)

℞ MENLOUGH CASTLE SIX PENCE WORK TOKEN 1819 *Unknown.*

PLATE J, no. 23.

KINGS COUNTY.

TULLAMORE.

ONE SHILLING AND ONE PENNY.

COPPER.

1. ☦ Arms, first and fourth quarterly vert, a cross crosslet; second and third azure, on a chief indented three mullets, a crescent, over all an escutcheon; supporters, two Moors in golden armour; crest, the coronet of a viscount; motto, VIRTUS SUB CRUCE CRESCIT (Virtue increases under a cross); over the crest, CHARLEVILLE Under the motto, FOREST All within a circle. Legend, INDUSTRY SHALL PROSPER· The date 1802 between sprigs of shamrock. There are *ten* shamrocks in the sprig at the left; and the end of the ribbon at the right lines with the *terminal* of E in PROSPER·

℞ PAYABLE AT TULLAMOORE FIRST TUESDAY IN EACH MONTH· Above PAYABLE a rose and branches of shamrock; under MONTH olive branches; all in a circle. Legend, ONE SHILLING AND ONE PENNY· A conventional scroll divides the legend; the Y in TUESDAY lines *between* P and E of PENNY· and the terminal shamrock at the left is under the O in ONE

PLATE G, no. 7.

2. ☦ Similar to last, but with only *eight* shamrocks in the sprig at the left; and the ribbon at the right, lines to the *first* limb of E in PROSPER· There are *two* tassels on the coronet, whereas in the last there is only *one*.

℞ Similar, but the top of Y in TUESDAY lines to the *first* limb of E in PENNY· *R.r.r.*

3. Similar, but the top of Y in TUESDAY lines to the P in PENNY and the terminal shamrock at the left *extends* to the first limb of N in ONE *Soho Mint. T. Wyon.*

In Mr. Norman's cabinet.

The arms, crest, etc., are intended to be those of Charles William Bury, Viscount Charleville, and Baron Tullamore. The token is one of the best executed of the nineteenth century; and, fortunately, the finest examples are the commonest variety.

Lindsay, *Coinage of Ireland*, p. 64, says: "A proof in copper gilt of a Charleville *shilling* token, 1802, is in the Dean of St. Patrick's cabinet." But Lindsay's description of the reverse is ONE SHILLING AND ONE PENNY· It is unfortunate that an author, writing on tokens only 37 years after they were issued, did not obtain the information as to why and under what conditions a copper piece was circulated for about twelve times more than its intrinsic value..

Charleville was born 1764, made a Viscount 1800, died 1835. The Forest mansion was burned down in 1808.

LONDONDERRY.

COLERAINE.

PENNY.

COPPER.

1. ☉ A female robed and seated to left on a corded bale; in her right hand a pair of scales, a cornucopia of fruit over her left arm, a harp at the side, a ship in the distance, and a sword on the ground; D between the harp and the bale. Legend, W · M^C·KENZIE · COLERAINE ·

℞ ONE PENNY TOKEN 1813 within a wreath of shamrock and laurel. There are *three* berries in the laurel branch. *Davies.*

Sharp 237, 1.

Co. LOUTH.

DROGHEDA.

HALFPENNY.
COPPER.

1. O Hibernia seated to left supporting a harp. LEINSTER × HALFPENNY × 1804 ×

℞ The monogram $I\,M\,C^o$ (Irish Mining Company) Legend, PAYABLE AT DROGHEDA OR DUBLIN ✶   *R.r.*   *Unknown.*
Atkins 331, 3.

HALFPENNY.

2. TATE & LILL LOUTH in a rectangle (*M.* 2), countermarked on George III halfpence. *R.r.*

PLATE J, no. 4.

This should have been included in the Countermarked section.

Co. MAYO.

WESTPORT.

ONE SHILLING.

TIN.

1. O + MARQUIS OF SLIGO + TOKEN FOR ONE SHILLING STERLING ✱
℞ PAYABLE AT KELLY'S ESTATE + + + EACH FRIDAY EVEN^G 6 O'CLOCK ✱ (*M.* 11). *R.r.r.*

SIXPENCE.

2. O Similar, but STERLING *omitted*, value SIX PENCE
℞ Similar, but EVENING *instead* of EVEN^G (*M.* 9). *R.r.*

THREEPENCE.

3. O Similar, but *without* the star and crosses in the legend, value THREEPENCE
℞ Similar, but *a period* instead of a star after O'CLOCK · (*M.* 8½). *R.*

These three pieces have holes in the centre, *Mionnet* 1, down in proportion. The legends on the tokens very much resemble in character those of Charleville Forest, King's County.

"I much regret that I am unable to give you any satisfactory information about the family 'Tokens.' There is only a vague tradition that, during the last 25 years of the eighteenth century and the first 25 years of the nineteenth century, these were issued in place of money. Those in the eighteenth century would be in the name of Lord Monteagle, Viscount Westport, or the Earl of Altamont, as the Marquisate was not created till 1800. We did not know that any of the tokens existed, and I am much interested to hear that you have some."—Earl of Altamont, heir to the Marquis of Sligo, to the author, Jan. 22, 1904.

Co. TYRONE.

STRABANE.

COPPER.

1. O Similar to the Coleraine Penny, female seated, etc., but the harp has *eight* strings instead of *seven*; the D again *appears*, but its bow is partly *hidden* by the sound board. Legend, G · IRVINE STRABANE

℞ ONE PENNY TOKEN 1812 within a wreath of shamrock and laurel, *four* berries in the wreath. *R*.   *Davies*.

2. Similar, but dated 1813
        PLATE G, no. 8.

Atkins, p. 347, gives a list of Irish leaden tokens, and says they were issued in Dublin towards the close of the eighteenth century. Lindsay, in his advertisement, p. 139, states that they were struck at Cork between 1809 and 1813. As there is a doubt, and none of them are dated, they are omitted.

From a Plate in the possession of the Author.

EIGHTEENTH CENTURY IRISH TOKENS.

Co. ANTRIM.

BALLYMENA.

TWOPENCE.

COPPER.

1. ☉ A hare lodged; below 2 · P (two pence). Legend, · I · MAKE · GOOD · SPEED · The *right* ear of the hare *touches* the P in SPEED ·
℞ · I · PROMISE TO · PAY · THE BEARER · ONE (*sic*) DEMAND · TWO PENCE · IA^S · ADAIR · B · MENA 1736. *R.r.*
Aquilla Smith 1.
PLATE N, no. 9.

2. ☉ Similar, but the *right* ear is *some distance* from the P
℞ Similar, but · IAM^S ADAIR · The ND in DEMAND *not* joined. *R.r.*
PLATE N, no. 10.

3. Similar, but the *left* ear of the hare is *under* the S in SPEED ·
In Mr. Fletcher's cabinet.
PLATE N, no. 11.

4. ☉ Similar, but the *right* ear of the hare is *under* the ·I·
℞ Similar, but the last letter in BEARER · is under the T in THE *whereas* in the preceding it is under the Y in PAY ·
In Mr. Fletcher's cabinet.
PLATE N, no. 12.

The following extract from Benn's History of Belfast is of interest:—"It cannot be discovered that any bank was established in Belfast prior to the year 1752. In that year the earliest bank, which is known, was formed, the partners in which were Daniel Mussenden, *James Adair* and Thomas Bateson, three of the principal merchants in the town."

Probably James Adair here referred to was the issuer of the token, as he occupied a good social status at the time. The successors of James Adair still hold a leading position in Ballymena. The representative of the family is Frederick Adair of Ballymena Castle. In the "Mc Donnells of Antrim," it is mentioned that William Adair, who died in 1626, purchased the estate of Sir Faithful Fortescue.

5. ☉ A double-headed eagle displayed, dividing 2 · P Legend, · READY · AY · READY . ° .
℞ · I · PROMISE TO · PAY · THE BEARER · TWO PENCE · ALEX · BEITH · B : MENA 1735 *R.r.*
Aquilla Smith 2.
PLATE N, no. 13.

Advertisement from the *Belfast News Letter*, from the 16th to the 27th of Feb., 1739:
"TICKETS LOCAL.—Whereas there are some Persons betwixt *Lisburn* and *Belfast*, who have counterfeited my Tickets with a Dye and Press, and sell them to the Country People, at half what they pass for. Therefore these are to give Notice to all Persons who have any of my Tickets, that they bring them unto me at any time before the first of *March* next (Counterfeits excepted) and I will pay them in Gold or Silver, and will give two Guineas reward to any Person or Persons, who will discover the Person or Persons who made these Counterfeit Tickets with the Die and Press, so that they may be convicted of said cheat.
ALEXANDER BEITH."

BELFAST.

TWOPENCE.

6. O A falcon volant, trussing a mallard (wild duck) NEVER · WITHOUT · MY · PREY   Only *one* wing of the falcon is seen.
℞ · I · PROMISE TO · PAY · THE BEARER · TWO · PENCE · IOHN · KNOX · BELFAST 1735   The H in IOHN is over the E and L in BELFAST   *R.r.*

Aquilla Smith 4.
PLATE N, no. 14.

7. O Similar, but the falcon exhibits *both* its wings.
℞ Similar, but the H in IOHN is over B and E of BELFAST

PLATE N, no. 15.
In Mr. Fletcher's cabinet.

"John Knox, watch maker, Belfast, was sworn to the 'Roll of Freemen' on the 11th of September, 1729."—*Town Book of Belfast, R. M. Young.*

8. O A wolf rampant, gorged and chained, dividing 2 P · Legend, · FIERCE AND · STRONG · · The hind feet of the animal are over the *space* between STRONG · and FIERCE ·
℞ · I · PROMISE TO · PAY · THE BEARER · TWO PENCE · HUGH MAGARRAGH BELFAST · 1736 ·   The A and S in BELFAST do *not touch*.   *R.r.*

Aquilla Smith 5.
PLATE N, no. 16.

9. O Similar, but the hind feet of the animal are over AND · and there is *no period* after P   R.
℞ As last.

Aquilla Smith 6.
PLATE N, no. 17.

10. O As last.
℞ Similar, but the A *touches* the S in BELFAST

In Mr. Fletcher's cabinet.

The wolf figures as a supporter in the arms of Belfast.

11. O A dove displayed, in its bill a sprig of olive. GOOD TIDINGS Above the wing at the left ⸵
℞ · · I · · PROMISE TO · PAY · THE BEARER · TWO PENCE : W^M·· RING LAND BELFAST 1734   *R.r.r.*

12. Similar, but value expressed ⸵   *R.*

Aquilla Smith 7.
PLATE N, no. 18.

13. Similar, but dated 1735   *R.r.*

Aquilla Smith 8.

14. Similar, but the value *omitted*, date 1734   *R.*

Aquilla Smith 9.

IRISH TOKEN COINAGE. 231

15. ☊ A lion rampant, supporting a wheatsheaf above a leopard's head. Legend *detrited*.

℞ I PROMISE TO PAY THE BEARER ON DEMAND TWO PENCE (name *detrited*) BELFAST

> In Mr. Fletcher's cabinet.
> PLATE N, no. 19.

PENNY.

16. ☊ Similar to no. 13, except in size:

℞ · I · PROMISE TO · PAY · THE BEARER · ONE PENNY ·· W:^{M} RING LAND BELFAST 1734 *R.r.*

> Aquilla Smith 10.
> PLATE N, no. 20.

HALFPENNY.

17. ☊ View of the High Street, showing on the principal building a centre tower with weather vane. BELFAST TICKET · 1734 · all within a cable border.

℞ I'L PAY THE BEARER ONE · HALF PENNY · W IOHNSTON 1/2 · ⅌ P.^{d} FOR THIS CO ⅌ (One shilling and two pence per lb. for this Copper Paid).

> Aquilla Smith 3.
> PLATE N, no. 21.

There are only two specimens of this token known, one being in the Belfast Museum and the other in Mr. Fletcher's cabinet. The two last, and the Maculla halfpennies are included in order to keep together this section of the Irish Tokens.

In the *Ulster Journal of Archæology*, of January, 1903, Mr. Lionel L. Fletcher has an article on this token. He says :—"The most interesting feature is the representation of Belfast. It shows a part of High Street and the end of one of the bridges which crossed the open river. The lofty steeple figure in the view was considered by George Benn to be the old market-house which formerly stood at the corner of the Corn Market." Mr. Fletcher however, expresses the opinion that the "building more probably represents the old Parish Church, in High Street, which was taken down in 1774, and which stood on the site now occupied by St. George's Church."

Mr. Fletcher thinks the issuer was "William Johnston, Baker, who it is recorded in the Town Book of Belfast, was admitted in 1729, to the freedom of the town."

BELLYLONAGHAN.

TWOPENCE.

18. ☊ A peacock 2 · P Legend, YOUTH AND BEAUTY

℞ I PROMISE TO · PAY · THE BEARER · TWO PENCE · ALLEX M^C CLURE · BELLYLONA GHAN · 1735

> Aquilla Smith 11.
> In the Dublin Museum.

Aquilla Smith mentioned that the name of Ballyloghnegany occurred in the *Index Locorum* of the Ulster Inquisitions, but he was unable to locate it.

BREBY.

19. ☉ A pelican in its piety. WITH MY BLOOD I FEED MY YOUNG

℞ * I * PROMISE TO PAY · Y^E BEARER ON DEMAND TWO PENCE PATRICK BROWN · BREBY · (?) *

Aquilla Smith 12.
PLATE N, no. 22.
In the British Museum.

This token may belong to Bready, Co. Tyrone, but spelled *BREDY.* The reverse is rather indistinct, especially so in the name of the town.

GLENARM.

20. ☉ An anchor and cable, between two fleurs-de-lis. 2 · P below. Legend, · I · LIVE · IN · HOPE · The *links* in the cable *are joined,* and the o in HOPE is the same size as the other letters.

℞ · I · PROMISE TO · PAY · THE BEARER · TWO PENCE · HUGH MOUNT GOMERY GLENARM · 1736 · The period after TO *touches* the P in PAY · *R.r.*

PLATE N, no. 23.
In Mr. Fletcher's cabinet.

21. ☉ Similar, but the *links* in the cable are *not joined,* and a small o in HOPE

℞ Similar, but the period is *equidistant* from TO · and PAY

Aquilla Smith 19.
PLATE N, no. 24.

Hugh Montgomery of the Ardes was the first Earl of Mount Alexander in the seventeenth century, and the name Hugh occurs in " Burke."

LISBURN.

22. ☉ Unicorn's head to left couped. Legend, ∴EDW=D smyth * · ·

℞ A minute eagle between two small circles. I · OWE THE · BEARER · TWO · PENCE LISBURN · 1736 · *R.r.*

Aquilla Smith 21.
PLATE N, no. 25.

" The issuer was High Sheriff of Co. Antrim in 1738." *Young's Historical Notices of Old Belfast.*

The same Journal copies an entry, dated August, 1744 : " To Edward Smyth for repairing 1000 Perches of the Road from Lisburn to Antrim £15."

MALONE.

23. ☉ A dolphin embowed. Under, 2 · P Legend, WITH · COVNC ILE · AND · COVRAGE

℞ · I · PROMISE TO · PAY · THE BEARER · TWO PENCE ⚏ AARON · KEAN MALLONE · (*sic*) 1735 ·

Aquilla Smith 25.
PLATE N, no. 26.

IRISH TOKEN COINAGE.

Co. ARMAGH.

THREEPENCE.
SILVER.

24. ☊ ALEX : MORTON ARMAGH ⊙ .ⁱ₈. ⊙ 1736
℞ I PROMIS : (*sic*) TO : PAY : THE : BEARER : THREE : PENCE : the A in BEARER : is under the *last* limb of the A in PAY : *R.*
PLATE I, no. 18.

25. Similar, but a small *scroll* after MORTON and ARMAGH ⊙

26. Similar, but the A in BEARER : is under the *first* limb of the A in PAY :

27. Similar, but the A in BEARER : is under the *colon* after TO :

The issuer was "a famous clockmaker, in the year 1717; he lived in Market Street, where he struck off a number of silver tokens, which were being used as current coin in Armagh."—*Stuart's Historical Memoirs of the City of Armagh.*

PORTADOWN.

28. ☊ IOHN · OUEREND · PORTADOWN ✱ · P · ✱ III · 1736 ·
℞ I PROMISE TO · PAY · THE · BEARER · THREE PENCE   *R.r.*
PLATE I, no. 19.

"John Overend, Merchant, died at Portadown, 1758."—*Monthly Chronicle, Ireland, Feb:* 1758.

RICHHILL.

29. ☊ SAM MACKIE : ✱ ᴾIII ✱ RICHHILL 1736
℞ · I · PROMIS · (*sic*) TO · PAY · THE · BEARER · · THREE · · PENCE ·
R.r.
PLATE I, no. 20.

30. Similar, but reads RICHILL (*sic*)   *R.r.*
Boyne, 4.

31. Similar, but the P over III *omitted* and reads RICHHILL   *R.r.*

32. ☊ SAM MACKIE ᴾIII RICHHIL (*sic*) 1736 within an inner circle.
℞ · I · PROMIS · (*sic*) TO · PAY · THE · BEARER · THREE · · PENCE · within an inner circle. *R.*

LURGAN.

THREEPENCE.
COPPER.

33. ☊ A roll of linen 3. P above. Legend, · THE · DRAPER · · ∘∘ ✱ ∘∘
℞ · I · PROMISE TO · PAY · THE · BEARER · THREE · PENCE IAM^S GREER LURGAN 1736 *R.r.r.*
Aquilla Smith 24.

It is stated in Knox's *History of the County Down* that this family descended from Henry Greer, who came to Ireland from Dumfriesshire and settled in Lurgan in 1653 The family is now represented by Captain J. W. Greer, The Wilderness.

H H

TWOPENCE.

34. ○ A stag at gaze; at the left, 2 P   The antlers have each *four* branches.
℞ · I · PROMISE · TO · PAY · THE BEARER : TWO   PENCE · THO^S : O : BRIEN ✻ LVRGAN 1736
Aquilla Smith 22.
In the Dublin Museum.

35. Similar, but with *six* branches in each antler.   *R.r.r.*
Aquilla Smith 22a.
PLATE N, no. 27.

36. ○ A horse's head to left, bridled.   Below 2 ✻ P ·
℞ · I · PROMISE TO · PAY · THE ·:· BEARER ·:· TWO · PENCE IOS· WILSON LURGAN 1735
Aquilla Smith 23.
PLATE N, no. 28.
In the British Museum.

Co. DOWN.

DROMORE.

TWOPENCE.

COPPER.

37. ○ A griffon, passant.   FOR · Y^E PARISH · OF · DROMORE ·
℞ · I · PROMISE TO · PAY · THE BEARER · TWO · PENCE · WILL · HALL DROMORE 1736   *R.r.*
Aquilla Smith 13.
PLATE N, no. 29.

The griffon was supposed to be a guardian of mines and hidden treasures. One Edmund Hall issued a token at Dromore about 1663.—*Vide Williamson*, 256.

GILFORD.

THREEPENCE.

38. ○ A man riding at speed; under the horse, dividing the date, 17 36 a horseshoe.   Legend, LOUSE · RUN · FOR · EVER
℞ · I · PROMISE TO · PAY · THE · BEARER · THREE · PENCE IN^O COCHRAN · GILLFORD · (*sic*) 1736 ·
Aquilla Smith 18.
PLATE N, no. 30.
In the British and Dublin Museums.

Aquilla Smith has the following note : "In the year 1685, James II incorporated by charter the Governor and Freemen of the Corporation of Horse Breeders in the County of Down." In the Gilford Directory, the Rev. John Cochrane, Presbyterian Minister, occurs, and the family, since this token was issued, has been an important one in this town.

KILLYLEIGH.

39. ○ A messenger with cudgel running, 2 · P · · BEWARE · OF · COVNTERFITS · (sic)
℞ · I · PROMISE TO · PAY · THE BEARER · TWO PENCE · IOHN STEWART · KILLILEAGH · (sic) 1735 · ·
Aquilla Smith 20.
In the Dublin and Belfast Museums.

George Benn, in the *Ulster Journal of Archæology*, July, 1855, says: "The hurrying messenger impressed upon it imaginative people might describe as the figure of Mercury; those who knew better would say it was the very image of a County Down 'boy,' bred and born in Killinchy, with a little round cap on his head,—probably a scratch wig underneath, a bunch of ribbons flying behind, loose jacket, short tights, home made hose,—his headlong speed, his determined look, and above all the stout cudgel in his hand, plainly intimating that the argument in the last resort would be brought to bear upon every caitiff guilty of forging the tokens of Mr. John Stewart of Killileagh."

NEWTOWNARDS.

40. ○ A kingfisher, a fish in its bill. No legend. There are *five* feathers in the tail of the bird, the fish does *not exhibit* its fins; all within a toothed border.
℞ I PROMISE TO PAY THE BEARER ON DEMAND TWO PENCE THOMAS FISHER The first upright limb of the M in THOMAS is over the *first* limb of H in FISHER *R*.
Aquilla Smith 32.
PLATE N, no. 31.

41. Similar, but there are *eight* feathers in the bird's tail, and the fish *exhibits* its fins. *R*.

42. ○ Similar, but there are *six* feathers in the tail.
℞ Similar, but the O in THOMAS is over the *first* limb of H in FISHER *R*.

43. ○ Similar, but a bird of *closer* plumage, the feathers in the tail are *short*; all within a cable circle.
℞ Similar, but the upright limb of H in FISHER is under the *space between* O and M of THOMAS *instead* of as previously being under the *first* limb of M *R.r.*
Aquilla Smith 32a.

The late Mr. Gillespie, in the list of his collection, placed the Kingfisher tokens to Newtownards.

44. ○ A cask dividing 2 P Legend, IOHN M^{C} CULLY BREWER A rose at the bottom. The H is over U in M^{C} CULLY
℞ I PROMISE TO · PAY · THE BEARER TWO · PENCE ON · ᴅEMANᴅ IOHN · M^{C} CULLY NEWTOWN (sic) · : 1761 : · A rose before and after BEARER The T in NEWTOWN is under the C in M^{C} CULLY *R*.
Aquilla Smith 27.
PLATE N, no. 32.

45. ℞ Similar, but the P is at the *right* of Y *whereas* in the last it is *under* that letter.
℞ As last.
In Mr. Fletcher's cabinet.

46. ℞ Similar, but the H is over ÜL and the P under Y in M^C CÜLLY
℞ Similar, but the T in NEWTOWN is under M in M^C CÜLLY R.r.
Neumann 24948a.

In the copy of *The Ancient and Present State of the County of Down*, in the British Museum, there is a MS. note, that in 1754 William McCully was one of the Churchwardens of Newtown(ards).

47. ℞ A lion's face between flags, 2 · * P · below. HOLD FAST · above.
℞ · I · PROMISE TO · PAY · THE BEARER · TWO PENCE · WILL^M M^C QUOID NEWTOWN (*sic*) 1736 R.r.r.
Aquilla Smith 26.
PLATE N, no. 33.

PORTAFERRY.

48. ℞ A ship under sail. · I · COME · SPEED — 2 · P
℞ · I · PROMISE TO · PAY · THE BEARER · TWO PENCE · IOHN GALLOWAY PORTAFERRY · 1735 · R.r.
Aquilla Smith 28.
PLATE N, no. 34.

The issuer of the token found it necessary to follow the example of Alexander Beith of Ballymena, and gave notice : " Tickets Local—Whereas some Persons with a Dye and Press have counterfeited the Tickets put out by *John Gallway* (sic) of *Portaferry*, Merchant, and sell them to severals at half what they pass for. Now I do give this public notice to all Persons who have any of my Tickets, that they may bring them unto me at any time before the first of May next (Counterfeits excepted) and I will pay them in Gold or Silver, and will give two Guineas Reward to any Person or Persons who will discover the Person or Persons that made these Counterfeit Tickets with the Dye and Press, so as they may be convicted of the said Cheat. John Gallway."—*Belfast News Letter, from March 13th to April 27th*, 1839.

49. ℞ A stag tripping. 2 · P TRUTH · OVER · COMES ·
℞ · I · PROMISE TO · PAY · THE BEARER · TWO PENCE · ROB^T · MILLER · PORTFEERY (*sic*) 1736 R.r.r.
Aquilla Smith 29.
PLATE N, no. 35.

Co. DUBLIN.
DUBLIN.

SILVER.
50. ℞ A hart statant, pierced with an arrow.
℞ BEN BOWEN DUBLIN Legend, I · OWE · THE · BEARER · III^D STER · R.r.
Boyne 2.
PLATE I, no. 21.

COPPER. PENNY, 1729.

51. ♉ CASH NOTES VAL RECEIVED DUBLIN 1729 JAMES MACULLA PENNY

℞ I PROMISE TO PAY · THE BEARER · ON DEMAND 20 PENCE · A · POU ND · FOR · THESE

Aquilla Smith 16.
PLATE N, no. 36.
In the British and Dublin Museums.

The die was originally intended for a halfpenny. It will be seen from the illustration in the plate that the first N in PENNY is engraved over ½

1731.

52. ♉ A large fleur-de-lis. CASH · NOTES · VALUE · RECD · I · MACULLA ·

℞ A female standing between two pillars, holding in her right hand a sword erect, in the left a pair of scales; the head of the figure divides the date 17 31. Legend, I · PROMISE · 20 · SHILLINGS · POUND · STR · *R.r.*

PLATE N, no. 37.

Aquilla Smith thought that this piece was intended to pass as a shilling. This is inconsistent with the idea of the period. The issuer probably intended to convey that he was prepared to pay, on return of the tokens, either in regal silver or cash notes.

HALFPENNY, 1728.

53. ♉ PROMESARY (*sic*) NOTES VALUE RECEIVED : DUBLIN · 1728 · IAMES · MACULLA

℞ I PROMISE TO · PAY · UNTO BEARER · ON · DEMAND · 20 · PENCE · A · POU ND FOR · THESE ·

Lindsay 119.
In the British Museum.

54. ♉ CASH NOTES · VAL, RECEIVED DUBLIN · 1728 IAMES · MACULLA

℞ I PROMISE TO · PAY · THE BEARER · ON DEM A ND · 20 · PENCE · A · POU ND · FOR · THESE · *R.r.*

Aquilla Smith 14.

1729.

55. ♉ CASH NOTES · VAL, RECEIVED · DUBLIN 1729 IAMES MACULLA ½ The A and L in VAL, *touch*.

℞ As last. *R.r.*

56. ♉ As last.

℞ I PROMISE · TO · PAY · THE BEARER · ON · DEMAND · 20 · PENCE · A · POU ND · FOR · THESE The O in TO is over E and A of BEARER *R.*

Aquilla Smith 15c.

This is also struck from the same die on a much thicker flan.—*Vide Aq. Smith* 15b.

57. ♉ Similar, but the A and L in VAL, do *not touch*, most of the letters in the inscription are *without* their *ceriphs*.

℞ As last.

In Mr. Fletcher's cabinet.

58. ⟋ As no. 55.
℞ Similar to last, but the o in TO is over the E in BEARER. *R.*
Aquilla Smith 15a.

59. ⟋ Similar to last, but the I in ½ is directly under the U instead of *between* C and U in MACULLA · which *has* a period after it.
℞ As last. *R.r.*
Aquilla Smith 15.

60. As no. 52, except in size. *R.*
Aquilla Smith 17.

James Maculla was a brazier in Dublin.

Maculla proposed to supply the coinage on a plan which he publicly stated. It was to circulate copper tokens for pennies and halfpennies stamped with a promissory to pay twenty pence for every pound of copper notes whenever they should be returned. There was to be forty-eight halfpence to the pound, avoirdupois, which he undertook to sell at two shillings. This he calculated would allow little more than sixteen *per cent.*, provided the tokens should be returned without loss of metal by circulation, and provided the expense of stamping should amount to sixpence each pound.

Maculla submitted this plan to Dean Swift, who disapproved it *as but little* security would be given to the public "that the tokens should always be made of the intrinsic value which was proposed in the project."

Swift proposed a counter plan. It was to form a Society of ten gentlemen to issue tokens of increased specific gravity to Maculla's, *vide Swift's Works*, vol. XV, p. 260. This project was not taken up and Maculla issued his tokens, notwithstanding the criticism to which the plan had been subjected by Swift, who, Ruding says, " was absolute monarch over all those who were likely to be much affected by the circulation of the tokens."—*Vide Ruding, vol. IV, p.* 3.

Co. LONDONDERRY.
KILREA.
TWOPENCE.

COPPER.

61. ⟋ A halberdier crowned, girt with a sword, in his right hand a halberd. 2 · P at the right. Legend, VIRTUE MINE · HONOUR
℞ · I · PROMISE TO · PAY · THE BEARER · TWO PENCE · IAM^S HENRY · KILLREA (*sic*) 1736 *R.r.r.*
Aquilla Smith 31.
PLATE N, no. 38.

The specimen which Aquilla Smith had was so detrited, that he placed this token in his Not Local section.

Macaulay, in the *Spanish Armada*, says—" Behind him march the halberdiers, before him sound the drums."

Co. TYRONE.
DUNGANNON.
THREEPENCE.

COPPER.

62. ⟋ A stag tripping; below ○ 3 ○ P ○ Legend, FIDES · NON · TIMET (Faith knows not fear).
℞ · I · PROMISE TO · PAY · THE BEARER · THREE PENCE THOM^S REA · DVNGA NNON · 1736 · *R.r.r.*
Batty 1562.
PLATE N, no. 39.

STEWARTSTOWN.

63. ☉ A view of the Market House.

℞ I PROMISE TO · PAY · THE BEARER · TWO PENCE IAM^S TEM PLETON STEWARTS TOWN 1736 *R.r.r.*

Aquilla Smith, in his introduction, gives an account of the state of the copper coinage of Ireland when these tokens were in circulation. He says, "the coinage of the fine copper halfpence by George the Second, in 1736 and 1737, and of farthings in 1737, put an end to the issue of private tokens...They were withdrawn from circulation, and full value given for them in gold or silver, which accounts for the extreme rarity of the greater number of the tickets, as they were designated. The weight or intrinsic value of the tickets, being nearly the same as that of the new halfpenny, gave rise to the once common saying 'not worth a two-penny ticket.'" How one could expect a halfpenny to be worth twopence is not explained.

"It is said that our good halfpence are carried to the West of England and to Scotland by the colliers and other dealers, which is a good trade for them, as they get thirteenpence for a shilling, which is eight and one-third profit, so that, unless Irish halfpence are prohibited in Great Britain, we shall be constantly drained of our Copper Coin, great quantities of which are likewise exported to America."

This interesting note, quoted by Aquilla Smith, from *Falkner's Dublin Journal, Sep.* 2, 1760, shows how difficult was the coinage question in those days. The same journal had a week before announced : " We are assured that several casks of halfpence, amounting to £15,000, lately coined at the Tower, for the use of this Kingdom, are shipped on board a London trader, and are daily expected here." This assurance was of no value, as the coinage dated 1760 was not sent to Ireland until 1762.

COUNTY UNKNOWN.

TWOPENCE.

COPPER.

64. ☉ I˙ PROMISE TO PAY THE BEARER ON DEMAND TWO PENCE FRAN M^C MINN 1760 The final letter in PROMISE is over the *last* limb of H in THE

℞ Similar to the obverse, countermarked F

Aquilla Smith 33.

This is supposed to be the specimen which Aquilla Smith described.

65. ☉ As last.
℞ Blank.

PLATE N, no. 40.

66. Similar to last, but the 2 in PROMISE is *inverted*, the final E *spans* the H in THE

In Mr. Fletcher's cabinet.

67. ☉ A greyhound to left at speed; 2 P above. Legend detrited.

℞ I PROMISE TO PAY THE BEARER TWO PENCE The remainder of legend detrited.

Aquilla Smith 30.
In the Dublin Museum.

THE CHANNEL ISLANDS.

Although the Channel Islands are not within the Constitution of Great Britain, their insular tokens are sought after and included in British collections.

The Islands were taken by Rolf, or Rollo, in the ninth century, and William the Conqueror was the first monarch to unite them to the Crown of England.

GUERNSEY.

FIVE SHILLINGS.

SILVER.

1. O Arms of Jersey, gules; three leopards passant gardant in pale, in a circle. BISHOP DE JERSEY & C? A rose ornament divides the legend.

℞ TOKEN OF FIVE SHILLINGS within a wreath of oak. Legend, BANK OF GUERNSEY 1809 *R.r.r.* *T. Wyon.*

PLATE I, no. 23.

This piece is struck on a Spanish dollar.

Bishop de Jersey & Co. also issued at their bank in Guernsey one pound notes. The following notice is of interest;

"CREDITORS OF BISHOP DE JERSEY AND CO. GUERNSEY.

"Notwithstanding Mr. Bishop has engaged to devote the profits of his business to the liquidation of any defalcification that might arrise in the concerns of the Bank, he is credibly informed that several malicious persons mean to proceed against him, as soon as the terms of the Royal Court opens, and endeavour to molest his person and trade; he therefore takes this opportunity to request those who wish to take advantage of the above engagement, to sign or cause to be signed the agreement entered upon before the 13th of October next, in default of which he will take the advantage of the regulations of the Laws of the Island, and shall not consider himself bound to any person having neglected to close with this offer. Guernsey, 7th September, 1811."—*The Star, Sep. 14th,* 1811.

THE STATES OF JERSEY.

THREE SHILLINGS.

2. O Arms as last, but not in a circle. Legend, STATES OF JERSEY 1813

℞ THREE SHILLINGS TOKEN within a wreath of oak. *R.*

Atkins (Colonial Tokens) 6, 45.

EIGHTEENPENCE.

3. O As last, except in size.

℞ As last, but legend, EIGHTEEN PENCE TOKEN *T. Wyon.*

PLATE G, no. 9.

Struck by order of Council.—*Vide* Ruding, vol. V, p. 368.

PENNY.

COPPER.

4 O Profile of George III laureated. JERSEY BANK TOKEN 1812
℞ ELIAS NEEL JERSEY Legend, A BANK OF ENGLAND NOTE FOR 240 TOKENS *R.r.* *Unknown.*
Atkins 7, 47.

5. O Draped and laureated bust to right of George III JERSEY BANK 1813
℞ A robed female figure seated to left on a bale, holding scales and cornucopia. ONE PENNY TOKEN *R.r.* *Halliday.*
Atkins 7, 48.

JERSEY, GUERNSEY AND ALDERNEY.

6. O Laureated and draped bust to right (George III), within a wreath of oak.
℞ ONE PENNY TOKEN in a circle. Legend, JERSEY GUERNSEY AND ALDERNEY · *R.* *Halliday.*
Atkins 7, 50.

7. O A druid's bust to left. PURE COPPER PREFERABLE TO PAPER · PENNY TOKEN ·
℞ As last. *R.* *Turnpenny and Halliday.*
Atkins 7, 52.

This obverse die is used on a Burton token.

8. O As last.
℞ A robed female figure seated to left on a bale of merchandise, holding an olive branch and cornucopia, a ship in the distance. Legend, COMMERCE *Turnpenny and Halliday.*

9. O As last.
℞ A robed female figure seated to left, holding in her right hand a sprig of olive, and in her left a palm branch; a shield at the side. Legend, COMMERCE 1814 *Turnpenny and Halliday.*

10. O The Prince of Wales' feathers issuant from a coronet. Motto on a ribbon, ICH DIEN Under the crest, 1813 Legend, TO FACILITATE TRADE · * ·
℞ ONE PENNY TOKEN in a circle. Legend, JERSEY GUERNSEY AND ALDERNEY · *Halliday.*
PLATE G, no. 10.

11. O As last.
℞ A female seated to left on a bale of merchandise, holding an olive branch and cornucopia, a ship in the distance. Legend, COMMERCE 1814 *R.* *Halliday.*

12. Similar, but the date *omitted* on the reverse.

13. ⊙ As reverse no. 10 ONE PENNY TOKEN in a circle. Legend, JERSEY GUERNSEY AND ALDERNEY ·
℞ ONE PENNY TOKEN in a wreath of oak. *R.r.* *Halliday.*
Atkins 7, 51.

HALFPENNY.

14. Similar to no. 10, except in size. HALF PENNY TOKEN *R.r.r.* *Halliday.*

The Channel Islands form the one exception where no seventeenth century tokens were issued.

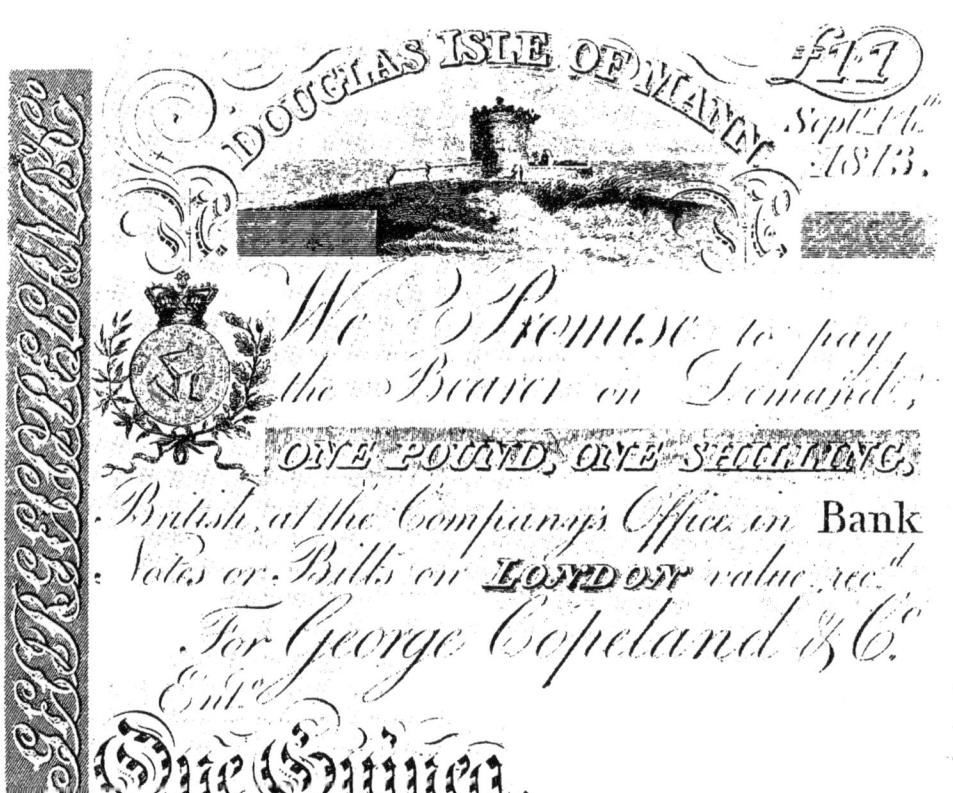

From a Print in the possession of the Author.

THE ISLE OF MAN.

Like the Channel Islands, the Isle of Man is not within the Constitution of Great Britain, but the Tokens form a most interesting section, and are eagerly sought after by English and American numismatists.

The Isle of Man having been for a long period the seat of an extensive smuggling trade, to the detriment of the Imperial revenue, the sovereignty of it was purchased by the British Government, in 1765, for £70,000 and an annuity of £2,000 a year to the Duke of Athol, he still retaining certain manorial rights, church patronage, etc. The last remaining interest of the Athol family in the island was transferred to the British Crown in 1829; the amount paid for the island having amounted in the aggregate to £493,000.—*Vide Chambers's Encyclopædia, vol. VII*, 1901.

Charles Clay, in his admirable work, commences the chapter on the Insular Tokens by quoting Dr. Combe: "Though at present no high value be set upon town pieces and tradesmen's Tokens by men of learning, a time will come when these Coins will be as much esteemed in this Country as the town pieces of the Greeks." This forecast, quoted as recently as 1869, has already been realised.

Three years after this opinion was quoted, the Collection of Tokens formed by Sir George Chetwynd was dispersed by Christie, Manson & Woods, and lot 545, which contained three fine specimen pieces, the Peel Castle crown, half crown and shilling, were sold for £1 17s. to Mr. Webster. It is no exaggeration to estimate their value to-day at thirty guineas, and that a similar relative appreciation has followed tokens generally which possess some degree of rarity.

In the Isle of Man, tokens were resorted to for precisely the same reason which caused their production in Great Britain and Ireland. Clay says: "For instance, in the time of Elizabeth, tradesmen's tokens were numerous, but it was the necessity for a small Coinage that forced them on the public," and, he goes on to say, that both the eighteenth and nineteenth century tokens were the result of Government neglect. So much so that "Before the issue of the Victoria coins (1839) the currency of the Island was utterly exhausted; and almost every kind of token was circulated, even to buttons with the shanks rubbed off. Dr. Clay illustrates one of these buttons, which represents the device and motto of the Isle of Man.

DOUGLAS.

SILVER.   FIVE SHILLINGS.

1. ☉ View of a castle and vessel from the quay, two mariners on the harbour watch. Legend, PEEL CASTLE ISLE OF MAN

℞ PROMISE TO PAY THE BEARER ON DEMAND 5 SHILLINGS BRITISH 1811 in a circle. Legend, THE DOUGLAS BANK C?. * AT THEIR BANK, DOUGLAS * *R.r.*   *Halliday.*

PLATE M, no. 10.

TWO SHILLINGS AND SIXPENCE.

2. ☉ Similar, except in size.

℞ PROMISE TO PAY THE BEARER ON DEMAND 2^S . 6^D BRITISH 1811 Legend as on the five shillings; the first numeral in date is over the *space* between B and A in BANK, *R.r.r.*

Boyne 71.

3. Also in Copper. *R.r.*

4. Similar, but the first numeral in date is over the *first limb* of B in BANK, *R.r.r.*

PLATE M, no. 11.

5. Also in Copper. *R.r.r.* *Halliday.*

SHILLING.

6. ☉ Similar view of Peel Castle, but the quay, harbour watch; and the legend are *omitted*.

℞ DOUGLAS BANK TOKEN ONE SHILLING BRITISH 1811 *R.r.*

Halliday.

Boyne 72.

7. ☉ As last.

℞ S · ASH occupying the field. *R.r.r.* *Halliday.*

Atkins 12, 25.

See also Countermarked Tokens no. 136.

This is in copper, and may exist in silver, but all efforts to discover it in that metal have failed.

C. Clay, on June 17th, 1864, stated to the Manchester Numismatic Society that the Douglas tokens were issued by Littler, Dove & Co., bankers, of Douglas. The bank did not survive the issue of the tokens for many months, nor were they circulated in large numbers, except the copper tokens hereafter described. On the currency of the Isle of Man Clay gives the following additional information :

"In the month of November, 1811, a new bank was opened in Douglas, under the firm of Littler, Dove & Co. Its claims on the public confidence were set forth in the following advertisement :

"'To counteract the Effects of many false Reports which have been circulated respecting the Plans and Intentions of the Douglas Bank Company, they feel it a duty they owe themselves and the Public to declare their Readiness to meet their tokens to any Amount above Twenty Pounds by Bills upon London, at the usual Exchange of the Island. Under that sum they propose to issue their own Notes, but as they are not quite in Readiness, they are prepared with Notes and Cards current in the Island. The Office of the Bank is at present in Fort Street, until the House they have taken of Messrs. Callows, in Duke Street, be finished. They have no other Office in Town. Littler, Dove & Co., Douglas, Nov. 29th, 1811.'

"It appears that disputes very soon arose between the members of the new banking firm of Littler, Dove & Co. The firm consisted of William Scarlett Littler, James Dove and the Rev. Robert Littler. The latter being about to leave the Island, his partner James Dove sued out an action against him for £1,000, under which he was arrested, and imprisoned. This led to the adoption of proceedings in the Chancery Court, on the part of the Rev. Robert Littler, against Dove, and which came before the Court on the 3rd January, 1812, when the arrest was set aside. The consequence was that the banking establishment was brought to an abrupt close."

CASTLETOWN.

ISLE OF MAN BANK.

PENNY.

COPPER.

8. ☉ The triune armoured and spurred with feet to *left*. Legend, QVOCVNQVE IECERIS STABIT· (Wherever you may cast it, it will stand).

℞ BANK PENNY in a circle. ISLE OF MAN 1811 *Halliday.*

PLATE M, no. 12.

C. Clay, June 17, 1854, said "The Isle of Man Bank Tokens were issued by George

Quayle & Co., bankers, Castle Town." The London agents of Quayle & Co., were Masterman & Co., 2, Whitehart Court. Subsequently, in the currency of the Isle of Man, Clay amplifies the information, as follows :—

"The Isle of Man Bank commenced business at Castletown, in the year 1802. The partners were Mark H. Quale, George Quale, John Taubman, and James Kelly. These constituted the firm until 1805. Then the bank was carried on by George Quale alone until January 1st, 1811 ; afterwards George Quale, Edward Cotteen, and Patrick Townsend Lightfoot continued it till about 1816, when Edward Cotteen retired ; and the above George Quayle and P. T. Lightfoot conducted it to its close in November, 1818. The first set of partners of this bank issued the Isle of Man Bank Penny and Halfpenny Tokens, although they have usually been attributed to George Quayle alone. I am indebted for the above information to the kindness of M. H. Quayle, Clerk of the Rolls, through J. F. Crellin, Esq., M.H.K. (Member of the House of Keys), Orrysdale.

HALFPENNY.

9. ☌ Similar to last, except in size.
℞ Similar to last, but BANK HALF PENNY in a circle. *Halliday*.
PLATE M, no. 13.

DOUGLAS.
PENNY.

10. ☌ View of Peel Castle, without the harbour watch, as no. 6. The building at the right of centre tower is *nearly* as *tall* as the tower, there are *four* stays to the mast, which *touches* the land.
℞ DOUGLAS BANK TOKEN ONE PENNY 1811 No inner circle. The tops of the ones in date *slope*. *R.*
PLATE M, no. 14.
In the Haw sale, Sotheby, Wilkinson & Hodge, no. 304, Jan. 20th, 1904, was a proof of this piece struck on a thin flan, penny size.—*Vide also Dr. Nelson, p.* 35.

11. ☌ As last, but the building extends *only half-way* up the centre tower, and there are *two* stays to the mast, which does *not touch* the land. The F of OF is under the ship.
℞ Similar, but BANK *omitted*. The upright limb of the T in TOKEN is over the *last* limb of the N in ONE The tops of the ones in date are *flat*. *R.r.r.*
This is a proof, of excellent workmanship.

12. ☌ Similar to last, but the *end* of F in OF is at the right of the ship, the mast *touches* the land.
℞ Similar, but the upright of the T in TOKEN is over the *space* between N and E in ONE *R.*
PLATE M, no. 15.
This is of inferior workmanship.

ATLAS.

13. ☌ The figure of Atlas kneeling; on his shoulder the globe. Legend, PAYABLE AT THE OFFICE DOUGLAS
℞ The triune armoured to the knee piece and spurred; with feet to *right*. Legend, MANKS TOKEN ONE PENNY 1811
PLATE M, no. 16.
C. Clay, June 17, 1864, says the penny and halfpenny "were issued by Beatson and Copeland, Bankers." John Beatson and George Copeland also issued Bank Notes for various sums ; were the agents of the Atlas Fire Office ; and, in addition, kept a Wine and Liquor Stores at Douglas.

246   NINETEENTH CENTURY TOKEN COINAGE.

God Save the King.

14. ○ Bust to right (George III) GOD : SAVE : THE : KING 1830 The figure 1 in date is *curved*.

℞ FOR ✺ PUBLICK ACCOMMODATION ✺   An ornament above and below PUBLICK   The bottom ornament *lines* to the I in ACCOMMODATION

PLATE M, no. 17.

This is also found in gunmetal.

15. ○ Similar, but the figure 1 in date is *straight*.

℞ Similar, but the bottom ornament *lines* to the T in ACCOMMODATION   *Unknown.*

Atkins 33.

This is in brass, and a contemporary forgery.

"God save the King Token. There was a report that an issue of Coins for the Isle of Man had occurred during the reign of George IV, but it was simply this token. It certainly appeared in his reign, but was in no way connected with the Government, except by having a badly executed head of George III on it. This token has also had the name of McTurk's Token, by others it was known as Caine's (Banker) Token, and again as Carter's Token.

"It is now easily explained how this piece became associated with the names beforementioned; the issuers being relatives, or connected in business, the dies consequently came into the possession of different persons at different times. Some time back, evidence was furnished me from the daughter and son-in-law of John McTurk (the former still living), confirming the above facts. This token was looked upon by English numismatists as an English token; and I believe I was the first to discover the error generally made."— *Charles Clay, p.* 102.

HALFPENNY.

16. ○ View of a castle *without* the quay and the harbour watch. Legend, PEEL CASTLE ISLE OF MAN

℞ DOUGLAS BANK TOKEN HALFPENNY 1811 No *inner* circle. *R. Halliday.*

PLATE M, no. 18.

ATLAS.

17. ○ The figure of Atlas kneeling, on his shoulders the globe. PAYABLE AT THE OFFICE DOUGLAS   The *right* foot of the figure is over the *space* between C and E in OFFICE

℞ The triune armoured and spurred with feet to right. MANKS TOKEN HALFPENNY 1811   The foot at the left of date points to the *first* limb of N in MANKS   *R.*

Atkins 12, 30.

THE ISLE OF MAN. 247

18. ○ Similar, but the *right* foot of the figure is over the *centre* of the E in OFFICE
℞ As last. *R.r.*

19. ○ Similar, but the *right* foot of Atlas is over the o in DOUGLAS
℞ Similar, but the foot of the triune points to the *first limb* of the A in MANKS *R.r.r.*
Nelson 49.

GOD SAVE THE KING.

20. ○ Bust to right. GOD : SAVE : THE : KING 1830 The top of the I in date is *flat*. The centre laurel leaf is *under* the *colon* after SAVE:
℞ FOR PUBLICK ACCOMMODATION as no. 13. An ornament above and below PUBLICK The K in PUBLICK lines to the *last limb* of N in ACCOMMODATION
PLATE M, no. 19.

21. Similar, but the 1 in date is *pointed*.
Nelson 52a.

22. ○ Similar, but the centre laurel leaf *lines* to the *first limb* of H in THE : The top of I in date *flat*.
℞ Similar, but the K lines to the *first* limb of N in ACCOMMODATION *R.* *Unknown.*
A forgery of the period.

23. ○ Similar to last reverse.
℞ A ship under sail. SHIPS COLONIES AND COMMERCE 1815 *R.*
Unknown.
Atkins 307, 230.
The last two are in brass.

RAMSAY.

FOUR SHILLINGS.

24. ○ Head of a king. HIARE SKILLIN PEESH (Four Shilling piece).
℞ St. George and the Dragon.
Nelson 56.
Dr. Nelson, in a note respecting this piece, which is in copper, says it was found in 1892, at Ballaugh, near Ramsay.

HALFPENNY.

25. ○ The triune armoured and spurred, with feet to *left*. On a raised rim in *incuse* letters, QUOCUNQUE · IECERIS · STABIT ·
℞ HALF PENNY TOKEN On a raised rim in incuse letters, PRO BONO PUBLICO 1831 *Halliday.*
PLATE M, no. 20.
" William Callister, of Ramsay, was the issuer."—*Vide Clay.*

26. O A man beside a horse. Legend detrited.
℞ The triune. Legend detrited.

Nelson 57.

Dr. Nelson says this is in brass and of rude execution.

As it is customary to complete the list of tokens issued in the Isle of Man, the solitary seventeenth century Penny of John Murrey with its variety are included.

27. O HIS PENNY I ✪ M Legend, IOHN · MURREY ·:· 1668 ✪
℞ The triune spurred to the *right*. QVOCVNQVE · GESSERIS ✪ STABIT ✪ *R.r.*

Williamson 1.

28. O Similar, but *reads* MURRAY ·:·
℞ Similar, but the triune *omitted*, and OF DOVGLAS IN · MAN · *substituted. R.r.r.*

Williamson 2.

Clay thinks the Token was made in Birmingham. He questions the statement of Oswald, in *Vestigia*, that the penny was a legal tender issued by Governor Murrey in 1669, and in support of his contention states: "The first governor of the name was the Hon. James Murray, but who was not appointed until 1739." The eminent author in all matters relating to the Isle of Man coinage, did not know at the time of the variety IOHN MURRAY. This, however, strengthens rather than weakens his knowledge on the subject, as the christian name of the variety being the same is a confirmation.

Boyne, quoting Snelling, says: "John Murray (*sic*) gave security to exchange his pennies, which his executors performed, when the copper money of the Earl of Derby was issued in 1709."

Clay gives the following table from Feltham's work on the relative value of the Manx Coinage to that of Gt. Britain and Ireland until it was assimilated to the English standard in 1840.

£				£	s.	d.	
100	English,	is equal to		116	13	4	Manx.
100	Manx,	,,	,,	85	14	3	English.
100	Irish	,,	,,	107	13	10	Manx.
100	Manx,	,,	,,	92	17	1	Irish.
1	English,	,,	,,	1	3	4	Manx.
1	Manx,	,,	,,	0	17	1½	English.
1	Irish,	,,	,,	1	1	6	Manx.
1	Manx,	,,	,,	0	18	7	Irish.
SHILLINGS.							
1	English,	,,	,,	0	1	2	Manx.
1	Manx,	,,	,,	0	0	10¼	English.
1	Irish,	,,	,,	0	1	1	Manx.
1	Manx,	,,	,,	0	0	11¼	Irish.

NOT LOCAL, OR TOKENS OF GENERAL CIRCULATION.

THREE SHILLINGS AND FOURPENCE.

SILVER.

1. ○ A beehive upon a wreath, surrounded by bees. No legend.

℞ THREE SHILLINGS & FOUR PENCE within a wreath of laurel and roses. *R.r.r.* *Unknown.*

The Lawrence sale, lot 357, May 1900.

THREE SHILLINGS.

2. ○ The golden fleece suspended from a ribbon. SHIPS COLONIES & COMMERCE 1811

℞ The Prince of Wales' feathers issuant from a coronet. On the ribbon, ICH DIEN within a garter inscribed THREE SHILLING TOKEN *R.r.*

PLATE G, no. 11.

3. The same in copper. *R.r.r.* *P. Wyon.*

Boyne, in his *Yorkshire Tokens*, 1858, p. 45, claims this for that county, the One Shilling and Sixpence of the same design, and the Sixpence with obverse fleece suspended, as described hereafter. In his general work on silver tokens, eight years later, he adds them to the section "without names." Somersetshire might claim them, as the obverse of the Three Shilling Piece has since been found muled with the Bath Four Shilling token issued by C. Culverhouse & Co. Boyne, and all token experts, have failed to trace their *locale*, therefore, they are included in this division.

4. ○ The Prince of Wales' feathers issuant from a coronet, and motto, ICH DIEN Legend, LONG LIVE THE PRINCE

℞ The star and garter. Motto, HONI SOIT QUI MAL Y PENSE Legend, REGENCY TOKEN *R.r.r.*

The Lawrence sale, lot 357, May, 1900.

5. The same in Copper. *Unknown.*

In Mr. Norman's cabinet.

EIGHTEENPENCE.

6. ○ Similar to no. 2, except in size.

℞ Similar to no. 2, but the motto *omitted*, and the garter inscribed ONE SHILLING & SIXPENCE *R.r.* *P. Wyon.*

Boyne 241.

SHILLING.

7. ○ A beehive and bees. FOR USE AND ACCOMMODATION Under the beehive, 12 PENNY TOKEN

℞ A female seated to left; in the right hand an olive branch, in the left a trident, a shield at the side. BRITANNIA *Unknown.*

Boyne 239.

8. ♁ ONE in large letters, inscribed SHILLING SILVER TOKEN Above, 1811 Below, w   All within a wreath of oak.

℞ Female seated to left on a cannon; in the left hand an olive branch, the right resting on a wheel.   BRITANNIA ·   *R.* *Unknown.*
Boyne 236.

SIXPENCE.

9. ♁ A head to right.   COMMERCIAL · T · OK · EN

℞ The rose and shamrock, between *J ℬ*   SIXPENCE 1811 Olive branches at the sides.   *Unknown.*
PLATE M, no. 21.

Boyne surmised the two last tokens were made to circulate in Ireland. The initials may be for Irish Bullion (Company).

10. ♁ A fleece suspended from a ribbon, 1811 in a circle. Legend, FOR PUBLIC ACCOMMODATION ✶

℞ SILVER TOKEN SIX PENCE in a wreath of oak.
PLATE G, no. 12.

11. Also in Copper.   *R.r.r.*   *P. Wyon.*

12. ♁ A beehive and bees.   1812 under.   Legend, FOR USE & ACCOMODATION (*sic*) 6 PENNY TOKEN

℞ Female seated to left on a cannon, as on no. 8, but without a period after BRITANNIA   *Unknown.*
Boyne 238.

13. ♁ A large 6 inscribed SIX PENNY TOKEN   On the ceriph of the figure 6 the letter w   Within a wreath of oak.

℞ As last.
PLATE K, no. 24.

14. ♁ As last.

℞ Similar, but the top leaves of the olive branch are between the I and the T *instead* of the R and I of BRITANNIA   *Wyon.*
PLATE K, no. 25.

15. ♁ A crescent and seven stars.   PRO BONO PUBLICO · 1812

℞ G between the all-seeing eye, and a hand holding a baton. SIX PENCE · SILVER TOKEN ·
Boyne 243.

16. Also in Copper.   *R.r.r.*   *Unknown.*

This device suggests the motto: "The clasping hand is under the all-seeing eye."

TWO SHILLINGS AND SIXPENCE.
COPPER.

17. ♁ TWO SHILLINGS AND SIXPENCE 1804   Outer legend, REMMINGTON & SMITH

℞ WE PROMISE TO PAY THE BEARER ON DEMAND A ONE POUND NOTE FOR EIGHT OF THESE PIECES   *R.r.*

Vide "Spink's Circular," Dec. 1895.

NOT LOCAL.   251

ONE SHILLING.

18. O Similar to last, but ONE SHILLING
   ℞ Similar to last, but TWENTY OF THESE PIECES *R.r.*
                                                Unknown.
      Vide Davis sale, no. 791.
   These tokens are of fine workmanship, and remarkable in consequence of the similarity to the tokens of 1811-12, although dated 1804.

PENNY.

BUST TO RIGHT.

DATE 1812 ON REVERSE ONLY.

19. O Bust (George III), laureated and draped, within a wreath of oak. On the shoulder, H The nose of the effigy *points* to a leaf, the H is over an *acorn*, and the bust *touches* the wreath.
   ℞ Female seated to left on a bale of merchandise; in the right hand a pair of scales, in the left a cornucopia, in the distance a ship, H on the ground at the right. ONE PENNY TOKEN 1812 The foot of Y is over the *head* of the figure at the left.
         Sharp 206, 6.

20. O Similar, but the H on the shoulder is *over* a *leaf*, and the bust is *distant* from the wreath.
   ℞ As last.

21. O Similar, but the H is over the *stem* of the acorn.
   ℞ Similar, but the foot of Y is over the *centre* of the head of the figure, the hand of the figure points to the *end* of E instead of *between* E and P in ONE PENNY
         PLATE G, no. 13.

22. O Similar, but the H on the shoulder *omitted*, *six* leaves in the laurel wreath instead of *nine*.
   ℞ Similar, but without the H on the ground, and the hand points to the *centre* of the E in ONE

1814.

23. O Similar, but with *eight* leaves in the laurel wreath.
   ℞ Female seated on a shield to left, holding in her right hand an olive branch, in the left a sprig of palm. COMMERCE 1814

NO DATE.

24. O As last.
   ℞ A female seated on a bale to the left; in her right hand an olive branch, in her left a cornucopia. COMMERCE *R.   Halliday.*

DATE ON OBVERSE AND REVERSE.

25. O Bust laureated and draped to right (George III). H on the shoulder; a wreath of oak divided by 1812 surrounds the bust; the H on the shoulder is over the first *numeral* of date.

℞ A female seated to left on a bale of merchandise; in her right hand a pair of scales, and in her left a cornucopia of fruit; in the distance, a ship; at the right, H on the ground. ONE PENNY TOKEN 1812

26. Similar, but the H on the shoulder is over the first *acorn stem* to left.

NO DATE ON REVERSE.

27. O As last.
℞ Similar, but date *omitted*.
Sharp 206, 7.

1813.

28. Similar, but date on obverse, 1813 On the shoulder H The laurel branch at the right terminates with *two acorns* and *one leaf*. R.
Sharp 206, 8.

29. Similar, but without the H on the shoulder, and the laurel branch terminates with *three leaves*. R.   *Halliday.*

OBVERSE 1811, REVERSE 1814.

30. O A robed bust (George III) unlaureated. ONE PENNY TOKEN 1811

℞ A female seated to left; in her right hand a spray of laurel; in her left a palm branch. COMMERCE 1814 The palm lines to the C in COMMERCE
Sharp 206, 17.

OBVERSE, 1811; NO DATE ON REVERSE.

31. O As last.
℞ Similar, but the palm lines to the last letter in COMMERCE The date is *omitted*.   *Halliday.*

WELLINGTON.

NO DATE.

32. O Bust to left *laureated*. FIELD MARSHAL WELLINGTON *Crossed* laurel branches under the bust.

℞ Britannia seated, in the right hand an olive branch; in the left a trident; a shield at the side, a ship in the distance; *crossed* laurel branches under the figure; the barb of the trident at the right touches the *first limb* of K in TOKEN
Sharp 207, 22.

33. O As last.

℞ Similar, but the *crossed* laurel branches *omitted*; the barb of the trident touches the O in TOKEN   R.r.

Sharp 207, 24.

1812.

34. O As last.

℞ A female seated on a bale of merchandise; in the left hand a pair of scales; in the right a cornucopia of fruit; a ship in the distance. ONE PENNY TOKEN 1812   R.r.

1813.

35. O A similar bust, but *unlaureated*, decorated with the order of the star and garter; the date 1813 under; the *crossed* laurel branches *omitted*.

℞ Similar to 32, but the centre barb of trident is under the O in TOKEN   The *crossed* laurel branches *omitted*.   *Halliday*.

PLATE G, no. 14.

SHIPS.

36. O A ship under full sail to right.   ONE PENNY TOKEN 1813

℞ ONE PENNY TOKEN within a wreath of oak   R.   *Halliday*.

PLATE G, no. 15.

37. O A larger ship sailing in the same direction; without the legend.

℞ ONE PENNY within a wreath of laurel.   R.   *Halliday*.

PLATE G, no. 16.

38. O A ship under top sails to left, in a circle. ONE PENNY TOKEN 1814.

℞ *R H* within a wreath of oak.   R.   *Halliday*.

WITHOUT BUSTS.

39. O A female seated to left on a bale of merchandise; an olive branch in her right hand, in her left a cornucopia of fruit; a ship in the distance.   COMMERCE

℞ ONE PENNY TOKEN within a mixed wreath of oak and laurel.   H on the laurel leaf opposite the N in TOKEN   *Halliday*.

The reverse appears also at Sedbury, Burton and Sheffield.

40. O *J J C* 1812 occupying the field.

℞ ONE PENNY TOKEN   No inner circle.   R.   *Unknown*.

PLATE G, no. 17.

41. ○ ℋ ℋ Above, a segment engrailed, gules; below, on a similar segment, 1814.
℞ ONE PENNY TOKEN   No inner circle.   *R.*   *Unknown.*

Sharp 206, 4.

This token is on a flan the size of a halfpenny, and of excellent workmanship. It was probably rejected as not being " good value " for " exchange."

42. ○ A female seated to left; in her right hand an olive branch, in the left a winged caduceus; a ship in the distance. H on the ground at the right.   TRADE & NAVIGATION 1812
℞ ONE PENNY TOKEN in a circle.   Legend, PURE COPPER PREFERABLE TO PAPER ·   *R.*

Breton 962.

43. Similar, but dated 1813

Sharp 205, 3.

44. ○ Similar, but the top of & is *rounded*, whereas in the last it is *flat*.
℞ Similar, but the P in PENNY lines to the *upright* of the second P in COPPER instead of to *a little* above it.

PLATE M, no. 22.

45. ○ Similar to last, but dated 1814
℞ Similar to last, but the P in PENNY lines *between* the P and E in COPPER

46. ○ Similar to last, but the top of the & is *flat*.
℞ As last.   *Halliday.*

HALFPENNY.

BUST TO RIGHT.

47. ○ Bust to right, laureated and robed (George III). H on the shoulder in a wreath of oak. There are *four* pearls in the shoulder brooch.
℞ A female seated to left on a bale of merchandise; in her right hand a pair of scales; in the left a cornucopia of fruit; in the distance a ship. On the ground at the right H Legend, HALFPENNY TOKEN 1812

Sharp 212.

48. ○ Similar, but the brooch on the shoulder has *six* pearls.
℞ As last.

49. Similar, but there are *no* pearls in the brooch.

50. Similar, but the head of the figure on the reverse, instead of being some *distance* from the Y in HALFPENNY *nearly touches* it.

Halliday.

The following ten varieties of inferior work, are forgeries of the time.

51. ○ Bust to right, laureated and robed (George III), within a wreath of oak containing *thirty-nine* acorns; *no* legend.
℞ A female seated, similar to those previously described HALFPENNY TOKEN 1812 The Y of HALFPENNY *touches* the head of the figure at the *right*, and the hand points to the F

52. ○ Similar, but the wreath has *twenty-four* acorns, the projecting laurel leaf points *to* an acorn.
℞ Similar, but the Y does *not touch* the head, and the hand points to the L of HALFPENNY

53. ○ Similar bust, but the leaf projecting points to a *leaf*.
℞ Similar, but the Y *touches* the head at the *right*; the hand points to the first limb of F

54. ○ Similar bust, but the leaves and acorns have *short stems*.
℞ Similar, but the Y does *not touch* the head.

55. ○ Similar bust, but the leaves have *no stems*.
℞ Similar, but the head of the figure is under the N and Y of HALFPENNY

56. Similar, but the Y *touches* the head of the figure.

57. ○ Similar bust, but the wreath is *reversed*, the leaves being arranged from left to right.
℞ Similar, but the Y does *not touch* the head. R.

58. ○ Similar bust, but the wreath has *thirty-four* acorns.
℞ Similar, but HALFPENNY TOKEN *omitted*.

59. Similar, but with *thirty-two* acorns in the wreath.

60. Similar, but the cornucopia *touches* a cord on the bale, whereas in the last it *rests between* the cords. *Unknown.*

TRADE AND COMMERCE.

61. ○ Bust to right, laureated and draped. SUCCESS TO TRADE 1812
℞ Britannia seated to left; in her right hand an olive branch, in the left a trident, a shield at the side. A ship (looks like a rock) in the distance. COMMERCE RULES THE MAIN

62. ○ As last.
℞ Similar, but legend, HALFPENNY R. *Halliday.*

63. ○ Similar bust, but legend, GREAT BRITAIN

℞ A female seated to left; in her right hand an olive branch of *seven* leaves, in the left a sprig of palm; at her side the union shield. COMMERCE 1814

64. Similar, but the olive branch has only *six* leaves.

65. ○ Similar bust, but legend, HALF PENNY TOKEN · 1814 ·

℞ A ship sailing under canvas. FOR THE CONVENIENCE OF TRADE ✱   R.   *Unknown.*

66. ○ Bust to right, laureated. GEORGE III RULES 1806

℞ Britannia seated with her usual attributes; in the distance a ship. BRITANNIA FOR EVER   In the exergue, MEDAL   *R.r.*
Halliday.

SHIPS.

67. ○ Bust to right (George III), laureated and draped. HALF PENNY TOKEN 1815   There are *two* projecting laurel leaves.

℞ A ship under canvas sailing to right. SUCCESS TO NAVIGATION & TRADE ✱   The bowsprit points to the T in TRADE ✱

68. Similar, but the bowsprit points to the &

69. Similar bust, but with only *one* projecting laurel leaf.

70. Similar, but the bowsprit points to the T in TRADE ✱ *Halliday.*

GENUINE BRITISH COPPER.

71. ○ Similar bust, but on a smaller flan. The projecting laurel leaf points to the *second* N in PENNY

℞ A female seated to left; an olive branch in her right hand, a trident in the left; the union shield at her side; in the distance a ship. GENUINE BRITISH COPPER   There are *nine* leaves in the olive branch.   *Halliday.*

PLATE G, no. 18.

72. ○ Similar bust, but the projecting laurel leaf points *between* the N and Y

℞ Similar, but there are *five* leaves in the olive branch.

73. Similar, but there are *four* leaves in the olive branch.

74. ○ Similar bust, but the projecting laurel leaf points to the *foot* of Y

℞ Similar, but there are *five* leaves in the olive branch.
Unknown.

75. ○ Similar bust, but on a *larger* flan. Legend, GENUINE BRITISH COPPER 1815

℞ Britannia seated with her attributes as before, but legend, HALFPENNY   *Halliday.*

NOT LOCAL. 257

76. ☉ Similar bust, but *without* legend. Under the bust, 1820
℞ Similar to last, but legend, GENUINE BRITISH COPPER

77. ☉ As last.
℞ Female seated to left on a bale of merchandise; in her right hand a pair of scales, in the left a cornucopia; a ship in the distance. No legend. *R.*

78. ☉ Similar bust, but *without* legend *or* date.
℞ Similar to last, but the date 1820 *added. R. Unknown.*

WELLINGTON.

79. ☉ Bust to right in military uniform. VICTORIA NOBIS EST (Victory is for us) Under the bust, laurel branches. The coat has *no* button.
℞ A female seated to left, in her right hand an olive branch, in the left a spear, at her side the union shield; a ship in the distance. Legend, HALFPENNY TOKEN In the exergue, sprigs of olive. *R.* *Unknown.*

80. ☉ Bust to right, laureated and robed. MARQUIS WELLINGTON 1813.
℞ A female seated to left; in her right hand an olive branch, in the left a spear, the union shield at her side, a ship in the distance. Legend, COMMERCE *Parkes.*

81. ☉ Bust to right, unlaureated, in military uniform. No legend. There are *eight* buttons on the coat.
℞ WELLINGTON WATERLOO 1815 No device. *R. Unknown.*

BUST TO LEFT.

82. ☉ Bust laureated to left, in military uniform, between branches of laurel. No legend, and *without* buttons on the coat.
℞ A female seated to right on a bale of merchandise; in the left hand a spear, in her right a pair of scales, a ship in the distance. Legend, TRADE & COMMERCE 1811 *R. Unknown.*

83. ☉ Bust laureated in military uniform. WELLINGTON HALFPENNY TOKEN The projecting laurel points to the second L There is *one* button on the coat.
℞ Britannia seated to left; in her right hand an olive branch, in the left a trident, a ship in the distance, within a wreath of oak In the exergue, 1814 The left barb of trident does *not quite* touch a leaf, and the right and centre barbs *touch* a leaf.

84. Similar, but the left barb *touches* a leaf, and the right an *acorn.* *Unknown.*

L L

85. Similar, but the right and left barb *each touch a leaf*, the centre barb is *between* two leaves.

86. ○ Similar, but with *two* projecting laurel leaves, one pointing to I and the other to N
℞ Similar, but the left barb of trident does not *quite touch a leaf*.

87. Similar, but Britannia surrounded by a wreath of oak, and the date *omitted*.

88. ○ Similar bust, but legend, FIELD MARSHAL WELLINGTON Sprigs of laurel under the bust. There are *two* buttons on the coat.
℞ Britannia seated to left with her usual attributes. Legend, HALFPENNY TOKEN Under the figure branches of laurel.

89. Similar, but sprigs of laurel in the exergue.

90. Similar, but Britannia holds a spear *instead* of a trident.

91. Similar, but Britannia with trident surrounded by a wreath of oak.

92. ○ Similar bust, but only *one* button on the coat.
℞ Similar, but the date 1813 *added* to the legend, the sprigs of laurel *omitted*. *Unknown.*

WELLINGTON AND BLUCHER.

93. ○ An unrobed and unlaureated head to left. WELLINGTON above. 1815 below.
℞ A robed unlaureated bust to left. Above, BLUCHER R.
Turnpenny.

This piece is of fine workmanship.

SHIP SAILING TO RIGHT.

94. ○ A ship sailing to right. No legend.
℞ WELLINGTON WATERLOO 1815 No device. *Halliday.*

95. ○ A ship sailing, no legend; the sails are *plain*
℞ A female seated to left on a case of merchandise labelled S J & Cº In her right hand a pair of scales, in her left a cornucopia, a ship in the distance. Legend, HALFPENNY TOKEN 1812 R.

96. Similar, but *dated* 1815
Sharp 212, 5.

Sharp attributes this piece to Halliday, but he could not have been guilty of so mean a production.

97. ○ Similar ship, but the flag is *smaller*.
℞ Similar, but the date and the initials on the bale *omitted*.

98. Similar, but *legend* and date *omitted*. Unknown.

99. O A ship sailing. Legend, FOR GENERAL ACCOMMODATION · The sails are *striped*.

℞ HALF PENNY TOKEN in a circle. Legend, PURE COPPER PREFERABLE TO PAPER · *Halliday*.

100. O A ship sailing, *plain* sails; *no* legend.

℞ *B M C⁰* in a circle. *R*. Unknown.

SHIPS SAILING TO LEFT.

101. O A ship sailing under top sails in a circle. Legend, TRADE & NAVIGATION 1813 The rope nearest the foremast leads from the spritsail-yard to the top of the *shrouds*.

℞ HALF PENNY TOKEN in a circle. Legend, PURE COPPER PREFERABLE TO PAPER ·

102. Similar, but the rope leads to the *bowsprit*.

103. Similar, but the rope leads from the spritsail-yard to the *foremast*. *Halliday*.

104. O Ship under topsails in a circle. Legend, HALF PENNY TOKEN 1814

℞ *R H* within a wreath of oak. *Halliday*.

Sharp 212, 6.
This piece is also claimed for Canada.

BEEHIVE AND BEES.

105. O A beehive and bees within a wreath, the rose, thistle and shamrock. Legend, INDUSTRY THE SOURCE OF CONTENT *T. S*

℞ A shield azure, inscribed FOR CHANGE IN TRADE. In base a rose between branches of oak. Crest, a knotted ribbon. Legend, TO CONVENIENCE THE PUBLIC 1801 *Dixon*.

Atkins 372, 120 *bis*.
This token in design and motto is similar to eighteenth century work.

106. O A female seated to left on a bale of merchandise; in her right hand an olive branch, in the left a caduceus, a ship in the distance. On the ground at the right H Legend, TRADE & NAVIGATION 1812

℞ HALF PENNY TOKEN in a circle. PURE COPPER PREFERABLE TO PAPER ·

Sharp 212, 3,

107. Similar, but dated 1813 *Halliday*.

108. O An anchor and cable in a circle. HALFPENNY TOKEN · 1816·

℞ A large H within an olive wreath. *R.r*.

The Spread Eagle.

109. O An eagle volant, in its right talon *four* arrows, in its left an olive branch of *five* leaves, a ship in the distance. HALFPENNY TOKEN 18 13 The date *divided* by the tail.

℞ Britannia seated to left within a wreath of oak, in her right hand an olive branch of *five* leaves, in the left a trident. The *centre* barb of the trident is under an acorn.

110. O As last.

℞ Similar, but the olive branch has *seven* leaves, the *first* barb of the trident at the left is under an *acorn*.

111. O Similar to last, but dated 18 14

℞ Similar, but the olive branch has *five* leaves, the *centre* barb of the trident *touches* an acorn.

112. Similar, but the head of Britannia is directly under an *acorn*, whereas in the others it is under a *leaf*.

113. O Similar, but 1815 *under* the tail of the eagle, with only *three* arrows and *six* leaves to the olive branch in its talons.

℞ Similar, but the centre barb of the trident is *shorter* than the other two, and is under a *leaf*.

114. O As last.

℞ Similar, but the wreath arranged from *left* to right, whereas previously from *right* to left. *R*. *Unknown.*

FARTHING.

115. O A draped bust to right. No legend.

℞ COMMERCIAL CHANGE occupying the field. *R*.

116. O Over a cask, TOBACCO Legend, PRO · BONO · PUBLICO ✶

℞ *HB* FARTHING 1803 in a circle. *R*. *Unknown.*

117. O A ship sailing to left under top sails. FARTHING TOKEN 1812

℞ *BH* within a wreath of oak. *R*. *Halliday.*

118. O A view of rocks. Legend, PURE COPPER PREFERABLE TO PAPER ·

℞ A female seated on a bale of merchandise; in her right hand an olive branch, in the left a caduceus; a ship in the distance. Legend, TRADE & NAVIGATION 1813 *R*. *Halliday.*

PLATE G, no. 19.

WORKS OF REFERENCE.

Aitken (W. C.) Brass and Brass Manufacturers, *sm. 4to*, 1865.
Atkins (J.) The Coins and Tokens of the Possessions and Colonies of the British Empire, 8*vo*, 1889.
Atkins (J.) The Tradesmen's Tokens of the Eighteenth Century, 8*vo*, 1892.
Batty (D. T.) Descriptive Catalogue of the Copper Coinage of Great Britain, 3 vols., *sm. 4to*, 1868, 1894.
Blades (W.) A List of Medals, Jettons, etc., in connection with Printers and the Art of Printing, 8*vo*, 1869.
Bowles (H. B.) Bristol Coins and Tokens, 8*vo*, (1900).
Boyne (W.) Silver Tokens of Great Britain and its Dependencies, *4to*, 1866.
Boyne (W.) The Tokens of Yorkshire, *4to*, 1858.
Burn (J. H.) London Tradesmen's Tokens, 8*vo*, 1855.
Clay (C.) Currency of the Isle of Man, 8*vo*, 1869.
Cotton (W. A.) Coins, Tokens and Medals of Worcestershire, 8*vo*, 1885.
Chaffers (W.) Marks and Monograms on Pottery and Porcelain, *roy. 8vo*, 1903.
Davis (W. J.) Token Coinage of Warwickshire, *4to*, 1895.
Davis (W. J.) Short History of the Brass Trades, 1892.
Evelyn's Discourse of Medals, 1697.
Goulding (C.) The Coinage of Suffolk, *4to*, 1868.
Grueber (H. A.) Handbook of the Coins of Gt. Britain and Ireland in the B. Museum, 8*vo*, 1899.
Heaton (R.) Birmingham Coinage, 8*vo*, 1865.
Holinshed (R.) Chronicles. England, Scotland and Wales, 1577.
Lindsay (J.) The Coinage of Ireland, *4to*, 1839.
Manchester Numismatic Society, Proceedings of, *4to*, 1871.
Meili (J.) Die Munzen der colonie Brasilien, 1645-1822, 8*vo, Zurich*, 1897 (Describes and Illustrates some English Countermarks).
Montagu (H.) Copper Coins of England, 8*vo*, 1893.
Nelson (P.) Coinage of the Isle of Man, 8*vo*, 1899.
Nelson (P.) Coinage of William Wood, 8*vo*, 1903.
Neumann (J.) Beschreibung der Bekanntesten, 6 vols., 8*vo, Prague*, 1858-72.
Numismatic Chronicle. The Proceedings of the Numismatic Society of London.
Numismatic Magazine, 8*vo and sm. 4to*, 1886 *to* 1903.
Palmer (A. N.) John Wilkinson and Old Bershaw Iron Works, 8*vo*, 1899.
Phillips (M.) The Token Money of the Bank of England, 8*vo*, 1900.
Pye (C.) Complete Representation of all the Provincial Copper Coins, *4to*, (1801).
Pye (C.) Modern Birmingham, *post 8vo*, (1818).
Randall (J.) The Wilkinsons, 12*mo, Madeley*, (1870).
Ruding (Rev. R.) Annals of the Coinage of Great Britain, 6 vols., 8*vo*, 1819.
Sharp (T.) Catalogue of the Coins and Tokens in the Collection of Sir G. Chetwynd, *4to*, 1834.
Simon (J.) Essay Historical Account of Irish Coins, *4to, Dublin*, 1810.
Spink's Numismatic Circular, *folio*, 1892 *to* 1903.
Smith (Aquilla) Irish Tokens and Jettons, 8*vo*, 1869.
Smith (Aquilla) Papers on Irish Coinage, 8*vo*, 1855.
Snelling (T.) The Coins of Great Britain and Ireland, *folio*, 1766.
Sykes (W.) Hull Coins and Tokens, 8*vo*, 1892.
Thomason (Sir Edward) Memoirs, 2 vols., 1845.
Waters (A. W.) The Token Coinage of South London issued in the Eighteenth and Nineteenth Centuries, 8*vo, Leamington*, 1904.

Besides the above Numismatic Books, there have been consulted Pamphlets, Coin Sale Catalogues, Files of old Newspapers, Directories, etc.

INDEX I.

Places at which Tokens were issued; or were current.

⁂ The numbers in this, and following Indexes, refer to the *page* in the book.

Abercarne, 196.
Adelphi Cotton Works, 22, 23.
Alderney, 241, 242.
Alford, 66.
Alloa Colliery, 20.
Andover, 57, 60, 97.
Anglesea, 146.
Antrim, county of, 229.
Armagh, county of, 233.
Arnold, 92.
Ashbourn, 38.
Attleborough, 80.
Ayrshire, 19, 199, 200.

Ballindalloch, 20.
Ballymena, 229.
Bank of England, 1-8, 11, 12.
Bank of Ireland, 8, 9, 10.
Barnsley, 166, 175.
Barnstaple, 34, 40.
Basingstoke, 60.
Bath, 53, 95-98, 109, 110, 249.
Bedworth, 143.
Belfast, 230, 231.
Bellylonaghan, 231.
Benhall, 136.
Berkshire, 29.
Bersham, 145.
Berwickshire, 201.
Beverley, 175.
Bewdley, 161.
Bilston, 118, 121-126.
Birmingham, 17, 121, 143, 144, 146-157, 161, 162.
Birmingham Workhouse, 17, 143, 144, 146-149.
Blandford, 43.
Bolton, 17.
Bolton, Ireland, 26.
Bradford, 18, 166, 176.
Bradford Workhouse, 176.
Bradley, 121, 145.
Breby, 232.
Brechin, 206.

Brecknock, 187.
Bridlington, 166, 167.
Brierley, 133.
Brighton, 140.
Bristol, 98-107, 110-115, 193.
Buckinghamshire, 30.
Bucklersbury—*see* London.
Burslem, 127.
Burton, 38, 55, 121, 127, 183, 241, 253.
Bury St. Edmunds, 16, 82.
Buteshire, 19.

Calton, 210.
Cambrian Pottery, Swansea, 195.
Cambridgeshire, 31.
Canada, 259.
Cark-in-Cartmell, 15.
Carmarthen, 188, 189.
Carmarthenshire, 188, 189.
Castlecomer, 27.
Castlecomer Colliery, 27.
Castletown, 244, 245.
Catrine Works, 19.
Chard, 108.
Charing Cross, London, 70, 71, 73.
Charlotte-street—*see* London.
Channel Islands, The, 240.
Chatteris, 31.
Cheadle, 128.
Cheltenham, 53-55, 72.
Cheshire, 32.
Chesterfield, 38.
Chichester, 140, 141.
Christ's Hospital—*see* London.
Cinque Ports, 63.
Clackmannanshire, 20.
Coleraine, 225.
Cornwall, 33, 34, 39, 71.
Coseley, 133.
Coventry, 23, 157, 158.
Cromford, 14.
Culgreuch, 25.
Culgreuch Mill, 25.
Cumberland, 37.

INDEX I.

Dalkeith, 203.
Dalzield Farm, 20, 21.
Darlaston, 128.
Dawley, 94.
Deanston, 23.
Deanston Cotton Mill, 23.
Denbighshire, 190.
Derby, 38, 65.
Derbyshire, 14, 38, 65.
Devonshire, 39-42, 98.
Diss, 81.
Dolcoath Mine, 34.
Doncaster, 167, 176.
Dorchester, 43.
Dorsetshire, 14, 43-46.
Douglas, 243-247.
Down, 26.
Down, county of, 234.
Drogheda, 226.
Dromore, 234.
Dublin, 26, 212-222, 226.
Dublin, county of, 236, 237.
Dudley, 161, 162.
Dundee, 206.
Dunfermline, 205.
Dungannon, 238.
Duns, 201.
Durham, 15, 47, 86.

East Retford, 16.
Edinburgh, 22, 202, 203.
Edinburghshire, 202, 203.
Elgin, 20.
England, Bank of—*see* B. of England.
Epping, 48.
Epworth, 66.
Eskmills, 203.
Essex, 48-51, 80.
Exeter, 40, 41.
Exeter Change—*see* London, Strand.
Fazeley, 118, 119.
Fifeshire, 205.
Fintry, 25.
Flint, 191, 192.
Flintshire, 191, 192.
Folkestone, 63.
Forfarshire, 206.
Frome, or Frome Selwood, 97, 108, 109.

Gainsborough, 67, 91.
Galston Society, 19.
Galway, 223.

Gateshead, 47.
Gilford, 234.
Glamorganshire, 193-195.
Glanclydwedog, 190.
Glasgow, 21, 25, 209, 210.
Glemham, 136.
Glenarm, 232.
Gloucester, 53, 54, 97.
Gloucestershire, 53, 54, 98, 105, 107.
Godalming, 138.
Goodman's Fields—*see* London.
Gosport, 56.
Greenock, 23, 24.
Guernsey, 240, 241, 242.

Haddingtonshire, 207.
Halesowen, 94.
Hamilton, 210.
Hampshire, 56-60, 135.
Happing—*see* Tunstead and Happing.
Haverford West, 198.
Hereford, 61.
Herefordshire, 61.
Hertfordshire, 62, 74, 75, 78.
High Wycombe, 30.
Hill of Down, 27.
Holbeach, 68, 135.
Hotcheson-town, 25.
Houndsditch, 15, 16.
Hoxne, 137.
Hull, 168, 176-179.
Hull Lead Works, 176-179.

Inverness-shire, 208.
Ipswich, 135, 141.
Ireland, 26, 212-239.
Ireland, Bank of—*see* Bank of Ireland.
Isle of Ely, 31.
Isle of Man, 27, 243-248.
Isle of Wight, 56.

Jersey, 240, 241, 242.

Keighley, 18, 180.
Kent, 63.
Kilkenny, 27.
Killyleigh, 235.
Kilrea, 238.
King's County, 224.

Lanark, 21.
Lanark Mills, 21, 22.
Lanarkshire, 20-22, 209, 210.
Lancashire, 15, 64.

264 INDEX I.

Launceston, 33.
Leeds, 73, 168, 169, 171, 180.
Leicester, 38, 65.
Leicestershire, 38, 65.
Leith, 203, 204.
Lemonsley Mill, 128.
Levernbank, 24.
Levern Mill, 24.
Lichfield, 38, 128, 129.
Limekilns, 205.
Lincoln, 68.
Lincolnshire, 66-69.
Lisburn, 232.
Liverpool, 64, 146.
Locality unknown, 28, 55, 239, 249-260.
Lochearn, 23.
Lochwinnoch, 24.
London, 13, 16, 33, 53, 54, 56, 65, 70-79, 81, 86, 88, 91, 112, 114, 115, 146, 189.
   „ Exeter Change, Strand, 75, 76, 78, 79.
   „ 10, Charlotte-street, 53, 54.
   „ Soho, 74, 78.
   „ 12, Rathbone-place, 33, 56, 65, 70-73.
   „ Goodman's Fields, 74.
   „ Charing Cross, 70, 71, 73.
   „ Christ's Hospital, 74.
   „ Bucklersbury, 71, 73.
   „ Thames-street, 74.
   „ St. Martin's Lane, 72, 77.
   „ Cheapside, 77.
   „ Lad Lane, 77.
   „ Old Stock Exchange, 77.
Londonderry, 225.
Londonderry, County of, 225, 238.
London-road, Southwark, 138.
Louth, county of, 226.
Louth, Lincolnshire, 68.
Lowestoft, 137.
Lurgan, 233, 234.
Lye, 162.
Lynn, 81, 91, 135.

Malone, 232.
Malton, 181.
Manchester, 15, 64.
Mansfield, 72, 81, 91.
Manx—*see* Isle of Man.
March, 31.
Marlborough, 97, 159.

Mayo, county of, 227.
Meath, 27.
Merthyr, 104.
Merthyr Tydvil, 193.
Menlough, 223.
Middlesex, 13, 15, 16, 33, 53, 54, 56, 65, 70-79, 81, 86, 88, 91, 112, 114, 115, 146, 189.
Midlothian, 22.
Monmouthshire, 196.
Montgomeryshire, 197.
Morriston, 195.
Muir Kirk Ironworks, 19.
Musselburgh, 204.

Nantwich, 32.
Neath, 150, 194.
Needham Market, 135.
Newark, 91, 92.
Newcastle-on-Tyne, 86-90.
Newcastle-under-Lyme, 129.
Newport, I. of W., 58.
Newtownards, 235, 236.
Norfolk, 80-84.
Northampton, 38, 65.
Northamptonshire, 85.
North Cornwall, 33.
North Lopham, 81.
North Shields, 16.
Northumberland, 16, 86-90.
Norwich, 83, 84.
Not locals—*see* Unknown locality.
Nottingham, 38, 93.
Nottinghamshire, 16, 38, 65, 91-93.

Oldbury, 133.

Paisley, 24, 25.
Peebles, 211.
Peebleshire, 211.
Pembrokeshire, 198.
Perry Barr, 129.
Perthshire, 22.
Peterborough, 85.
Phœnix Iron Works, Glasgow, 209.
Phœnix Iron Works, Sheffield, 184, 185.
Poole, 14, 43.
Portadown, 233.
Portaferry, 236.
Portsea, 58.
Portsmouth, 56, 59.
Potteries, Staffordshire, 130.
Poulton, 64.

INDEX I.   265

Powell, 26.
Prestonpans, 207.
Priestfield, 121, 123.

Ramsay, 247, 248.
Rathbone-place—*see* London.
Reading, 29.
Redditch, 162.
Renfrewshire, 23.
Retford—*see* East Retford.
Richhill, 233.
Richmond, 139.
Ripley, 138.
Risca, 150.
Romsey, 59, 60.
Roscoe Mills, Sheffield, 184-186.
Rothsay Cotton Works, 19, 20.
Rothsay Mills, 19.
Rowfant, 141.
Rugeley, 130.
Rutland, 38, 65.

St. Martin's Lane—*see* London.
Sawbridgeworth, 62, 74, 75, 78.
Scarborough, 170.
Scorrier House, 35, 36, 121.
Scotland, 19, 25, 199-208.
Sedbury, 55, 127, 253.
Shaftesbury, 44-46, 71.
Sheffield, 55, 152, 153, 166, 170-172, 181-185, 253.
Sheffield Workhouse, 172, 181-183.
Sherborne, 14.
Shoreham, 135, 141.
Shropshire, 94.
Snedshill, 145.
Soho—*see* London.
Somersetshire, 39, 95-117, 249.
Southampton, 56, 60.
South Shields, 15, 47.
Sowerby Bridge, 186.
Stafford, 119, 130, 131.
Staffordshire, 118-134.
Stamford, 69.
Stanley Colliery, Bewdley, 161.
Staverton, 159, 160.
Stewartson, 239.
Steyning, 142.
Stirlingshire, 25.
Stockport, 32.
Stockton, 47.
Strabane, 228.

Strand—*see* London.
Stratton, 33, 34.
Suffolk, 16, 80, 82, 135-137.
Surrey, 138, 139.
Sussex, 140-142.
Swanage, 46.
Swansea, 73, 114, 154, 155, 189, 194, 195.
Swords, 222.

Taunton, 109, 116.
Tavistock, 42.
Teignmouth, 41.
Thirsk, 18, 172.
Thistle Bank, 21.
Tipton, 133.
Trowbridge, 104, 107.
Tullamore, 224.
Tunstead and Happing, 84.
Tyrone, county of, 228, 238.

Unknown locality, 28, 55, 239, 249-260.
Vigornia, 164, 165

Wales (North and South), 98, 104-107, 113, 150, 151, 153, 187, 193-198.
Walsall, 14, 131-133.
Walthamstow, 48-52.
Walworth, 139.
Warwickshire, 17, 143-158.
Wednesbury, 133.
Welshpool, 197.
West Bromwich and Coseley, 133.
West Bromwich, Oldbury, Tipton and Brierley, 133.
Westport, 227.
West Wheal Mine, 34, 35.
Weybridge, 138.
Whitby, 173.
Whitehaven, 37.
Willey, 145, 146.
Wiltshire, 97, 98, 104, 105, 107, 159-160.
Withymoor, 134.
Wiveliscombe, 116, 117.
Wolverhampton, 121, 134.
Woodbridge, 136.
Worcester, 161, 163-165.
Worcester Porcelain Company, 165.
Worcestershire, 161-165.
Wroxham, 84.

Yarmouth, 82.
Yorkshire, 17, 55, 73, 152, 166-186.
Yorkshire, West Riding, 166.
York, 73, 173-175, 186.

INDEX II.

Names of Issuers of Tokens.

A. on Isle of Man shilling, 27.
Adelphi Cotton Works, 22, 23.
Adair, James, 229.
Adams, W., 59.
Adams, Webster, 135.
Alloa Colliery, 20.
Altamont, Earl of, 227.
A. M. B., 27.
Andrews, J.—*see* Padley and Andrews.
Arkwright and Co., 14.
Arnold Works, 92.
Atherton, James, 122.
Avenell and Simmonds, 58.

Badger, T. and J., 161, 162.
Baker, William, 93.
Ballans, W., 64.
Ballindalloch Cotton Works, 20.
Bank of England, 1-8, 11-13.
Bank of Guernsey, 240.
Bank of Ireland, 8-10.
Barber—*see* Cattle and Barber.
Barker, E., 130.
Barker, Samuel, 83.
Bartleet, W., 162, 163.
Bastin, John and Co., 54.
Bastin, William, 53.
Baylis, H., 121.
B. C.—*see* J. T.
Berwick, or Bewicke Main Colliery, 86, 88.
Bean, James, 139.
Beatson and Copeland, 245.
Beck, Lant—*see* Garratt and Co.
Bedworth Mill, 143.
Beebee, Edward, 122.
Begg, W., 202.
Beith, Alexander, 229.
Bell, John, 88, 89.
Bently, W. F. and Co. (W. F. B. and Co.), 213.
Best, W., 14.
Best, W. B., 44.
Beverley, G., 208.
Beverley New Friendly Society 175.

Bevington—*see* Dillwyn and Bevingtons.
Bewley, Edward, 213.
Binns, William, 222.
Bird, Edward—*see* Garratt and Co.
Birkinshaw, 166, 167.
Birmingham and Sheffield Copper Co., 152, 153.
Birmingham and South Wales, 153.
Birmingham Union Copper Co., 150, 151.
Birmingham Workhouse, 17, 143, 144, 146-149.
Bishop and Co., 240.
Bishop, John, and Co., 55.
Blair, R. and G., 23.
Blake, Robert, 83.
Bluett, John, 109.
Blythe, John, 82.
B. M. Co., 259.
Board of Ordnance, 11.
Bohay—*see* Evans and Co.
Bone and Co., 210.
Booth, William, 129.
Bowen, Ben, 236.
Boxer, John, 63.
Bradford Workhouse, 18, 176.
Bragg, William, 37.
British Copper Co., 48-52.
Bristol Brass and Copper Co., 111, 114.
Broughton, Sprout, Garnet and Sutton, 32.
Brown, J., 202.
Brown, Patrick, 232.
Brumby Martin, 67.
Bryan, E., 98, 105.
Buchanan and Co., 23.
"Bull, John," 137.
Bunn, J. and Co., 138.
Butt, Edward and Francis, 69.
Butt—*see* Saunders and Butt.

Caffin, B. and J., Redman J., Halstead W., Shipman, C., 140, 141.
Calder, William, 202.
Callister, William, 247.

Cark Cotton Works, 15.
Carless and Co., 61.
Carter and Caine, 246.
Cartwright, T., 32.
Cartwright, T. and G. and R. Ferns, 32.
Castle Comer Colliery, 27.
Catrine Cotton Works, 19.
Cattle and Barber, 173-175.
Chapman—*see* Stovin and Chapman.
Charges, Benjamin, 140.
Charleville, Viscount, 224.
Chaston, J., 137.
Cheadle, Cooper and Brass Co., 128.
Cheesman, J., 142.
Ching—*see* Pearse and Co.
Christie, S. P., 202.
Christopher and Jennett, 47.
Christ's Hospital, 74.
Clarke, 16.
Clarke, J.—*see* Temlett and Clarke.
Clark, West and Co., 212.
Clayton and Hide, 141.
Clayton and Hydes, 135.
Cochran, John, 234.
Cole and Co., 85.
Collyer, Rev. Daniel, 84.
Comper, Henry, 140.
Cook and Harwood, 166.
Cooksey, James, 133.
Cooper, John and Co., 160.
Copeland—*see* Beatson and Copeland.
Corbe—*see* Forster and Corbe.
Corcer, 24.
Cowans, of Musselburgh, 204.
Cox, Merle and Pattison, 43.
Cox, Messrs., 116.
Crichton, Robert, 21.
Crown Copper Company, 150.
Culgreuch Mill, 25.
Culverhouse, C.; Orchard J.; and Phipps, J., 95, 97, 98, 249.
Curtis, W., 31.

Dally, T. and Co., 141.
Dalziel Farm, 20, 21.
Davidson, John, 90.
Davis, John, 15, 16.
Davis, W., at Worcester, 165.
Dawson, Edward, 91.
Deakin—*see* Younge and Deakin.
Deanston Cotton Mill, 23.

Devon Mines, 42.
Dillwyn, L. W., Bevington, T., and Bevington, J., 195.
Dolcoath Mine, 34.
Dorchester Bank, 43.
Dore, William—*see* Whitchurch and Dore.
Douglas Bank Co., 243, 244, 246, 247.
Douglass, A. D., 202.
Dove—*see* Littler, Dove and Co.
Dromore, Countess of, 27.
Dudley, John, 59.
Dunham and Yallop, 83.

Eccles of Duns, 201.
Eggo, John, 203.
Elam—*see* Ratcliffe, Elam and Thurbon.
Elliott, John, 89, 90.
Ellis, William—*see* Stanton and Co.
Emerton, Elizabeth and Sons, 66.
E. S., surmounted by a crown, 13.
Evans, Bohay, Nott, and Gribble, 40.
Evans—*see* Ricketts and Co.
Exeter Change, 16.

Featherstone, John, 116.
Fellowes, J. M., 93.
Fereday, Samuel, 121-124, 126.
Ferns—*see* Cartwright and Co.
Ferris, James, 43, 144.
Fillingham, William—*see* Stansall and Co.
Fisher, Richard—*see* Stansall and Co.
Fisher, Thomas, 235.
Fletcher and Sharratt, 131, 133.
Flint Copper Co., 131, 154.
Flint Lead Works, 191, 192.
Flintshire Bank, 191.
Forrest, J. and Co., 162.
Forster and Corbe, 25.
Francis, Richard, 80.
Frazer, Robert, 211.
Frazer, William—*see* McDonell and Frazer
Fullarton, Colonel, 199, 200.

Galloway, John, 236.
Galston Society, 19.
Gamson, John, 67.
Garnett—*see* Broughton and Co.
Garratt and Grigg, 104, 106.
Garratt, Fcs.; Terrell, Wm.; Bird, Edw.; Beck, Lant.; and Grigg, Fcs. H., 98-103, 106.

INDEX II.

Gateis, S., 142.
Gibbons, M. D., 26.
Gibson, A. and Co., 24.
Gibson, Thomas, 149.
Gilpin, Gilbert, 94.
Glanclywedog Factory, 190.
Glasgow Bank, 21.
Glover, Samuel, 196.
Gomme, James, 30.
Gosling—*see* King and Co.
Gough—*see* Willoughby and Co.
Gray, John, 208.
Gray, of Dunse, 201.
Gray, W., 204.
Greer, James, 233.
Gregory—*see* Longden and Gregory.
Gribble—*see* Evans and Co.
Griffith, J. and S., 53.
Griffith, W. Gerrard—*see* Willoughby and Co.
Griffiths, R., 197.
Griffiths—*see* King and Co.
Griffiths, W. and Co., 188.
Griffin, George, 85.
Griffin, James and Sons, 134.
Grigg, F. H.—*see* Garratt and Co.
Guppy, S., 112, 115.

H., 259.
Halesowen Workhouse, 94.
Hall, William, 234.
Halls, R. D., 64.
Halse—*see* Jacob and Halse.
Halstead, W.—*see* Caffin and Co.
Hamilton, retailers, 210.
Hampson, Mary and Son, 15.
Hancock, J. Gregory, 156, 157.
Hancock—*see* Stanton and Co.
Harding—*see* Peels, Harding and Co.
Harrop, John, 47.
Harwood—*see* Cook and Harwood.
H. B., 260.
Hedley, Isaquey, 81, 91.
Hemming, W., 162, 163.
Henderson and Co., 46.
Henrickson, John, 128, 129.
H. H., 254.
Hicks, Joseph, 41.
Hide—*see* Clayton and Hide.
Hilles, James, 213, 219.
Hobson, S. and Sons, 183.

Hoff, R. B., 68.
Holland, J., 41.
Horton and Co., 130, 131.
Horsfall, William, 166.
House, W., 16.
Hunton, John, 82.
Hunt, Henry, 141.
Hyde—*see* Clayton and Hyde.

I. B., 250.
I. B. Co. (Irish Bullion Co.), 212, 250.
I. M. Co. (Irish Mining Co.), 226.
Innocent, Robert, 139.
I. P. R., 16.
I. T., 26.
Irvine, G., 228.

Jackson and Lister, 175.
Jackson, William, 180.
Jacob and Halse, 189.
Jardine—*see* Thomas and Co.
Jennett—*see* Christopher and Jennett.
Jerrems, William, 67, 91.
Jersey, States of, 240.
Jobson—*see* Shaw, Jobson and Co.
Johnston—*see* Bunn and Co.
Johnston, W., 231.
Jones, W. and Co., 71.
Jordan and Co., 74.
J. T., B. C., 202.

Kean, Aaron, 232.
Keighley Overseers, 18.
Kelty, Alexander, 86.
Kiddell, Robert, 80.
Killrea, James Henry, 238.
King, A., 24.
King, Gosling, Tanner and Griffiths, 159.
King, John, 138.
Kirk, J., 205.
Kitchin, William, 37.
Knapp and Co., 71.
Knapp John, junior, 164, 165.
Knox, John, 230.

Lanark Mills, 21.
Lane, H. P., 143.
Lang, John, 24.
Langm. . . ., W., 25.
Latham—*see* Niblock and Latham.
Laycock, James, 166.
Leck, Thomas, 175.

Leith, W. C., 203.
Lill—*see* Tate and Lill.
Lister—*see* Jackson and Lister.
Lintott and Sons, 60.
Littler, Dove and Co., 244.
Lloyd, S., 44.
Lloyd, Samuel and Co., 71, 73.
Lomer and Son, 60.
Longden and Gregory, 184.
Lord and Marshall, 170.
Lumb—*see* Smalpage and Lumb.

McClure, Alexander, 231.
McCully, John, 235, 236.
McDonell, Angus, and Fraser, William, 208.
McEwen, A., 203.
McFie, Lindsay and Co., 24.
Machin—*see* Riley and Machin.
McIntosh, W., 208.
McK., J. and Son, 24.
McKenzie, W., 225.
Mackie, Samuel, 233.
McLaren, Duncan, 23.
McMillan and Co., 210.
McMinn, Fran., 239.
McNee, Robert, 25.
McO'Grady, 26.
McPherson, Alexander, 208.
McQuoid, William, 236.
McQuoid, J., 26.
McTurk, 246.
Maculla, James, 237, 238.
McVicar, Duncan, 208.
Magarragh, Hugh, 230.
Maillers, R., 205.
Marlborough Bank, 97.
Marshall—*see* Lord and Marshall.
Mathews—*see* Studd and Mathews.
Meeson, James, 28.
Menelaws, of Edinburgh, 202.
Merle—*see* Cox and Co.
Miller, J., 203.
Miller, Robert, 236.
Miller, W., senior, 204.
Millson and Preston, 68.
Mirfin and Parker, 167.
Mitchell, J., 27.
Moline and Co., 138.
Monck, J. B., 29.
Monteagle, Lord, 227.
Montgomery, Hugh, 232.

Moor, Charles—*see* Stansall and Co.
Morgan, H., of London, 33, 38-40, 54, 56, 65, 71-4, 81, 91, 103, 104, 106.
Morgan, of Bristol, 106.
Morgan, D.—*see* Rees and Morgan.
Morgan, M. L.; Williams, M.D.; Williams, Wm., 193.
Morris, of Carmarthen, 188.
Morton, Alexander, 233.
Moss, William, 189.
M. and S., of Musselburgh, 204.
Muir Kirk Iron Works, 19.
Muir, J. and A., 24.
Muir, A., 24.
Muir, J., 25.
Murphy, McC. W., 26.
Murrey or Murray, John, 248.
Muskett, William, 80.
Muskett and Sons, 81.

Nantrhydnyvilas Air Furnace Company, 195.
Nantwich Old Bank, 32.
Neel, Elias, 241.
Nevill and Co., 219.
Newton, 83, 84.
Niblock and Latham, 104, 107.
Nicols—*see* Pearce and Co.
Nimmo, G., 207.
North, R. and Co., 116.
North, George, 187.
Nott—*see* Evans and Co.

Oakley and Co., 191.
Oates and Co., 28.
O'Brien, 26.
O'Brien, Thomas, 234.
Oliver, Robert, 88, 89.
O'Neill, 26.
Orchard, J.—*see* Culverhouse and Co.
Orchard Robert, 62, 74, 75, 78.
Ordnance, Board of, 11.
Ords, George, 222.
Overend John, 233.
Overseers of—*see* Birmingham Workhouse.

Padley and Andrews, 194.
Paisley Society, 25.
Papin, W. J., 203.
Pardoe, James, 127.
Parker, Joseph, 132.
Parker—*see* Mirfin and Parker.
Parson, William and Son, 80.

Patent Sheathing Nail Manufactory, 112, 114, 115.
Pattison—*see* Cox and Co., 203.
Pearse, Ching, Nicols and Prockter, 33.
Peel Castle, Isle of Man, 27.
Peels, Harding and Co., 118, 119.
Percy, E. W., 157, 158.
Peterborough Bank, 85.
Phœnix Iron Works, Sheffield, 183, 184.
Phœnix Iron Works, Glasgow, 209.
Phœnix Glass Works, 114.
Phillips, W. and J.—*see* Thomas and Co.
Phillipson, J. B., 140.
Phillipson, Robert, 140.
Phipps, J.—*see* Culverhouse and Co.
Picard, J. K., 176-180.
Pidcock, Gilbert, 75, 76, 78, 79.
Pinkerton, John, 60.
Pollock, James, 204.
Porter, Samuel, 81.
Powell, 26, 27.
Preter, Pew and Whitty, 14.
Prockter—*see* Pearse and Co.
Proddy, A., 89.
Preston—*see* Millson and Preston.
Preston—*see* Rudston and Preston.
Purdie, D., 202.

Quayle, George and Co., 245.

Ratcliffe, Elam and Thurbon, 31.
Ratley, 77.
Rawsons, I. W. and W., 65.
Rea, Thomas, 238.
Read, T. and W., 66.
Readett, William—*see* Stansall and Co.
Redman, J.—*see* Caffin and Co.
Rees and Morgan, 194.
Reid, Henry, 210.
Remmington and Smith, 250, 251.
Retford—*see* East Retford.
Revolution Mill, 16.
Reynolds, F. R., 82.
R. H., 253, 259, 260.
Ricketts, Evans and Co., 114.
Riley, J. and R., and Machin, 127.
Ringland, William, 230, 231.
Risca Union Copper Co., 150, 151.
Robb, Alexander, 202.
Robertson, John, 86-88.
Robinson, Francis, 47.

Romains, 77.
Rose Copper Co., 154-6.
Rose, P., 103.
Rothsay Cotton Works, 19, 20.
Rothsay Mills, 19, 20.
Round, Abel, 133.
Rudston and Preston, 168.
Rushbury and Woolley, 118, 122, 124-6.
Ryall, H.—*see* Willoughby and Co.

Sandars, Samuel, 67.
Saunders and Butt, 54.
Scott, A. and J., 203.
Scott, I. and W., 24.
Scurr, Richard, 18, 172.
S. D. and Co., 24.
Sedbury Iron Works, 55.
Shaftesbury Bank, 44-6.
Sharratt—*see* Fletcher and Sharratt.
Shaw, Jobson and Co., 183, 184, 186.
Shephard, Watts and Co., 33.
Sheppard, W., 105-7.
Sheffield Overseers, 172, 181-3.
Shipham, C.—*see* Caffin and Co.
Short, J., 26.
Simmonds—*see* Avenell and Simmonds.
Sinkins, Mrs.—*see* Willoughby and Co.
Sizers, W., 136.
Sligo, Marquis of, 227.
Smalpage and Lumb, 168, 169.
Smith and Wilson, 206.
Smith, John, 31.
Smith—*see* Remington and Smith.
Smyth, Edward, 232.
Somervills, Mrs., 26.
Sparks, W.—*see* Willoughby and Co.
Spence, 48.
Sprout—*see* Broughton and Co.
Staffordshire Pottery, 130.
Stansall, Moor, Fisher, Fillingham, Readett and Wilson, 91, 92.
Stanton, Hancock, Wakefield and Co., and William Ellis, 91.
States of Jersey, 240.
Staverton Factory, 159, 160.
Steele, John, 202.
Stephens, Edward, 214-6, 218.
Stephens, J. M., 59.
Stephenson, James, 167.
Steven, A. and Sons, 21.
Steward, J., 135.

Stewart, A., 208.
Stewart, John, 235.
Stovin and Chapman, 68.
Studd and Mathews, 136.
Sutton—*see* Broughton and Co.
Swanage Friendly Society, 46.

Tanner—*see* King and Co.
Tate, John and Son, 16.
Tate and Lill, 226.
T. C. (Stafford), 119.
T. C. S. (Ripley), 138.
Teignmouth Bank, 41.
Temlett and Clarke, 117.
Templeton, James, 239.
Terrell, William—*see* Garratt and Co.
Thirsk Association, 18, 172.
Thistle Bank Company, 22.
Thom, J, 263.
Thomas and Phillips; Jardine; Lloyd and W. and J. Phillips, 198.
Thomason, Sir Edward, 149.
Thomson, T., 204.
Thompson, I. and B., 161.
Thompson, J. H., 129.
Thurbon—*see* Ratcliffe and Co.
T. I. C., 253.
Toole, 26.
T. P., 259.
Tripp and Co., 105, 107.
Tunstead and Happing Corporation, 84.
Tullamore, Baron, 224.

Union Copper Co., 150-152, 156.
Upcott, W., 41.

Voss, John, 195.

Wade, Francis, 136.
Wade, J. S., 136.
Wainwright and Co., 61.
Wakefield and Co.—*see* Stanton and Co.
Wakeford, W. S. and J., 57, 60.
Wallis, Richard, 161, 162.
Walsall Church, 14.
Ward, H., 43.
Warren, Robert, 72, 77.
Waters, Messrs. Robert, 188.
Watts—*see* Shephard and Co.
W. C.—C., 31.
Westport, Viscount, 227.

West Wheal Mine, 34, 35.
West—*see* Clark, West and Co.
W. F. B. and Co., 219.
W. H. Co., 222.
Whalley and Co., 74.
Whalley, J., 53, 54.
Whitby Association, 173.
Whitchurch and Dore, 96-98, 109, 110.
White, James, 203.
Whitehouse and Co., 133.
Whitty, 14.
Whyte, Thomas, 25.
Wilkins, R. B., 58.
Wilkes, Job, 128.
Wilkinson, James, 162.
Wilkinson, John, 145, 146.
Wilkison, 22.
Will, J., 203.
Williams, John, 35, 36.
Williams—*see* Morgan and Co.
Willoughby, Messrs.; Sinkins, Mrs.; Ryall; Sparks; Griffith, and Gough, 109.
Willoughby and Sons, 108, 109.
Wilson, 26.
Wilson, Joseph, 234.
Wilson, Robert, 186.
Wilson, R., 204.
Wilson—*see* Smith and Wilson.
Wilson, T. and Co., 64.
Wilson, T.—*see* Stansall and Co.
Wilson, W. "Swan with two necks," 77.
Wilsons — *see* Younge, Wilsons and Younge.
Wise, Alexander, 203.
Wood, Thomas, 77.
Wood, T., and Co., 162.
Woolley—*see* Rusbury and Woolley.
Worcester Overseers, 161.
Worcester House of Industry, 164.
Worcester Porcelain Co., 165.
W. R., 26.
Wright, Edward, 143.
Wright, J., Junior, 206.

Yallop—*see* Dunham and Yallop.
Younge, Wilsons and Younge, 170.
Younge and Deakin, 170, 172.
Younge and Co., 171.
Younge, S. C. and Co., 171, 172.

INDEX III.

Miscellaneous Subjects.

A. B. Token Issuer, 101.
Adair, James, 229.
Adams, Webster, 59, 135.
Adams, W., 59.
Air Furnace Co., 195.
Allan's History of the County of York, 167.
Altamont, Earl of, xlviii, 227.
Ampers' and (&), 16.
Andover Bank, 57.
Andover "Star and Garter," 57.
Angell's History of Halesowen, 94.
Armagh, Stuart's Historical Memoirs of, 233.
Arnold Works, 92.
Arts, Society of, 94.
Atherton James, 122.
Atkins' 18th Century Tokens, 13, 16, 17, 48, 58, 62, 75-9, 107, 137, 141, 146, 157, 200, 202-4, 206, 210, 211, 222, 226, 228, 246, 247.
Atkins' Coins of British Possessions, 240-2, 244, 246, 247.
Auction Mart, London, 88.
Avenell, William, 58.
Ballaugh, Ramsay, I. of M., 247.
Ballyloghnegany, 231.
Bank Note of the Token Bank, 101.
Bank of England dollar, 1, 2.
Bank Quay, Warrington, 128.
Banks Collection, 208.
Banks, Miss, 75.
Banks, Sir Joseph, 200.
Barge Yard, 44.
Barker, Samuel, 83.
Barnstaple Bank, 40.
Basingstoke Canal, 60.
Bastin and Co., 54.
Bath Chronicle, 5, 7, 95-8, 101, 105, 160, 170, 175, 191, 213.
Bath Journal, 98, 100.
Bath City Bank, 96.
Bath, 96-8, 104.
Batty's Tokens, 88, 89, 114, 156, 175, 202, 203, 238.
Bauert, Mr., 75.
Bazaar Articles, 121, 122, 129, 180, 192, 195, 209, 217, 222.

Beck, Launcelot, 100-2.
Beckett and Co., Bankers, 169.
Bedworth Mill, 143.
Beebee, Edward, 122.
Beith, Alexander, 229.
Belfast News Letter, 229, 236.
Belfast Town Book, 230.
Belfast, Young's Historical Notices of Old, 232.
Belfast Museum, 235.
Bell, John, 86-9.
Benn's History of Belfast, 229.
Beverley Brothers Society, 175.
Bewicke Main Colliery, 88.
Bindley, James, 75.
Bird, Edward, 100-2.
Birkinshaw, of Doncaster, 167.
Birmingham Mining and Copper Co., 156
Bishop de Jersey and Co., 240.
Bishop, John, 55.
Black Prince-row, Walworth, 139.
Blake, Robert, 83.
Bliss Collection, 4, 11, 14, 19, 20, 26, 27, 32, 40, 41, 45, 171, 194.
Bluett, John, 109.
Blythe and Co., 82.
Board of Ordnance, 11.
Booth, William, of Perry Barr, 129.
Boulton and Co., 5.
Boulton, Mathew, 149, 154, 220.
Bowles' Collection, 3, 4, 7, 11, 13, 14, 22, 28, 34, 99, 101, 138, 145, 187.
Boyne's 17th Century Tokens—see Williamson.
Boyne's Silver Tokens, 1, 2, 4-12, 14, 16, 17, 22, 23, 26, 29-34, 38-40, 43-6, 54-9, 64-8, 70-4, 80-82, 85-7, 91, 92, 95, 96, 98-100, 103-9, 118, 119, 135, 136, 140-3, 145, 146, 159, 166-74, 178, 188, 191, 194, 195, 199, 212, 213, 222, 233, 236, 243, 244, 249, 250.
Boyne's Yorkshire Tokens, 18, 180, 249.
Bracteate Tokens, 208.
Bready, co. Tyrone, 232.
Breton, 222, 254.
Brewer, Dr., 23.
Bristol and South Wales, 113.

INDEX III.

Bristol Bridge, 104.
Bristol Token Co., 101.
Bristol Tokens—opposition to, 107, 108.
Bristol—want of silver coin, 107, 108.
Britannia dollar, 1.
British Copper Co., 48, 49-52.
British Museum Collection, 6, 16, 75, 83, 89, 90, 94, 145, 165, 201, 208, 232, 234, 237.
Broughton and Garnett, 32.
Brumby, Martin, 67.
Bryan, E., 98.
Burn's London Traders' Tokens, 77.
Bury, Gillingwater's History of, 16.
Butt, Messrs., 69.

Camborne, 34.
Cambrian Pottery, 195.
Canterbury, Archbishop, 43.
Card Tokens, 164.
Carless and Co., 61.
Carless, T., 61.
Cartwright, Thomas, 32.
Cattle and Barber, 175.
Chaffers—Marks and Monograms on Pottery, etc., 165, 195.
Chambers' Encyclopædia, 243.
Channel Islands, 240-2.
Chapman—*see* Stovin and Chapman.
Charge, Benjamin, 140.
Charing Cross, 33.
Charles I., 61, 70.
Charles II., 15.
Charleville, Viscount, 224.
Chaston, John, 137.
Cheadle Copper and Brass Co., 128.
Cheesman, John, 142.
Cheltenham, 54, 55, 91.
Chetwynd Sir George, 34, 49, 94, 200, 243.
Christie, Manson and Woods, 243.
Clark and West, 212.
Clay, Dr. Charles, 243-8.
Clayton, Thomas, 141.
Cochran, John, 234.
Clocks, 43.
Cole and Co., 85.
Collyer, Rev. Daniel, 84.
Commercial Bristol Token Co., 101.
Comper, Henry, 140.
Conder, James, 75.

Cook, Samuel, 86.
Cooksey, James, 133.
Cooper, Good and Co., 149.
Copper Companies, 156.
Copper (old Tower) halfpennies, 103.
Cornish Mines, 34.
Cotton, William—*Tokens of Worcestershire*, 164.
Countermarked Tokens, 14-28, 226.
Countermarks, 5.
Coventry, 23.
Crown Copper Co., 150, 155, 156.

Dally and Co., 141.
Davidson, John, 90.
Davies, die sinker, 41, 43, 70, 71, 135, 225, 228.
Davis, W. J.—*see Token Coinage*.
Davis, W. J., sale, 16, 17, 200, 214, 251.
Dawson, Edward, 91.
Dean of St. Patrick's collection, 224.
de Birmingham's Arms, 144.
Dent's glove factory, 165.
Derbyshire Peak, 40.
Devil, the, 43.
Devonshire Bank, 40.
Devonshire Arms, 72.
Dickens, Charles, 77.
Die Sinkers, indexed under their names.
Dixon, die sinker, 146, 259.
Dollar, Bank of England, 1, 2.
  „ Shield, 1, 4.
  „ Britannia, 1.
  „ Garter, 3.
  „ Countermarked, 11.
Dore, William, 96, 97.
Dorrien, Magens, and Mello, 118.
Down co. *Ancient and present state of*, 236.
  „ *Knox's History of*, 233.
  „ Horse Breeders' Corporation, 234.
Dromore, Countess of, 27.
Dublin Museum collection, 231, 234-7, 239.
Dudley, John, 59.
Dunstan, Saint, 43.

East India Co., 77.
East London Waterworks, 49.
Eddystone Lighthouse, 39, 40-2, 80.
Edward I., 16.
Edward III., 23.

Eighteen-pence Token, armoured bust, 6, 7.
Eighteen-pence Token, laureated head, 7.
Elam, Edward, 31.
Elizabeth, Queen, 23, 29.
Ellis, William, 91.
Evening Sun newspaper, 82.
Every Day Book, 43.
Exeter, 34, 39, 41.
Exeter Change, *see* London.

Falkner's Dublin Journal, 239.
Falstaff, Sir John, 15, 16.
Fellows and Co., 93.
Fereday, Samuel, 121, 122, 124.
Ferns, Messrs., 32.
Fillingham, William, 92.
Fisher, Richard, 92.
Five shillings and sixpence Token, 3, 4, 5.
Five pence Token, 10.
Fletcher collection, 27, 204, 208, 210, 211, 216, 229, 230-2, 236, 237, 239.
Flint Lead Works, 192.
Forster, John, 77.
Fort William, 208.
Franks, Sir A. W., collection, 165.
Fraser, William, 208.
Frome, 109.

Gamson, John, 67.
Garratt, Francis, 100-3.
Garraways, 78.
Garter dollar, 3.
Gateis, Samuel, 142.
Gentleman's Magazine, 2, 3, 42, 77, 78, 86, 206.
"George" Inn, Portsmouth, 58.
Gerrard, William, 109.
Gillespie collection, 27, 235.
Gillingwater's History of Bury, 16.
Gilpin, Gilbert, 94.
Glasgow Bank Co., 21.
Glastonbury, Abbot of 43.
Glendining and Co., 3.
Glyn and Co., 85.
Golding, Charles—*Coinage of Suffolk*, 82, 136.
Goldsmiths' Company, 11-13.
Greer, Captn. J. W., 233.
Griffiths, R., 197.
Griffith and Gough, 109.

Griffon, 234.
Grigg, F. H., 100-102.
Grimsby, 67.
Grueber, H. A., 12, 118.
Guppy, Samuel, 112.

Halesowen, 94.
Halliday, Thomas, die sinker, 27, 29, 30-32, 34-40, 43-47, 53-55, 57-61, 63-68, 70-74, 77, 80-88, 90-92, 94, 95, 97-99, 103-110, 112-130, 133, 135, 136, 138, 140-142, 146, 149-155, 159, 161-167, 169-195, 198, 209, 213-215, 219-221, 241-247, 251-256, 258-260.
Hancock, die sinker, 146, 157, 158.
Hancock, John Gregory, die sinker, 156, 157, 212.
Hancock, Mr., 75.
Hancock, Wakefield and Co., 91.
Harrison, Cooke and Co., 88.
Hase, Henry, 12.
Heaton, Mr., 70.
Hedley, Isaquey, 81.
Hilles, James, 213.
Historical Chronicle, 42.
Hodgson, S., printer, 87, 88.
Hoff, R. B., 68.
Holinshed, 40.
Holland, Philemon, 158.
Holywell and Flintshire Bank, 191.
Horsfall and Co., 166.
Houndsditch, 15, 16.
House of Commons, 12.
House of Lords, 23.
Hull Advertiser, 180.
Hunter, John, 76.
Hunton, John, 82.
Hyde (or Hide), John, 141.

Illustrated London News, 149.
Ingleby, S. and J., 12.
Inglis motto, 202.
Ipswich, 59, 141.
Isle of Man, 243.

Jackson and Listers, 175.
James III, 22.
James, die sinker, 48, 62, 75, 76.
Jerrens, W., 67.
Jesus College, Bury, 16.
Johnston, William, 230.
Jones, Promoter of British Copper Co., 49.

INDEX III.

Jones, John, 160.
Jordan and Co., 74.

Keene's Bath Journal, 98, 100.
Kempson and Son, die sinkers, 44.
Kempson, Peter, ditto, 44, 137, 212.
Kilkenny Traders, 27.
Knapp, John, Junior, 164.
Knox, John, 230.
Küchler, die sinker, 1, 3, 4, 8, 9, 183, 217, 220, 221.

Lane, H. P., 143.
Latham, R. S., 104.
Lawrence sale, 9, 249.
Lea, River, 49.
Leather Note for five shillings, 146.
Lichfield, 128.
Lincoln, 73.
Lindsay's Coinage of Ireland, 224, 228, 237.
Liverpool, 64.
Lomer, W., 60.
London Carriers' Directory, 75.
London, Exeter Change, 16, 75, 76, 79.
London Gazette, 31, 32, 59, 80, 88, 166, 172, 178, 197.
Lord and Marshall, 170.
Lutwych, 76.

M ; 2 × 2½ H. C. T. Co., 11
Macaulay, Lord, 238.
Macfadyen collection, 89.
Mackintosh's Inverness-shire Antiquarian Notes, 238.
Madden, Mr., 75.
Mainwaring, 58.
Mansfield Postmaster, 91.
Manx Coinage—Relative values, 248.
Marazion Road, 35.
Marlborough Bank, 97, 159.
Marshall sale, 12.
Mayo co., xlviii, 227.
Meili, 11-13, 19, 25.
Mihell's Caravan Ticket, 75.
Miles, Mr., 75.
Millar, T., of Bungay, 77.
Miller, 75.
Millson and Preston, 68.
Milton, Mr., 75.
Milton, die sinker, 46, 74, 75, 78, 84, 199, 200.
Minories, London, 74.

Mionnet's scale, 11.
Modern Birmingham, 1818, 151.
Monck, J. B., M.P., 29.
Montagu collection, 8.
Montgomery, Hugh, 232.
Monthly Chronicle, 233.
Monthly Magazine, 136.
Moor, Charles, 92.
Morgan, H. and Co., die sinkers, 70, 101, 103, 104, 106.
Morland, Henry, 77.
Morland, Ransom and Co., 21.
Morning Chronicle, London, 76, 78.
Morris Family Arms, 188.
Morton, Alexander, 233.
Mossop, die sinker, 213, 219-222.
Mount, Alexander, Earl of, 232.
Munn, auctioneer, 88.
Murdoch collection, 13, 15, 19-22, 24, 193, 200.

Neath Abbey, 128.
Nelson, Lord, 17, 185.
Nelson, Dr., 27, 247, 248.
Neumann, 201-204, 236.
Nevill, Brent, 219.
Newcastle Chronicle, 76.
Newport, 33.
Newport, I. of Wight, 58.
Newton, silversmith, 84.
Niblock, J., 104, 107.
Nightingale, Benjamin, 149.
Ninepence Token, 8, 9.
Norman collection, 15, 16, 23, 25, 49, 52, 89, 132, 157, 161, 196, 206, 210, 224, 249.
Norman Survey, 109.
North, George, 187.
North Lopham, 81.
Nottingham, 92, 93.
Numismatic Magazine, 66, 80, 82, 109.

Old Stock Exchange, 77, 78.
Ordnance—*see* Board of Ordnance.
Orchard, Isaac, 95.
Orchard, Robert, 75.
Order of St. Andrew, 22.
Order of the Thistle, 22.
Otho de Tilli, 167.
Overend, John, 233.

Padley, Sylvanus, 194.
Palmer's *John Wilkinson*, 146.
Parker, Joseph, 132.

Parkes, die sinker, 213, 215, 217, 218, 257.
Parliament and Tokens, 97.
Parsons, 80.
Paterson, William, 25.
Patrick, die sinker, 56, 60, 120, 121, 129.
Peak in Derbyshire, 40.
Peel, Sir Robert, 118.
Pelham's Chronicles of Crime, 82.
Peterborough Cathedral, 38, 85.
Peterborough, 53, 85.
Phillips, 8.
Phillipson Brothers, 140.
Philp, die sinker, 3, 4, 9, 10.
Phipps, J., 95.
Picard, J. K., 178-180.
Phœnix Glass Co., 114.
Phœnix Iron Works, Glasgow, 209.
Pidcock, Gilbert, 76, 78, 79.
Pingo, die sinker, 5-7, 9.
"Plough" Hotel, Cheltenham, 55.
Polito, 79.
Ponthon, die sinker, 200.
Portsmouth, "The George" Inn, 58.
Porter, Samuel, 81.
Port Augustus, 208.
Portuguese Dollars, 96.
Poulton, 64.
Preston—*see* Millson and Preston.
Preston's sale, 1.
Prince Regent's tailor, 55.
Pye, Charles, 74, 146, 151, 157, 158.
Randall's Life of Wilkinson, 94.
Ratcliffe, Stephen, 31.
Ratley, 77.
Rawsons, Messrs., 65.
Read, T. and W., 66.
Readett, William, 92.
Reading Arms, 29.
Rebello, D. A., 75.
Redruth, 36.
Reeves, Mr., 75.
Revolution Mill, 16.
Reynolds, F. R., 82.
Richardson, John, *Hull Coinage*, 179.
Ricketts, Evans and Co., 114.
Riley, J. and R., 127.
Robertson, T. G., 27.
Robertson's Tokens, 86-88.
Rolling Mills, Walthamstow, 49.
Romanis, Robert, 77.
Romsey, 59.

Rose Copper Co., 154, 156.
Roskell, Tipton and Co., 192.
Rothschild, N. M., 82.
Round, Abel, 133.
Royal Exchange, 121.
Ruding, *Annals of the Coinage*, 238, 240.
Rushbury and Woolley, 118.
Ryall, Henry, 109.

St. Andrew, Order of, 22.
St. Michael Mount, 34, 35.
St. James Street, Walthamstow, 49.
Sanders, Samuel, 67.
Saunders and Butt, 54.
Scurr, Richard, 172.
Searle, W. G., 31.
Shakespeare Token, 156.
Sharp, T., *Catalogue of Provincial Copper Coins*, 34-36, 41, 42, 48, 52, 55, 60, 74, 77, 83, 84, 92-94, 109-114, 116, 117, 120-129, 132-134, 137, 146-155, 160-165, 175-178, 181, 183-185, 188, 189, 192, 195, 209, 213, 214, 221, 225, 251-254, 258, 259.
Sheffield, Meeting with reference to Tokens, 170.
Sheppard, William, 105.
Sherriff, die sinker, 129, 134.
Shield dollar, 1, 4.
Shuttleworth, Mr., 78.
Sinkins, Mrs. Jane, 109.
Six shillings Token, 8.
Sizer, W., 136.
Smallburgh, 84.
Smalpage and Lumb, 169.
Smeaton, J., 41.
Smith, Aquilla, 27, 212, 214, 229-239.
Smith, Payne and Co., 22.
Smyth, Edward, 232.
Society of Arts, 94.
Soho, 5.
Sotheby and Co., 9, 12, 16, 200, 206.
Sparks, William, 109.
Spink's Circular, 210, 250.
Spooner, Attwood and Co., 159.
Stafford, Sir Henry de, 131.
Staffordshire Knot, 39, 131.
Stalham Railway Station, 84.
Stanley Colliery, Bewdley, 161.
Stansall, Thomas, 92.
Stanton, Messrs., 91.
Star newspaper, 22, 70, 78, 88, 129, 143, 240.

INDEX III.

Statesman, The, newspaper, 40.
Stephens, Edward, 216, 218.
Stephens, J. M., 59.
Stevenson and Salt, 32.
Stewart, John, 235.
Storrs, Fry and Sons, 101.
Stovin and Chapman, 68.
Stuart—*see* Armagh.
Summergang's House, Hull, 179.
Sun newspaper, 77.
Surrey Zoological Gardens, 76.
Sydney Gardens, Bath, 98.
Sykes, W., *Hull Coins and Tokens*, 178.
"Swan with two necks," 77.

Tamworth Old Bank, 118.
Taylor, Hanbury and Co., 93.
Taylor, W. J., die sinker, 42, 200.
Teath river, 23.
Tenpenny Token, 9, 10.
Terrell, William, 100-2.
Thames Street, London, 52.
Thistle Bank Co., 21, 22.
Thistle, Order of, 22.
Thomason, Sir Edward, 29, 122, 149, 180, 186.
Three shillings Token, armoured bust, 5.
Three shillings Token, laureate head, 6.
Thurbon, John, 31.
Times newspaper, 82.
Token bank note, 101.
Token Coinage of Warwickshire, 129, 148, 157, 158.
Tokens, Collections of, indexed under owners' names.
Tokens, Notices referring to, 107, 108, 115, 116, 134, 143, 170, 180, 229, 236.
Tokens supplied to order, 70, 98.
Tower halfpennies, 103.
Treasury, 12.
Tripp, Robert, and Co., 105.
Tunstead and Happing Corporation, 84.
Turnpenny, die sinker, 93, 120, 122, 125, 127, 131, 133, 195, 241, 258.

Ulster Journal of Archæology, 231, 235.
Union Copper Co., 150-152, 156.
Upcott, W., 41.

Voss, John, 195.

Wade, J. S., 136.
Wainwright, B., 61.
Wainwright and Co., 61.
Wakeford, Messrs., 57.

Wallace Halfpenny, 200.
Warberg, Mr., 75.
Ward, Henry, 43.
Warren, James, 77.
Warren, Robert, 77.
Warwick Assizes, 12.
Washington, 12.
Waters, 138, 139.
Waters, Robert, banker, 188.
Weare, G. E., 107.
Weare, Mr., 115.
West, Admiral, 42.
Whalley, James, 53.
Whitchurch, Samuel, 96, 97.
Whitehouse and Co., 133.
Wilkes, Job, 128.
Wilkins, R. B., 58.
Wilkinson, John, 94, 146.
Wilkison, 22
Willets, die sinker, 145, 147-149, 206.
William III., 22, 42.
Williamson's Boyne's Tokens, 234, 248.
Willoughby and Son, 109.
Wills, Sir W. H., Bart., collection, 106, 112.
Wilson, Thomas, 92.
Wilson's Dublin Directory, 213, 216.
Winchester, Bishop of, 94.
Windsor, Sir William, 165.
Winstanley, Mr., 42.
Wood, T., 78.
Woodward, Thomas, 75.
Woolsack, The, 23.
Worcester Herald, 134.
Worcester House of Industry, 164.
Worcester Porcelain Co., 165.
Wright, Edward, 144.
Wright, James, 206.
Wyon, die sinker, 77, 92, 136, 137, 143-146, 148, 167, 175, 206, 216, 219.
Wyon, Peter, die sinker, 47, 49, 83, 86, 87, 93, 95, 96, 110, 116, 121, 127, 128, 130-132, 136-138, 141, 217, 218, 222, 249, 250.
Wyon, Thomas, die sinker, 6, 9, 17, 42, 50-52, 60, 83, 159, 160, 185, 224, 240.

Y. and D.—*see* Younge and Deakin, Sheffield.
Yarmouth coach, 82.
Young, Mathew, 75, 200.
Younge and Deakin, 186.
York.—*see* Allan.

J. DAVY AND SONS, 137, LONG ACRE, LONDON.

Lightning Source UK Ltd.
Milton Keynes UK
UKHW02f2158110518
322462UK00006B/829/P